The Cambridge Handbook of
Cognitive Science

Cognitive science is a cross-disciplinary enterprise devoted to understanding the nature of the mind. In recent years, investigators in philosophy, psychology, the neurosciences, artificial intelligence, and a host of other disciplines have come to appreciate how much they can learn from one another about the various dimensions of cognition. The result has been the emergence of one of the most exciting and fruitful areas of interdisciplinary research in the history of science. This volume of original essays surveys foundational, theoretical, and philosophical issues across the field, and introduces the foundations of cognitive science, the principal areas of research, and the major research programs. With a focus on broad philosophical themes rather than detailed technical issues, the volume will be valuable not only to cognitive scientists and philosophers of cognitive science, but also to those in other disciplines looking for an authoritative and up-to-date introduction to the field.

Keith Frankish is Visiting Senior Research Fellow at The Open University UK, and Adjunct Professor with the Brain and Mind Program in Neurosciences at the University of Crete. He is the author of *Mind and Supermind* (Cambridge, 2004) and *Consciousness* (2005), and he is co-editor of *In Two Minds: Dual Processes and Beyond* (with Jonathan St. B. T. Evans, 2009) and *New Waves in Philosophy of Action* (with Jesús H. Aguilar and Andrei A. Buckareff, 2010).

William M. Ramsey is Associate Professor of Philosophy at the University of Nevada at Las Vegas. He is the author of *Representation Reconsidered* (Cambridge, 2007), and co-editor of *Philosophy and Connectionist Theory* (with David Rumelhart and Stephen Stich, 1991) and *Rethinking Intuition* (with Michael DePaul, 1998).

The Cambridge Handbook of
Cognitive Science

EDITED BY

Keith Frankish and William M. Ramsey

CAMBRIDGE
UNIVERSITY PRESS

CAMBRIDGE UNIVERSITY PRESS
Cambridge, New York, Melbourne, Madrid, Cape Town,
Singapore, São Paulo, Delhi, Mexico City

Cambridge University Press
The Edinburgh Building, Cambridge CB2 8RU, UK
Published in the United States of America by Cambridge University Press, New York

www.cambridge.org
Information on this title: www.cambridge.org/9780521871419

First published 2012

Printed in the United Kingdom at the University Press, Cambridge

A catalogue record for this publication is available from the British Library

Library of Congress Cataloguing in Publication data
The Cambridge handbook of cognitive science / edited by Keith Frankish and
William M. Ramsey.
     pages   cm
Includes bibliographical references and index.
ISBN 978-0-521-87141-9 (hardback) – ISBN 978-0-521-69190-1 (paperback)
1. Cognitive science.   I. Frankish, Keith.   II. Ramsey, William (William M.)
BF311.C186   2012
153 – dc23   2012013654

ISBN 978-0-521-87141-9 Hardback
ISBN 978-0-521-69190-1 Paperback

Contents

List of figures and tables

Figures

Tables

Contributors

Adele Abrahamsen is a Project Scientist in the Center for Research in Language at the University of California, San Diego. She is the author of *Child Language: An Interdisciplinary Guide to Theory and Research* (1977) and co-author of *Connectionism and the Mind* (2nd edn., 2002).

H. Clark Barrett is Associate Professor of Anthropology at the University of California, Los Angeles. He is the author of numerous articles and book chapters on evolutionary psychology and cross-cultural studies of development and cognition.

William Bechtel is Professor in the Department of Philosophy, the Center for Chronobiology, and the Interdisciplinary Program in Cognitive Science at the University of California, San Diego. He is the co-author of *Discovering Complexity* (2nd edn., 2010) and *Connectionism and the Mind* (2nd edn., 2002), and author of *Mental Mechanisms* (2008) and *Discovering Cell Mechanisms* (2006).

Nick Chater is Professor of Cognitive and Decision Sciences at UCL. He is the co-author of *Bayesian Rationality* (2007) and *Rationality in an Uncertain World* (1998), both with Mike Oaksford. He has written over 200 publications, primarily on the cognitive science of reasoning, decision making, and language, combining mathematical, computational, and experimental work.

Andy Clark is Professor of Logic and Metaphysics in the School of Philosophy, Psychology and Language Sciences, at Edinburgh University in Scotland. He is the author of *Being There: Putting Brain, Body And World Together Again* (1997), *Mindware* (2001), *Natural-Born Cyborgs: Minds, Technologies and the Future of Human Intelligence* (2003), and *Supersizing the Mind: Embodiment, Action, and Cognitive Extension* (2008).

Keith Frankish is Visiting Senior Research Fellow at The Open University UK and Adjunct Professor with the Brain and Mind Program in Neurosciences at the University of Crete. He is the author of *Mind and Supermind* (Cambridge, 2004) and *Consciousness* (2005), and he is co-editor of *In Two Minds: Dual Processes and Beyond* (with Jonathan St. B. T. Evans, 2009) and *New Waves in Philosophy of Action* (with Jesús H. Aguilar and Andrei A. Buckareff, 2010).

Aaron B. Hoffman is a senior quantitative analyst at Frank N. Magid Associates, Inc., Los Angeles.

Ray Jackendoff is Seth Merrin Professor of Philosophy and Co-Director of the Center for Cognitive Studies at Tufts University. His most recent books are *Foundations of Language* (2002), *Simpler Syntax* (with Peter Culicover, 2005), *Language, Consciousness, Culture* (2007), *Meaning and the Lexicon* (2010), and *A User's Guide to Thought and Meaning* (2012).

Laura A. Libby is a graduate student in the doctoral program in psychology at UC Davis.

William G. Lycan is the William Rand Kenan, Jr. Professor of Philosophy at the University of North Carolina. He is the author of *Logical Form in Natural Language* (1984), *Consciousness* (Cambridge, 1987), *Judgment and Justification* (1988), *Modality and Meaning* (1994), and *Consciousness and Experience* (1996).

Gregory L. Murphy is Professor of Psychology at New York University. He is the author of *The Big Book of Concepts* (2002).

Mike Oaksford is Professor of Psychology and Chair of the Department of Psychological Science at Birkbeck College, University of London. He is the joint author of *Rationality in an Uncertain World* (1998), and *Bayesian Rationality* (2007), and joint editor of *Neurodynamics and Psychology* (1994), *Rational Models of Cognition* (1998), *Emotional Cognition* (2002), *The Probabilistic Mind* (2008), and *Cognition and Conditionals* (2010), as well as numerous articles and book chapters.

Casey O'Callaghan is Associate Professor of Philosophy at Rice University. He is the author of *Sounds: A Philosophical Theory* (2007) and co-editor, with Matthew Nudds, of *Sounds and Perception: New Philosophical Essays* (2009).

Elisabeth Pacherie is senior researcher in philosophy at Institut Jean Nicod, (École Normale Supérieure, Centre National de la Recherche Scientifique) in Paris. She is the author of *Naturaliser l'intentionnalité* (1993) as well as of numerous papers and book chapters.

Jesse Prinz is Distinguished Professor of Philosophy at The City University of New York, Graduate Center. His books include *Furnishing the Mind* (2002), *Gut Reactions* (2004), *The Emotional Construction of Morals* (2007), and *Beyond Human Nature* (2012).

William M. Ramsey is Associate Professor of Philosophy at the University of Nevada at Las Vegas. He is the author of *Representation Reconsidered* (Cambridge, 2007), and co-editor of *Philosophy and Connectionist Theory* (with David Rumelhart and Stephen Stich, 1991) and *Rethinking Intuition* (with Michael DePaul, 1998).

Charan Ranganath is Professor of Psychology and Neuroscience at the University of California at Davis. He has written or co-written over sixty papers on human memory processes and co-edited the book *Neuroimaging in Human Memory: Linking Cognitive Processes to Neural Systems* (2009).

Sara J. Shettleworth is Professor Emerita in the Departments of Psychology and of Ecology and Evolutionary Biology at the University of Toronto. She is author of *Cognition, Evolution, and Behavior* (2nd edn., 2010) and of many articles and chapters on animal behavior and cognition.

Dominic Standage is a postdoctoral research fellow at the Centre for Neuroscience Studies, Queen's University, Canada. His research addresses the neural mechanisms underlying cognitive phenomena including memory formation, working memory, decision making, attention, and executive control.

Neil Stewart is Professor of Psychology at Warwick University. His recent publications examine the psychology of credit card repayments, a review of evidence for contextual effects in risky decision making, and the design of fair police lineups for suspects with distinctive features.

Paul Thagard is Professor of Philosophy and Director of the Cognitive Science Program at the University of Waterloo, Canada. His books include *The Brain and the Meaning of Life* (2010), *Hot Thought* (2006), and *Mind: Introduction to Cognitive Science* (2005).

Thomas Trappenberg is Professor of Computer Science and a member of the Neuroscience Institute at Dalhousie University, Canada. He has published numerous papers and is author of *Fundamentals of Computational Neuroscience*, now in its second edition (2010).

Barbara Von Eckardt is Dean of Liberal Arts and Professor of Philosophy in the Department of History, Philosophy, and the Social Sciences at the Rhode Island School of Design. She is author of *What is Cognitive Science?* (1993) as well as numerous articles and entries.

Ling Wong is a graduate student in the doctoral program in neuroscience at UC Davis.

Acknowledgments

Many people contributed, directly and indirectly, to the production of this volume. First, we would like to thank the contributors for their expertise, hard work, and responsiveness to our sometimes exacting requirements. We are also grateful to Hilary Gaskin at Cambridge University Press for inviting us to compile the volume, and for her patience when the project took longer than expected; to Pashawna Miller and Alma Johnson for their hard work in preparing the index; and to Anna Oxbury for her scrupulous and thoughtful copyediting of the text.

We also wish to thank our home institutions and others who have assisted our work on this volume. Keith is grateful to The Open University for support during some difficult personal times, to the Department of Philosophy and Social Studies at the University of Crete for hosting him as a Visiting Researcher, and to Professor Adonis Moschovakis, Professor Helen Savaki, and the other members of the Brain and Mind Program at the University of Crete for making him welcome in the strong cognitive science community in Crete. Finally, and most importantly, he thanks his partner, Maria Kasmirli, for her patience, support, and excellent advice on philosophical matters. William is grateful to both the University of Notre Dame and the University of Nevada at Las Vegas, and especially would like to thank Notre Dame for its Associative Professor's Special Leave, which helped support work on this project.

INTRODUCTION

Keith Frankish and William M. Ramsey

Overview

Cognitive science is a cross-disciplinary enterprise devoted to exploring and understanding the nature of the mind. In recent years, investigators in psychology, the neurosciences, artificial intelligence, philosophy, and a host of other disciplines have come to appreciate how much they can learn from one another about the various dimensions of cognition. The result has been the emergence of one of the most exciting and fruitful areas of interdisciplinary research in the history of science.

This volume of original essays is designed to describe the state of the art in cognitive science and to survey the major theoretical, philosophical, and foundational issues across the field. With a focus on theory rather than technical and applied issues, the volume is designed to appeal to both cognitive scientists and philosophers of cognitive science. Each chapter is a specially commissioned article from a leading writer in the area – either a philosopher of cognitive science or a scientist with strong theoretical interests. These writers cover the foundations of cognitive science, the principal areas of study, major research methodologies, and the philosophical implications of current research. The chapters are largely thematic rather than historical, and although the essays are primarily survey pieces, readers will find important critical insights, assessments, and analyses included in each essay. Readers are not expected to have extensive background in the primary subject areas.

This volume is distinctive in several ways. First, its coverage is both broad and authoritative. Its fifteen chapters provide a concise, up-to-date survey of a field that is developing and expanding rapidly, written by leading philosophers of cognitive science and front-line researchers with important and broad-ranging perspectives. Second, it is designed to be widely accessible. The contributors present scientific work in a form that is comprehensible to a humanities audience and focus on theoretical issues and applications rather than the details of experimental work. Third, the contributions are written at an intermediate level, suitable for both advanced students and scholars new to the area, and the book includes supporting materials, such as a glossary and chapter-specific 'Further Reading' sections, that make it an ideal teaching text. A companion handbook to artificial intelligence has also been compiled, which has similar scope and aims and is designed to complement this one.

The philosophy and science of cognition

A number of the chapters in this volume are written by people who are usually characterized, not as cognitive scientists *per se*, but as *philosophers of* cognitive science. Moreover, the volume's co-editors both have their primary homes in philosophy departments. Thus, one might wonder why a volume about the *science* of the mind is so heavily infused with input from philosophers.

In truth, the distinction between cognitive science and the philosophy of cognitive science is not nearly as sharp as one might suppose. First, there really is no clear demarcation between empirical investigation on the one hand and philosophical reflection on that investigation on the other. Cognitive scientists must reflect on the broader implications of their findings, speculate about more abstract matters such as hidden assumptions and overarching themes, appeal to thought-experiments in arguing for their positions, and invoke traditional philosophical concepts such as knowledge, representation, and consciousness. In other words, there is a lot of philosophical reasoning involved in being a cutting-edge scientist. At the same time, philosophers of cognitive science must be well versed in the empirical theories and methods of investigation, so that their own contributions are relevant and beneficial. In fact, there is often little difference between doing, say, theoretical psychology and the philosophy of psychology.

Secondly, the philosophy of cognitive science involves two features that provide scholars in the discipline with a unique perspective on cognitive science itself. One is a broad-based understanding of the more general metaphysical, epistemological, and even ethical issues that arise in cognitive science. These include questions about the nature of mind–brain identity, reductionism, cognitive explanation and modeling, appropriate taxonomies for mental states, types of mental content, and so on. The other feature is an appreciation of the specific foundational issues associated with particular areas of cognitive research. For centuries, philosophers have been thinking and writing about a wide array of mental phenomena that different empirical researchers are now exploring. Aspects of the mind such as consciousness, mental representation, perceptual experience, and human action are traditional areas of philosophical analysis *and* the target of increased scientific scrutiny. The philosophy of mind has been dramatically transformed by scientific findings and theories, and, at the same time, philosophers have a unique vantage from which they can elucidate empirical work.

Thus, not only is there no sharp distinction to be made between science and philosophy (in this area at least), but researchers with a background in philosophy are particularly well placed to provide an overview of the science and to draw out the foundational issues.

The future of cognitive science

Because the essays in this volume present state of the art research and theorizing, they also provide a glimpse of where things are heading in the discipline of cognitive science. It is, of course, always difficult to predict the future of any field, but we can see certain trends that we expect to continue. For example, in their chapter on core themes, Abrahamsen and Bechtel discuss the expansion of cognitive science both downward and outward. The expansion is downward in the sense that more and more work in psychology is informed by discoveries and findings in the neurosciences. As many of the chapters here reveal, current work on consciousness, perception, learning, and a host of other aspects of cognition is increasingly being influenced by our growing knowledge of the brain. We fully expect this trend to continue and, indeed, to strengthen as neuroscientific knowledge develops. Expansion in cognitive science is outward in at least two senses. First, as Clark's chapter on embedded and extended cognition reveals, there is a growing movement to treat things beyond the cranium as vitally important to, and perhaps even constituent of, cognitive processes and states. This movement will no doubt continue as more investigators come to view cognitive agents as inextricably embedded in a web of complex interactions with a broader external environment. Second, over time cognitive science itself has increasingly interfaced with other disciplines and subdisciplines, expanding both the range of research it draws upon and the extent of its own influence. The chapters here strongly suggest that this theoretical expansion will continue, and, with it, the vital importance of cognitive science as the field that is at the heart of our understanding of ourselves.

Summary of the volume

The volume is composed of fifteen chapters divided into three main sections: *Foundations*, *Aspects of cognition*, and *Research programs*. We selected these sections because, taken together, they provide an excellent overview of the theoretical landscape of cognitive science. Each section and each chapter stands alone and can be read individually, though the sections and chapters are designed to complement each other, and the collection as a whole provides a systematic and comprehensive survey of the field.

Part I: Foundations

This section is devoted to the foundational issues of cognitive science. The first chapter, which is by Adele Abrahamsen and William Bechtel, provides a brief history of the cognitive revolution and the emergence of cognitive science. It also introduces some of the foundational issues, such as the philosophical roots of cognitivism, the computer model of the mind, and the merits of cross-disciplinary research. The second chapter, by Barbara Von Eckardt, introduces the representational theory of the mind and explains the role that representationalism has played in the development of cognitive science. It explains some of the arguments for and against representationalism and looks at philosophical work on the problem of naturalizing intentionality. The third and final chapter of this section is by Paul Thagard. It deals with cognitive architectures – general models of processing and representation, which serve as paradigms in cognitive science. Thagard surveys the two most influential architectures – rule-based and connectionist – and considers the prospects for developing a general cognitive theory that combines aspects of both.

Part II: Aspects of cognition

This section is devoted to recent research on various aspects of cognition. The authors present a survey of recent findings and theories and discuss the more significant philosophical implications of this research. Readers can use this section of the volume to gain both a good grasp of specific areas of cognitive research and an understanding of the philosophical issues surrounding them.

The chapters, written by leading specialists in each field, cover a variety of topics. Casey O'Callaghan looks at perception, explaining traditional philosophical problems which form the backdrop to contemporary scientific research and introducing empirically motivated theoretical issues, such as the relationship between perception, cognition, and action. Elisabeth Pacherie discusses action, showing how a more comprehensive, integrative picture of action is gradually emerging which draws on both conceptual frameworks developed by philosophers and empirical investigations into motor cognition. Charan Ranganath, Laura A. Libby, and Ling Wong survey modern memory research and introduce key issues in the field, stressing the theoretical advances that are resulting from collaboration between psychologists and neuroscientists. Mike Oaksford, Nick Chater, and Neil Stewart introduce some recent developments in the large and complex field of human reasoning and decision making, explaining both the main normative theories and important experimental paradigms, findings, and interpretations. In the next chapter, Gregory L. Murphy and Aaron B. Hoffman look at work on concepts and category learning. They identify and survey two main strands of contemporary research, one concerned with formal models of category learning, and the other focusing on the content of concepts and the interaction between learning and prior knowledge. Progress in the field, Murphy and Hoffman suggest, requires further integration of these two strands. The study of language has always had a central role in cognitive science, and linguists have developed detailed models of the mental structures involved in language processing. In his chapter, Ray Jackendoff surveys this work and seeks to integrate linguistic theory with wider issues in cognitive science. Next, Jesse Prinz reviews recent research on the emotions, focusing on their causes, constituents, and effects, and introducing a major dispute over the role of cognition in emotion. Finally in this section, William G. Lycan looks at the aspect of the mind often regarded as the most resistant to scientific understanding: consciousness. Lycan disentangles different facets of consciousness and distinguishes empirical issues, on which cognitive scientists are making progress, from purely philosophical issues, which, he suggests, are likely to remain contentious.

Part III: Research programs

This section introduces readers to some broader research programs and their particular methodological and theoretical commitments. In the first chapter Dominic Standage and Thomas Trappenberg provide an overview of developments in the growing field known as computational neuroscience, which aims to provide explanations of cognitive phenomena that are rooted in models of brain structure and functioning. In the next chapter, H. Clark Barrett explores the developing and controversial discipline of evolutionary psychology and discusses why evolution is relevant to understanding the mind. The penultimate chapter, by Andy Clark, focuses on the boundaries of cognition. Clark explores the claim that cognitive systems and processes can be understood only by including the surrounding environment in which the system is embedded, along with the provocative suggestion that cognitive systems themselves actually extend out into the world. The volume concludes with a chapter on animal cognition, in which Sara J. Shettleworth presents some of the more significant findings in the field of cognitive ethology and discusses the different ways in which the study of animal brains and behavior has helped shape our understanding of cognition.

This choice of chapter topics is, we feel, sound and as comprehensive as possible given the size of the volume. Of course, there are other topics we would have liked to have included, in particular some alternative and emerging research programs. However, given the limitations of space, we decided to focus on mainstream cognitive science and established programs (though non-mainstream work is touched on in many places). We do not suggest that no work of value is being done outside this mainstream, nor do we deny that cognitive science may take a very different turn in the future. But the topics covered here are undeniably central to the discipline, and it is not our job as editors of a handbook to impose a vision of how the field will develop. Moreover, as mentioned earlier, this volume is one of a pair, and some alternative approaches to cognition are discussed in detail in the companion volume, *The Cambridge Handbook of Artificial Intelligence* (also edited by us). This contains chapters on, among many other things, challenges to traditional AI conceptions of cognition, dynamical systems and embedded cognition, robotics, and artificial life.

We have enjoyed putting this volume together, and we hope it will introduce many readers to the rich and exciting work being done in contemporary cognitive science. Some readers, we hope, will be spurred to join the enterprise, and others to apply insights and ideas from cognitive science in their own fields. All, we hope, will benefit from an increased understanding of the complex cognitive machinery that makes us what we are.

Part I

Foundations

1 History and core themes

Adele Abrahamsen and William Bechtel

1.1 Overview

Two characteristics of cognitive science are central and obvious.

First, it is *cognitive*, aiming toward empirical and theoretical understanding of cognition. Its founding disciplines addressed intelligence in humans (cognitive psychology) and computers (artificial intelligence), with special scrutiny given to language as a paradigmatic domain of human competence (linguistics). Over time, the understanding of what it is to be cognitive has expanded, diversified, and become more contentious.

Second, it is *interdisciplinary*: ideas and methods of inquiry propagate across traditional boundaries, and collaborations thrive among the founding fields and also philosophy, sociology, anthropology, developmental psychology, education, and neuroscience. Some of these collaborations have created or reinvigorated interdisciplinary fields such as psycholinguistics, language acquisition, linguistic anthropology, cognitive sociology, computational linguistics, and cognitive neuroscience; others have contributed research strategies, especially computer simulation of mental activity; and many more have contributed to particular strands of inquiry.

Beyond these, there are few if any core characteristics embraced by all cognitive scientists. Instead, there are themes that emerge as important in particular eras or approaches and also some dichotomies that unify advocates on each side but divide them from each other. To get more of the full story, see the Further Reading at chapter's end. Here we situate the mutable themes of cognitive science within a brief historical tour, organized as follows:

- Cognitive science has deep roots in several fields, but the most relevant advances were largely abandoned in the United States during the first half of the twentieth century as psychology became behaviorist, linguistics became structuralist, and what later became known as neuroscience was limited by the available methods and by anti-localizationist leanings.
- Key innovations in the 1940s – the idea of information and the advent of electronic computers – gave rise to new fields, such as information theory, artificial intelligence, and artificial neural networks, and set the stage for

interdisciplinary ferment and a "cognitive revolution" in psychology and linguistics.

- By the late 1950s pioneers in several fields were embarking on a vigorous pursuit of what is now called symbolic architecture, in which representations and the rules specifying operations on them consist of discrete symbols. This took the form of information-processing models in psychology, computer programs in artificial intelligence, generative grammar in linguistics, and the language of thought hypothesis in philosophy. In this volume, there is more extensive discussion of representation in Chapter 2 and of organized operations ("procedures") in Chapter 3.
- By 1975 "cognitive science" had a name, but its focus on symbolic rules and representations was challenged when some key cognitive scientists took another look at artificial neural networks and adapted them to obtain statistical, "subsymbolic" connectionist models in the early 1980s. Ever since, symbol manipulation and statistical approaches have offered quite different insights into perception, action, learning, memory, reasoning, decision making, concepts and language – aspects of cognition covered in Chapters 4–9. Moreover, certain alternatives to generative grammar – especially cognitive linguistics and optimality theory – had an impact beyond linguistics.
- Since the 1990s cognitive science has expanded in ways making it even more diverse and increasing the salience of previously peripheral fields, as discussed in Chapters 10–15.

Throughout this history, philosophy has been a player at arm's length from day-to-day empirical research. However, its concepts, theories, and tools often get adapted or applied by researchers in other cognitive science disciplines, and philosophers reciprocate by collaborating and by probing those disciplines. Moreover, philosophy of mind has provided an ongoing forum for interdisciplinary conversation and inspired certain lines of empirical research.

1.2   The roots of cognitive science

Theoretical inquiries into mental phenomena date back at least 2,500 years, but substantial lines of empirical research first developed in the nineteenth century – an era in which disciplinary boundaries were being established as universities grew dramatically. Contributions that are still relevant today were made by European researchers trained in biology or physics, notably Weber's and Fechner's psychophysical laws, Helmholtz's and Hering's accounts of color perception, Donders' techniques for inferring mental processes from reaction times, and (on a wider canvas) Darwin's insightful observations and theory of evolution. Certain philosophical frameworks were influential, including J. S. Mill's "mental chemistry" and Brentano's introspective analyses of mental acts and their "intentionality" (being about something). These strands converged in a new discipline when two young scholars established psychology laboratories and began publishing in the 1870s. At Harvard University, William James arrived at rich characterizations of consciousness, memory, habit, sensation, emotion, and other mental functions. In Leipzig, Wilhelm Wundt's great breadth, ranging from neural to cultural investigations, precluded a unitary legacy. Most students pursued either his program of experimentation or his use of systematic introspection for inferring mental content. By 1900 psychology was a thriving discipline, complete with factional disputes.

Research emphasizing the physical facets of the mind/brain followed a separate trajectory. The idea that different brain areas subserve different functions (localizationism) goes back at least to the early nineteenth century, when Gall's *phrenology* was built on apparent associations between size of particular brain areas (as inferred from the skull) and differences in ability to recall words, perform music, show kindness, and so forth. There was popular uptake but strong scientific opposition. By the 1860s, influential autopsy studies by Paul Broca had associated lesions with patients' loss of articulate speech (*Broca's aphasia*). In the early twentieth century, anatomist Korbinian Brodmann was able to use the layout and layering of different types of neurons to map areas of neocortex precisely enough that his numerical designations are still in use. Concurrently, neurophysiologists began using behavioral effects of lesions and electrical stimulation in animals to successfully identify brain areas for vision (striate cortex), motor control (precentral gyrus), and finally other sensory systems. Their attempts to localize memory or other higher functions in parts of the large "association cortex" that remained were less well received. Karl Lashley famously concluded that this brain tissue exhibited (1) *equipotentiality*, the ability to take on different functions (e.g., following damage); and (2) *mass action*, in which it is the total area available, not location, that matters. Today localizationism dominates neuroscience, ranging from single-cell recording to functional magnetic resonance imaging (fMRI), while anti-localizationism has a new home in dynamical systems modeling. Cognitive science encompasses both.

The prevalence of anti-localizationist views like Lashley's through the first half of the twentieth century minimized neurophysiology's influence on psychology. However, another part of physiology – Pavlov's studies of salivation in Russia – helped to shape an entirely new school of thought that came to dominate psychology in the United States during that period. *Behaviorism* originated in John Watson's growing conviction that both Jamesian functionalism and Wundtian introspectionism suffered from insufficient empirical grounding and objectivity, largely in consequence of their focus on mental activity or contents. Once Watson learned of Pavlov's classical conditioning (in which, e.g., a bell repeatedly paired with food can itself elicit salivation), he embraced it as a tool by which psychologists could obtain objective accounts of observable behavior. Soon he had narrowed psychology's focus to learning and promoted the use of animals as model organisms. In mid-century B. F. Skinner championed operant conditioning (in which reinforcing an act brings it under control, e.g., increasing the rate at which a rat presses a bar). Although Skinner was also known for his *radical behaviorism*, which repudiated appeals to inner states in explanations of behavior, during the same period Watson's approach was further developed by the less restrictive *neo-behaviorists*. In particular, Clark Hull allowed intervening variables for *drive* and other unobservables in his influential mathematical laws of learning, but he stopped short of overtly mentalistic constructs such as memory, attention, or representation. Edward Tolman went that extra step by positing cognitive maps in explaining the navigational behavior of rats (making him a maverick), and other less behaviorist research paths were pursued in psychophysics and parts of developmental, social, and clinical psychology.

Outside the United States, behaviorism had little impact on psychology. A variety of approaches that emerged in the 1920s and 1930s continued to advance in the UK (e.g., Sir Frederic Bartlett's appeal to schemata to explain memory distortions), Germany and Austria (Gestalt psychology's emphasis on organized wholes), Switzerland (Jean Piaget's genetic epistemology, in which schemata develop into stably organized systems), and the Soviet Union (Lev Vygotsky and Alexander Luria's studies of language and thought). These proceeded independently until all found a degree of uptake in cognitive psychology in the 1960s.

One other discipline with deep historic roots played a major role in early cognitive science: linguistics. As far back as the eighth century BCE, Panini systematically described the phonology (sound structure) and morphology (word structure) of Sanskrit, and touched on its syntax (sentence structure). His counterparts in the first half of the twentieth century were the *structural linguists*, many of whom showed an affinity with behaviorism. Leonard Bloomfield, for example, was influential in his insistence on cataloguing and analyzing only directly observed speech.

There were two periods of especially fertile interaction between psychology and linguistics. Around the turn of the twentieth century in Europe, certain linguists and psychologists shared an interest in mechanisms of change based on analogy or association. Other linguists were influenced by two of the many strands of Wundt's work: his emphasis on holistic creative mental processes and his use of tree notation to convey grammatical structure as hierarchical (vs. the flat but less constrained structures implied by associationism). The second period of interaction began in the early 1950s in the USA and relied on empiricism as a common ground between neo-behaviorist psychologists and structural linguists. Participants in a 1953 summer seminar reintroduced the term *psycholinguistics* and set an ambitious agenda for cooperative research. Although many of the specific theories from both linguistics and psychology were soon to be replaced in the cognitive revolution, the major research goals they set, such as establishing the psychological reality of *phoneme* and other linguistic constructs, would continue to be pursued.

1.3   Information, computation, and the cognitive revolution (1940–1956)

It is sometimes said that the cognitive revolution stemmed from seizing on a new technology – the digital computer – as a metaphor for the mind. This indeed was the dominant metaphor by the 1960s, but earlier technologies – the telegraph and telephone – provided a transitional metaphor in which certain human systems were likened to electronic communication channels. Formal engineering analyses of communication, especially in the 1920s to 1960s at Bell Laboratories, gave rise to a cluster of fields which changed the intellectual landscape. Those making the greatest impact on psychology included *information theory* (a quantitative treatment of information transmission across channels subject to capacity limits, rate limits, and noise) and *coding theory* (concerned with the form of the message, especially ways of recoding it into a compressed format – such as today's MP3 – that can be transmitted and stored more efficiently). Ignoring semantic content, a message was taken to be informative to the extent that it reduced uncertainty: the more possible messages, the greater the uncertainty. Claude Shannon (1948) introduced the *bit* (from *bi*nary digi*t*, 0/1) to quantify this; for example, if there are two equally likely messages, one bit is sufficient to distinguish them, but eight messages (2^3) require at minimum a three-bit encoding.

George Miller began a long, influential career in cognitive science by bringing Shannon's framework to bear on data he collected for his 1946 PhD dissertation in S. S. Stevens' psychophysics laboratory at Harvard. Specifically, he showed that spoken English messages that were most intelligible in noise were those that were more redundant – that is, those requiring fewer bits of information to narrow the interpretations to one. A small stream of research in what Miller called *statistical behavioristics* ensued. Within the next decade the computer metaphor began overtaking the communication metaphor, ultimately favoring a less statistical notion of information as mental content held in computer memory-like storage registers and manipulated by program-like processes. Both metaphors gave rise to *information processing* by offering engineering-based ways to open the "black box" between stimuli and responses and model mental activity. Two communication-based accounts in the 1950s helped shape the research paradigms and computer-based models of the 1960s. First, British psychologist Donald Broadbent posited multiple sensory channels, each with a memory buffer feeding into a central attentional filter that selects (and can switch) which channel's input gets sent through a limited-capacity information channel for further processing. His research paradigms and use of flow charts were as influential as his model. Second,

Miller (1956) himself offered "the magical number seven plus or minus two" as the capacity limit of immediate memory (Broadbent's information channel, redubbed *short-term memory* in the 1960s) and proposed that humans often deal with this by "chunking" incoming information. As a simple example, 149217761860 exceeds capacity unless we recode the twelve digits as three familiar dates (1492, 1776, 1860). Miller presented this work to a Symposium on Information Theory at MIT on September 11, 1956.

Two other papers at the same symposium (by Noam Chomsky and by Allen Newell and Herbert Simon) advanced the computer metaphor by focusing on symbolic rules and representations. The roots of this approach lie in symbolic logic as formulated by Frege and further developed by Whitehead and Russell near the turn of the twentieth century; we use a simpler formulation to provide a glimpse. First, in *propositional logic*, symbolic expressions composed of propositions and connectives, such as ∨ ("or"), ∧ ("and"), and ⌐ ("not"), can be derived using rules of inference such as:

$$p \rightarrow (q \vee p)$$

where p and q are any two propositions, (q ∨ p) indicates that q or p or both are true, and → ("implies") indicates that if the expression on the left is true, then the expression on the right must be true. Second, in *predicate logic*, propositions are replaced by predicates (F, G,...) taking one or more arguments, each of which is a constant or a variable (x, y,...) that can be bound by the quantifiers "for all" (∀) and "there exists" (∃). For example:

$$\forall x \; \forall y \; Fxy \rightarrow \forall x \; \forall y \; (Gxy \vee Fxy).$$

A more immediate influence is automata theory, a mathematically rigorous exploration of virtual machines for computation. A *finite state automaton* takes as input symbols from a finite set; each of its rules specifies transition to its next state based solely on its current state and current symbol (i.e., "if state A and symbol S at time t, then state B at time $t + 1$"). In the 1930s Alan Turing proposed a more powerful type of automaton with an indefinitely extendable tape holding symbols. Each rule specifies, based on the current state and symbol, a state transition and also actions with respect to the tape (writing or deleting a symbol, moving left or right) – actions that amount to adding a memory. This abstract class of *Turing machines* influenced John von Neumann's design work on the overall architecture that has dominated computer design for decades and, in turn, cognitive scientists' conceptions of mind and language.

Chomsky had the revolutionary idea of construing the grammar of a natural language as equivalent to an automaton capable of generating the sentences of that language – a *generative grammar* – and asked what sort of grammar would be adequate. He used the 1956 symposium and the book *Syntactic Structures* (Chomsky 1957) to persuade key thinkers beyond linguistics to accept the question itself and his answer. As explained in Chapter 9, he concluded that a transformational grammar was required. By 1965 he described this as a grammar in which *phrase structure rules* such as S → NP VP and VP → V (NP) generated a sentence's *deep structure* (a tree suitable for computing meaning) and then *transformational rules* altered it to obtain the *surface structure* (a tree suitable for computing how the sentence should sound). When assessed as automata, transformational grammars were shown to have the power of a Turing machine. However, Chomsky's furthest-reaching impact beyond linguistics was that deep structure trees and transformations offered a specific vision of how mental representations and operations might look.

The symposium paper by Newell and Simon offered another such vision, as realized in the first functioning computer program in the new field of *artificial intelligence (AI)*. The historical background overlapped with that of generative grammar, and they shared Chomsky's basic commitment to rules specifying operations on symbols. But Newell and Simon anchored their work to digital computers – physical realizations of the kinds of devices abstractly explored in automata theory. Shannon had shown in the late 1930s that electric switches could be arranged to turn one another on and off so as to perform arithmetic operations, and World War II made this a priority. The first general-purpose digital computer, ENIAC, was delivered in 1946. The first with the serial von Neumann architecture was EDVAC in 1949–51: in the computer's memory are stored programs, data, and the results of each processing step, and these communicate (at the next step) with the central processing unit that carries out computations. Just ten years after ENIAC, Newell and Simon (with J. C. Shaw) wrote the first AI program (Logic Theorist) in the first list-processing language (IPL) and had it running on a digital computer. The influence of symbolic logic was obvious in its task: discovering proofs for theorems in propositional logic.

Looking back on his excitement at the nascent symbol-processing approaches in linguistics, AI, and his own corner of psychology, Miller (1979) identified September 11, 1956, as the birthday of cognitive science. It is important to note, though, that the information sciences were making connections not only with these fields but also with neuroscience during the 1940s and 1950s. A key example is the joint work by neurophysiologist Warren McCulloch and logician Walter Pitts on formal networks of simplified neuron-like units (*McCulloch–Pitts neurons*). Each unit could fire or not at each time-step, based on whether the sum of its individually weighted excitatory inputs across connections from other units exceeded a threshold. In 1943 they showed that any logical function could be computed by a network with this kind of parallel architecture, and by 1947 they were designing networks to simulate real-life tasks like sensory-motor mappings in the superior colliculus. McCulloch also helped organize an interdisciplinary conference on *cybernetics* that thrived from 1945 to 1953. For Norbert Wiener (1948), who coined the term and defined the field of cybernetics, the central concern was the role of feedback in controlling natural and artificial systems and guiding them toward goals. Cybernetics did not endure as a unified movement, but sent splinters of influence into a variety of fields. Most notably *artificial neural networks* were vigorously pursued in the 1940s through 1960s and revived in the 1980s. They represent a counterpoint to discrete computation (the von Neumann computer architecture and the symbolic models it inspired). We return to them in a later section.

This period saw the introduction or increased salience of a number of dichotomies that were inherited by cognitive science. Among them are content (the meaning of a symbol) vs. form (the "shape" of a symbol); digital/discrete vs. analog representation (some of the earliest computer designs were analog, as are mental images); serial vs. parallel processing; symbolic vs. statistical/quantitative models; and artificial vs. human intelligence.

1.4   Building symbolic models (1956–1975)

What are now called symbolic architectures or models continued to develop in generative grammar and artificial intelligence, and by the 1960s they were reshaping the information-processing approach in psychology as well. A *symbol* is a discrete form (e.g., the word "stop" or a stop sign) that stands for (represents) something else. Symbolic architectures share a commitment to (1) *representations* whose elements are symbols and (2) *operations* on those representations that typically involve moving, copying, deleting, comparing, or replacing symbols. A *rule* specifies one or more operations (e.g., S → NP VP). Typically the result is a different representation which then triggers a different rule, and so on until no further rules apply. An organized rule sequence such as this may be called a *process*, *procedure*, or (in linguistics) *derivation*. In many fields structured representations (rather than flat symbol sequences) are involved. For example, grammatical rules provide a combinatorial capacity that is constrained but productive, yielding sentences ("The car should stop here") along with trees indicating their structure, but not word salad ("stop the should here car"). Overall, the rules and representations approach is *formal* in that rules focus on the form of symbols, not what they represent, and *computational* in that it involves the manipulation of discrete forms.

As it became once again respectable to inquire into the inner workings of the mind, a major challenge was to develop tools for characterizing information processing. Taking inspiration from Weiner's cybernetics, George Miller, Eugene Galanter, and Karl Pribram (1960) proposed to model purposive human action using hierarchically organized goal structures that were flexible and recursive and that repeatedly assessed their own success. This book marked a turning point in North American psychology.

Miller next collaborated with social psychologist Jerome Bruner in creating the Center for Cognitive Studies at Harvard, an important influence on a new generation of cognitive psychologists. Bruner's own work in the previous decade – the "New Look" – had emphasized that a person's internal values and expectations affected their perception of external stimuli, and in the 1950s he pushed further into the mind by examining strategies of concept acquisition. A frequent visitor at the Center was Ulric Neisser, whose landmark *Cognitive Psychology* (Neisser 1967) emphasized the constructive nature of cognitive processes and brought European frameworks (e.g., Broadbent's attention filter, Bartlett's and Piaget's schemata, and gestalt psychology) to bear on the new information-processing approach in North America. The book served both to provide a name for the new subfield and to initiate the next generation of students into it; by 1970 there was a journal of the same name.

Harvard was not the only university at which strong faculty–student collaborations produced rapid advances in cognitive psychology in the late 1960s and early 1970s. Several psychology faculty at Stanford University whose original training was in mathematical and behavioral approaches to learning, most prominently William Estes, made a brilliant transition to innovative experiments and mathematical and computer models that were increasingly cognitive. Here are just three examples: Richard Atkinson and Richard Shiffrin developed an especially influential model of memory processes in which flexible control structures were involved in converting information from sensory to short-term to long-term memory stores. John Anderson and Gordon Bower proposed a pioneering semantic network model of human associative memory (HAM) that was the forerunner of Anderson's (1983) architecture ACT* (Adaptive Control of Thought). And Roger Shepard and Lynn Cooper asked people to mentally rotate geometric figures; finding a linear relation between the amount of rotation required and reaction times, they argued for analog mental operations.

Also influential was the new University of California at San Diego (UCSD). George Mandler, known for his work on active organization of memory, became first chair of its psychology department in 1965 and hired three young cognitive psychologists: Donald A. Norman, David E. Rumelhart, and Peter Lindsay. They and their graduate students (Norman, Rumelhart, and the LNR Research Group 1975) developed models of word recognition, analogy, memory, and semantic interpretation of verbs, sentences, and even brief stories. Underlying much of the work was a computer-implemented semantic network model of memory (ELINOR) that brought together influences from artificial intelligence, psychology, and linguistics.

During the same period research on memory continued within cognitive psychology (see Chapter 6), yielding more detailed characterizations of sensory, short- and long-term memory and of recognition and recall processes, plus discernment of procedural, episodic, and working memory. Research on reasoning gained traction, e.g., by positing mental models (see Chapter 7). But the greatest impact on cognitive science came from the rapid development of artificial intelligence within the new discipline of computer science. Embarking on a four-decade collaboration that made Carnegie-Mellon University a major incubator of cognitive science, Newell and Simon followed their landmark Logic Theorist program with General Problem Solver (GPS) in 1957. Both were written in their innovative Information Processing Language (IPL), which stored symbols in a *list structure* (i.e., one item was linked to another by specifying at the first site the address of the second item). In GPS they added their powerful idea of a *production system* architecture, in which conditional rules operate on representations in working memory (e.g., if expressions X and Y are in working memory, delete X and add Z). Newell and Simon (1972) asked people to think aloud while solving a problem and incorporated some of the strategies (e.g., reasoning backward from a goal state) in their models. Another AI pioneer, John McCarthy, created LISP (*LISt Processing language) in 1958; it incorporated some of IPL's features and became a standard tool. At MIT, Marvin Minsky (1968) introduced a wider readership to LISP programs adapting predicate logic toward simulating semantic activities such as solving analogies, proving theorems, and answering questions. The simplest example is in F. Black's chapter: "Where is my pencil?" was represented as a predicate with two arguments, **at (pencil, *y*)**, and answers were deduced from stored statements, e.g., **in (pencil, desk), at (desk, home)**. In an outlier chapter M. Ross Quillian pioneered a different format – *semantic networks* – that found uptake in the 1970s (initially in HAM and ELINOR).

A related endeavor, *robotics*, began the transition from science fiction to engineering project in the 1960s. Minsky's group designed a Blocks Micro-World in which robots must see and move blocks (not simply cogitate like most AI programs). At Stanford, Charles Rosen's group endowed "Shakey" with wheels, a TV camera, and control by rules akin to a production system. However, what many regarded as the most impressive research with a blocks world did not involve a robot. Focusing on natural language processing (NLP) at MIT in 1972, Terry Winograd wrote a program, SHRDLU, that could follow commands and answer questions in English regarding a simulated blocks world displayed on a monitor. Its large number of specialist subprograms picked out aspects of the syntax and semantics of a command and combined them with constraints from the current situation to arrive at its response.

Significantly, Winograd did not find Chomsky's generative grammar a suitable tool in writing these subprograms, and even the one he chose (Halliday's functional grammar) required extensive adaptation. A distinction made by Chomsky (1968) – *competence* versus *performance* – suggested one way to think about this. Generative grammar was offered as a formalization of people's tacit knowledge of language – their linguistic competence. Chomsky did not regard it as the linguist's job to study individual acts of comprehending or producing particular sentences in real time – linguistic performance – or to ask how a competence theory might be applied in explaining performance.

It was psycholinguists who faced that question, beginning with Miller's 1962 finding that sentences with more transformations were harder to process and remember. He inferred a close alignment between competence and performance, but later studies yielded mixed results. Moreover, it became clear that the ways of organizing a grammar that worked best for most linguistic purposes were awkward for modeling sentence production or comprehension. By 1970 cognitive scientists favorable to Chomsky had concluded that the relation of competence to performance was more abstract than originally thought, and most others found the notion of competence superfluous. In retrospect, Winograd's SHRDLU was a harbinger of numerous performance-oriented natural language processing systems implemented on computers in the 1970s (e.g., parsers using Aravind Joshi's Tree Adjoining Grammar).

Chomsky found greater uptake among the new *developmental psycholinguists* – those students of child language who signed onto the assault against behaviorism in Chomsky's (1959) review of Skinner's book *Verbal Behavior* (1957). One line of Chomsky's argument emphasized the essential creativity of language, in that there is no bound to the novel but grammatically well-formed sentences of a given language. He also argued for nature (language acquisition constrained by innate knowledge) over nurture (language acquired solely by learning – Skinner's position). David McNeill boldly brought this nativist perspective to bear on toddlers' earliest two-word utterances. More pragmatically, Roger Brown and others adapted such rules as Chomsky had proposed toward writing grammars for individual toddlers as they progressed toward more complex utterances. Views became more diverse as this field grew, and today it is a major nexus of ideas and data in cognitive science. (See Chapter 9 for more on adult and developmental psycholinguistics.)

1.5   Cognitive science gets its name and identity (1975–1980)

Cognitive science flourished for some years before it acquired a name and institutional identity. The term *cognitive science* first appeared in print in two 1975 books. The LNR group's *Explorations in Cognition* ended (p. 409) with the suggestion that the "concerted efforts of a number of people from . . . linguistics, artificial intelligence, and psychology may be creating a new field: *cognitive science*." The same term appeared in the subtitle of a book by computer scientist Daniel Bobrow and cognitive psychologist Allan Collins. The term caught on quickly, and the Alfred P. Sloan Foundation spearheaded interdisciplinary centers at selected universities. One product of its grant to UCSD was the 1979 La Jolla Conference on Cognitive Science, announced as the first annual meeting of the Cognitive Science Society. In 1980 the Society assumed ownership of the journal *Cognitive Science* (launched in 1977).

Roger Schank, who played a central role in the early days of the society and journal, constructed highly original computer simulations that offered an alternative to Chomsky's separation of syntax from meaning. He put his first major computer program through its paces in the early 1970s at Stanford, where he had a joint appointment in linguistics and computer science. MARGIE took in and produced English sentences and made inferences using semantic representations built from eleven primitive predicates and their arguments (e.g., PTRANS linked an actor, an object to be transferred, source, and goal). It worked surprisingly well but tended to license too many plausible inferences. Having already combined AI and linguistics, Schank moved to Yale in 1974 and began collaborating with psychologist Robert Abelson. They developed higher-order knowledge structures, *scripts*, which characterized common experiences. Their well-known restaurant script, for example, specified multiple roles (e.g., diner, server) and scenes (e.g., entering, ordering, eating, and exiting) and the typical sequence of primitive actions for each scene. Schank and Abelson (1977) reported that computer simulations incorporating scripts could read simple stories, infer unmentioned primitive actions to answer questions, and include such inferences in paraphrases.

Symbol-based computational models of mental representations and operations were the high-energy core of the newly named cognitive science. This bridge between psychology and artificial intelligence was constructed not only by computer scientists like Schank, but also by psychologists. We have already noted the wide-ranging models by Norman and Rumelhart (ELINOR) and by Anderson (a colleague of Newell and Simon by the time he created ACT by adding a production system to a HAM-style associative memory). These emerged amid a good deal of interdisciplinary crosstalk and occasional collaboration that was largely limited to the two disciplines. A look at the first volume of *Cognitive Science* (1977) reveals that the affiliations of the authors were either computer science (eight articles), psychology (six articles), or both (one article), and most of the articles concerned computational models.

Nonetheless, cognitive science (narrowly construed) has enjoyed a good deal of interdisciplinary crosstalk with what we might call the cognitive sciences (broadly construed). Consider the active engagement of philosophers of science who have taken cognitive science as an object of analysis. Some have assessed whether the cognitive revolution was a Kuhnian paradigm shift; others (Bechtel 2008; Thagard 2006) have examined the role of mechanistic explanation in cognitive science. A few also have made direct contributions; for example, Paul Thagard collaborated with psychologists Keith Holyoak and Richard Nisbett and computer scientist John Holland on a computer simulation of inductive learning and reasoning. Philosophers of mind have been active as well, forming interdisciplinary collaborations (e.g., Lakoff and Johnson 1980), or initiating debates that engage nonphilosophers (e.g., Fodor's language of thought and Putnam's thought experiments; see Chapter 2). Finally, certain longstanding contributions in philosophy have had an impact within cognitive science. Notably, formats for representing information were adapted from predicate logic not only by early computational modelers but also by cognitive psychologists studying knowledge representation, reasoning, and decision making (e.g., Walter Kintsch; also see Chapter 7). Moreover, philosophical proposals regarding concepts have found uptake in psychology. Eleanor Rosch (1973) propelled "west coast" research on concepts away from necessary and sufficient conditions toward a more Wittgensteinian emphasis on family resemblance and typicality (see Chapter 8). More classic "east coast" paths were pursued by Frank Keil, Elizabeth Spelke, and Susan Carey. For example, Carey (2009) credits children with a substantial core of Kantian a priori concepts, augmented with Quinean bootstrapping as a mechanism for conceptual change.

Together, these examples illustrate the complex relationship between various parts of philosophy and cognitive science from its early years to the present. At the other extreme are disciplines in which just one specialized subfield has had an ongoing participation in cognitive science. Examples include anthropology (beginning with Roy D'Andrade's cognitive treatment of kin terms) and sociology (e.g., Aaron Cicourel's reconstrual of social interaction). Cognitive scientists also monitored developments in neuroscience, but during this period made no major attempt to build bridges.

It gets tricky placing linguistics in this picture. Chomsky's earliest impact was on nonlinguists with an interdisciplinary orientation – nascent cognitive scientists – but he absorbed very little reciprocal impact as he riveted his own attention on generative grammar (and on provocative political essays). By the late 1960s he was succeeding in reshaping theoretical linguistics but also confronting a schism in his own ranks. It was the rebel "west coast" linguists who most directly interacted with and influenced the computational modelers at the core of the newly named cognitive science. Most notable (as discussed in Chapter 9) was the interlacing of semantics and syntax championed by generative semanticists such as George Lakoff and Ronald W. Langacker (giving rise later to cognitive linguistics) and the widely adopted *deep case* categories of Charles J. Fillmore, such as agent, instrument, object, and location. Lakoff and Fillmore had a strong presence in the early years of the Cognitive Science Society and were colleagues at University of California-Berkeley. By the 1980s a broader range of interdisciplinary researchers identified themselves as cognitive scientists, including many influenced by Chomskian linguistics.

Psycholinguists (of both coastal persuasions) were major contributors to cognitive science as it grew and matured, though few found their primary identity there. With the psychological reality of something akin to deep structure already well supported, attention turned to how adults parse, comprehend, and produce sentences (see Chapter 9). For example, Thomas Bever championed strategies such as (1) breaking complex sentences into simple sentoids and (2) conjecturing that a sentoid's N–V–N order corresponds to actor–action–object, which works well for active but not passive sentences. For those focusing on children rather than adults, Chomskian developmental psycholinguists confronted the emergence of semantic, cognitive, and social perspectives. Some debated, for example, whether early sentences like "Mommy eat" were produced from syntactic rules (S → NP + VP), semantic rules (actor + action), or narrow word-based formulae (Mommy + X); others sought universals by expanding inquiry beyond English. Most salient to cognitive scientists were increasingly precise data and arguments regarding acquisition processes that emphasized nurture (Catherine Snow), nature (Lila Gleitman), or a dynamic interplay with cognition (Elizabeth Bates).

Cognitive psychologists offered a variety of ingenious strategies for inferring aspects of adults' mental representations or operations. With the transition from behaviorism achieved, their battles now focused on those inferences. There was a long debate, for example, whether all mental representations were composed from discrete symbols or, as held by Alan Paivio and Stephen Kosslyn, some were visual images appropriate for analog operations such as scanning. Another dichotomy productive of research was top-down vs. bottom-up processing (e.g., to what extent is perception driven by expectation?). Also, a trend toward investigating larger units of cognitive activity yielded experimental paradigms based on Schank's scripts or the new *story grammars*.

Finally, artificial intelligence generally proceeded as its name suggests – most researchers directed to computational virtuosity rather than human simulation – but the performance of AI programs was improving only incrementally and it was a particular challenge to scale up from highly constrained domains such as the blocks micro-world. Philosopher Hubert Dreyfus pronounced symbolic AI's core strategy of symbolic rules and representations doomed to fail. Unbeknownst to him and to most cognitive scientists, their friends, and their critics, an alternative was about to shake up the field.

1.6 The connectionist challenge: artificial neural network models (1980 to present)

Information-processing models based on symbolic rules and representations opened mental life to serious inquiry and still are advantageous for many purposes. By the late 1970s, however, there had been little progress in equipping them to learn from experience or in overcoming their brittleness. A few key cognitive scientists took a new look at artificial neural networks and saw in them a promising alternative to stepwise operations on symbols. Such networks had been pioneered in the 1940s by McCulloch and Pitts, as noted above, and were a promising, active research area until the late 1960s. Frank Rosenblatt (1962) developed a training procedure for pattern classification networks in which the key components were McCulloch–Pitts neurons (linear threshold units) that provided one layer of connections with modifiable weights. His *perceptron convergence theorem* proved that if a solution existed, this procedure would find it. However, Minsky and Papert (1969) mathematically dissected important classes of perceptrons, demonstrating no solution (or no tractable solution) for whether or not a geometric figure is connected, parity is odd or even, etc. With this formal justification in place for the emerging dominance of serial, symbolic architectures, only a few dedicated researchers pursued neural network research through the 1970s (most notably Stephen Grossberg).

Within a decade artificial neural networks began their comeback (for more of this story, see Chapters 3 and 12 and Bechtel and Abrahamsen 2002). The turning point was a small, ad hoc conference in June 1979 at UCSD in which neuroscientists, cognitive psychologists, AI researchers, mathematicians, and electrical engineers became aware of common threads in their diverse projects. Visiting scholars Geoffrey Hinton (a computer scientist) and James A. Anderson (a psychologist) served as conference organizers and edited the presentations into a game-changing book (Hinton and Anderson 1981), with an introduction by conference hosts Rumelhart and Norman. UCSD assistant professor James L. McClelland had already developed an influential, transitional *interactive activation* model with Rumelhart, and by January 1982 they had reinvented the LNR research group as the PDP (*parallel distributed processing*) group. Its fluid membership included Hinton, Terrence J. Sejnowski, Paul Smolensky, and Jeffrey L. Elman – recent PhDs whose conceptual and computational virtuosity would soon help shape the new era of network modeling.

The PDP group focused on *distributed networks* in which the task-relevant information is encoded across multiple units, in contrast not only to symbolic architectures but also to the *localist networks* preferred by most other *connectionists* (the name adopted by many using artificial neural networks for cognitive modeling). One key contribution was *backpropagation*, a network learning procedure that finally made it possible to train multiple layers of connections (and hence find solutions where simple perceptrons could not). It was unveiled in a chapter in the first volume of a landmark publication by Rumelhart, McClelland and the PDP research group (1986a), titled *Parallel Distributed Processing: Explorations in the Microstructure of Cognition*. The two PDP volumes elicited a barrage of critical responses from symbolic theorists, especially Jerry Fodor and Zenon Pylyshyn. The lengthiest and best-known exchange (see Chapter 9) began with Rumelhart and McClelland's (1986b) single-network model of past tense acquisition in the second PDP volume and Pinker and Prince's (1988) defense of the classic claims that past tense forms are generated by a rule for regular verbs but retrieved from memory for irregular verbs and that two-year-olds' overregularization errors (e.g., *falled* rather than *fell*) signal that they have induced the rule.

Today there is less debate, and cognitive scientists can choose from a variety of neural network and symbolic architectures developed in the 1980s and 1990s. For example, some networks gradually increase the weights between pairs of units that become active together; this is called *Hebbian learning* in recognition of Donald Hebb's proposed synaptic modification mechanism. Others self-organize in other ways (e.g., Kohonen feature maps yield spatially organized two-dimensional sheets of units). Elman's simple recurrent networks retain traces of previous activity, and with Bates and others he developed a nuanced, connectionist perspective on the issue of innateness (Elman *et al.* 1996). For symbolic modeling, production systems continue to play a major role in Newell's SOAR and Anderson's ACT-R (see Chapter 3). Choices in linguistics and psycholinguistics include Chomsky's government binding theory (including a notion of parameter setting frequently applied to acquisition), his more recent minimalism, and alternatives better suited to processing (e.g., functional, cognitive, and construction grammars and head-driven phrase structure grammar). Of special note, *optimality theory* is a constraint-based linguistic theory that interfaces well with PDP networks as an underlying mechanism (see Smolensky and Legendre 2006). Within psychology, statistical approaches have diversified beyond artificial neural networks. Bayesian models offer a competing probabilistic framework for inductive learning and inference (Tenenbaum, Griffiths, and Kemp 2006), while language researchers have grappled with the implications of infants' knack for statistical learning of word boundaries (Saffran, Aslin, and Newport 1996).

1.7   Cognitive science expands downward and outward (1990s to present)

Since 1990 cognitive science has given increased attention to phenomena of emotion (Chapter 10), consciousness (Chapter 11), and animal cognition (Chapter 15) and incorporated new methods and perspectives from cognitive neuroscience (Chapter 12), evolutionary psychology (Chapter 13), embedded and extended cognition (Chapter 14), and dynamical systems theory. This has brought connections with a wider variety of research fields, such as clinical psychology, behavioral biology, human evolution, and artificial life. Regrettably, we cannot discuss all of these developments. Instead we highlight just two trends: the expansion of inquiry down into the brain (cognitive neuroscience) and out into the body and world (embedded and extended cognition).

To begin with the expansion downward, this would seem most naturally to involve artificial neural networks, but that came later; in fact it was a convergence between neuroscience and information processing that ignited cognitive neuroscience in the 1980s. Neuroscientist David Marr played a key transitional role by moving beyond single-cell recording to pursue neurally informed computational models of vision, especially focusing on object representation (see Chapter 4). Marr's life ended prematurely, but his former student Shimon Ullman made his own major contributions. Other neuroscientists redirected the partnership with information processing by bringing in new technologies. In particular, positron emission tomography (PET), and subsequently functional magnetic resonance imaging (fMRI), made blood flow available as a proxy in localizing neural activity while humans performed cognitive tasks. Electrophysiological studies (ERP) offered higher temporal, but lower spatial, resolution. These became the core of the new cognitive neuroscience. Initially regarded as a distraction or competitor by most cognitive scientists, by the twenty-first century these fields increasingly overlapped.

The expansion outward has been more diverse, but the transitional figure clearly is James J. Gibson (see Chapter 4 regarding both Marr and Gibson). He emphasized the rich information in the world outside the perceiver ("in the light") and argued that it was directly *picked up*, not processed step by step in the head. His successors are cognitive scientists who, in varied ways, have focused on cognition as embodied, situated, and extended beyond the individual. Embodied approaches to concepts have ranged from Lawrence Barsalou's perceptual symbol system to the more abstract image-schemas of cognitive linguistics, including Jean Mandler's (2004) nuanced treatment of their onset in infancy. Situatedness is added to embodiment, and physically realized, in robotics. For Rodney Brooks, who designs robots in which a hierarchy of controllers are coupled directly to the sensory-motor apparatus, the seamless, dynamic interaction between agents and the world demonstrates that intervening representations are unnecessary. Anthropologist Edwin Hutchins takes a different tack by adding to situatedness and embodiment the idea that cognitive activities extend beyond a single brain. He examines the coordination of multiple agents and instruments in real-world tasks such as navigating a large ship.

Overall, these avenues of inquiry have made space in cognitive science for a focus on real-time activities of embodied agents, but the more specific claims have been controversial. For example, Andy Clark advocates a philosophy of mind in which mind extends out into the world, but defends representations. In contrast, many advocates of another framework, *dynamical systems theory*, reconceptualize the mind and explicitly deny representations. They contend that coordinated interactions between the world and an agent can best be explained by identifying a small number of critical variables and capturing their evolving relation over time in differential equations. (For discussion, see Chapters 2 and 14.)

1.8   Conclusion

We have followed cognitive science from its historical roots through the cognitive revolution, symbolic rules and representations, subsymbolic artificial neural networks, and its most recent expansions down to the brain and out to the body, world, and other agents. One way of viewing this history is not as a series of polarized proposals and debates, but rather as a dynamic interplay of ideas and approaches. The claim that cognitive science is especially notable for its varied and changing *integrations* of diverse approaches both within and across disciplines is further developed and illustrated by Abrahamsen and Bechtel (2006).

Further reading

Bechtel, W., Abrahamsen, A., and Graham, G. (1998). The life of cognitive science, in W. Bechtel and G. Graham (eds.), *A Companion to Cognitive Science* (pp. 1–104). Oxford: Basil Blackwell. This opening chapter presents a detailed historical overview of cognitive science. The other chapters address a variety of research areas, methods, theoretical stances, controversies, and applications, followed by biographies of 138 early contributors to cognitive science.

Mandler, G. (2007). *A History of Modern Experimental Psychology: From James and Wundt to Cognitive Science*. Cambridge, MA: MIT Press/Bradford. A historical tour of the theoretical and experimental traditions in twentieth-century psychology that emphasizes their social and cultural context, by a leading contributor to the cognitive revolution.

Nadel, L. (ed.) (2003). *Encyclopedia of Cognitive Science*. London: Nature Publishing Group. A four-volume encyclopedia that offers detailed analysis of recent research and theoretical traditions in cognitive science.

Stainton, R. J. (ed.) (2006). *Contemporary Debates in Cognitive Science*. Oxford: Blackwell. Prominent advocates and critics of nativism, modularity, rules and representations, extended cognition, the irreducibility of consciousness and other controversial positions make their arguments accessible to graduate and advanced undergraduate students.

Thagard, P. (2005). *Mind: Introduction to Cognitive Science* (2nd edn.). Cambridge, MA: MIT Press/Bradford. This book provides a highly accessible introduction to representation and computation, including analogical reasoning and reasoning based on images. In the second edition Thagard adds discussion of how the brain and the social and material context of cognitive agents figure in current cognitive science.

Wilson, R. A. and Keil, F. C. (eds.) (1999). *The MIT Encyclopedia of the Cognitive Sciences*. Cambridge, MA: MIT Press/Bradford. This excellent one-volume resource offers approximately 450 one- to three-page articles by experts on such topics as memory, cognitive development, and dynamic approaches to cognition. It also features longer overviews of six major disciplines comprising cognitive science.

MITCogNet. http://cognet.mit.edu. A large online resource including access to many journals, books, reference works, and conference proceedings in cognitive science as well as free courseware for MIT courses in brain and cognitive science.

References

Abrahamsen, A. and Bechtel, W. (2006). Phenomena and mechanisms: Putting the symbolic, connectionist, and dynamical systems debate in broader perspective, in R. Stainton (ed.), *Contemporary Debates in Cognitive Science* (pp. 159–86). Oxford: Blackwell.

Anderson, J. R. (1983). *The Architecture of Cognition*. Cambridge, MA: Harvard University Press.

Bechtel, W. (2008). *Mental Mechanisms*. London: Routledge.

Bechtel, W. and Abrahamsen, A. (2002). *Connectionism and the Mind: Parallel Processing, Dynamics, and Evolution in Networks* (2nd edn.). Oxford: Blackwell.

Carey, S. (2009). *The Origin of Concepts*. Oxford University Press.

Chomsky, N. (1957). *Syntactic Structures*. The Hague: Mouton.

  (1959). Review of *Verbal Behavior, Language* 35: 26–58.

  (1968). *Language and Mind*. New York: Harcourt, Brace, and World.

Elman, J. L., Bates, E. A., Johnson, M. H., Karmiloff-Smith, A., Parisi, D., and Plunkett, K. (1996). *Rethinking Innateness: A Connectionist Perspective on Development*. Cambridge, MA: MIT Press.

Hinton, G. E. and Anderson, J. A. (eds.) (1981). *Parallel Models of Associative Memory*. Hillsdale, NJ: Lawrence Erlbaum.

Lakoff, G. and Johnson, M. (1980). *Metaphors We Live By*. University of Chicago Press.

Mandler, J. M. (2004). *The Foundations of Mind*. Oxford University Press.

Miller, G. A. (1956). The magical number seven, plus or minus two: Some limits on our capacity for processing information, *Psychological Review* 63: 81–97.

  (1979). *A Very Personal History* (Occasional paper No. 1). Cambridge, MA: Center for Cognitive Science.

Miller, G. A., Galanter, E., and Pribram, K. (1960). *Plans and the Structure of Behavior*. New York: Holt.

Minsky, M. (ed.) (1968). *Semantic Information Processing*. Cambridge, MA: MIT Press.

Minsky, M. and Papert, S. (1969). *Perceptrons*. Cambridge, MA: MIT Press.

Neisser, U. (1967). *Cognitive Psychology*. New York: Appleton-Century-Crofts.

Newell, A. and Simon, H. A. (1972). *Human Problem Solving*. Englewood Cliffs, NJ: Prentice-Hall.

Norman, D. A., Rumelhart, D. E., and the LNR Research Group (1975). *Explorations in Cognition*. San Francisco: Freeman.

Pinker, S. and Prince, A. (1988). On language and connectionism: Analysis of a parallel distributed processing model of language acquisition, *Cognition* 28: 73–193.

Rosch, E. (1973). Natural categories, *Cognitive Psychology* 4: 328–50.

Rosenblatt, F. (1962). *Principles of Neurodynamics: Perceptrons and the Theory of Brain Mechanisms*. Washington: Spartan Books.

Rumelhart, D. E., McClelland, J. L., and the PDP Research Group (1986a). *Parallel distributed processing*, vol. 1: *Foundations*. Cambridge, MA: MIT Press.

Rumelhart, D. E. and McClelland, J. L. (1986b). On learning the past tenses of English verbs, in J. L. McClelland, D. E. Rumelhart, and the PDP Research Group, *Parallel Distributed Processing*, vol. 2: *Psychological and Biological Models*. Cambridge, MA: MIT Press.

Saffran, J. R., Aslin, R. N., and Newport, E. L. (1996). Statistical learning by 8-month-old infants, *Science* 274: 1926–8.

Schank, R. C. and Abelson, R. P. (1977). *Scripts, Plans, Goals, and Understanding.* Hillsdale, NJ: Lawrence Erlbaum.

Shannon, C. E. (1948). A mathematical theory of communication, *Bell System Technical Journal* 27: 379–423, 623–56.

Skinner, B. F. (1957). *Verbal Behavior.* New York: Appleton-Century-Crofts.

Smolensky, P. and Legendre, G. (2006). *The Harmonic Mind: From Neural Computation to Optimality-Theoretic Grammar.* Cambridge, MA: MIT Press.

Tenenbaum, J. B., Griffiths, T. L., and Kemp, C. (2006). Theory-based Bayesian models of inductive learning and reasoning, *Trends in Cognitive Science* 10: 309–18.

Thagard, P. (2006). *Hot Thought.* Cambridge, MA: MIT Press.

Wiener, N. (1948). *Cybernetics.* New York: Wiley.

2 The representational theory of mind

Barbara Von Eckardt

2.1 Two conceptions of RTM

The phrase "the Representational Theory of Mind" (RTM) is used in two different but related ways. To understand the difference, we must distinguish two "levels" at which human beings can be described.[1] The first is *personal* and belongs to common sense or "folk psychology." At this level people are said to *act* (rather than simply behave) and to have propositional attitudes, emotions, sensations, character traits, and an impressive array of cognitive capacities, such as perceiving, understanding and speaking language, remembering, imaging, reasoning, etc. The second level, in contrast, is *subpersonal* and scientific. This is the "information-processing" level of cognitive science, at which a person's cognitive mind is theorized to be both a computational and representational system. It is at this level that most scientific hypotheses of cognitive psychology, traditional AI, and connectionism are formulated, hypotheses designed to explain our cognitive capacities, as conceived, initially, at the folk psychological level.

Given the above distinction, the two uses of RTM are this. On the first use, RTM is a thesis about just the subpersonal level, viz., that there are mental representations at that level. This is a working assumption about the mind/brain, held by many cognitive scientists. On the second, due largely to Fodor (1975) and much discussed by philosophers, RTM is a theory about the *relationship* of the personal to the subpersonal levels, specifically, that propositional attitudes are computational relations to subpersonal mental representations.[2] In this chapter, we will focus exclusively on the first use.

Contemporary treatments of the history of RTM typically trace that history back to the seventeenth and eighteenth century, with occasional mentions of Aristotle. In fact, many aspects of the contemporary discussion were anticipated well before the seventeenth century not only by Aristotle but also by

---

[1] There are also multiple subpersonal neural levels. How explanations and descriptions at the information-processing level relate to those at the neural level is an important foundational question for cognitive science.

[2] More specifically, Fodor (1987)'s proposal is that for each propositional attitude PA that *p*, there exists a computational relation C and a representation R such that a person has PA just in case his or her mind/brain bears C to R and R has the content that *p*.

the Arabic philosopher Ibn Sina (980 CE – 1037 CE) and a host of medieval philosophers, including Aquinas (1225–74), and, especially, Ockham (1285–1347/49).[3]

2.2   What is a mental representation?

Cognitive scientists and philosophers of cognitive science have offered various characterizations. I'll begin with my own view (Von Eckardt 1993), based on Peirce's *general* theory of representation, and then use that as a basis of comparison to other views. Representation, according to Peirce, always involves a triadic relation. He writes:

[a sign is] anything which is related to a Second thing, its *Object*, in respect to a Quality in such a way as to bring a Third thing, its *Interpretant*, into relation to the same object ... (2.92)[4]

In contemporary terms, we would say that a representation is constituted by a *representation-bearer* that represents some object (or has some *content*), where this representing has *significance* for some interpreter.

The representation-bearer. Although something is a full-blown representation only if it has content and significance, we can view representations in terms of only their material or formal properties. For example, the representation bearer of the following word token

"DOG"

is either a set of ink marks on paper or a set of pixels on a monitor screen. The representation-bearer of the Mona Lisa is a painted canvas hanging in the Louvre.

The represented object. When Peirce talks about "the" represented object, the definite article is not intended very seriously. A representation may have multiple objects, which can be treated as one complex object. For example, a representation might have something akin to reference (or extension) and something akin to sense (or intension) or represent a "target" under an aspect (Cummins 1996). Contemporary theorists often use the term *content* to capture the meaning of representations in the most generic sense. Peirce distinguishes two kinds of relations to represented objects – semantic relations (representing, referring, expressing a sense) and the relation that "grounds" these semantic relations. There are, on Peirce's view, only three possible kinds of pure ground:

---

[3] Lagerlund (2008) writes that "medieval theories are more than a match for anything advanced by the most important modern philosophers." An excellent place to begin in exploring the history of RTM is with entries in the online *Stanford Encyclopedia of Philosophy.*

[4] References to Peirce are to his collected papers (Peirce 1931–58). Specific passages are noted by volume and paragraph number (e.g., 5.346).

iconic, indexical, and symbolic. An *icon* is a representation that represents its object in virtue of being similar to the object in some respect (2.282, 3.556). The ground of an *index* is supposed to be an "existential" relation or a real connection between the representation and its object (2.243), including a causal relation. Finally, *symbols* represent by virtue of a convention. We'll discuss the contemporary versions of the first two below.

Significance. Peirce's "interpretant" is whatever it is that makes a representation-bearer's representing some object significant for an "interpreter." Typically, it is a "mental effect" in the mind of the interpreter for whom the representation is a representation. In his earlier writings, he considered this mental effect always to be a thought (for example, the thought involved in understanding a text); in later writings, other kinds of effects (emotional, energetic, and involving a habit) were allowed. He recognized that identifying the interpretant for mental representation posed special problems (more on this later).

If we accept Peirce's theory of representation in general, a *mental* representation becomes, simply, a representation that is mental. In other words, it is a representation whose representation-bearer, content, significance, and ground are appropriate to its being a representation in the mind/brain. Although there is fairly widespread agreement that each of these is a key feature of mental representations, not everyone follows Peirce in taking significance to be *essential* for representation (e.g., Mandik 2003). On Peirce's triadic view, a state with content that no longer has an interpretant mental effect, due perhaps to disease, would no longer be a representation; on a dyadic view, it still would be. In addition, some theorists add other requirements: that a representation must be capable of misrepresenting; that a representation must be part of a representational "scheme" (Haugeland 1991; van Gelder 1995); that a representation must have combinatorial structure (Wheeler and Clark 1999); that the representational system must be "arbitrary" in the sense that "what matters [for the system to exhibit the intelligent behavior and environmental coordination it does] is not the shape or form of the individual representations themselves, but rather their role as content-bearers" (Wheeler and Clark 1999, p. 124). For current purposes, the Peircian view will suffice. We'll refer to the entire system of mental representations as "MRS" (for "Mental Representation System").

2.3 Representation-bearers in cognitive science

Cognitive scientists, who conceptualize the mind/brain as, or as substantially like, a computer, take the representation-bearers of mental representations to be computational structures or states. If one assumes the mind/brain to be a "classical" von Neumann computer, its representation-bearers will be data structures; if one takes it to be a connectionist computer, its *explicit* representation-bearers will be patterns of activation of nodes in a network. Some people also claim that connectionist computers *implicitly* represent by means of their connection weights. Churchland and Sejnowski (1994) and Rolls and colleagues (reviewed in Rolls 2001) have explored the application of these ideas to actual neural networks in the brain. An alternative to both the classical computational and the connectionist views is the *dynamical systems approach* (DST). Although some who advocate DST are against representations, van Gelder (1995, p. 377) notes that DST is not necessarily anti-representationalist and that there are many entities and structures within a dynamical system that can serve as representation-bearers, including individual state variables, parameters, points in state space, trajectories, attractors, or "even such exotica as transformations of attractor arrangements as a system's control parameters change."

The data structure representation-bearers of the classical approach are often described as falling into *formal* kinds. For example, if one thinks of MRS as something like a language (e.g., Fodor 1975's "language of thought"), then there will be formal kinds akin to the syntactic types of natural language (names, definite descriptions, pronouns, predicates, sentences, etc.). Thagard (2005) takes there to be six main kinds of representations: sentences or well-formed formulae of a logical system; rules; concepts such as frames, schemata, or scripts; analogies; images; and connectionist representations. Each can be described formally but each also typically represents a certain kind of content. For example, sentences typically represent propositions; scripts usually represent typical action sequences; and imagistic representations typically represent scenes.

2.4   The semantics of mental representations

As we have seen, there are *two* sorts of relations that can exist between a representation-bearer and its representational object or content: *semantic* relations of representing, referring, expressing, etc.; and *ground* relations, such as similarity or causality, in virtue of which these semantic relations hold. Theories of both sorts are often referred to as "semantics." To avoid confusion, I'll use that term to refer only to theories of the first kind. A theory of this sort for English would, for example, tell us that the word 'cat' refers to the set of all cats. Similarly a semantics for MRS might tell us that the representation-bearer <CAT> expresses the property *cat*. (Angle brackets will be used to pick out kinds of representations in MRS, with capital letters for formal kinds and lower-case letters for semantic kinds. Thus <CAT> picks out a "word" in MRS, analogous to the word "cat" in English, and <cat> refers to any representation in MRS expressing the property *cat*.) In contrast, a *theory of content determination* (TCD) will be a theory of how the properties and relations described in a semantics are grounded. (Block 1986, p. 639, and Cummins 1989, pp. 10–11, also make this distinction.)

There is nothing even approximating a systematic semantics for even a fragment of MRS. Nevertheless, there are ways to inductively infer to some global semantic features MRS, arguably, must have. One way is to extrapolate, via a form of "transcendental" reasoning, from features of cognitive science's *explananda* (what it is trying to explain). The other is to look at the kinds of representational contents cognitive scientists have in fact posited. Von Eckardt (1993), following the lead of Lloyd (1987), adopts the first strategy as follows. Cognitive science's explananda include basic questions about the human cognitive capacities, i.e.: What, precisely, is the capacity to *X*? How does a person, typically, exercise his/her capacity to *X*? In virtue of what (in the mind/brain) does a person have the capacity *X*? Answering such questions involves, among other things, explaining the *intentionality* of the capacities (that they involve states that have content), their *pragmatic evaluability* (that they can be exercised correctly or incorrectly), their *opacity* (that the ways a person thinks about something will not capture everything that is true of it), their *productivity* (that having once mastered a capacity, a person can exercise it in novel ways), and their *systematicity* (that certain capacities go hand-in-hand with certain others). The cognitive science explanation of these features relies, in part, on the positing of representations. Assuming the correctness of this representational strategy, we can inductively infer that MRS must have certain general *semantic* properties, specifically, those that make intentionality, evaluability, opacity, productivity, and systematicity *possible*.[5] A related strategy is to infer from the semantics of natural language: assuming that we can think (that is, mentally represent) everything we can *say*, one can infer that the semantics of MRS must be at least as rich and complex as the semantics of natural language. Reasoning in these ways, we arrive at the following conclusions about the semantics of MRS. Each conclusion is also supported by representational contents cognitive scientists in fact posit.

1 Mental representations are *semantically selective*. The "aboutness" of perception, memory, and linguistic understanding is, typically, experienced as being quite specific. I perceive a clear (not opaque) bottle (not a cup or dish) on the desk (not the floor or suspended in the air). Since cognitive scientists take the content of intentional (i.e., propositional attitude) states

---

[5] The first three features of mental representations – semantic selectivity, semantic diversity, and semantic complexity – explain the analogous features of the intentional states involved in our capacities. Semantic complexity is also needed to account for opacity. Semantic evaluability explains pragmatic evaluability and semantic compositionality is needed to explain the semantic features of productivity and systematicity.

to be "inherited" from the content of mental representations, the latter must be similarly specific.

2 Mental representations are *semantically diverse*. We can perceive, imagine, and think about many different types of things – concrete objects, events, situations, properties, and sets in the world; concrete objects, events, situations, properties, and sets in possible and fictional worlds; and abstract objects such as universals and numbers. A similar diversity emerges from studying the semantics of natural language. If we can think everything we can mean in natural language, MRS must be similarly semantically diverse.

3 Mental representations are *semantically complex*. The intentionality of our capacities is complex. We can believe *of* something that it is so-and-so. Similarly, not only do the representations of MRS, taken as a whole, have many different kinds of content, many representational tokens have more than one kind of content simultaneously. For example, many are representations *of* something (the "target") *as* such-and-such, i.e., a representation of a read sentence in terms of its syntactic structure. Another kind of complexity is analogous to the sense/reference or intension/extension distinction found in semantic theories of natural language. Note that the target of a representation is often not the same as its extension. The representation <horse> has as its extension the set of all actual horses. When used on a particular occasion for perceptual recognition, its target (if used veridically) would be a particular horse. If used incorrectly, its target might be a cow.

4 Mental representations are *semantically evaluable*. The intentional states involved in our cognitive capacities are, typically, propositional attitude states, and such states are *evaluable*. We can perceive veridically and non-veridically, have true or false beliefs, and carry out our intentions to act either successfully or unsuccessfully. To account for such pragmatic evaluability, cognitive science needs representations that are *semantically* evaluable. The evaluability feature most often discussed is our capacity for *misrepresentation*, representing a target *t* that is actually *G*, as *H*. Examples from cognitive science include: perceptual illusion, false memories, speech errors. Note that there can be no misrepresentation without semantic complexity since misrepresentation always involves a mismatch between a target and properties attributed to that target. There are other kinds of evaluability besides misrepresentation. One is vacuous representation, when a mental predicate that has an extension has no target, as in "hearing" a missing phoneme. Another is using a mental predicate, such as <unicorn>, with no extension at all.

5 Mental representations are *compositional*. Fodor and Pylyshyn (1988) argue, based on the productivity and systematicity of our capacities, that our representations must be structured. Since this productivity and systematicity is not only formal but also semantic, it provides the basis for inferring to the compositionality of mental representational content as well, viz., that the

content of complex representations is "composed from" the contents of their representational constituents. Just as the meaning of "John loves Mary" is derived from the meanings of the individual words "John," "loves," and "Mary," so the content of the complex representation <<John> <loves> <Mary>> is presumably derived from the contents of the constituent representations <John>, <loves>, and <Mary> (plus order information). Although the compositionality of MRS is questioned by some connectionists, it is widely supported by the kinds of representational posits actually found in cognitive science, including in vision research, semantic memory research, psycholinguistics, theory of mind, study of reasoning, and many other areas. Furthermore, all agree that the contents of our propositional attitudes are clearly compositional.

2.5   The ground of mental content

Cognitive scientists explain various aspects of human cognition, in part, by positing representations with content. But what is it about these representations that gives them this content? This is the problem of content determination, arguably, *the* foundational problem for cognitive science – to identify a general "ground" for MRS, that is, a set of naturalistic (i.e., non-intentional, non-semantic, non-normative) properties and relations possessed by the representation-bearers of MRS that *determine* their semantic properties and relations.

Peirce hypothesized two broad kinds of ground for representation – similarity and causation. Contemporary TCDs embrace both of these and have added two other types, functional role (although the main version of this – "conceptual role semantics" – is actually a form of resemblance theory) and biological function.

2.5.1   The resemblance approach

Resemblance TCDs claim that a representation-bearer R represents a target t as a G in virtue of a resemblance relation between R and Gs. Two kinds of resemblance have been invoked: first-order resemblance, in which Rs and Gs share one or more properties (such as shape or color); and, second-order resemblance, in which they share a relational structure. Contemporary resemblance TCDs focus on second-order resemblance (Shepard and Chipman 1970; Palmer 1978; Swoyer 1991; Cummins 1996; O'Brien and Opie 2004). For such theories, both R and the Gs must be conceived as sets of objects plus relations defined over those objects. R then represents t as a G if the abstract relational structure of R "mirrors" the relational structure of Gs. Once such a representation relation exists for R and the Gs, one can get derivative representation relations between the constituent objects in R and the Gs, the specific relations in R and the Gs, and specific states-of-affairs in R and the Gs (Cummins 1996, p. 96).

Everyone agrees that first-order resemblance theories are highly problematic since they require representation-bearers to actually have the sensory properties they represent (triangular, smooth, polka-dotted), which, in most cases, they simply don't. Second-order resemblance theories overcome this problem. In addition, since there is no restriction on the kinds of constituent objects and relations that can constitute the represented object, they are able to handle a fair amount of diversity, including the representation of Gs that are concrete, abstract, actual, possible, fictional, present, past, or future. What they can't do is pick out *individuals*, a point noted by Peirce (3.434). As Stampe (1977) makes clear, a picture of a person who is an identical twin cannot, on purely resemblance grounds, pick out one twin rather than another. Rather relational structure representations always express the property of having a certain relational structure and, hence, extensionally, pick out *all things* having that structure.

Second-order resemblance theories also fall short with respect to selectivity. Because the structures involved are defined abstractly, any given relational structure will, typically, apply not only to many things but also to many *sorts* of things (e.g., people, plants, numbers). Finally, second-order resemblance theories, like any theory positing only one *specific* kind of ground (like second-order resemblance), cannot handle misrepresentation since misrepresentation always requires two grounds, one to determine the representation's target and one to determine the content of the mental predicate being misapplied to the target. This is not to say, of course, that second-order resemblance, were it satisfactory in other respects, couldn't be combined with another "factor" such as a singular causal relation to determine the target, so that it could handle misrepresentation.

2.5.2   The indicator approach

Indicator (also called "informational," and "causal") theories attempt to ground the semantics of MRS on either an informational or causally lawful relation between R and Gs (Stampe 1977; Dretske 1981; Fodor 1987).[6] Again, there are several versions. The core idea of Dretske (1981) is that R represents a target t as being G if and only if Rs *carry information* about Gs, that is, given an R, it is certain that t will be G.[7] Although an R can carry information about a G

---

[6] Dretske and Stalnaker advance their theories as theories of content determination for the propositional attitudes rather than as TCDs for the representations of cognitive science. However, their views can easily be reconstructed as the latter.

[7] This is a simplification. The view is actually that "a signal r carries the information that s is G = The conditional probability of s's being G, given r (and k), is 1 (but, given k alone,

without that *G* actually causing the *R* (the two might be correlated by sharing an underlying cause), such causation would be the typical case. Fodor's (1987) "crude causal theory" is that a representation *R* expresses a property *G* if "it's nomologically necessary that *all* and *only* instances of the property cause tokenings of the symbol" (p. 100). Since clearly cats in South Africa don't cause instantiations of <cat> in me in Rhode Island, the "all" clause gets restricted in his "slightly less crude causal theory" to all G instances that are "causally responsible for psychophysical traces" to which the person "stands in a psychophysically optimum relation" (p. 126).

Indicator TCDs makes the most sense for perceptual representations of properties, but even when thus restricted they face problems. Selectivity poses a problem because perceptual representations carry information about or co-vary with more instantiated properties than they supposedly represent. As a result, the challenge is to distinguish those informational or co-variation relations that determine content from those that don't. For example, even when I'm perceiving veridically, <cat> carries information about not only the presence of a cat but also the presence of a mammal, the existence of various background conditions (my eyes being open, there being adequate lighting), and the presence of various proximal states (a retinal image of a cat, neural signals in my optic nerve, etc.). But my representation expresses the property of being a cat, not any of these other things. Dretske (1981, chs. 6 and 7) provides interesting suggestions on how to deal with these problems.

Taken simply as a TCD for mental *predicates*, an indicator theory is, obviously, missing a key ingredient for handling a lot of misrepresentation, namely, picking out a target. But even with this missing ingredient, misrepresentation raises a problem – the infamous "disjunction problem" (Fodor 1987, 1991). Suppose there is a solution to the selectivity problem; it will still be the case that, occasionally, a person will token <CAT> in the presence of a dog. Now, of course, this tokening of <CAT> counts as a case of *mis*representation only if the content of <CAT> in fact expresses the property of being a cat rather than the property of being a dog. But what gives it feline content rather than canine content? According to the indicator approach, it has feline content because <CAT>s indicate the presence of cats. But, if the content of the representation is determined by what <CAT> *in fact* co-varies with or carries information about, then insofar as there is an occasional dog causing <CAT>, the ground will actually consist of cats *or* dogs and, hence, <CAT> will actually express the property of being a cat or a dog. But if the representation in question has this *disjunctive* content, then, of course, the tokening of <CAT> in the presence of a dog doesn't count as misrepresentation at all!

less than 1)" (p. 65). The variable *k* stands for background knowledge. One question is whether including *k* threatens the view's naturalism.

Generalizing this reasoning for every putative case of misrepresentation, it will turn out that we never actually misrepresent anything! Several solutions have been offered to this problem, all involving ways of ruling out the "wild" tokens (the dogs, etc.) from contributing to the content. See Godfrey-Smith (1989) for an overview of some proposed solutions, and Fodor (1990a, 1990b) and Loewer and Rey (2001) for critical responses to these proposals.

What are the prospects of extending the account beyond the representation of properties in perception? There are two kinds of extension required: to non-perceptual representations (e.g., in memory, reasoning, etc.) of immediately observable properties and to representations, in perception and elsewhere, of non-observable properties. Consider the first. I can *remember* a red dress I bought twenty years ago, I *know* that red is a color, and I can *intend* to wear red tomorrow. Determining the content of <red> in non-perceptual cognitive roles directly by an indicator ground gets more and more problematic with respect to selectivity as the causal distance (and, hence, the number of causal intermediaries) between the distal property instantiations and the cognitive use increases. A more promising approach is to say, as Dretske (1981, p. 193) does, that *types* of representations of immediately observable properties, e.g., <RED>, get their content via indication in perception, but that once that content is fixed, tokens of that type can be used (by the same person), outside of perception, with the same content. Note, however, that this move introduces an element other than indication as part of our TCD, namely, the inheritance story just mentioned.

What about the second type of extension to the representation of properties not immediately observable? Many kinds of properties fall into this category. The obvious candidates are abstract, merely possible (hence, actually uninstantiated), theoretical, and fictional properties. A natural suggestion for handling all of these is to opt for some form of content empiricism, and distinguish primitive representations, whose content is determined by indication, from complex representations, which are "built" out of primitive ones. But such a program faces significant challenges.

2.5.3   The biological function approach

Biological function or "teleosemantic" TCDs come in various forms but all use the notion of biological function. The biological function *indicator* approach attempts to ground content on the *function* to indicate rather than simply on indication (Dretske 1986, 1988), where the notion of function is biological and related to evolutionary selection. Neander (1991, p. 74) explicates the relevant notion of function as follows:

It is a/the proper function of an item (X) of an organism (O) to do that which items of X's type did to contribute to the inclusive fitness of O's ancestors, and which caused the genotype, of which X is the phenotypic expression, to be selected by natural selection.

(For other views, see Allen, Bekoff, and Lauder 1998 and Ariew, Cummins, and Perlman 2002.)

Content theorists have been attracted to the biological function indicator approach in the hope that it will solve the disjunction problem but, unfortunately, difficulties remain. For a representation R to acquire the function of indication, R-type representations in a person's evolutionary ancestors must have actually indicated. But it is implausible that there were no cases of "misrepresentation" during that period. However, if that is the case, making the ground the function to indicate rather than simply indication pushes the disjunction problem back into human prehistory.

Millikan (1984, 1989) has argued for an alternative biological function approach that combines a structural isomorphism approach with the "proper function" of the "consumer" of the representation. Suppose that a representation-bearer R in an organism O belongs to a family of representation-bearers such that the family bears a second-order structural resemblance relation to some set of states-of-affairs in the world. Her view is, (very) roughly, that R (from the family) represents a state-of-affairs p (from the relevant set) if R maps to p and p's being the case is a *normal* condition for the consumer of R to successfully carry out its biological function F, where "normal" is unpacked as a condition necessary for the consumer systems in O's ancestors exercising F in a way that contributed to fitness of those ancestors. For example, the perceptual system of the frog generates representation-bearers that map onto moving black spots in its visual field. The content of a specific representation in this family is moving-frog-food-at-point-x-in-the-frog's-visual-field because the proper function of the motor mechanism consuming these representations is to snap at frog food and a normal condition of successful execution of that function is that the representations actually map onto frog food rather than things that look like frog food but are not edible.

Millikan's emphasis on consumption solves some problems plaguing the other approaches but leaves others untouched. Her view solves the disjunction problem because "wild" tokens are now irrelevant to content determination. It also cuts down on some of the selectivity problems facing the indicator approach and straightforward resemblance theories (the frog's representations mean frog-food not moving-black-spots). But, like simple resemblance theories, it can't handle singular representation and the close tie to evolution limits content in fairly serious ways to those properties that contributed to the fitness of the organism (hence, not *telephone, bank rate, condo*, etc.). Another serious question is whether the account, which makes sense for simple systems in which the consumption of a representation is directly linked to behavior, will work for systems, like human mind/brains, where the "consumption" process is extremely complex and often only very indirectly connected to behavior.

2.5.4 The causal historical approach

In the late 1960s, several prominent philosophers argued that referring expressions in natural language, such as proper names and natural-kind terms, attach to the world not by means of any implicit description but rather by means of actual causal links to the objects and phenomena being referred to (Kripke 1980; Putnam 1975). Theories of this sort are called "causal theories of reference." This approach to referring expressions in natural language has been extended to representations in MRS by Field (1978), Devitt (1981), and Sterelny (1990). The basic idea is that some of our representations function like proper names and get their content not by a general causal dependency on what they represent but from a singular causal connection, which functions something like a natural language naming event.

Insofar as the basic grounding property for causal historical TCDs is causation, the approach faces the same selectivity problems as does the indicator approach. Whether singular or general, the causation in question is made up of multiple links. For example, when my grandson Jack was born, why did the original tokening of <Jack> in my mind name Jack rather than my retinal image of Jack? There is also serious indeterminacy of reference. How is the object in the world to be delimited? Why does <Jack> name Jack rather than Jack + hospital crib or Jack + his mother's arms? Why Jack rather than just Jack's head? Why not human baby? And as a single-factor account, the causal historical approach also can't deal with misrepresentation although it does avoid the disjunction problem since no causal connections beyond the original (and, hence, no "wild" tokenings) count toward determining content.

Singular causal relations have been used not only to ground the content of MRS names but also to ground the representation of a target. Although sometimes not distinguished, the two are different. The name "Madonna" refers to the singer Madonna, but I can still apply it to someone else, say, Brittany Spears. In this case of misapplication, Brittany Spears is the target and is not identical to the name's referent, Madonna. The difference between the ground of a name and the ground of a name's target is that, whereas both involve singular causal connections, the ground of a name is the causal connection that occurred at the original naming event whereas the ground of a target is the connection occurring at the moment the object is being "targeted." Both Dretske (1981) and Cummins (1996) explore the nature of grounds for targets.

2.5.5 The functional role approach

The core idea of a functional role TCD is that a representation-bearer R represents some object O in virtue of the functional role of R in the mind/brain "mirroring" the role of O in some other domain of objects to which it belongs.[8] There are several versions of functional role TCDs. We'll focus here on "conceptual role semantics" (Field 1977; Field 1978; McGinn 1982; Loar 1982; Block 1986; Block 1987; Schiffer 1987). An alternative view is Cummins' (1989) "interpretational semantics."

Conceptual role TCDs are best suited for grounding propositional representations. The claim is that a propositional representation R represents a proposition p if the conceptual role of R in the mind "mirrors" the logical role of p in the Platonic space of propositions. More precisely, R represents p if R belongs to the causal network of representation-bearers R-net underlying inference and reasoning, p belongs to a logical network of propositions, p-net, and there exists an isomorphism between R-net and p-net such that R maps onto p. Formulated thus, the theory encompasses only "narrow" functional role. A "wide" two-factor version extends the input and output arms of functional role to include causal relations to the world.

The content-determination story offered by conceptual role accounts suffers from selectivity and diversity problems. Given that content determination is, ultimately, based on similarity, conceptual role TCDs, like structural similarity theories, have a serious problem with selectivity since there will be many (probably, indefinitely many) propositional networks with the same relational structure as a given causal network of representation-bearers. With respect to diversity, there is an obvious problem since the approach is only worked out for the representation of propositions. Some philosophers (Block 1986, p. 628; Schiffer 1987, p. 92) have suggested that the view might extend to the components of propositions but that suggestion is, at this point, simply a promissory note. Thus, at present, there is no account of the vast majority of entities cognitive science claims we represent – edges, scenes, objects, color, space, remembered episodes, intended actions, etc.

2.5.6   Multiple-factor approaches

To handle misrepresentation, some forms of diversity, and even selectivity, some TCD theorists have turned to approaches which encompass more than one type of ground. Dretske (1981), for example, combines an information-based indicator approach for predicate content with a singular causal account (also making use of the notion of information) for the *target*. Cummins (1996) opts for a structural isomorphism theory for predicate content and a biological function approach for the target. Finally, there are "two-factor" functional

---

[8] The fact that functional role TCDs implicitly or explicitly invoke a mirroring or isomorphism relation raises the question of whether they should be categorized as "resemblance" views. The literature has, generally, distinguished accounts in which the relational structure being mirrored is internal to the representation ("resemblance" accounts) from those in which the relational structure involves the relations of representations to each other ("functional role" accounts) and I do the same here.

role theories (Field 1977, 1978; McGinn 1982; Loar 1982) that combine both functional role and a causal relation to the world. It is quite possible that all of the above kinds of ground will have to play some role. In addition, on my view, TCD theorists need to take more seriously the role of natural language in determining mental content as the child acquires linguistic ability.

2.6   The significance of mental representations

Peirce recognized that the interpretants of representations cannot always be thoughts. For if thoughts are themselves (or involve) mental representations and all representations (including the mental ones) must have interpretants to be representations, then there will be infinite regress of interpretation. Peirce considered several solutions to this problem, two of which have close analogues in the contemporary cognitive science discussion. The first consists in pointing out that since the characterization of a representation doesn't require that interpretants be *actual* but only *potential*, the infinite regress is not really that problematic (Cummins 1983, p. 114). The second seeks to eliminate the regress altogether by proposing that the interpretant of a mental representation is *ultimately* a habit change (a disposition to behave, in modern parlance) rather than another representational state (5.491). On the information-processing paradigm, this amounts to the fact that for each representation there will be a set of computational consequences contingent upon entertaining that representation and responsive to its content (Von Eckardt 1993, pp. 290–302). How this is spelled out in detail depends on the computational architecture of the system in question.

2.7   The role of mental representations in cognitive science explanations

Mental representations play multiple roles in cognitive science explanations, which themselves come in many kinds. The kind most studied by philosophers explains in virtue of what a typical, normal adult has a certain complex cognitive capacity C, where the answer takes the form of a "functional analysis" of C in terms of the ordered exercise of a set of less complex capacities that constitute C (Cummins 1975, 1983). But there are other kinds as well, including explaining what precisely a certain capacity C *is* (including in virtue of what it is intentional, coherent, etc.), how C normally develops, how C typically breaks down, how C varies across individuals (between males and females, and cross-culturally), how C is typically realized in the brain, how various capacities interact, and why the "effects" psychologists discover about particular capacities occur. The key (intended) roles of representations in these explanations include explaining in virtue of what our cognitive capacities are intentional (answer: because they involve representations which, like intentional states, have content), making evident how the processes involved in the exercise of our cognitive capacities are intelligible (because the sequence of representations makes a certain sense), and explaining why some psychological effects, such as certain error patterns, occur in certain experimental tasks (because the subject lacked certain representations or represented a target in a certain way).

2.8   Challenges to RTM

Philosophers have challenged RTM by challenging (1) whether it is even *possible* (conceptually or metaphysically) for representations to play the above intended roles; (2) whether, even if it is possible, it is explanatorily necessary; and (3) whether states claimed to be representations are, in fact, suited for these roles. Regarding possibility, Horst (1996) argues that none of the plausible senses in which mental representations can be said to have content can account for the intentionality of our capacities, as they are supposed to do. Another possibility challenge rests on the claim that *no* mental state (thus, no representational state) can have causal powers (Kim 1993, 1998, 2005) and, hence, can play a role in causal explanation. Fortunately, neither of these arguments is decisive. (See Von Eckardt 2002 for a reply to Horst, and Robb and Heil 2009 for a helpful overview of the mental causation literature.)

Necessity challenges have been made by both cognitive science insiders and outsiders. As an insider, Stich (1983) argues that cognitive scientists can make do with a purely "syntactic theory of mind" and, hence, don't need any representations. (For responses, see Possin 1986, Egan 1999, and Von Eckardt 2002.) Outsiders claim that competing research programs can explain everything cognitive science seeks to explain without resort to representations. The earliest, post-behaviorist, scientific challenge of this sort came from Gibson's (1966, 1979/1986) "ecological" approach to perception. Currently, the biggest challenges come from the *dynamic systems approach* (DST) (Thelen and Smith 1993; van Gelder 1995; Kelso 1995), robotics and "autonomous agent theory" (Brooks 1991; Beer 1995), "artificial evolution" (Cliff and Noble 1997), "non-computational cognitive neuroscience" (Globus 1992), and "ruthless reductionism" (Bickle 2003), which advocates the explanation of behavior directly from molecular and cellular neuroscience.

Space does not permit evaluation of the pros and cons of these competitor approaches here. (For responses to DST, see Clark 1997 and Bechtel 1998, with a reply in Ramsey 2007; to "embodied cognition" approaches generally, including robotics and artificial evolution, see Clark and Toribio 1994, Wheeler and Clark 1999, and Wheeler 2001; to "ruthless reductionism," see van Eck, Looren de Jong, and Schouten 2006 and Looren de Jong 2006.)

However, for readers interested in exploring this literature, there are a couple of points to keep in mind. Anti-representationalists, typically, argue in two steps. First, they describe a small number of phenomena that have purportedly been explained non-representationally. Examples include a robot navigating toward a goal while avoiding obstacles, the development of infant walking, female crickets tracking male auditory signals, and the consolidation of memory. They then *generalize* from the research cases to claim that all of cognition can be similarly explained. There are two critical questions to ask. First, is it true that the sample explanations don't invoke representations? And, second, is the generalization step justified? Exploration of the first reveals that anti-representationalist cases often show only that certain *kinds* of representations aren't needed (e.g., detailed, viewer-independent models of the environment, detailed instructions for action) but that on a plausible conception of mental representation, there are plenty of representations involved (Clark and Toribio 1994; Clark 1997; Wheeler and Clark 1999). Consideration of the second has led to the identification of kinds of cognitive behaviors that are, in Clark's words, "representation hungry," that is, extremely unlikely to fall to the anti-representationalist's challenge, even if some online intelligent behaviors do. These include reasoning about absent, non-existent, or counterfactual states of affairs and perception of more abstract properties (Clark and Toribio 1994). Another consideration is whether the explanandum is couched in terms of behavior (albeit intelligent) or the cognitive capacities. If the latter and these are conceptualized to include the property of intentionality, and other intentionality-based properties, such as pragmatic evaluability, cogency, reliability, and systematicity, then it can be argued (Von Eckardt 1993, pp. 330–9) that anti-representational approaches simply don't have the conceptual resources to provide the required explanations.

A third kind of challenge comes from Ramsey (1997, 2007), who has argued for a more limited thesis: that not all the "representational" states cognitive scientists have posited *in fact* merit being considered representations. Those that don't pass muster, on his view, include indicators (those underwritten by an indicator TCD), including connectionist, hidden unit representations, and "tacit" representations. (For a response to Ramsey 1997, see Von Eckardt 2003.)

2.9   Concluding summary

Much cognitive science assumes that human cognition involves both unconscious and conscious use of mental representations. Hypotheses in cognitive science are often framed in representational terms and representational posits play important roles in cognitive science explanation. It is thus important for cognitive scientists to understand both the precise nature of RTM, and the challenges to it. The biggest foundational challenge is to develop an adequate naturalistic theory of how representational content is determined. Philosophers have proposed several ingenious theory-sketches of content determination but none accounts for the full range of semantic features mental representations arguably have. Another major challenge is the existence of non-representational competitor research programs. A likely future scenario is that we will be able to explain certain "low-level" aspects of cognition without resort to representations but that representational hypotheses will still be needed to account for the intentionality-based features of cognition and "representation hungry" higher-level processes.

Further reading

Primary works

Bickle, J. (2003). *Philosophy and Neuroscience: A Ruthlessly Reductive Account.* Norwell, MA: Kluwer Academic Press. An important challenge to the idea that mental representations are needed to account for cognition.

Block, N. (1986). Advertisement for a semantics for psychology, *Midwest Studies in Philosophy* 10: 615–78. A classical statement of the functional role theory of content determination.

Dretske, F. (1981). *Knowledge and the Flow of Information.* Cambridge, MA: MIT Press. An important systematic treatment of the information version of the indicator theory of content determination.

Fodor, J. (1987). *Psychosemantics: The Problem of Meaning in the Philosophy of Mind.* Cambridge, MA: MIT Press. Fodor's initial statement of his causal indicator theory of content determination.

(1990). *A Theory of Content and Other Essays.* Cambridge, MA: MIT Press. An elaboration of Fodor's theory of content determination with discussion of asymmetrical dependence.

(2008). *LOT 2: The Language of Thought Revisited.* Oxford University Press. An update of Fodor's 1975 *The Language of Thought* with special attention to concepts, nativism, and reference.

Millikan, R. (1984). *Language, Thought, and Other Biological Categories.* Cambridge, MA: MIT Press. A detailed presentation of Millikan's teleosemantic approach to content determination.

(1989). Biosemantics, *Journal of Philosophy* 86: 281–97. The most accessible statement of Millikan's teleosemantic approach to content determination.

van Gelder, T. (1995). What might cognition be if not computation? *The Journal of Philosophy* 92: 345–81. A defense of the dynamical-systems approach.

Secondary works

Adams, F. and Aizawa, K. Causal theories of mental content, in Edward N. Zalta (ed.), *The Stanford Encyclopedia of Philosophy*, http://plato.stanford.edu. A nice review of recent literature on causal approaches to content determination.

Cummins, R. (1989). *Meaning and Mental Representation*. Cambridge, MA: MIT Press. An overview of major theories of content determination.

Neander, K. Teleological theories of mental content, in Edward N. Zalta (ed.), *The Stanford Encyclopedia of Philosophy*, http://plato.stanford.edu. An excellent review of recent literature on the teleosemantic approach to content determination.

Pitt, D. Mental Representation, in Edward N. Zalta (ed.), *The Stanford Encyclopedia of Philosophy*, http://plato.stanford.edu. An overview of the mental representation literature with more emphasis on philosophy of mind issues.

Von Eckardt, B. (1993). *What is Cognitive Science?* Cambridge, MA: MIT Press. A systematic treatment of the foundations of cognitive science including several chapters on mental representation.

References

Allen, C., Bekoff, M., and Lauder, G. (eds.) (1998). *Nature's Purposes: Analyses of Function and Design in Biology*. Cambridge, MA: MIT Press.

Ariew, A., Cummins, R., and Perlman, M. (eds.) (2002). *Functions: New Readings in the Philosophy of Biology and Psychology*. Oxford University Press.

Bechtel, W. (1998). Representations and cognitive explanations: Assessing the dynamicist's challenge in cognitive science, *Cognitive Science* 22: 295–318.

Beer, R. (1995). Computational and dynamical languages for autonomous agents, in R. Port and T. van Gelder (eds.), *Mind as Motion: Explorations in the Dynamics of Cognition* (pp. 121–47). Cambridge, MA: MIT Press.

Bickle, J. (2003). *Philosophy and Neuroscience: A Ruthlessly Reductive Account*. Norwell, MA: Kluwer Academic Press.

Block, N. (1986). Advertisement for a semantics for psychology, *Midwest Studies in Philosophy* 10: 615–78.

(1987). Functional role and truth conditions, *Proceedings of the Aristotelian Society*, Supplement 61: 157–81.

Brooks, R. (1991). Intelligence without representation, *Artificial Intelligence* 47: 139–59.

Churchland, P. and Sejnowski, T. (1994). *The Computational Brain*. Cambridge, MA: MIT Press.

Clark, A. (1997). The dynamical challenge, *Cognitive Science* 21: 461–81.

Clark, A. and Toribio, J. (1994). Doing without representing, *Synthese* 101: 401–31.

Cliff, D. and Noble, J. (1997). Knowledge-based vision and simple visual machines, *Philosophical Transactions of the Royal Society: Biological Sciences*, 352, 1165–75.

Cummins, R. (1975). Functional analysis, *The Journal of Philosophy* 72: 741–65.

(1983). *The Nature of Psychological Explanation*. Cambridge, MA: MIT Press.

(1989). *Meaning and Mental Representation*. Cambridge, MA: MIT Press.

(1996). *Representations, Targets, and Attitudes*. Cambridge, MA: MIT Press.

Devitt, M. (1981). *Designation*. New York: Columbia University Press.

Dretske, F. (1981). *Knowledge and the Flow of Information*. Cambridge, MA: MIT Press.
  (1986). Misinformation, in R. Bogdan (ed.), *Belief* (pp. 17–36). Oxford University Press.
  (1988). *Explaining Behavior: Reasons in a World of Causes*. Cambridge, MA: MIT Press.
Egan, M. (1999). What's wrong with the syntactic theory of mind, *Philosophy of Science* 56: 664–74.
Field, H. (1977). Logic, meaning, and conceptual role, *Journal of Philosophy* 74: 379–409.
  (1978). Mental representation, *Erkenntnis* 13: 9–61.
Fodor, J. (1975). *The Language of Thought*. New York: Thomas Y. Crowell.
  (1987). *Psychosemantics: The Problem of Meaning in the Philosophy of Mind*. Cambridge, MA: MIT Press.
  (1990a). *A Theory of Content and Other Essays*. Cambridge, MA: MIT Press.
  (1990b). Information and representation, in P. Hanson (ed.), *Information, Language, and Cognition* (pp. 175–90). Vancouver: University of British Columbia Press.
  (1991). Replies, in B. Loewer and G. Rey (eds.), *Meaning in Mind: Foder and this Critics* (pp. 255–319). Oxford University Press.
Fodor, J. and Pylyshyn, Z. (1988). Connectionism and cognitive architecture: A critical analysis, *Cognition* 28: 3–71.
Gibson, J. (1966). *The Senses Considered as a Perceptual System*. Boston, MA: Houghton Mifflin Company.
  (1979/1986). *Ecological Approach to Visual Perception*. Hillsdale, NJ: Lawrence Erlbaum.
Globus, G. (1992). Towards a non-computational cognitive neuroscience, *Journal of Cognitive Neuroscience* 40: 299–310.
Godfrey-Smith, P. (1989). Misinformation, *Canadian Journal of Philosophy* 19: 533–50.
Haugeland, J. (1991). Representational genera, in W. Ramsey, S. Stich, and D. Rumelhart (eds.), *Philosophy and Connectionist Theory* (pp. 61–89). Hillsdale, NJ: Lawrence Erlbaum.
Horst, S. W. (1996). *Symbols, Computation, and Intentionality*. Berkeley: University of California Press.
Kelso, J. (1995). *Dynamic Patterns*. Cambridge, MA: MIT Press.
Kim J. (1993). *Supervenience and Mind: Selected Philosophical Essays*. Cambridge University Press.
  (1998). *Mind in a Physical World*. Cambridge, MA: MIT Press.
  (2005). *Physicalism, or Something Near Enough*. Princeton University Press.
Kripke, S. (1980). *Naming and Necessity*. Cambridge, MA: Harvard University Press.
Lagerlund, H. (2008). Mental representation in medieval philosophy, in Edward N. Zalta (ed.), *The Stanford Encyclopedia of Philosophy* (Fall 2008 edn.), http://plato.stanford.edu/archives/fall2008/entries/representation-medieval/.

Lloyd, D. (1987). Mental representation from the bottom up, *Synthese* 70: 23–78.

Loar, B. (1982). Conceptual role and truth conditions, *Notre Dame Journal of Formal Logic* 23: 272–83.

Loewer, B. and Rey, G. (2001). *Meaning in Mind: Fodor and His Critics*. Oxford University Press.

Looren de Jong, H. (2006). Explicating pluralism: Where the mind to molecule pathway gets off the track – Reply to Bickle, *Synthese* 151: 435–43.

Mandik, P. (2003). Varieties of representation in evolved and embodied neural networks, *Biology and Philosophy* 18: 95–130.

McGinn, C. (1982). The structure of content, in A. Woodfield (ed.), *Thought and Content* (pp. 207–58). Oxford University Press.

Millikan, R. (1984). *Language, Thought, and Other Biological Categories*. Cambridge, MA: MIT Press.

  (1989). Biosemantics, *Journal of Philosophy* 86: 281–97.

Neander, K. (1991). Functions as selected effects, *Philosophy of Science* 58: 168–84.

O'Brien, G. and Opie, J. (2004). Notes toward a structuralist theory of mental representation, in H. Clapin, P. Staines, and P. Slezak (eds.), *Representation in Mind: New Approaches to Mental Representation* (pp. 1–20). Amsterdam: Elsevier.

Palmer, S. (1978). Fundamental aspects of cognitive representation, in E. Rosch and B. Lloyd (eds.), *Cognition and Categorization* (pp. 259–302). Hillsdale, NJ: Lawrence Erlbaum.

Peirce, C. S. (1931–58). *Collected Papers of Charles Sanders Peirce* (8 vols.), eds. P. Hartshorne, P. Weiss, and A. Burks. Cambridge, MA: Harvard University Press.

Possin, K. (1986). The case against Stephen Stich's syntactic theory of mind, *Philosophical Studies* 49: 405–18.

Putnam, H. (1975). The meaning of "meaning", in *Philosophical Papers*, vol. 2: *Language, Mind and Reality* (pp. 215–71). Cambridge University Press.

Ramsey, W. (1997). Do connectionist representations earn their explanatory keep? *Mind & Language* 12: 34–66.

  (2007). *Representation Reconsidered*. Cambridge University Press.

Robb, D. and Heil, J. (2009). Mental causation, in Edward N. Zalta (ed.), *The Stanford Encyclopedia of Philosophy* (Summer 2009 edn.), http://plato.stanford.edu/archives/sum2009/entries/mental-causation/.

Rolls, E. (2001). Representations in the brain, *Synthese* 129: 153–71.

Schiffer, S. (1987). *Remnants of Meaning*. Cambridge, MA: MIT Press.

Shepard, R. and Chipman, S. (1970). Second-order isomorphism of internal representations: Shapes of states, *Cognitive Psychology* 1: 1–17.

Stampe, D. (1977). Toward a causal theory of linguistic representation, in A. French (ed.) (pp. 81–102). Minneapolis: University of Minnesota Press.

Sterelny, K. (1990). *The Representational Theory of Mind: An Introduction*. Cambridge, MA: Basil Blackwell.

Stich, S. P. (1983). *From Folk Psychology to Cognitive Science: The Case Against Belief.* Cambridge, MA: MIT Press.

Swoyer, C. (1991). Structural representation and surrogative reasoning, *Synthese* 87: 449–508.

Thagard, P. (2005). *Mind: Introduction to Cognitive Science* (2nd edn.). Cambridge, MA: MIT Press.

Thelen, E. and Smith, L. (1993). *A Dynamic Systems Approach to the Development of Cognition and Action.* Cambridge, MA: MIT Press.

van Eck, D., Looren de Jong, H., and Schouten, M. (2006). Evaluating new wave reductionism: The case of vision, *The British Journal for the Philosophy of Science* 57: 167–96.

van Gelder, T. (1995). What might cognition be if not computation? *The Journal of Philosophy* 92: 345–81.

Von Eckardt, B. (1993). *What is Cognitive Science?* Cambridge, MA: MIT Press.

(2002). In defense of mental representation, in P. Gardenfors, K. Kijania-Placek, and J. Wolenski (eds.) (pp. 471–96). *Proceedings of the 11th International Congress of Logic, Methodology and Philosophy of Science.* Dordrecht: Kluwer.

(2003). The explanatory need for mental representations in cognitive science, *Mind & Language* 18: 427–39.

Wheeler, M. (2001). Two threats to representation, *Synthese* 129: 211–31.

Wheeler, M. and Clark, A. (1999). Genic representation: Reconciling content and causal complexity, *British Journal for the Philosophy of Science* 50: 103–35.

3 Cognitive architectures

Paul Thagard

A cognitive architecture is a general proposal about the representations and processes that produce intelligent thought. Cognitive architectures have primarily been used to explain important aspects of human thinking such as problem solving, memory, and learning. But they can also be used as blueprints for designing computers and robots that possess some of the cognitive abilities of humans. The most influential cognitive architectures that have been developed are either rule-based, using if-then rules and procedures that operate on them to explain thinking, or connectionist, using artificial neural networks. This chapter will describe the central structures and processes of these two kind of architectures, and review how well they succeed as general theories of mental processing. I argue that advances in neuroscience hold the promise for producing a general cognitive theory that encompasses the advantages of both rule-based and connectionist architectures.

What is an explanation in cognitive science? In keeping with much recent philosophical research on explanation, I maintain that scientific explanations are typically descriptions of mechanisms that produce the phenomena to be explained (Bechtel and Abrahamsen 2005; Machamer, Darden, and Craver 2000). A mechanism is a system of related parts whose interactions produce regular changes. For example, to explain how a bicycle works, we describe how its parts such as the pedals, chain, and wheels are connected to each other and how they interact to produce the movement of the bike. Similarly, explanation in physics, chemistry, and biology identifies relevant parts such as atoms, molecules, and cells and describes how they interact to produce observed changes in things and organisms. Explanations in cognitive science are typically mechanistic in that they describe how different kinds of thinking occur as the result of mental representations (parts) operated on by computational procedures (interactions) that change mental states.

A cognitive architecture is a proposal about the kinds of mental representation and computational procedure that constitute a mechanism for explaining a broad range of kinds of thinking. A complete unified general theory of cognition would provide mechanisms for explaining the workings of perception, attention, memory, problem solving, reasoning, learning, decision making, motor control, language, emotion, and consciousness. Let us now review the history of cognitive architectures.

3.1 Brief history of cognitive architectures

The term "cognitive architecture" developed from the idea of a computer architecture, which originated with a description of the first widely used computer,
the IBM 360 (Amdahl, Blaaw, and Brooks 1964). A computer architecture is
the conceptual structure and functional behavior of a system as seen by a
programmer, not the computer's physical implementation. John Anderson's
1983 book, *The Architecture of Cognition*, was the main text that introduced
the term "cognitive architecture," defined (p. ix) as a "the basic principles of
operations of a cognitive system." That book describes the ACT architecture,
which is a synthesis of Anderson's earlier ideas about propositional memory
with previous ideas about rule-based processing. The idea of a cognitive architecture was already implicit in the rule-based information-processing theories
of Newell and Simon (1972). Allan Newell further popularized the idea in his
1990 book, *Unified Theories of Cognition*, which described his work with John
Laird and Paul Rosenbloom on a particular rule-based architecture, SOAR
(Rosenbloom, Laird, and Newell 1993). Rule-based systems were originally
used by Newell and Simon to explain problem solving, but later work has
applied them to account for a much broader range of psychological phenomena, including memory and learning. The rule-based approach continues to
thrive in ongoing research by proponents of ACT, SOAR, and related cognitive
architectures; for more references, see the discussion below of psychological
applications of rule-based systems.

Rule-based systems are not the only way to think about cognition. In the
1970s, researchers such as Minsky (1975) and Schank and Abelson (1977) proposed a different way of understanding cognition as involving the matching
of current situations against concept-like structures variously called frames,
schemas, scripts, and prototypes. On this view, the fundamental kind of mental representation is a schema that specifies what holds for a typical situation, thing, or process. Proponents of schemas have used them to explain
such phenomena as perception, memory, and explanation. For example, you
understand what happens when you go out to eat by applying your restaurant
schema, which specifies the typical characteristics of restaurants. However,
schema-based systems have not survived as general theories of cognition,
although they have been included in hybrid systems that use both rules and
schemas such as PI ("processes of induction"), which models aspects of scientific reasoning such as discovery and explanation (Thagard 1988).

Another supplement to the rule-based approach involves analogical reasoning, in which problems are solved not by the application of general rules
but by the matching of a stored mental representation of a previous case
against a description of the problem to be solved. For example, you might
understand a new restaurant by comparing it to a highly similar restaurant
that you have previously experienced, rather than by using a general schema

or rule. Although analogical reasoning has been much discussed in psychology (Holyoak and Thagard 1995), and in artificial intelligence under the term "case-based" reasoning (Kolodner 1993), it is implausible to base a whole cognitive architecture on just schema-based or case-based reasoning.

The major alternative to rule-based cognitive architectures emerged in the 1980s. Neural network models of thinking had been around since the 1950s, but they only began to have a major impact on theorizing about the mind with the development of the PDP (parallel distributed processing) approach (Rumelhart and McClelland 1986). This approach is also called *connectionism*, because it views knowledge as being encoded not in rules, but via the connections between simple neuron-like processors. More details will be provided below about how such processors work and how connectionist architectures differ from rule-based architectures. Connectionism has been applied to a broad range of psychological phenomena ranging from concept learning to high-level reasoning. Like rule-based cognitive architectures, connectionist ones are a thriving intellectual industry, as seen for example in the applications to categorization and language found in Rogers and McClelland (2004) and Smolensky and LeGendre (2006). We can conduct a more systematic comparison of rule-based and connectionist approaches to explaining cognition by reviewing what they say about representations and procedures.

3.2   Representations

Since its origins in the mid-1950s, cognitive science has employed a fundamental hypothesis, that thinking is produced by computational procedures operating on mental representations. However, there has been much controversy about *what kind* of representations and *what kind* of procedures are best suited to explain the many varieties of human thinking. I will not attempt to review all the different versions of rule-based and connectionist architectures that have been proposed. Instead, I will provide an introduction to the representations and procedures used by rule-based and connectionist systems by showing how they can deal with a familiar area of human thinking: personality and human relations.

In thinking about all the people you know, you employ a familiar set of concepts, describing them as kind or cruel, intelligent or dumb, considerate or self-centered, polite or crude, outgoing or antisocial, confident or fearful, adventurous or cautious, conscientious or irresponsible, agreeable or difficult, and so on. Rule-based and connectionist approaches offer very different pictures of the nature of these concepts. From a rule-based perspective, your knowledge about other people consists of a set of rules, that can be stated as

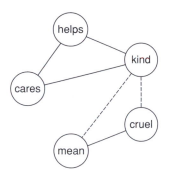

Figure 3.1 Localist network showing some of the connections between social concepts. The solid lines indicate excitatory links and the dotted lines indicate inhibitory links. Links in this network are symmetric, that is, they run in both directions.

if-then structures. For example, here are some rules that might capture part of your knowledge about kindness, letting P stand for any person.

> If P is kind, then P helps other people.
> If P is kind, then P cares about other people.
> If P is kind, then P is not cruel.
> If P cares about other people and helps other people, then P is kind.
> If P has the goal of being kind, then P should think about the feelings of others.
> If P is cruel, then avoid P.

As an exercise you should try to write down rules for a few other social concepts such as *outgoing* and *polite*. Unless you find it terribly difficult to construct such rules, you should find it plausible that the representations in your mind of social concepts consist of rules.

Connectionist cognitive architectures propose a very different kind of mental representation. As a first approximation, we can think of a concept as a node in a network that is roughly analogous to networks of neurons in the brain. Figure 3.1 shows a very simple network that has a few nodes for the concepts *kind*, *cruel*, and *mean*. But these concepts are not related by if-then rules that employ word-like symbols, but instead by simple connections that can be either positive or negative, just as neurons in the brain are connected by synapses that enable one neuron to either excite or inhibit another. The network in Figure 3.1 uses a kind of representation called *localist*, which means that each concept is represented by a single neuron-like node.

Much more radically, connectionism can represent concepts by *distributed* representations that use many nodes for each concept. Figure 3.2 shows a typical three-layer network that consists of an input layer of simple features

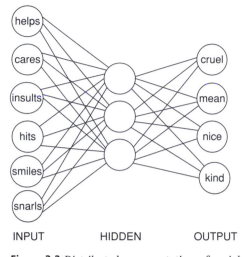

INPUT   HIDDEN   OUTPUT

Figure 3.2 Distributed representation of social concepts. The links are not symmetric, but feed activation forward from left to right. Weights on the links are learned by training.

and an output layer of concepts, with an intervening layer called *hidden* because it is neither input nor output. As in the localist network in Figure 3.1, the nodes are connected by links that are positive or negative depending on how the network is trained. Whereas if-then rules and localist connections are typically specified in advance, connections in a distributed representation are usually learned by experience. I will say more about how such networks are trained in the section below about procedures. The key point to note now is that a concept such as *cruel* is not the single node in the output layer, nor any simple rule connecting the input and output layers. Rather, it is a whole pattern of connections involving the input, output, and hidden layers; the nodes in the hidden layer do not need to acquire any specific interpretation. Neural networks in the brain are much more complicated than the simple three-layer network in Figure 3.2, but they share the property that representation of concepts is distributed across many neurons.

To summarize, social and other concepts in a rule-based cognitive architecture primarily consist of sets of if-then rules, but in a connectionist architecture concepts are patterns of connections between nodes in a network, including hidden nodes that by themselves do not have any specific interpretation. Rather, they serve by virtue of their links to input and output layers to furnish a statistical connection between inputs and outputs that is often hard to characterize in words and is rarely replaceable by general if-then rules. To appreciate fully the difference between rule-based and connectionist representations, it is crucial to notice how they support different kinds of procedures for reasoning, problem solving, and learning.

3.3   Rule-based procedures

Just as you cannot make a cake without doing things to the ingredients, you cannot think without mental procedures that operate on your representations. For rule-based systems, the simplest kind of procedure is the obvious one where you match the IF part against something you know and then fill in the THEN part. For example, you might make the following inference:

> If P cares about other people and helps other people, then P is kind.
> Sandra cares about other people and helps other people.
> Therefore, Sandra is kind.

In a computational model of a rule-based system, this sort of inference is made by having a list of facts of current interest, such as that Sandra cares about other people, in addition to a large set of rules that encapsulate information about social concepts. Here is the main forward procedure performed by a cognitive architecture based on rules:

1 Match what is currently known (the facts) against a database of rules.
2 If the facts match the IF parts of a rule, then infer the THEN part.
3 Repeat.

The repetition is crucial, because a rule-based system usually needs to make a whole series of inferences to come to an interesting conclusion. For example, having inferred that Sandra is kind, we could then use the rule *if P is kind then P is not cruel* to infer that Sandra is not cruel. Thus if-then rules can be chained together to produce complex inferences.

   Often it is useful to chain rules backward instead of forward in order to answer questions or solve problems. Suppose, for example, your aim is to answer the question whether Sandra is cruel and you want to find rules that can answer it. You can then work backward using the following procedure:

1 Match what you want to know (the goals) against a database of rules.
2 If the goal matches the THEN part of a rule, then add the IF part to the set of goals.
3 Repeat.

This procedure may enable you to chain backward from the goals you want to accomplish to find aspects of the current situation that would identify the information you need to then chain forward to provide an answer to your question or a solution to your goal. For example, generating the goal to determine if Sandra is cruel may lead you to retrieve rules such as *If P insults people then P is cruel* that can then spur you to ask whether Sandra insults people.

Thus a rule-based system accomplishes reasoning and problem solving by forward or backward chaining using a sequence of rules. To make such reasoning psychologically effective, other procedures are needed for retrieving rules from memory, resolving conflicts between competing rules, and learning new rules. First, consider retrieval from memory. My description of the procedures for forward and backward chaining assumed that there is an accessible list of relevant rules, but an educated adult has accumulated many thousands of rules constituting the thousands of concepts that have been acquired. (It has been estimated that the typical vocabulary of an adult is more than 100,000 words, so there must be least this many concepts and rules.) It would be too slow and awkward to match thousands of rules one by one against the rule-based system's list of known facts or goals to be solved. Hence there needs to be a procedure to ensure that the matching is only done against a set of rules somehow selected to be potentially relevant. Anderson's (1983) ACT architecture uses spreading activation among the constituents of rules, facts, and goals as a way to select from memory a set of rules that appear relevant for matching. For example, if the concepts *cruel* and *insult* are associated in your memory because of your previous experiences, then activating one of them can lead to the activation of the other, making available a new set of relevant rules.

Second, additional procedures are needed to determine what rules to apply in cases where they provide conflicting answers. Suppose you want to determine whether Solomon is outgoing, and you have the following rules in your memory base:

If P likes to go to parties, then P is outgoing.
If P likes to read a lot of books, then P is not outgoing.

If you know that Solomon likes to go to parties *and* to read lots of books, your rules suggest that you should infer that Solomon is both outgoing and not outgoing. To resolve this conflict, which is even more acute when the THEN part of the rules suggests incompatible actions such as both talking to someone and walking away, there needs to be a procedure to select which rules apply best to the problem situation. Procedures that have been used in various cognitive architectures include using rules that are most specific to the current situation and using rules that have been highly successful in past problem-solving episodes.

The third sort of procedure that is important for rule-based cognitive architectures involves learning new rules and new strategies for solving problems more effectively. How did you acquire rules like *If P is kind, then P helps homeless people*? This rule is not part of the central meaning of the concept *kind*, so it is unlikely that you were simply told it as part of learning what kindness is. Instead, you may have learned it from experience, seeing a collection of examples of people who are both kind and help homeless people, producing a new rule by generalization. Another way of acquiring a rule is by stringing together other rules you already have, perhaps reasoning as follows:

> If P is kind, then P cares about people.
> If P cares about people, then P helps homeless people.
> So: If P is kind, then P helps homeless people.

Here a new rule is acquired by combining two or more other rules. In sum, rule-based architecture can have various procedures for learning new rules, including being given the rule, generalizing from experience, and compiling new rules from previous rules.

Thus rule-based systems can employ many powerful procedures for problem solving and learning: forward and backward chaining, retrieval by spreading activation, conflict resolution, and generation of new rules.

3.4   Connectionist procedures

Connectionist cognitive architectures have very different methods for reasoning and learning. In rule-based systems, problem solving consists primarily of using rules to *search* a space of possible actions. In contrast, the connectionist perspective conceives of problem solving as *parallel constraint satisfaction*. Suppose your problem is to categorize someone as either kind or cruel, perhaps as part of a hiring decision. Instead of using rule-based reasoning, you might apply the kind of network shown in Figure 3.1. The excitatory links in the network represent positive constraints, factors that tend to go together, such as being kind and helping others. The inhibitory links represent negative constraints, factors that tend not to go together, such as being kind and being cruel. The inference problem here is to figure out the best way to satisfy the most constraints, which is done in parallel by spreading activation through the network. Activation is a property of each node in the network, roughly analogous to the firing rate of a neuron (how many times it fires per second compared to how fast it could fire). Activation of a node represents the acceptability of the representation to which the node corresponds. Just as the brain operates by parallel activity of multiple neurons, constraint satisfaction in a neural network should be a parallel process that takes into account all relevant constraints simultaneously.

Here is an outline of the procedure used to solve a constraint satisfaction problem in connectionist fashion:

1 Express the problem as a set of nodes connected by excitatory and inhibitory links.
2 Establish the givens of the problem as inputs to some of the nodes.

3 Spread activation among the nodes based on their excitatory and inhibitory inputs, until the network settles, i.e., all nodes have reached stable activation.

4 Read off the network's solution to the problem as represented by the nodes that have highest activation.

For example, the network shown in Figure 3.1, with inputs from the evidence that a person helps others and cares about them, will settle with the node for *kind* having high activation and the node for *cruel* having low activation. The next section lists many other kinds of problems that can be solved by parallel constraint satisfaction, from decision making to vision to language comprehension.

In the connectionist procedure I just sketched for solving parallel constraint satisfaction problems, the links between the nodes are given, but how might they be learned? Moreover, how do the nodes in networks with distributed representations like those in Figure 3.2 acquire meaning? The most common connectionist procedure used to learn weights is called *backpropagation*, because it propagates errors back from output nodes to adjust all the weights in the network. Here is a simple description of how backpropagation works:

1 Assign weights randomly to all the connections in the network.

2 Provide inputs to the input units, feed activation forward through the network, and see whether the outputs produced are correct.

3 If the outputs are wrong, then change the weights that produced them, including weights between the input and hidden layer and between the hidden and output layer.

4 Repeat with many input examples until the network has acquired the desired behavior.

This procedure is a kind of supervised learning, in that it requires telling the network whether it is getting the right answer. There are also learning procedures for artificial neural networks that do not require a supervisor. The simplest is one proposed by Hebb (1949) that has been found to operate in real neural networks: if two neurons are connected and they fire at the same time, then increase the strength of the connection between them; whatever fires together, wires together. More complicated procedures for unsupervised learning using an internal model of the task to be completed have also been developed.

To sum up, connectionist networks make inferences and solve problems by parallel constraint satisfaction, and they learn to improve their performance by procedures that adjust the weights on the links between nodes. I will now review some of the many psychological applications that have been found for rule-based and connectionist cognitive architectures.

3.5 Psychological applications

Both rule-based and connectionist architectures embody powerful theories about the representations and procedures that explain human thinking. Which cognitive architecture, which theory of thinking, is the best? There have been many great battles in the history of science between competing theories, for example heliocentric Copernican astronomy vs. Ptolemy's geometric theory, the wave theory of light vs. particle theories, and Darwin's theory of evolution vs. creationism. These battles are adjudicated by evaluating how well the competing theories explain all the relevant evidence.

Both rule-based and connectionist architectures have had many impressive applications to psychological phenomena. Table 3.1 shows that rule-based architectures have had explanatory successes in many psychological domains, especially problem solving and language. Table 3.2 shows that connectionism has also done very well in generating explanations. Which kind of cognitive architecture is the best explanation of the full range of psychological phenomena? Neither Tables 3.1 and 3.2 nor the very large additional literature espousing these two approaches establishes a winner. I see no immediate prospect of one of the two kinds of cognitive architecture superseding the other by showing itself capable of explaining everything that the other one does in addition to what it currently explains. Moreover, there are some aspects of thinking such as consciousness that have largely been neglected by *both* approaches.

The current battle between rule-based and connectionist architecture is analogous to a previous episode in the history of science, the controversy between wave and particle theories of light. From the seventeenth through the nineteenth centuries, there was an oscillation between the wave theory, advocated by scientists such as Huygens and Young, and the particle theory, advocated by Gassendi and Newton. The battle was only settled in the twentieth century by the advent of quantum theories of light, according to which light consists of photons that exhibit properties of *both* particles and waves. Similarly, I think that the most reasonable conclusion from the current impasse of rule-based and connectionist architectures is that the mind is both a rule-based and a connectionist system, and that problem solving can sometimes be search through a space of rules and sometimes parallel constraint satisfaction.

3.6 Neural architecture

How can the brain be both a rule-based and a connectionist system? It might seem that connectionism has a head start in taking into account knowledge about the brain, given that its parallel processing seems to employ a kind of brain-style computation. But there are many respects in which connectionist

Table 3.1 **Selection of psychological phenomena that can be explained by processing of rules**

Domains	Applications	References
Problem solving	Domains such as logic and chess	Newell and Simon (1972), Newell (1990)
	Human–computer interaction	Kieras and Meyer (1997)
	Perceptual-motor system	Anderson *et al.* (2004)
Learning	Arithmetic procedures	Anderson (1983)
	Scientific discovery	Langley *et al.* (1987), Thagard (1988)
	Skill acquisition	Newell (1990)
	Tutoring	Anderson (1993)
	Induction	Holland *et al.* (1986)
Language	Acquisition	Anderson (1983), Pinker (1989)
	Regular and irregular verbs	Pinker (1999)
Reasoning	Syllogisms	Newell (1990)
	Statistical heuristics	Nisbett (1993)
Memory	List memory	Anderson *et al.* (1998)
Explanation	Hypothesis generation	Thagard (1988)
Emotion	Cognitive appraisal	Scherer (1993)

cognitive architectures have not accurately captured how the brain works. First, at the level of individual neurons, connectionist models usually describe neural activity in terms of activation, understood as the rate of firing. But there are both neurological and computational reasons to think that it matters that neurons show particular patterns of spiking (Maass and Bishop 1999; Rieke et al. 1997). Imagine a neuron whose firing rate is fifty times per second. Such a rate is consistent with many very different patterns of firing, for example (FIRE REST FIRE REST ...) versus (FIRE FIRE REST REST ...). Biologically realistic neural networks encode information using spiking patterns, not just rates of firing. A population of neurons can become tuned to a set of stimuli such as faces by acquiring synaptic connections that generate different spiking patterns.

Second, neural networks are not simply electrical systems, sending charges from one neuron to another; they are also chemical systems employing dozens of neurotransmitters and other molecules to carry out signaling in complex ways. Important neurotransmitters include glutamate for excitatory connections, GABA for inhibitory connections, and dopamine for circuits that evaluate the reward potential of stimuli. A single synaptic connection can involve multiple neurotransmitters and other chemicals operating at different time scales (Leonard 1997).

Table 3.2 **Selection of psychological phenomena that can be explained by parallel constraint satisfaction**

Domains	Applications	References
Vision	Stereoscopic vision	Marr and Poggio (1976)
	Figure interpretation	Feldman (1981)
	Visual expectation	Bressler (2004)
Language	Letter perception	McClelland and Rumelhart (1981)
	Discourse comprehension	Kintsch (1998)
	Irony	Shelley (2001)
	Grammar	Smolensky and Legendre (2006)
	Semantic cognition	Rogers and McClelland (2004)
Concepts	Schema application	Rumelhart *et al.* (1986)
	Impression formation	Kunda and Thagard (1996)
Analogy	Mapping and retrieval	Holyoak and Thagard (1989, 1995)
Explanation	Theory evaluation	Thagard (1992, 2000)
	Social explanations	Read and Marcus-Newhall (1993)
Social behavior	Cognitive dissonance	Shultz and Lepper (1996)
	Personality	Shoda and Mischel (1998)
	Social perception	Read and Miller (1998)
	Attitude change	Spellman, Ullman, and Holyoak (1993)
Decision	Plan selection	Thagard and Millgram (1995)
	Preference construction	Simon, Krawcyyck, and Holyoak (2004)
Emotion	Appraisal and inference	Nerb and Spada (2001), Thagard (2000, 2006)

Third, the brain should not be thought of as one big neural network, but as organized into areas that have identifiable functions. For example, the occipital area at the back of your head is the main visual processing center. The prefrontal cortex, the part of your brain roughly behind your eyes, is important for high-level reasoning and language. More specifically, the ventromedial (bottom–middle) prefrontal cortex facilitates decision making by providing connections between high-level reasoning in the dorsolateral (top-sides) prefrontal cortex and emotional reactions in the amygdala, which lies below the cortex. Hence traditional connectionist models are typically not biologically realistic either at the level of individual neurons or at the level of brain organization.

There is, however, a wealth of current research aimed at producing more biologically realistic models of cognitive processes. Whether these models

Table 3.3 **Some prominent work in the emerging field of theoretical neuroscience, which develops biologically realistic computational models of cognition**

Researcher	Applications	Sample publications
Jonathan Cohen, Princeton University	Decision making, attention, categorization	Miller and Cohen (2001)
Chris Eliasmith, University of Waterloo	Perception, memory, motor control	Eliasmith and Anderson (2003)
Stephen Grossberg, Boston University	Perception, attention, learning	Carpenter and Grossberg (2003)
Randy O'Reilly, University of Colorado	Learning, memory, attention	O'Reilly and Munakata (2000)
Terry Sejnowski, University of California-San Diego	Learning, memory, motor control	Quartz and Sejnowski (2002)

should currently be called "cognitive architectures" is not clear, because they have mostly been applied to low-level kinds of cognition such as perception and memory, rather than to high-level kinds of inference such as problem solving. But these models have the potential to develop into broader accounts of human thinking that I hope will supersede the current apparent conflict between rule-based and connectionist approaches. Table 3.3 points to the work of five researchers in theoretical computational neuroscience who are pursuing promising directions.

Research in theoretical neuroscience along the lines of Table 3.3 is highly technical, and I will not attempt to summarize the similarities and differences among the various researchers. Instead, I will return to my previous example and indicate how concepts such as *kind* and *cruel* might be represented in a more biologically realistic fashion than is possible in rule-based and connectionist cognitive architectures. Eliasmith (2003) provides a more specific argument about the advantages of theoretical neuroscience for going beyond the limitations of rule-based and connectionist approaches.

Concepts in human brains are represented in a distributed fashion across multiple neurons, just as in the parallel distributed processing version of connectionism. Whereas connectionist models distribute a concept such as *kind* across a small number of closely attached units, a more biologically realistic model would have thousands or millions of spiking neurons distributed across multiple brain areas. Using spiking neurons has the computational advantage of making it possible to model the dynamic properties of neural networks such as temporal coordination of different neural populations. Moreover, in some models (e.g., ones by Cohen and O'Reilly) the role of particular neurotransmitters such as dopamine can be emphasized. Dopamine is associated with positive emotional reactions, so it is likely involved in the fact that the concept of kindness is for most people a positive one. When you think of someone as kind, you usually have a positive feeling toward them, whereas applying the concept *cruel* prompts negative emotions for most people. Thus theoretical neuroscience is developing models that take into account the spiking and chemical properties of neurons.

In addition, theoretical neuroscience can describe the contributions to the representation of a concept from different brain areas. The semantic characteristics of *kind* and *cruel* that are captured by approximate rules describing the behavior of people are probably represented in the prefrontal cortex, which plays a large role in reasoning. But other brain areas are likely involved too, for example the primary visual cortex which would be activated if you created a mental image of a person being kind or cruel, perhaps by kicking a homeless person. Some concepts, e.g., *automobile*, are closely tied to specific modalities such as vision (Barsalou *et al.* 2003). Moreover, the emotional component of concepts such as *kind* and *cruel* suggests the involvement of brain areas that are known to be active in positive emotions (e.g., the nucleus accumbens, which is tied to various pleasurable activities) and negative emotions (e.g., the insula which has been found to be active in both physical and social pain). Thagard and Aubie (2008) show how satisfaction of both cognitive and emotional constraints can be performed in a neurally plausible manner. In sum, from the perspective of theoretical neuroscience, a concept is a pattern of spiking and chemical behaviors in a large population of neurons distributed across multiple brain areas.

Rule-based models have also been moving in the direction of greater neurological plausibility. John Anderson and his colleagues have used brain-scanning experiments to relate the ACT system to specific brain regions such as the prefrontal cortex, used for memory and matching of rules against facts, and the basal ganglia, used for the implementation of production rules (Anderson *et al.* 2004). Other brain areas they postulate to be involved in the matching and firing of rules include the striatum for selection of rules and parts of the prefrontal cortex for memory buffers. Thus rule-based cognitive architectures are becoming neural architectures, just as connectionist approaches are giving way to computational neuroscience.

Earlier, I mentioned the great synthesis accomplished by the quantum theory of light, according to which light consists of photons, which have properties of both particles and waves. A similar synthesis has yet to occur in cognitive science, as no one has figured out fully how to blend the ideas emerging from theoretical neuroscience about the behavior of spiking chemical neurons in multiple brain areas with the more high-level behavior of neurally grounded rule-based systems. Among the exciting new ideas are mathematical ways of showing how artificial neurons can implement features of rules such as their complex symbolic structure (e.g., Smolensky and Legendre 2006). My hope is that a grand synthesis will be accomplished by identifying how neural mechanisms that are well suited for low-level operations such as perception can also serve to support high-level kinds of symbolic inferences. Such a synthesis will show that the competition that raged in the 1980s and 1990s between rule-based and connectionist cognitive architectures was merely a prelude to deep reconciliation by virtue of a unified theory of neural mechanisms.

Accomplishment of this synthesis would not eliminate the usefulness of rule-based and connectionist cognitive models, although it would undercut their claims to be universal cognitive architectures. Cognitive theories are claims about the mental representations and computational procedures that produce different kinds of thinking. Computational models implemented as running programs provide simplified approximations of such representations and procedures. Scientific models are like maps, in that different ones can be useful for different purposes. Just as you use different scales of maps depending on whether your aim is to travel across the city or to travel across the country, so different kinds of model are useful for explaining different aspects of human thinking. A full model of the brain, encompassing all of its billions of neurons, trillions of synapses, and hundreds of chemicals, would be as useless as a map of a country that was the same size and detail as the country itself. A cognitive or neural theory does not aim to describe everything about thought and the brain, but rather to describe the mechanisms that underlie the fundamental causal processes most relevant to explaining those aspects of thinking we find most interesting. Simplifications of the sort provided by rule-based and connectionist models will remain useful for explaining particular phenomena at comprehensible levels of detail. Current rule-based and connectionist models successfully capture many aspects of thinking, particularly sequential problem solving and parallel constraint satisfaction. Hence it will continue to be methodologically legitimate to employ them, even if it becomes established that the ultimate cognitive architecture is provided by theoretical neuroscience.

If principles of neuroscience make possible the unification of rule-based and connectionist explanations under a common framework, then they should also serve to bring into a single theoretical fold other aspects of cognition that have been discussed using different theoretical ideas. For example, it would be theoretically exciting to integrate ideas about probabilistic inference into a general framework that also applies to rule-based and connectionist processing. Reasoning involving mental models, which are rich psychological representations of real or imagined situations, should also be incorporated. Then cognitive science would have the sort of unifying theory that relativity and quantum theories provide to physics and that evolution and genetics provide to biology. Such a grand unification may, however, require decades or even centuries.

3.7 Artificial intelligence

If it turns out that the deepest cognitive architecture is furnished by theoretical neuroscience, what are the implications for artificial intelligence? When cognitive science began in the mid 1950s and got named and recognized as an interdisciplinary field in the mid 1970s, there was a common perception that psychology and artificial intelligence were natural allies. A unified cognitive architecture based on rules or other sorts of representation would provide a way simultaneously of understanding how human minds work and how computers and robots can be made to work in comparable ways. The reconceptualization of cognitive architectures as neural architectures raises the possibility that what kind of hardware an intelligent system is running on matters much more than the pioneers of cognitive science realized. Compared to computers, whose chips can perform operations more than a billion times per second, a neuron looks hopelessly slow, typically firing only around a hundred times per second. But we have billions of neurons, with far more biological and chemical complexity than research on simple neural networks has recognized. There are thousands of different kinds of neurons adapted for different purposes, and each neuron has thousands of chemical connections to other neurons that allow many kinds of chemical modulation as well as transmission of electrical impulses. The best way to get a computer to do things that are intelligent may be to develop software more suited to the extraordinary speed and lack of evolutionary history of its central processing unit. Then there will be a bifurcation of cognitive architectures into ones best suited for operating with the messy biological hardware of the brain and those best suited for operating with digital processing. Langley (2006) provides a thorough discussion of the role of cognitive architectures in artificial intelligence.

Another possibility besides bifurcation is that there will be a set of statistical principles that describe how both brains and intelligent machines operate in the world. Perhaps there is a convergence between the recent trend in neuroscience to describe what brains do as a kind of Bayesian statistical inference (Doya *et al.* 2007) and the major trend in artificial intelligence and robotics to approach problems statistically using Bayesian inference mechanisms (Thrun, Burgard, and Fox 2005). Bayesian inference is a way of evaluating a hypothesis about what is going on in an environment by mathematically taking into account the prior probability of the hypothesis, the probability of the evidence given the hypothesis, and the probability of the evidence. Perhaps then, at some level, both the human brain and digital computers can be viewed as engines for statistical inference. It remains to be seen whether that level will be the most fruitful for understanding human and artificial intelligence.

3.8 Conclusion

This chapter has reviewed the two main current approaches to cognitive architecture: rule-based systems and connectionism. Both kinds of architecture assume the central hypothesis of cognitive science that thinking consists of the application of computational procedures to mental representations, but they propose very different kinds of representations and procedures. Rule-based systems apply procedures such as forward chaining to if-then representations with word-like symbols, whereas connectionist systems apply procedures such as parallel activation adjustment to representations comprised of neuron-like units with excitatory and inhibitory connections between them. Both rule-based and connectionist architectures have had many successes in explaining important psychological phenomena concerning problem solving, learning, language use, and other kinds of thinking. Given their large and only partially overlapping range of explanatory applications, it seems unlikely that either of the two approaches to cognitive architecture will come to dominate cognitive science. I suggested an alternative scenario, consistent with current developments in both rule-based systems and connectionist modeling, that will see a reconciliation of the two approaches by means of theoretical neuroscience. Unified understanding of how the brain can perform both serial problem solving using rules and parallel constraint satisfaction using distributed representations will be a major triumph of cognitive science.

Further reading

Bechtel, W. and Abrahamsen, A. A. (2002). *Connectionism and the Mind: Parallel Processing, Dynamics, and Evolution in Networks* (2nd edn.). Oxford: Basil Blackwell. An introduction to connectionism.

Boden, M. (2006). *Mind as Machine: A History of Cognitive Science.* Oxford University Press. A review of the history of different approaches to cognitive science.

Dayan, P. and Abbott, L. F. (2001). *Theoretical Neuroscience: Computational and Mathematical Modeling of Neural Systems.* Cambridge, MA: MIT Press. An introduction to theoretical neuroscience.

Newell, A. (1990). *Unified Theories of Cognition.* Cambridge, MA: Harvard University Press. A good introduction to rule-based systems.

Thagard, P. (2005). *Mind: Introduction to Cognitive Science* (2nd edn.). Cambridge, MA: MIT Press. An accessible introduction to approaches to mental representation and computation.

References

Amdahl, G. M., Blaauw, G. A., and Brooks, L. R. (1964). Architecture of the IBM System/360, *IBM Journal of Research and Development* 4: 87–101.

Anderson, J. R. (1983). *The Architecture of Cognition*. Cambridge, MA: Harvard University Press.

(1993). *Rules of the mind*. Hillsdale, NJ: Erlbaum.

Anderson, J. R., Bothell, D., Byrne, M. D., Douglas, S., Lebiere, C., and Qin, U. (2004). An integrated theory of the mind, *Psychological Review* 111: 1030–60.

Anderson, J. R., Bothell, D., Lebiere, C., and Matessa, M. (1998). An integrated theory of list memory, *Journal of Memory and Language* 38: 341–80.

Barsalou, L. W., Simmons, W. K., Barbey, A. K., and Wilson, C. D. (2003). Grounding conceptual knowledge in modality-specific systems, *Trends in Cognitive Sciences* 7: 84–91.

Bechtel, W. and Abrahamsen, A. A. (2005). Explanation: A mechanistic alternative, *Studies in History and Philosophy of Biology and Biomedical Sciences* 36: 421–41.

Bressler, S. L. (2004). Inferential constraint sets in the organization of visual expectation, *Neuroinformaics* 2: 227–37.

Carpenter, G. A. and Grossberg, S. (2003). Adaptive resonance theory, in M. A. Arbiib (ed.), *Handbook of Brain Theory and Neural Networks*. Cambridge, MA: MIT Press.

Doya, K., Ishii, S., Pouget, A., and Rao, A. (eds.) (2007). *Bayesian Brain*. Cambridge, MA: MIT Press.

Eliasmith, C. (2003). Moving beyond metaphors: Understanding the mind for what it is, *Journal of Philosophy* 100: 493–520.

Eliasmith, C. and Anderson, C. H. (2003). *Neural Engineering: Computation, Representation and Dynamics in Neurobiological Systems*. Cambridge, MA: MIT Press.

Feldman, J. A. (1981). A connectionist model of visual memory, in G. E. Hinton and J. A. Anderson (eds.), *Parallel Models of Associative Memory* (pp. 49–81). Hillsdale, NJ: Lawrance Erlbaum.

Hebb, D. O. (1949). *The Organization of Behavior*. New York: Wiley.

Holland, J. H., Holyoak, K. J., Nisbett, R. E., and Thagard, P. R. (1986). *Induction: Processes of Inference, Learning, and Discovery*. Cambridge, MA: MIT Press/Bradford Books.

Holyoak, K. J. and Thagard, P. (1989). Analogical mapping by constraint satisfaction, *Cognitive Science* 13: 295–355.

(1995). *Mental Leaps: Analogy in Creative Thought*. Cambridge, MA: MIT Press/Bradford Books.

Kieras, D. E. and Meyer, D. E. (1997). An overview of the EPIC architecture for cognition and performance with application to human–computer interaction, *Human–Computer Interaction* 12: 391–438.

Kintsch, W. (1998). *Comprehension: A Paradigm for Cognition.* Cambridge University Press.

Kolodner, J. (1993). *Case-Based Reasoning.* San Mateo, CA: Morgan Kaufmann.

Kunda, Z. and Thagard, P. (1996). Forming impressions from stereotypes, traits, and behaviors: A parallel-constraint-satisfaction theory, *Psychological Review* 103: 284–308.

Langley, P. (2006). Cognitive architectures and general intelligent systems, *AI Magazine* 27: 33–44.

Langley, P., Simon, H., Bradshaw, G., and Zytkow, J. (1987). *Scientific Discovery.* Cambridge, MA: MIT Press/Bradford Books.

Leonard, B. E. (1997). *Fundamentals of Pharmacology* (2nd edn.). Chichester: John Wiley.

Maass, W. and Bishop, C. M. (eds.) (1999). *Pulsed Neural Networks.* Cambridge, MA: MIT Press.

Machamer, P., Darden, L., and Craver, C. F. (2000). Thinking about mechanisms, *Philosophy of Science* 67: 1–25.

Marr, D. and Poggio, T. (1976). Cooperative computation of stereo disparity. *Science* 194: 283–7.

McClelland, J. L. and Rumelhart, D. E. (1981). An interactive activation model of context effects in letter perception: Part 1: An account of basic findings, *Psychological Review* 88: 375–407.

Miller, E. K. and Cohen, J. D. (2001). An integrative theory of prefrontal cortex function, *Annual Review of Neuroscience* 24: 167–202.

Minsky, M. (1975). A framework for representing knowledge, in P. H. Winston (ed.), *The Psychology of Computer Vision* (pp. 211–77). New York: McGraw-Hill.

Nerb, J. and Spada, H. (2001). Evaluation of environmental problems: A coherence model of cognition and emotion, *Cognition and Emotion* 15: 521–51.

Newell, A. (1990). *Unified Theories of Cognition.* Cambridge, MA: Harvard University Press.

Newell, A. and Simon, H. A. (1972). *Human Problem Solving.* Englewood Cliffs, NJ: Prentice-Hall.

Nisbett, R. E. (ed.). (1993). *Rules for Reasoning.* Hillsdale, NJ: Lawrance Erlbaum.

O'Reilly, R. C. and Munakata, Y. (2000). *Computational Explorations in Cognitive Neuroscience.* Cambridge, MA: MIT Press.

Pinker, S. (1989). *Learnability and Cognition: The Acquisition of Argument Structure.* Cambridge, MA: MIT Press.

(1999). *Words and Rules: The Ingredients of Language.* New York: HarperCollins.

Quartz, S. R. and Sejnowski, T. J. (2002). *Liars, Lovers, and Heroes: What the New Brain Science Reveals about How We Become Who We Are.* New York: William Morrow.

Read, S. J. and Marcus-Newhall, A. (1993). Explanatory coherence in social explanations: A parallel distributed processing account, *Journal of Personality and Social Psychology* 65: 429–47.

Read, S. J. and Miller, L. C. (1998). On the dynamic construction of meaning: An interactive activation and competition model of social perception, in S. J. Read and L. C. Miller (eds.), *Connectionist Models of Social Reasoning and Behavior* (pp. 27–68). Mahwah, NJ: Erlbaum.

Rieke, F., Warland, D., de Ruyter van Steveninick, R. R., and Bialek, W. (1997). *Spikes: Exploring the Neural Code.* Cambridge, MA: MIT Press.

Rogers, T. T. and McClelland, J. L. (2004). *Semantic Cognition: A Parallel Distributed Processing Approach.* Cambridge, MA: MIT Press.

Rosenbloom, P., Laird, J., and Newell, A. (1993). *The SOAR Papers: Research on Integrated Intelligence.* Cambridge, MA: MIT Press.

Rumelhart, D. E. and McClelland, J. L. (eds.) (1986). *Parallel Distributed Processing: Explorations in the Microstructure of Cognition.* Cambridge MA: MIT Press/Bradford Books.

Rumelhart, D. E., Smolensky, P., Hinton, G. E., and McClelland, J. L. (1986). Schemata and sequential thought processes in PDP models, in J. L. McClelland and D. E. Rumelhart (eds.), *Parallel Distributed Processing: Explorations in the Microstructure of Cognition* (vol. 2, pp. 7–57). Cambridge, MA: MIT Press/Bradford Books.

Schank, R. C. and Abelson, R. P. (1977). *Scripts, Plans, Goals, and Understanding: An Inquiry into Human Knowledge Structures.* Hillsdale, NJ: Lawrence Erlbaum.

Scherer, K. R. (1993). Studying the emotion–antecedent appraisal process: An expert system approach, *Cognition and Emotion* 7: 325–55.

Shelley, C. (2001). The bicoherence theory of situational irony, *Cognitive Science* 25: 775–818.

Shoda, Y. and Mischel, W. (1998). Personality as a stable cognitive-affective activation network: Characteristic patterns of behavior variation emerge from a stable personality structure, in S. J. Read and L. C. Miller (eds.), *Connectionist Models of Social Reasoning and Behavior* (pp. 175–208). Mahwah, NJ: Lawrence Erlbaum.

Shultz, T. R. and Lepper, M. R. (1996). Cognitive dissonance reduction as constraint satisfaction, *Psychological Review* 103: 219–40.

Simon, D., Krawczyk, D. C., and Holyoak, K. J. (2004). Construction of preferences by constraint satisfaction, *Psychological Science* 15: 331–6.

Smolensky, P. and Legendre, G. (2006). *The Harmonic Mind.* Cambridge, MA: MIT Press.

Spellman, B. A., Ullman, J. B., and Holyoak, K. J. (1993). A coherence model of cognitive consistency: Dynamics of attitude change during the Persian War, *Journal of Social Issues* 49: 147–65.

Thagard, P. (1988). *Computational Philosophy of Science.* Cambridge, MA: MIT Press/Bradford Books.

(1992). *Conceptual Revolutions.* Princeton University Press.

(2000). *Coherence in Thought and Action.* Cambridge, MA: MIT Press.

(2006). *Hot Thought: Mechanisms and Applications of Emotional Cognition.* Cambridge, MA: MIT Press.

Thagard, P. and Aubie, B. (2008). Emotional consciousness: A neural model of how cognitive appraisal and somatic perception interact to produce qualitative experience, *Consciousness and Cognition* 17: 811–34.

Thagard, P. and Millgram, E. (1995). Inference to the best plan: A coherence theory of Decision, in A. Ram and D. B. Leake (eds.), *Goal-Driven Learning* (pp. 439–54). Cambridge, MA: MIT Press.

Thrun, S., Burgard, W., and Fox, D. (2005). *Probabilistic Robotics.* Cambridge, MA: MIT Press.

Part II

Aspects of cognition

4 Perception

Casey O'Callaghan

Perception drives discussion in philosophy and the cognitive sciences because it forms our most intimate sort of acquaintance with the world. In perception, the world appears before us as available to our thoughts and susceptible to our deeds. What we perceive shapes our thinking and guides our action. The variety and the flux are impressive.

Philosophical work on perception traditionally concerns whether perceptual *acquaintance* with things in the world is compatible with the possibility of illusions and hallucinations. Given that you cannot tell definitively if you are hallucinating, how are you acquainted with things like tomatoes, barns, collisions, colors, sounds, and odors?

The contemporary cognitive science of perception attempts to understand perceiving in naturalistic terms. Cognitive science aims to explain the *processes* and *mechanisms* by which perceiving takes place in organisms understood as biological systems. The objective is to describe and explain how a creature accomplishes the feat of perceiving given constraints imposed by its physiology, environment, and goals. How, for instance, do your body and brain, which are made of cells and neural tissue, ground your awareness of the sights and sounds of a tomato being squashed?

This chapter introduces the traditional philosophical problem of perception, which concerns whether our naïve sense of perceptual awareness survives arguments from illusion and hallucination. Though it may seem distant from empirical concerns, this problem holds important lessons about the nature of perception, and it provides the conceptual backdrop to contemporary discussions among philosophers and cognitive scientists about what it is to perceive. The chapter next turns to empirically motivated theoretical issues about perception. These concern how to characterize the tasks of perception, alternative ways to understand the role of processes and mechanisms involved in perceiving, and the relationships among perception, other forms of cognition, and action. In light of methodological concerns, the chapter concludes by discussing the role of phenomenology in perceptual theorizing.

4.1   The philosophical problem of perception

Philosophical worries over perception traditionally stem from a catalogue of real and imagined illusions and hallucinations. Sometimes, things are not as they appear. For instance, a straight stick half submerged looks bent. The Necker cube illusion involves a flat figure that looks three-dimensional. In the McGurk effect, audio of the syllable /ba/ sounds like /da/ when viewing a speaker's mouth pronounce /ga/. Such illusions involve perceiving a thing while misperceiving some of its features. Hallucinations, however, involve complete figments of experience, as when Macbeth seems to see a dagger, tinnitus sufferers hear ringing, or a lifelike experience turns out to be a dream.

Arguments from illusion and hallucination target the intuitive or naïve view underwritten by perception's phenomenology and aim to prove that perceptual awareness is not a direct relationship to mind-independent entities. If, in some perceptual experience, the world does not match how it seems to the subject, then that experience does not just consist in unmediated openness to things and features in the environment. How, then, since nothing subjective distinguishes illusory from veridical experience, could even accurate experience involve direct awareness of the world? If ordinary things and qualities (like tomatoes, colors, and sounds) are not the objects of illusory and hallucinatory perceptual experiences, and if nothing subjectively accessible indicates that you are aware of something different in illusion or hallucination than in genuine perception, then perception, too, might be something other than intimate, unmediated acquaintance with extra-mental items.

Philosophical theories of perception attempt to reconcile the phenomenology of perceptual experience with misperception. They are constrained on one hand by the relational or world-involving character of perceptual experience, and on the other by the possibility of illusion and hallucination that is undetectable by the subject. It is useful to classify them according to whether the objects of perception, if any, are internal or external (that is, whether they are mind-dependent or mind-independent), and according to whether perceptual awareness of things in the world is mediated awareness or not (that is, whether it is indirect or direct). The possibility of misperception forces us to take a stand on what sorts of things we are aware of when we perceive, and on that in virtue of which we are aware of them (see, e.g., Smith 2002; Crane 2008).

To preserve the intuition that you experience the same kind of thing in illusory and veridical perceptual experience, and to preserve experiential contact or acquaintance with the objects of perception, *sense-datum* theories deny that the immediate objects of perceptual experience are ordinary public things like tables and chairs. Instead, they are experience-dependent items of sense that are present to one equally in veridical and delusive experience. But citing private sense data does not suffice to capture how the experience seems. For that, we must mention ordinary public objects and qualities (Strawson 1979). According to sense-datum theories, if one ever perceives anything external and public, one perceives it by virtue of experiencing internal or private sense data. Perception thus is mediated by awareness of internal features present in sensation (see, e.g., Jackson 1977; Foster 2000).

Disjunctive theories respond that perception requires contact with ordinary, mind-independent objects, but deny that genuine perceptual experiences and subjectively indistinguishable hallucinations belong to a common fundamental psychological kind. Perceptual experiences require a certain kind of relation between a subject and an ordinary subject-independent object, in which the object is partly constitutive of the perceptual experience. Delusions do not involve such a constitutive relation to an ordinary subject-independent object. Perception on this account is direct because it requires no awareness of internal mediators. According to disjunctive theories, however, subjects are at best in a position to characterize what they undergo as, for example, *indistinguishable from when I see a tomato smash* – one either hallucinates or experiences a tomato (see Haddock and Macpherson 2008; Byrne and Logue 2009).

Intentional, or *representational*, theories, on the other hand, want it both ways. They attempt to capture both the impression that one enjoys perceptual awareness of the external world and the intuitive claim that veridical experiences and subjectively indistinguishable illusions belong to a common explanatory psychological kind. According to intentionalism, perceiving, like believing and desiring, involves representing things to be a certain way. Perceptual states thus have *content* corresponding to what they are about, in the sense in which newspapers, in contrast to buckets, have contents (Siegel 2005). Such states thus may or may not be satisfied depending upon how the world is. Perceiving, like believing, thus is a psychological attitude with accuracy conditions. It is, however, customary to reserve "perceive," as we reserve "know" and "regret," but not "believe," for success. Perception plausibly is *factive* in that one cannot genuinely perceive that which is not the case, just as one cannot know or regret that which is false. According to the intentionalist, however, *perceptual experience*, like belief, can go wrong. It might seem to you as if you see a cow even if there is no cow. Your perceptual experience might seem *as of* a cow, though you perceive a cow only if the cow unaccidentally causes your experience. Intentionalists embrace the possibility of misperception while explaining why perceiving seems to involve awareness of things independent from oneself. Illusory and veridical experiences share representational *content*, but among the *objects* of perception are ordinary external things and features. Awareness of public objects is mediated in the sense that it requires representing those objects, but this need not be mediation by some entity *of which one is aware*. Perceptual representation need not be like viewing a picture. It is more like *being* the picture (see Harman 1990; Tye 2000).

If perceptual experiences, as well as beliefs and judgments, can be characterized in terms of their content, what distinguishes perceptual states from other contentful cognitive states? First, perceptual experiences have vivid phenomenology in which things appear as present before you. In addition, perceptual experiences count as sources and reasons for judgments and beliefs, and bear distinctive evidential weight. Experiences, however, need not compel belief or judgment. One might withhold commitment to the truth of what one experiences, and perhaps one need not even acquire a disposition to judge or so commit. Conversely, knowing that you are experiencing an illusion may do nothing to change your perceptual experience. Finally, judging and having beliefs are straightforwardly conceptual achievements that require possessing concepts corresponding to what one believes. But, intuitively, people and animals perceive things for which they do not possess concepts: seeing a horseshoe does not require possessing the concept of a horseshoe. Perceiving, then, is not a form of judging or believing. It is an attitude marked by its phenomenology and functional role.

Their contents do, however, illuminate how perceptual experiences differ from mere sensations and from any purely qualitative features intrinsic to experiences. Conscious bodily sensations, such as those you are aware of when you experience pains, nausea, or dizziness, seem private or not independent from oneself. First, they do not seem to be located outside one's body. Second, their existence seems to depend on their being experienced: a pain exists if one hurts, and unfelt dizziness is no dizziness at all. Third, more controversially, their experience lacks accuracy conditions: one cannot misperceive a pain, and illusory nausea is just plain nausea.

Some philosophers hold that sense perception involves consciousness of purely qualitative features, or *qualia*, that are intrinsic to one's experience (see Jackson 1982). Though it is a matter of controversy whether any such features exist, they are at least quite difficult to discern *as such*. The fact that one "sees right through" one's experiences to the world has been dubbed the *diaphanousness* or *transparency* of perceptual experience. As a result, one's attempts to introspectively attend to features intrinsic to a perceptual experience nearly always deliver either features of things one seems to perceive, such as colors and shapes, or extrinsic, relational features of one's experience, such as that one experiences a red thing. According to intentionalists about the phenomenological character of perceptual experience, any qualia we do sense strike us either as qualities of things we perceive, or as representational features of experiences (see, e.g., Harman 1990; Tye 2003; cf. Loar 2003).

4.2   The mechanisms of perception

Perceptual experience may seem effortless, automatic, and directly responsive to the world. It nevertheless requires a complex battery of subperceptual processes. Sensory stimulation occurs when the environment disturbs a sensory surface, such as the retina, tympanum, skin, olfactory epithelium, or tongue. Receptive surfaces *transduce* chemical, mechanical, or electromagnetic energy into neural signals that initiate further sensory and subperceptual processes. How does the disturbance of a sensory surface come to regulate action, impact thought, and stimulate vivid experiences in which you seem to be aware of a richly detailed world independent from yourself? One facet of this puzzle is how processes initiated at the interface between the environment and your sensory surfaces recover aspects of the world just on the basis of retinal, tympanic, or dermal activity. Cognitive science attempts to illuminate how the feat is accomplished.

Why is this such a puzzle? In vision, the image projected by the lens of the eye upon the retina is quite different from what we see. The image is two-dimensional, and it is inverted. Due to constant eye movements (saccades and micro-saccades that occur up to sixty times per second) the image moves continuously relative to the retina. Rod and cone receptors, which are sensitive to different wavelengths of light, are distributed unevenly. Image information is lost where the optic nerve departs the retina, though we don't experience a "blind spot" in our vision. And, a different image strikes each of the two retinas. In audition, air pressure fluctuations set off intricate vibration patterns at the two eardrums. This leads ultimately to a spatial auditory experience comprising discrete sound streams characterized by discernible audible attributes. In olfaction, complex mixtures of chemical compounds cause a huge array of experiences of recognizable smells. The difficult empirical question is: What are the mechanisms by which stimulation of sensory surfaces and sensory transduction lead to perceptual awareness?

One might think that after such questions have been answered, we have explained all there is to understand about perceiving. Cognitive scientists and philosophers, however, recently have engaged in heated debate over exactly what these processes tell us about what it is to perceive. On one hand, we might view the evolving states and processes that occur "inside the head" as tantamount to perceiving. On the other hand, we might think that although these mechanisms reveal a critical part of what enables perception, citing internal processes as such misses some essential aspect of what it is to perceive. As the following three sections mean to make clear, how researchers view the role of activity subsequent to the event of sensory transduction increasingly marks an important theoretical rift concerning the nature of perception.

4.3   Perceiving as information processing

The mainstream of cognitive science understands perception as an *information-processing* problem. How does one construct a representation of a complex environment, which meets the demands of thought and action, from impoverished stimulation? Viewed as such, developing a theory of perceiving requires discovering the mechanisms responsible for our capacity to extract useful information from sensory stimulation and to present it in a form that suits the needs of other cognitive functions.

Early theorists underestimated how demanding the task is in two respects. First, they construed perceiving as discerning or grasping the significance of a sensory image of which one is already conscious or aware. But even consciously sensing an image requires extracting features such as color, shape, and motion from light. Illumination upon the retina, for instance, is a product of ambient light and surface reflectance, and thus underdetermines color experience. Even if a scene's colors were simply projected onto a retinal image, being conscious of them would require an additional mind's eye. The image theory begs an essential question about vision by assuming awareness of such features without explaining it. What is required is a story about how information is extracted from light to recover even the most basic sensible features.

Second, they took perception, in contrast to sensation, to be continuous with higher cognition and intelligence. As above, perceiving requires something akin to problem solving because the information on which it is based, even if that is an image, underdetermines what one perceives. Early theorists took perceiving, understood as discerning or grasping an image's significance, to deploy general-purpose cognitive capacities that are not peculiar to perceiving, but which are involved in many varieties of thinking and reasoning. Lewis (1966, p. 357) describes one version of the picture like this: "Those in the traditions of British empiricism and introspectionist psychology hold that the content of visual experience is a sensuously given mosaic of color spots, together with a mass of interpretive judgments injected by the subject." General-purpose cognitive capabilities, however, do not suffice to explain how information concerning public objects and things in the world is extracted exclusively from a private image or from sensory stimulation. One might suggest that perceptions, concerning, for instance, size and distance, result from mechanisms such as learning, association, inference, or intuition. But it is unclear how general-purpose cognitive capacities such as associative learning or inference by themselves could yield a robust perceptual judgment concerning three-dimensional arrangements of surfaces and objects if one only ever has immediate acquaintance with a two-dimensional color spot mosaic, or if the only information available is how a sense organ is stimulated.

Suppose you take vision to involve consciously sensing a two-dimensional image projected upon the retina, as did Descartes (1637/1988, p. 64). This two-dimensional image by itself drastically underdetermines the scene. First, the projection of a scene is geometrically consistent with an infinite number of three-dimensional arrangements. A given region may correspond to something small, nearby, square, and at an angle; or it may correspond to something large, distant, trapezoidal, and oblique. A colored image itself determines neither size, distance, shape, nor orientation. Second, the image, marked by color discontinuities, is not clearly carved into units such as surfaces or objects. It thus fails to account for a scene's discernible segmentation into bounded regions with three-dimensional contours and shadows. This deficit is somewhat difficult to appreciate given our facility with pictorial representations, but it is pressing. The capacity to resolve such dramatic ambiguity must be accommodated by any theory of the mechanisms of perceiving.

In a step toward resolving these puzzles, and toward the contemporary approach to perception, Helmholtz (1867/1910) suggested that vision involves a series of *unconscious inferences*. Since, according to Helmholtz, such inferences are based upon sensations that possess phenomenal features, and since Helmholtz relies on a general, associative model of inference, his view exhibits the failings characteristic of early theories. However, the view according to which perceiving involves *inference-like* transitions inaccessible to conscious experience anticipates what Fodor and Pylyshyn (1981) call the "establishment view" of perceiving. It prefigures contemporary accounts according to which *subpersonal* sensory processes fuel unconscious transitions akin to a form of deductive or inductive inference (see Rock 1983).

Contemporary theories differ in two critical respects from early image- and sensation-based theories. First, they recognize that even formulating a color mosaic requires extracting information from light and thus do not take for granted that consciously accessible images or sensations ground perceptual inferences. Second, they hold that perceptual processing is conducted by specialized subsystems, not by a general rational or cognitive faculty. Deploying general-purpose problem-solving strategies would be radically inefficient given the specificity and complexity of perceptual tasks. To efficiently transform light information into full-fledged perceptions of public objects and features requires extracting, representing, and putting to use specific kinds of information at different stages, and it requires specialized rules and assumptions to guide the transitions. As a result, perceptual systems are, to a significant degree, unaffected by one's beliefs and reasoning. Though they furnish materials for thought and action, they are to a great extent *modular* or informationally encapsulated (Fodor 1983; Pylyshyn 1984). Perceptual capacities on this model forfeit the generality of those proposed by Helmholtz and other early theorists.

According to the contemporary establishment view, perceiving involves processes that resemble judgment and reasoning. The degree of specialization in perceptual systems, however, makes perception more automatic than classic views supposed. Whether 'inference' is understood literally or less-than-literally is partly terminological. Clearly, perceptual processes are not *ordinary* inferences. They are neither conscious nor deliberate. They are suited to a particular kind of task, do not generalize to all varieties of information, and may incorporate little outside information. Even so, it is tempting to view what takes place in perception as a regimented progression of transitions from early sensory states that bear information about stimulation to later states that represent features of one's environment. Indeed, the received view is that perception involves the kind of information processing that is characteristic of representational systems, such as computers. Perceiving, on this account, is constructing a representation of one's environment from impoverished sensory information.

Hatfield (2002) suggests, nonetheless, that explaining perception in terms of unconscious inferences requires justifying why the cognitive machinery should be understood as conducting inferences, or reaching conclusions guided by premises or evidence. This requires establishing that subpersonal states of perceptual systems have *content* – that they represent, for example, intensity values, visual angle, and distance – and implement principles or rules for deriving one from the other. One might also wonder why *conclusions* of such inferences are identical with or lead to perceptual *experiences*.

4.4   Gibson and Marr: direct pickup and computation

The view that perceiving is mediated by unconscious inferences from sensory stimulation is not uncontroversial. Gibson (1979) famously suggested that visual perception involves the *direct pickup* of information about one's environment that is present in the ambient light. Perceiving, according to this account, is not a matter of representing, transforming, and augmenting impoverished information drawn from the senses. There is no need, Gibson claims, to infer or otherwise intelligently construct a rich internal description or representation of the world. The world, available directly to be perceived, eliminates the need for representations; it serves as its own model.

Gibson suggests that unconscious inferences are unnecessary for vision since information concerning features that matter to the creature is present in the pattern of light that reaches the eye, or the *ambient optical array*. The key is that resolving ambiguities in sensory information requires appreciating that such information is *dynamic* – sensory stimulation changes over time as a creature negotiates its shifting environment. Since the light that reaches the eye is determined by illumination, the surfaces that reflect and generate light, and a creature's position in the environment, the structure of the ambient optical array changes as a function of illumination and of the movements of both the objects and the animal. The resulting patterns of change, or *optic flow*, contain information about the objects and features in the environment. For instance, changes in illumination cause relatively uniform changes across the optic array. And the pattern of optic flow when an object moves differs from when the creature moves. When an object moves, it produces a local, relative change to an otherwise static optic array. When the creature moves, it produces a distinctive global pattern of optic flow. Walking forward, for instance, creates flow outward from a vanishing point in the direction of travel. Perceiving thus involves detecting, in the changing optic array over time as one negotiates the environment, information about invariant properties that correspond lawfully to objects and features. It is not a matter of constructing representations by means of unconscious inferences from impoverished, static sensory information. According to Gibson, subpersonal processes *enable* perceiving. However, for Gibson, perceiving is an achievement of nothing less than the creature in its environment.

Marr's seminal work, *Vision* (1982), begins to reconcile these divergent ideas, though it nonetheless belongs squarely with the establishment. Marr's approach likens perception to deriving representations of the world from sensory information according to rule-like constraints. According to Marr, Gibson's insight was to recognize that the senses are "channels for perception" of the outside world, and not simply sources for sensations that fuel cognitive processes. Perception of the environment must be understood in terms of the detection of invariant properties of sensory stimulation through movement and time (1982, p. 29). Marr, however, claims that, framed as such, "direct pickup" *is* an information-processing task that must be carried out by our perceptual systems and that Gibson drastically underestimates its difficulty (1982, p. 30). So Marr acknowledges Gibson's insight that the ambient optic array provides important information concerning invariants, and thus about the arrangement of the visible environment, but Marr also proposes an account of *how* this information is extracted from retinal stimulation and represented in a useful form. Marr thus understands perception in traditional terms: "Vision is a *process* that produces from images of the external world a description that is useful to the viewer and not cluttered by irrelevant information" (Marr and Nishihara 1978, p. 269).

Marr's innovation is the framework he proposes for understanding perception in *computational* terms. He proposes that explaining the information processing that takes place in perception requires understanding it at each of three levels of abstraction. First and foremost, the *task* or *computational problem* of perceiving is defined by a mapping from information about sensory stimulation to information about the environment that answers to a creature's needs. Second, the level of the *algorithm* (or program) addresses the format in which to represent each sort of information and articulates a specific solution or detailed strategy concerning how to transform one into another. Finally, the level of *implementation* (or hardware) concerns how physiological processes in the brain realize the computational algorithm.

What distinguishes Marr's account from previous theories is that, to perform the task, so defined, the visual system employs processing strategies that exhibit a grasp upon the *natural physical constraints* governing the sources of sensory stimulation. Since stimulation underdetermines its source, perceiving invokes subpersonal rules that are intelligible only as embodying general principles that reflect one's environment. Assumptions about the natural world – concerning, for example, how scene geometry projects to the retinal image (for instance, how a three-dimensional object projects to a two-dimensional array) or that rigid rather than flexible bodies produce a given pattern of stimulation over time – are encoded by the visual system and govern how visual processes transform representations of retinal stimulation into full-fledged representations of the visual world. Patterns of luminance intensity values are converted into representations of one's visual environment through the help of built-in rules concerning how illumination, scene geometry, surface reflectance, and viewpoint determine luminance (the ambient optic array). A sharp luminance gradient, for instance, corresponds to an edge and thus forms the basis of an edge representation. Perceptual systems resolve the radical ambiguity in sensory stimulation through processing strategies that exploit assumptions concerning its relation to the natural world.

The computational process Marr describes proceeds in stages. From retinal luminance values, a *primal sketch* representing *edges* and *blobs* is computed by detecting sharp intensity discontinuities. From the primal sketch, a $2\frac{1}{2}$-*D sketch* encodes information about *visible surfaces*. It represents the contours and arrangement of surfaces in a viewer-centered, or egocentric, framework that includes information about depth, orientation, and surface discontinuities (1982, p. 277). The $2\frac{1}{2}$-D sketch depends upon a number of image characteristics and natural constraints. For instance, assuming stereoscopic disparities stem from a common physical source yields distance information; that illumination patterns are generated by rigid bodies yields physical structure from motion and optical flow; that surface elements are uniform in size and distribution yields surface texture from luminance patterns (1982, p. 267). Finally, a *3-D model*, a detailed description of a scene's three-dimensional shapes, meets the needs for object recognition. The 3-D model comprises primitive volumetric shapes (such as cylinders, spheres, cubes, or cones) assembled with increasingly fine detail to recover the specific geometric structure of the objects in a scene. Object identification might then invoke higher-level cognitive processes, such as pattern recognition and memory, which are beyond the scope of perception.

The information-processing paradigm understands perceiving as transforming sensory information into increasingly rich representations of one's environment. Steps in this process, understood as computations, take place according to algorithms that amount to strategies for interpreting the environmental significance of sensory stimulation. If perceiving culminates with the experience of a visual scene populated by volumes, colors, and shadows, then perceptual systems, guided by natural constraints, must extract such information from retinal clues and build it into a consciously accessible representation.

Marr's computational approach to vision, which distinguishes the overall task of vision from the algorithms for its solution and from its neurophysiological implementation, exemplifies one predominant contemporary approach to perception in cognitive science.

4.5 Representing and enacting

According to the received approach, perceiving is tantamount to representing. It principally involves constructing a representation of the immediate environment from the noisy, ambiguous stimulation of sensory surfaces. According to this conception, all perceptual awareness is, in a sense that may not be phenomenologically accessible to the subject, mediated by representations derived subpersonally from sensory stimulation.

Understanding perception in such terms has come under fire from a growing anti-establishment. In the first place, vision may not require constructing a *detailed* representation of a scene, since we may see far less at any given moment than we take ourselves to see. For instance, it may seem right now that you are seeing all of the words on this page, and that the details are all present in your visual experience. However, fixating on the period at the end of this sentence frustrates your attempts to recognize more than just a few surrounding words on the page. Furthermore, recent work on *change blindness* demonstrates that frequently we fail to notice prominent changes to a visual scene, such as a sailboat disappearing from an image, the replacement of a person with whom we are conversing, or the swapping of faces in a photograph (see, e.g., Simons and Rensink 2005). Moreover, aspects of a scene to which we do not attend, including those as striking as a gorilla strolling across the court during a basketball game, escape our notice – a phenomenon known as *inattentional blindness* (Mack and Rock 1998; Simons and Chabris 1999). On these grounds, Noë (2004) criticizes what he dubs the "snapshot conception" of visual experience, according to which one enjoys uniformly detailed visual awareness of an entire scene at any given moment. Some have argued for similar reasons that rich representations are absent from vision altogether (e.g., O'Regan 1992; O'Regan and Noë 2001). The evidence, however, is consistent with our registering the relevant information at a subpersonal (or even conscious) level but failing to retain, attend to, or access it. Even granting that we neither visually experience nor, at any level, visually represent in information-rich detail, one might revise one's characterization of representations to include mere sparse or incomplete detail. Indeed, this eases the computational and the explanatory burdens.

A second type of concern is that the received model leaves out the contributions of some factor critical to perceiving, such as movement, action, or the body. Thus, for instance, the received model has been charged with failing to appreciate the dynamic quality of seeing as it unfolds over time or in response to a creature's engagement with its environment. The charge is that establishment theories fail because they consider vision merely as a *static* or *disembodied* phenomenon. Establishment theorists, however, might respond as follows. Such faults do not belong to the overall computational framework itself, but rather to specific algorithms within that framework. Amending an algorithm to incorporate the relevant contributions and constraints might repair the defect. Ongoing research attempts to discover just such contributions. Moreover, it is not even clear that current models entirely fail to consider such contributions. For instance, distinguishing global patterns of optic flow that result from movements of the head and eyes (saccadic and intentional) from patterns that correspond to relative motion among objects is critical to determining the size, shape, and movement of objects in a scene. So, on contemporary models, detecting invariant features of the environment by distinguishing patterns of stimulation caused by changes to the environment from those caused by a subject's activity is part of the task of perception. Thus, the proposed solutions might after all incorporate resources that help explain the dynamic and action-involving character of perception.

Some might still object that the information-processing accounts make perceiving an entirely *subpersonal* process, instead of an activity carried out by the creature itself. But subpersonal processes might be constitutive of perceiving, or might underlie it, without being identical with or providing the essence of perceiving. The representational view is compatible with understanding perception to involve the level of the person or creature, while particular informational theories of perceiving aim to explain how – by explicating the mechanisms by which – representing one's environment is possible given our more basic capacities and our physiology.

A related worry about the received view is that it construes perceiving as something that depends entirely upon what takes place *in the head*. Though characterizing or individuating perceptual content – what is represented – might require invoking external relations, perceptual experience on the received view itself depends or supervenes entirely upon one's physiology. Stimulating sensory surfaces causes brain activity; such brain activity grounds perceptual processing that suffices to generate a given perceptual experience. Critics, however, insist that neither brain activity nor internally grounded processing alone, considered in isolation from how it is embedded in a creature and an environment, constitutes perceptual experience. The *vehicles* of perceptual experience thus extend beyond the brain, or even beyond the skin.

A growing cadre of philosophers, psychologists, and neuroscientists takes the sum of these worries to constitute a strong case against the received view. They contend that no theory framed in terms of sensory surface stimulation and subsequent rule-driven processing of internal representations captures what is most distinctive about perceiving. Instead, an adequate understanding of perception requires appreciating how a creature *uses* its body and its senses to interact with its environment. There are two broad themes in this work. One is that deciphering perception requires comprehending "the level of detail of the biological machine" (Ballard 1996, p. 461) – how a creature is *embodied*. Another is that it requires appreciating the way in which a creature is *embedded* or *situated* in its environment.

According to one such theory, perceiving is a dynamic, purpose-driven way of interacting with the world. O'Regan and Noë's (2001) *sensorimotor account* holds that seeing, for instance, is an activity that consists in a creature's exploring its environment in a skillful manner (see also Hurley 1998; Noë 2004). They point out that although brain activity is a necessary part of what enables perception, no internal representation suffices for seeing. Moreover, seeing, for the sensorimotor theorist, is not essentially mediated by detailed internal representations constructed "at some specific stage of neural processing" (Noë and Thompson 2002, p. 6). It is essentially mediated only by the exercise of one's implicit grasp of *sensorimotor contingencies*, which are the ways that sensory stimulation varies in response to actions and movements. Perceiving thus exemplifies one's implicit understanding of the ways things look and feel from a variety of perspectives. One does not internally represent, but *enacts* perceptual content through skillful performance. Perceiving, according to such an *enactive* conception, is a skill-based way of coming into *contact* with one's environment.

What we do, of course, makes a difference to what we see: turning my head leads to my seeing a jukebox. Acting thus causally impacts what we perceive. But what we do may also be relevant to explaining *how* we see. At minimum, explaining vision requires positing perceptual principles that concern how sensory stimulation changes in response to what one does. Distinguishing subject-induced patterns of stimulation or optic flow from object-induced ones helps to ground visual awareness of a scene. Proponents of the establishment view may reasonably grant that implicitly grasping or subpersonally representing sensorimotor contingencies is necessary for perceiving. The conceptual rift between perceiving and acting, since it is bridged by principles of vision, therefore is less sharp than earlier inquiry supposed. Still, it is a stretch to say, on such a conception, that action itself is constitutive of perception. For the received view, the boundary between perceptual processes and action remains intact because the principles in question are internal to vision (see, e.g., Prinz 2006). In brief, the relationship between perception and action remains causal. According to certain dissenters from the received view, however, perceiving must be subsumed under acting.

With this in mind, two steps toward resolution nevertheless serve to sharpen the focus of the conflict. The first step is to address worries concerning *how much* we see in framing the informational task of vision. In particular, clarify the amount of detail (rich or poor) in visual representations; specify the level (subpersonal or personal) of given representational states; and state whether such representations are accessible to other cognitive operations and to which ones, such as short-term recall or explicit reasoning. This helps address concerns about the snapshot conception of experience, change blindness, and inattentional blindness. The second step is to recognize movement-involving or motor-based constraints in the solution of the information-processing problem. For instance, seeing external objects depends on grasping how not just the environment but also a creature's movements impact optic flow. Seeing involves distinguishing creature-generated from environment-generated patterns of sensory stimulation. This alleviates some pressure to capture perception's dynamic and enactive characteristics. While such conciliatory steps suggest fruitful avenues for future research, they by no means dissolve the foundational dispute. The remaining dispute turns on at least three questions. First, is action constitutive of perception? Second, does what occurs in the head suffice for having perceptual experiences? Third, is perception a subject's direct contact with the world, or is it mediated by representations?

4.6   The role of phenomenology

This chapter has discussed philosophical and theoretical questions about the nature of perception that emerge from considering the role of perceptual illusions, the functions perception performs, and the general problems perceptual mechanisms solve. To more carefully characterize perceptual content, specify perceptual functions, and explicate its mechanisms requires a scientific study of the sorts of things creatures perceive. So, at a more concrete level, cognitive science sheds light on what it is to perceive by demanding and providing a systematic, scientific *accounting* of what we are capable of perceiving. Experimental psychology and philosophy increasingly attempt to answer such questions such as: What kinds of particulars and properties can we perceive? And, how much detail and variety is evident in perception?

In each of these enterprises, philosophers and psychologists frequently rely on conscious or introspectible aspects of experience to launch or constrain theoretical discussion. What is the proper role of *phenomenology*, and what are the limits of appeals to phenomenology in theorizing about perception (see also Jack and Roepstorff 2003; Roepstorff and Jack 2004; Noë 2007)?

Non-veridical experiences such as illusions show that perceptual phenomenology does not suffice for perceiving. A more challenging question is whether phenomenology is necessary for perceiving. Perceptual experiences do frequently accompany perception, but are they required? Evidence suggests otherwise in at least some cases. Certain subjects with primary visual cortex damage respond to their environment in ways characteristic of perceiving without introspectible conscious experience. Such *blindsighted* subjects reliably form beliefs about things before their eyes without reporting seeing them (Weiskrantz 1986). Furthermore, patients with a form of visual agnosia report no awareness of certain spatial features, yet those features appear successfully to guide their action (Milner and Goodale 1995). Even ordinary perceivers subject to certain visual spatial illusions act in ways appropriate to the scene's true geometry, such as by adjusting grasp width to the actual size of Titchener circles rather than to their apparent size (Goodale and Humphrey 1998). Subjects sometimes make judgments and act on the basis of sensory information, though they lack corresponding conscious awareness. It would be dogmatic to deny that such subjects perceive in some fashion. If so, perceptual phenomenology is neither sufficient nor necessary for perceiving.

Nakayama, He, and Shimojo (1995, pp. 21–2) nevertheless argue that consulting phenomenology is an important tool for investigating perception. They claim that phenomenologically grounded results are more objective than many suppose and present three reasons phenomenological methods are valuable. First, well-crafted experiments and demonstrations lead to surprisingly wide agreement with respect to phenomenology. They note that numerous demonstrations evoke near universal agreement, in contrast to many other psychological methods which rely upon subtle statistical analysis of large data sets. Second, compelling phenomenological results are immediate and verifiable across subjects. Researchers and audiences can view results for themselves. Finally, such methods provide a large, diverse database of results with relative ease and little cost. Nakayama *et al.* argue that phenomenological methods are widespread for good reason and suggest that the results and conclusions they ground are well founded.

However, reliance upon introspection and reports of perceptual phenomenology has come under attack (see, e.g., Schwitzgebel 2008). Though the phenomenology of a perceptual experience is supposed to concern what it is like for a subject to have that experience, phenomenological reports often are incomplete, inaccurate, or unreliable. Though many of us take ourselves to have detailed awareness of our surroundings at any given moment, and believe we know just what we see, careful investigation challenges both of these beliefs. Some researchers suggest the impression that visual experience has a vivid, introspectible phenomenology is a "grand illusion" (see Noë 2002). How could any methodology that depends upon elusive phenomenology and unreliable introspection be trusted?

As a start, it is plausible that differences in phenomenology, or differences in what it is like to have a perceptual experience, imply differences in the content of perceptual experience, or in how things are perceptually represented to be (Byrne 2001). This does not by itself imply infallible introspective access to determinate phenomenological features or to the contents of experiences. But, suppose we are capable under some conditions of detecting phenomenological *contrasts*. One strategy that uses phenomenology reasonably to get at perceptual content is to point to some introspectible phenomenological contrast and to argue that a given representational difference best explains that contrast (see Siegel 2006). This requires from phenomenology only that phenomenological or introspective reports do not wildly over-ascribe apparent phenomenological differences. Both the explanation for the contrast and the claim about perceptual content must stand on further theoretical, and not mere phenomenological, grounds.

This does not justify using phenomenology and first-person methods to discover the deep mechanisms responsible for perceiving. The structure of experience need not match that of perceptual processes. Such methods nonetheless furnish data that somehow must be explained. If an experience report is accurate, it provides evidence about the product of perceptual mechanisms. Contrary to traditional views associated with Descartes, however, the phenomenology of experience often is not immediately obvious. Doing careful experience reporting takes considerable work. Responses based on phenomenological reflection should be treated as a kind of performance that might be attributed to a variety of factors apart from accurately reporting perceptual experiences. If reports might be infused with information from other sources, such as one's background beliefs concerning the items in a scene, or some strategy adopted to respond to ambiguous experiences, then perhaps no unique, epistemically privileged level of introspectively accessible phenomenology exists. It is unwise in both philosophy and in science to rely exclusively on phenomenological reports and reflections – someone else's or one's own. It is, however, compelling to understand introspective reports as data that inform the construction of philosophical and scientific theories of perception. It remains, after all, a goal of investigating perception to explain the seemings.

Further reading

Bregman, A. S. (1990). *Auditory Scene Analysis: The Perceptual Organization of Sound*. Cambridge, MA: MIT Press. Bregman's work brought techniques and theoretical resources familiar in contemporary cognitive science to bear on problems concerning auditory perception.

Gendler, T. S. and Hawthorne, J. (eds.) (2006). *Perceptual Experience*. New York: Oxford University Press. A collection of new essays that provides a cross-section of recent philosophical work on the nature of perceptual content and perceptual experience.

Gibson, J. J. (1966). *The Senses Considered as Perceptual Systems*. Boston, MA: Houghton Mifflin. One of the most influential books on sensory perception. It articulates the framework of Gibson's ecological approach to perception.

Heyer, D. and Mausfeld, R. (eds.) (2002). *Perception and the Physical World: Psychological and Philosophical Issues in Perception*. Chichester: John Wiley

& Sons, Ltd. A recent interdisciplinary collection of essays on foundational and theoretical issues in the cognitive science of perception.

Mack, A. and Rock, I. (1998). *Inattentional Blindness*. Cambridge, MA: MIT Press. Argues from evidence that subjects fail to notice features of a scene to which they do not attend that conscious perceptual awareness requires attention.

Marr, D. (1982). *Vision*. San Francisco, CA: W. H. Freeman. Marr's book is the seminal presentation of the computational approach to visual representation, information processing, and perception.

Noë, A. (2004). *Action in Perception*. Cambridge, MA: MIT Press. A vivid, influential, and accessible recent introduction and defense of the enactive view of perception.

Noë, A. and Thompson, E. (eds.) (2002). *Vision and Mind: Selected Readings in the Philosophy of Perception*. Cambridge, MA: MIT Press. A selection of classic contemporary essays concerning philosophical issues about the nature of visual perception.

Palmer, S. (1999). *Vision Science: Photons to Phenomenology*. Cambridge, MA: MIT Press. A tremendously informative book that deals with nearly every important empirical issue concerning the cognitive science of visual perception.

Rock, I. (1983). *The Logic of Perception*. Cambridge, MA: The MIT Press. In contrast to Gibson's ecological approach, this book presents Rock's defense of the view that visual perception results from unconscious inference and problem solving.

References

Ballard, D. (1996). On the function of visual representation, in K. Akins (eds.), *Perception*, vol. 5 of *Vancouver Studies in Cognitive Science* (pp. 111–31). Oxford University Press.

Byrne, A. (2001). Intentionalism defended, *Philosophical Review* 110: 199–240.

Byrne, A. and Logue, H. (eds.) (2009). *Disjunctivism: Contemporary Readings*. Cambridge, MA: MIT Press.

Crane, T. (2008). The problem of perception, in E. N. Zalta (ed.), *The Stanford Encyclopedia of Philosophy* (Fall 2008 edn.), http://plato.stanford.edu/archives/fall2008/entries/perception-problem.

Descartes, R. (1637/1988). Optics, in J. Cottingham, R. Stoothoff, and D. Murdoch (eds.), *Descartes: Selected Philosophical Writings* (pp. 57–72). Cambridge University Press.

Fodor, J. (1983). *The Modularity of Mind*. Cambridge, MA: MIT Press.

Fodor, J. A. and Pylyshyn, Z. W. (1981). How direct is visual perception? Some reflections on Gibson's "ecological approach," *Cognition* 9: 139–96.

Foster, J. (2000). *The Nature of Perception*. Oxford: Clarendon Press.

Gibson, J. J. (1979). *The Ecological Approach to Visual Perception*. Hillsdale, NJ: Lawrence Erlbaum.

Goodale, M. A. and Humphrey, G. K. (1998). The objects of action and perception, *Cognition* 67: 181–207.

Haddock, A. and Macpherson, F. (eds.) (2008). *Disjunctivism: Perception, Action, Knowledge.* Oxford University Press.

Harman, G. (1990). The intrinsic quality of experience, in J. Tomberlin (ed.), *Philosophical Perspectives*, vol. 4: *Action Theory and Philosophy of Mind* (pp. 31–52). Atascadero, CA: Ridgeview.

Hatfield, G. (2002). Perception as unconscious inference, in D. Heyer and R. Mausfeld (eds.), *Perception and the Physical World: Psychological and Philosophical Issues in Perception* (pp. 115–43). Chichester: John Wiley & Sons, Ltd.

Helmholtz, H. L. (1867/1910). *Handbuch der physiologischen Optik.* Leipzig: L. Voss.

Hurley, S. L. (1998). *Consciousness in Action.* Cambridge, MA: Harvard University Press.

Jack, A. I. and Roepstorff, A. (2003). Why trust the subject? *Journal Of Consciousness Studies* 10: v–xx.

Jackson, F. (1977). *Perception: A Representative Theory.* Cambridge University Press.

(1982). Epiphenomenal qualia, *Philosophical Quarterly* 32: 127–36.

Lewis, D. (1966). Percepts and color mosaics in visual experience, *The Philosophical Review* 75: 357–68.

Loar, B. (2003). Transparent experience and the availability of qualia, in Q. Smith and A. Jokic (eds.), *Consciousness* (pp. 77–96). Oxford University Press.

Mack, A. and Rock, I. (1998). *Inattentional Blindness.* Cambridge, MA: MIT Press.

Marr, D. (1982). *Vision.* San Francisco, CA: W. H. Freeman.

Marr, D. and Nishihara, H. K. (1978). Representation and recognition of the spatial organization of three-dimensional shapes, *Proceedings of the Royal Society of London, Series B, Biological Sciences*, 200(1140): 269–94.

Milner, A. D. and Goodale, M. A. (1995). *The Visual Brain in Action.* Oxford University Press.

Nakayama, K., He, Z. J., and Shimojo, S. (1995). Visual surface representation: A critical link between lower-level and higher-level vision, in S. M. Kosslyn and D. N. Osherson (eds.), *Visual Cognition, vol. 2 of An Invitation to Cognitive Science* (2nd edn., pp. 1–70). Cambridge, MA: MIT Press.

Noë, A. (2002). Is the visual world a grand illusion? *Journal of Consciousness Studies* 9: 1–12.

(2004). *Action in Perception.* Cambridge, MA: MIT Press.

(ed.) (2007). *Phenomenology and the Cognitive Sciences* (special issue on Dennett's heterophenomenology) 6: 1–270.

Noë, A. and Thompson, E. (2002). Introduction, in A. Noë and E. Thompson (eds.), *Vision and Mind: Selected Readings in the Philosophy of Perception* (pp. 1–14). Cambridge, MA: MIT Press.

O'Regan, J. K. (1992). Solving the "real" mysteries of visual perception: The world as an outside memory, *Canadian Journal of Psychology* 46: 461–88.

O'Regan, J. K. and Noë, A. (2001). A sensorimotor account of vision and visual consciousness, *Behavioral and Brain Sciences* 24: 939–1031.

Prinz, J. (2006). Putting the brakes on enactive perception, *PSYCHE*, 12.

Pylyshyn, Z. W. (1984). *Computation and Cognition: Toward a Foundation for Cognitive Science*. Cambridge, MA: MIT Press.

Rock, I. (1983). *The Logic of Perception*. Cambridge, MA: The MIT Press.

Roepstorff, A. and Jack, A. I. (2004). Trust or interaction? *Journal of Consciousness Studies* 11: v–xxii.

Schwitzgebel, E. (2008). The unreliability of naive introspection, *Philosophical Review* 117: 245–73.

Siegel, S. (2005). The contents of perception, in E. N. Zalta (ed.), *The Stanford Encyclopedia of Philosophy* (Summer 2005 edn.), http://plato.stanford.edu/archives/sum2005/entries/perception-contents.

(2006). Which properties are represented in perception? in T. S. Gendler and J. Hawthorne (eds.), *Perceptual Experience* (pp. 481–503). New York: Oxford University Press.

Simons, D. J. and Chabris, C. F. (1999). Gorillas in our midst: Sustained inattentional blindness for dynamic events, *Perception* 28: 1059–74.

Simons, D. J. and Rensink, R. A. (2005). Change blindness: Past, present, and future, *Trends in Cognitive Sciences* 9: 16–20.

Smith, A. D. (2002). *The Problem of Perception*. Cambridge, MA: Harvard University Press.

Strawson, P. F. (1979). Perception and its objects, in G. F. MacDonald (ed.), *Perception and Identity: Essays Presented to A. J. Ayer with his Replies* (pp. 41–60). Ithaca, NY: Cornell University Press.

Tye, M. (2000). *Consciousness, Color, and Content*. Cambridge, MA: MIT Press.

(2003). Qualia, in E. N. Zalta (ed.), *The Stanford Encyclopedia of Philosophy* (Summer 2003 edn.), http://plato.stanford.edu/archives/sum2003/entries/qualia.

Weiskrantz, L. (1986). *Blindsight: A Case Study and Implications*. Oxford: Clarendon Press.

5 Action

Elisabeth Pacherie

5.1 Introduction

My arm rises. Is my arm rising something happening to me – say, a movement caused by a muscle spasm or by somebody pulling a string attached to my wrist – or is it my own doing – am I raising my arm? What does it mean to say that I am raising my arm intentionally? Must it be the case that a conscious intention to do so causes my arm to rise? How do I know that I am raising my arm, and does that knowledge differ from the knowledge you may acquire by observing me? The nature of action, action explanation, and agency are central issues in philosophical action theory and have been systematically explored in the last fifty years.

On the empirical side, with the emergence of cognitive neuroscience in the 1980s, motor cognition became a very active area of research. Work in the field of motor cognition aims at uncovering and understanding the mechanisms and processes involved in action specification and control. The efforts made to interpret anatomical and physiological evidence using cognitive theories and methods, including computational modeling, and, conversely, to test and refine cognitive models of normal motor cognition using functional neuroimaging and data from brain-damaged patients have resulted in a vast array of exciting discoveries and in provocative hypotheses about the cognitive structure of the processes and representations underpinning action.

The scientific study of action yields insights, distinctions, as well as descriptions of the causal mechanisms underlying action that go beyond what conceptual analysis, however sophisticated, could alone reveal. Results and ideas drawn from the scientific study of action can thus offer new sources of inspiration for philosophers, evidence which may help overcome longstanding difficulties or redraw the lines on the philosopher's map by challenging certain widely received assumptions. Conversely, careful philosophical analysis can also lead to more sober assessments of over-enthusiastic claims about what some recent empirical data show.

In recent years, the integration of philosophical with scientific theorizing has started to yield new insights. This chapter will survey some recent philosophical and empirical work on the nature and structure of action, on conscious agency, and on our knowledge of actions.

5.2   The nature of action and action explanation

One important debate that arose in the early sixties was concerned with whether the agent's reasons for his or her action were also the causes of the action. Following Wittgenstein, some philosophers (Anscombe 1963) argued that to explain why an agent acted as he or she did involved identifying the normative reasons that made the action intelligible in the agent's eyes and claimed that such normative explanations were different in kind from causal explanations. Others (Taylor 1964) similarly argued that explanations of actions are teleological explanations – in other words, explanations in terms of goals – and are as such not analyzable as causal explanations. In contrast, Davidson (1980, ch. 1) argued that reason-explanations are causal explanations and did much to rebut the anti-causalist arguments that purported to show that reasons couldn't be causes. In particular, he pointed out that an agent may have several reasons to perform a certain action, but act only for one of those reasons. Challenging the non-causalists to provide an alternative explanation, he argued that what makes it true that the agent acts for this reason and not the other reasons he or she has is that this reason but not the others makes a causal contribution to the action. Similarly, most causalists will agree that reason-explanations for action are teleological but contend that teleological explanations are themselves kinds of causal explanations.

By reuniting the causal with the rational, the causalists opened the way for a naturalistic stance in action theory and thus for an integration of philosophical and scientific enquiries. The causal approach is today the dominant position in philosophical action theory. Broadly speaking, it considers that action is behavior that can be characterized in terms of a certain sort of psychological causal process. Yet, versions of the causal approach can take widely different forms depending on (1) what they take the elements of the action-relevant causal process to be, and (2) what part of the process they identify as the action. Thus, with respect to the first question, some theories countenance only beliefs and desires, while others view intentions, volitions or tryings as essential elements of the action-relevant causal structure. We can also distinguish three broad types of causal theories on the basis of their answer to the second question. On one view, one should characterize actions in terms of their causal power to bring about certain effects, typically bodily movements and their consequences. Accordingly, proponents of this view will tend to identify an action with mental events belonging to the earlier part of a causal sequence, such as tryings (Hornsby 1980). Conversely, one may hold that what distinguishes actions from other kinds of happenings is the nature of their causal antecedents. Actions will then be taken to be physical events (bodily movements and their consequences) with a distinctive mental cause. A third possibility is to consider actions as causal processes rather than just causes or effects and to identify them with, if not the entire causal sequence, at least a large portion of it.

The earlier belief–desire versions of the causal theory, made popular most notably by Davidson (1980, ch. 1) and Goldman (1970), held that what distinguishes an action from a mere happening is the nature of its causal antecedent, conceived as a complex of some of the agent's beliefs and desires. One attraction of the belief–desire theory was its elegant simplicity. The theory took the belief–desire complex to both rationalize the action and cause it, thus simultaneously offering an account of the nature of actions – as events caused by belief–desire complexes – and an account of the explanation of intentional action as explanation in terms of the agent's reasons for acting. Another important attraction of the theory was its ontological parsimony. It didn't postulate any special type of mental events such as willings, volitions, acts of will, settings of oneself to act, tryings, etc. It did not even postulate intentions as distinct states, since on the theory, to say that somebody acted with a certain intention was just to say that his action stood in the appropriate relation to certain of his desires and beliefs.

However, it soon appeared that this simple version of the causal theory had serious shortcomings and remained incomplete in a number of important respects. First, as several philosophers have pointed out, including Davidson himself (Davidson 1980, Ch. 5; Bratman 1987), the relational analysis of intentions is inapplicable to intentions concerning the future, intentions which we may now have, but which are not yet acted upon, and, indeed, may never be acted upon. Acknowledging the existence of future-directed intentions forces one to admit that intentions can be states separate from the intended actions or from the reasons that prompted the action. But, as Davidson himself notes, once this is admitted, there seems to be no reason not to allow that intentions of the same kind are also present in all or at least most cases of intentional actions.

Second, it was also pointed out (Brand 1984; Searle 1983) that the belief–desire theory does not account for "minimal" actions, i.e., actions that are performed routinely, automatically, impulsively or unthinkingly. To borrow an example from Searle (1983), suppose I am sitting in a chair reflecting on a philosophical problem, and I suddenly get up and start pacing about the room. Although my getting up and pacing about are actions of mine, no antecedent belief–desire complex prompted me to do so. The act was unpremeditated and spontaneous. Thus, it may be doubted whether being caused by a belief–desire complex is a necessary condition for an event to qualify as an action.

What these two objections suggest is that actions come in various grades, from routinely performed low-level purposive behavior to deliberately undertaken and consciously preplanned actions, and thus that their psychological structure may be more or less rich.

A third objection to the belief–desire version of the causal theory is that it doesn't have the resources to exclude aberrant manners of causation. This is the notorious problem of causal deviance or waywardness. Here's an example from Mele:

> Ann wants to awaken her husband and she believes that she may do so by making a loud noise. Motivated (causally) by this desire and belief, Ann may search in the dark for a suitable noise-maker. In her search, she may accidentally knock over a lamp, producing a loud crash. By so doing, she may awaken her husband, but her awakening him in this way is not an intentional action. (Mele 2002, pp. 21–2)

As this example illustrates, not every causal relation between seemingly appropriate mental antecedents and resultant events qualifies the latter as intentional actions. The challenge then is to specify the kind of causal connection that must hold between the antecedent mental event and the resultant behavior for the latter to qualify as an intentional action.

A fourth, related problem, concerns the explanation of failed actions. Some actions fail because some of the agent's beliefs are false. Thus, John may fail to turn the light on because he was wrong to believe that the switch he pressed commanded the light. The causal theory can account for failures of this kind, for it claims that the (non-accidental) success of an action depends on the truth of the beliefs figuring in the motivating belief–desire complex. Yet, as Israel, Perry, and Tutiya (1993) point out, the failure of an action cannot always be traced back to the falsity of a motivating belief. Here's their example. Suppose Brutus intends to kill Caesar by stabbing him. His beliefs that Caesar is to his left and that stabbing Caesar in the chest would kill him are both true, and yet Brutus fails to kill Caesar because he makes the wrong movement and misses Caesar completely. This is what they call the "problem of the wrong movement": when the agent's beliefs are correct, what ultimately accounts for the success or failure of an intended action are the bodily movements performed. If we consider that a theory of action explanation should aim at explaining the actual action, not just the attempt or volition, we should be ready to include in the motivating complex cognitions pertaining to movements. The motivating complex as it is conceived in the standard account is thus fundamentally incomplete, leaving a gap between the motivating cognitions and the act itself.

The various revisions and refinements the causal theory of action has undergone in the last three decades can be seen as attempts to overcome some of these difficulties and shortcomings. In particular, many philosophers have found it necessary to introduce a conception of intentions as distinctive, *sui generis*, mental states. They argue that intentions have their own complex and distinctive functional role and form an irreducible kind of psychological state, on a par with beliefs and desires. Thus, Bratman (1987) stresses three functions of intentions. First, they are *terminators of practical reasoning* in the sense that once we have formed an intention to *A*, we will not normally continue to deliberate whether to *A* or not; in the absence of relevant new information, the intention will resist reconsideration. Second, intentions are also *prompters of practical reasoning*, where practical reasoning is about means of *A*-ing. This function of intentions thus involves devising specific plans for *A*-ing. Third, intentions also have a *coordinative function* and serve to coordinate the activities of the agent over time and to coordinate them with the activities of other agents.

Philosophers also typically point out further functions of intentions (Brand 1984; Mele 1992). Intentions are also responsible for triggering or initiating the intended action (*initiating function*) and for guiding its course until completion. An intention to *A* incorporates a plan for *A*-ing, a representation or set of representations specifying the goal of the action and how it is to be arrived at. It is this component of the intention that is relevant to its *guiding function*. Finally, intentions have also been assigned a *control function*, involving a capacity to monitor progress toward the goal and to detect and correct deviations from the course of action as laid out in the guiding representation.

The first three functions of intentions just described – their roles as terminators of practical reasoning about ends, as prompters of practical reasoning about means and as coordinators – are typically played by intentions in the period between their initial formation and the initiation of the action. By contrast, the last three functions (initiating, guiding, and controlling) are played in the period between the initiation of the action and its completion. Attention to these differences has led a number of philosophers to develop dual-intention theories of action. For instance, Searle (1983) distinguishes between prior intentions and intentions-in-action, Bratman (1987) between future-directed and present-directed intentions, and Mele (1992) between distal and proximal intentions. In all cases, an intention of the former type will only eventuate into action by first yielding an intention of the latter type.

Dual-intention theories make available new strategies for dealing with the difficulties listed earlier. To begin with, they open up new prospects toward a solution to the problem of minimal actions (that many actions do not seem to be preceded by any intention to perform them). According to dual-intention theories, all actions have proximal intentions, but they need not always be preceded by distal intentions (from now on, I use Mele's terminology). For instance, when, reflecting on a philosophical problem, I start pacing about the room, I do not first engage in a deliberative process that concludes with a distal intention to pace; rather my pacing is initiated and guided by a proximal intention formed on the spot. Automatic, spontaneous, or impulsive actions may then be said to be those actions that are caused by proximal intentions but are not planned ahead of time.

Dual-intention theories also provide at least a partial answer to the problem of causal deviance. They suggest that for intentions to cause actions in the right way for them to count as intentional, two constraints should be met. First, the intended effect must be brought about in the way specified by the plan component of the intention. Second, it must also be the case that the causal chain linking the distal intention to the resultant bodily behavior include relevant proximal intentions.

5.3   Motor cognition

Although dual-intention theories sound more promising than the earlier belief–desire theory, more needs to be said about the ways intentions carry out their functions and about the nature of their contents. First, if proximal intentions are to be regarded as playing an essential role in the initiation of every action, one should identify the features of proximal intentions that allow them to play this role. Second, we need an account of the guiding and control functions of proximal intentions. Third, in cases where the agent is acting on his distal intention, there must be an appropriate transition between the distal intention and the proximal intention, and we need to clarify what constitutes an appropriate transition.

Work in the field of motor cognition is highly relevant to these issues. This field integrates research techniques and methods from cognitive psychology, behavioral neuroscience, and computational modeling in an attempt to provide a unified approach to the central questions of the organization of action, the nature and role of the different representations involved in the generation of action, and the contributions of different brain structures to the planning and execution of movement. Here, I will concentrate on the functional architecture of motor cognition, introducing some of the theoretical concepts, models, and hypotheses that play a central role in current thinking in the motor domain and are of particular relevance for philosophical theorizing on action.

Work on motor physiology started at the end of the nineteenth century and was long dominated by the sensory-motor theory of action generation that conceived of actions as reactions to changes in the external environment and as essentially a matter of movements and the muscles that power them. Thus Sherrington, the famous British neurophysiologist, considered the reflex action as the elementary unit of behavior and thought that all coordinated action was constructed through a process of sequential combination, where reflexes were chained into behavioral sequences in such a way that feedback from one movement stimulated the next in the sequence (Sherrington 1947). This view of complex actions as associative chains left little role for cognitive processes in the organization of action.

In the early 1950s Karl Lashley (1951) launched an attack against this view and argued that the action sequence is guided by plans and motor programs.

He pointed out that complex action sequences are characteristic of human behavior and that humans are remarkably adept at learning new skills and rearranging elementary movements to produce new action sequences. The fact that the same elementary movements can occur in different orders raises an obvious problem for the idea of serial chaining since a given movement may be followed by different movements on different occasions. Another argument in favor of the central organization of action (as opposed to peripheral chaining) comes from the fact that we do not simply react to external events but also actively initiate interactions with our environment.

Centralism, the idea that voluntary actions are largely driven by central internal representations rather than by external events, is one of the main tenets of contemporary theories of action generation. As Jeannerod (1997, 2006) points out, to be capable of internally generated purposive action, an organism must have internal models of how the external world is, how it will be modified by the action of the organism, and how the organism itself will be modified by this action. The modern idea of internal models had several precursors. One of them is the idea of a homeostatic device, where the signals that initiate a process originate from a discrepancy between a central signal and an input signal, the former corresponding to a fixed inbuilt reference value for some parameter, the other to the current value of the parameter. Homeostatic systems draw attention to the role of endogenous factors and imply the existence of a certain form of representation or stored knowledge of the reference value of a parameter. Another precursor of internal models is the concept of efference copy proposed by Von Holst and Mittelsteadt (1950). The idea is that when the motor centers send a motor command to the peripheral nervous system to produce a movement, they also send a copy of this command to other centers that can in this way anticipate the effect of the motor command. (A motor signal from the central nervous system to the periphery is called an *efference*, and a copy of this signal is called an *efference copy*.) The notion of an efference copy is of particular interest for two reasons. First, it is a centrally generated signal, and this suggests that the central nervous system can inform itself directly about its current state and activity without a detour through peripheral reafferences. Second, it constitutes an elementary instance of expectation or anticipation, where an internal model of forthcoming sensory experience arises in advance of actual feedback.

The concept of internal models was further developed by engineers who proposed computational theories incorporating the idea of control strategies based on internal models and have applied this approach in the fields of robotics, neural networks, and adaptive control. There is now growing evidence that similar strategies are used in human motor control (e.g., Jeannerod 1997; Frith, Blakemore, and Wolpert 2000).

Current computational theories of human motor control appeal to two main kinds of internal models, forward and inverse models, as illustrated in

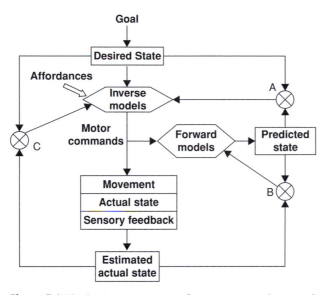

Figure 5.1 The basic components of a motor control system based on internal models. Adapted from Frith *et al.* (2000).

Figure 5.1. In a nutshell, an inverse model (or controller) computes the commands for achieving a desired state given the current states of the system and of the environment. An efference copy of these commands is fed to a forward model (also called predictive model) that represents the causal flow of a process in a system and can thus generate a prediction of the consequences of performing these commands. Of special interest is the idea that the control of action depends in a large part on the coupling of inverse and forward models through a series of comparators, i.e., mechanisms that compare two signals and use the result of the comparison for various kinds of regulation.

A first kind of comparator (labelled A in Figure 5.1) takes as input representations of the desired state and of the predicted state and sends an error signal to the inverse model if a difference is found. Such a mechanism can be used to maintain accurate performance in the presence of feedback delays. It can also be used for mental practise and planning, as forward models can predict the sensory outcome of an action without the action being actually carried out. A second kind of comparator mechanism (labelled B in Figure 5.1) compares the predicted consequences of a motor command with its actual consequences. The result of this comparison can be used to update the forward model and improve its functioning. It can also be used to filter sensory information and to distinguish the component that is due to self-movement from that due to changes in the world (Blakemore, Wolpert, and Frith 1999). Finally, a third kind of comparison is between desired state and actual feedback (labelled C in Figure 5.1). Errors derived from the difference between the desired state and the actual state can be used to update the inverse models and improve performance. This kind of comparison is therefore important for motor learning.

A third key tenet of current theorizing on motor cognition, besides the idea of central representations and the idea of control structures involving internal and external feedback loops, is the idea that action is hierarchically organized. The organization of action is commonly thought of as a functional hierarchy comprising three main levels, corresponding to the progressive specification of the action to be performed. At the highest level, action representations represent the whole action as a unit, in terms of its overarching goal and of the sequence of steps or subgoals needed to achieve that goal. At this level, the action is represented in a rather abstract, typically conceptual, format. The second level is concerned with the implementation of each step in the action plan and involves selecting an appropriate motor program given the immediate goal and contextual information about the current state of the agent and the current state of its environment. In other words, processes at this level are in charge of anchoring the successive steps of the action plan in the current situation and of selecting appropriate motor programs. Finally, once a motor program has been selected, the exact values of its parameters must still be set. This is done at the third level, where incoming sensory information about external constraints is used to specify these values.

This distinction of three levels is an oversimplification and should be qualified in several ways. First, the organization within each level can itself be decomposed into hierarchical stages. Second, the distinction between the first and second level is not always sharp. A given action may be planned to a greater or a lesser extent. Typically, how much is planned at the highest level depends on the agent's expertise. For instance, while the novice tennis player intent on performing a topspin serve may have to represent all the steps involved in performing such a serve in advance of acting, the expert tennis player need only represent his action as a topspin serve at the planning level, having already built through intensive training an appropriate motor program where these steps are stored. Third, talk of a hierarchical organization and of a series of levels may give the impression that the processing steps must be ordered serially – that planning must be over before programming starts, and that programming in turn must be over before the execution starts. As Jeannerod (1997) points out, however, activation in the cortical areas thought to correspond to the various levels of organization occurs simultaneously and the existence of a sequence can only be detected statistically. Yet, the existence of parallel processing in the motor system does not contradict the idea of hierarchy of levels. A hierarchy between levels implies degrees of specialization for each level but it does not imply a sequential order of activation.

One important source of evidence for the hierarchical organization of actions comes from neuropsychology, where lesions in different brain areas may lead to different types of impairments of motor cognition. Thus, patients with optic ataxia produce inaccurate reaching movements toward a target or object in space as well as inaccurate grasping of objects with incorrect orientating of the hand and inadequate pre-shaping with respect to the shape and size of the object (Rossetti, Vighetto, and Pisella 2003). Their visuomotor impairment affects the bottom level of the organization of action, concerned with appropriately setting the parameters of the selected motor programs. In contrast, patients suffering from ideomotor apraxia (Heilman and Rothi 1993) have no problem reaching for and grasping objects and can describe what their functions are, but they are not able to manipulate them according to their function. Their deficit relates to the second level of action organization: they seem to have lost the motor programs associated with various kinds of objects. Finally, patients with utilization behavior reach out and automatically use objects in an instrumentally correct manner that is inappropriate for the particular context (Lhermitte 1983). For instance, a patient seeing a pair of glasses placed in front of him may pick it up and put it on. Moreover, if a second and then a third pair of glasses are placed in front of him, he will put them on and will end up wearing all three. In contrast, when they lack external stimulation to steer them into action, these patients exhibit mental inertia and apathy. They seem to be impaired at the highest level of action organization: they have lost the capacity to generate and act on endogenous intentions and, as a result, to inhibit stimulus-driven actions that are normally kept in check by endogenous plans.

The three notions of central representations of action, control structures making use of internal models, and hierarchical organization of action are highly relevant to the concerns of philosophers of action. Firstly, the idea of a hierarchical organization of action representations and control structures helps flesh out the idea that actions come in various grades, from minimal, automatic, highly routinized actions to carefully preplanned actions with long-term and complex goals, and can have a psychological structure whose richness varies accordingly. The two highest levels in this hierarchy echo the distinction of distal and proximal intentions proposed by dual-intention theorists. However, with but a few exceptions (Pacherie 2008) philosophers ignore the third and lowest level of the hierarchy. Secondly, the idea that action representations are associated with control structures involving inverse and forward models coupled through comparators helps make sense of the idea that representations of actions can be both teleological and causal. They are representations of action goals that both cause action specification and execution and control progress toward the goal through internal and external feedback loops. Thirdly, careful attention to the way action representations control the performance of the agent may also give us a solution to problems of causal deviance. Yet, as we will now see, recent empirical work can also yield results that appear to challenge deeply entrenched philosophical assumptions.

5.4   Conscious agency

Libet (1985) suggested that the results of his studies on brain activity during the preparation of voluntary acts seriously questioned the idea that conscious intentions have any causal role in the initiation of action and therefore threatened the notion of free-will as traditionally understood. More recently, Wegner's psychological experiments led him to claim that the conscious will is an illusion (Wegner 2002). These attacks on the traditional view of the role of conscious agency did much to reawaken the interest of philosophers in the phenomenology of action. At the same time, further empirical investigations aimed at probing in more detail the phenomenology of action and its disorders have started yielding a wealth of new data, suggesting that extreme skepticism vis-à-vis conscious agency may rest in part on too simplistic a view of the phenomenology of agency.

In his famous studies, Libet (1985) asked subjects to move a hand at will and to note when they felt the urge to move by observing the position of a dot on a special clock. While the participants were doing this, the experimenters recorded their readiness potential, i.e., the brain activity linked to the preparation of movement. What they found was that the onset of the readiness potential predated the conscious awareness of the urge to move by about 350 milliseconds, while the actual onset of movement measured in the muscles of the forearm occurred around 150 milliseconds after conscious awareness. Libet and others have claimed that these results provide evidence in favor of a skeptical attitude toward conscious mental causation: since the conscious awareness of the urge to move occurs much later than the onset of the brain activity linked to the preparation of movement, it could play no causal role in the production of the intentional arm movement. Libet himself suggested that consciousness may still intervene and veto the unconsciously initiated action, providing a kind of conscious "free won't."

Several philosophers have criticized Libet's interpretation of the bearing of his experiments on conscious agency and free will. First, it is worth noting that although the conscious urge to move may lag behind the onset of brain activity, it still precedes the actual onset of movement. Libet's interpretation of his finding is premised on the view that only the initial element in a causal chain, i.e., only a cause uncaused, may genuinely qualify as a cause. Yet, the notion of a cause uncaused is metaphysically dubious and certainly hard to square with a naturalistic stance. A conscious mental state may play a causal role in the production of an action even though it doesn't trigger the whole causal process. If it makes a difference whether or not a causal chain contains conscious mental states as elements, and in particular if there are differences in the kinds of actions that can be the outcome of such chains or in the conditions in which such actions can be successfully performed, then it is fair to say that conscious mental states make a difference and are causally efficacious. One may also note that the unconscious processes that precede conscious awareness are not themselves uncaused and that, by parity of reasoning, Libet should also deny that they initiate the action.

Second, as Mele (2003) points out, it is unclear whether the readiness potential constitutes the neural substrate of intentions or decisions rather than of desires or urges. If the latter, no one should be surprised to find that desires precede conscious intentions, and finding that we have such desires does not commit us to acting upon them. For all Libet has shown, it may be that another conscious act is necessary before the event associated with the readiness potential leads to action. Third, Libet's analysis focuses on proximal intentions (the proximal causes of overt behavior, whose content in this case may be expressed as "I flex my wrist thus and thus now"), but it neglects distal intentions (whose content may be expressed as "I will flex my wrist when I feel the urge"). Yet, it is quite implausible that the participants in his studies would have produced hand movements at will unless they had formed the distal intention to do so in compliance with the experimenter's instructions. This suggests that distal intentions are not causally inert.

Wegner's claim that the conscious will is an illusion would seem, if empirically warranted, even more damaging to our traditional concept of will and conscious agency than Libet's findings. One line of argument Wegner advances in favor of this claim appeals to dissociations, i.e., cases in which agency and the experience of agency come apart. For instance, in his I-spy experiment (Wegner and Wheatley 1999), a participant and a confederate of the experimenter had joint control of a computer mouse that could be moved over any one of a number of pictures on a screen. When participants had been primed with the name of an item on which the mouse landed, they showed an increased tendency to self-attribute the action of stopping on that object (when in fact the stop had been forced by the confederate). In other words, they experienced conscious will for an action they had not actually controlled. Wegner also argues that many apparently occult phenomena, such as table turning and the ouija board, are instances of the reverse dissociation: the agents in question are doing things that they are not aware they are doing. Wegner seems to think that since the mechanisms responsible for the phenomenology of agency are fallible, we have no reason to think that our experience of agency can ever be trusted. This inference appears less than compelling. To show that the experience of willing is not always errorless is certainly not to show that it is always in error. Indeed, it may well be highly reliable most of the time.

Two further lines of argument for the illusory character of conscious will come from Wegner's account of how the experience of conscious will is generated, what he calls the theory of apparent mental causation. According to this theory, conscious will is experienced when we infer, correctly or not, that our thought has caused our action. We draw such an inference when we have thoughts that occur just before the actions, when these thoughts are consistent with the actions, and when other potential causes of the actions are not present. In actual fact, however, our actions spring from subpersonal causal processes and the conscious ideas that we mistakenly experience as their causes are themselves caused by subpersonal processes which may have only indirect links to the subpersonal processes causing the action.

Wegner's thought here seems to be that the real causal work is done by subpersonal processes and that subpersonal explanations pre-empt personal-level explanations. However, as Bayne (2006) points out, an alternative to this eliminativist position is to see these explanations as complementary. One might regard subpersonal explanations as explaining how intentional agency is realized rather than explaining it away. Wegner also seems to think that the conscious will is an illusion insofar as our experience is inferentially mediated rather than being a direct report of the processes whereby action is produced. If "direct report" is taken to mean that no subpersonal processes or inferential mechanisms of any kind are involved in generating the experience of agency, it is far from clear that a direct report view is a plausible view of the experience of agency or of any other kind of conscious experience. More importantly, Wegner offers no good reason for thinking that the experience of agency could be reliable only if it were a direct readout of action–production processes.

As Jeannerod and others have demonstrated, our conscious access to the representations and processes involved in action specification and control gets more and more limited as we go down the hierarchy of action organization, with the processes and representations at the lowest level being typically unavailable to consciousness. Thus, Wegner may well be right that the experience of conscious will is typically not a direct phenomenal readout of action–production processes and must be theoretically mediated. Yet, there are reasons to doubt that, as Wegner's model suggests, the experience of conscious will arises solely or primarily when there is a match between a prior thought and an observed action. First, prior thoughts or awareness thereof do not seem to be necessary for the sense of agency. On many occasions, we cannot remember what our prior intentions were and yet do not disown our actions. Furthermore, many of our actions, impulsive, routine or automatic, are not preceded by conscious previews and yet we own them. Second, awareness of a match between a prior thought and an action does not seem sufficient for a sense of agency. For instance, schizophrenic patients suffering from delusions of control may lack a sense of agency for a given action despite being aware that what they are doing matches their prior intention (Frith *et al.* 2000).

Recent empirical work suggests that other types of matches than just the match between a prior intention and an observed action play a role. One such match is between a voluntary movement and its consequences. Haggard and colleagues (Haggard and Clark 2003; Moore and Haggard 2008) have shown that when a voluntary act (a button press) causes an effect (a tone), the perceived time of initiating the act is closer to the perceived time of the effect. Specifically, the action (the button press) is shifted forward in time toward the effect it produces, while the effect is shifted backward in time toward the action that produces it. Haggard calls this phenomenon intentional binding.

Several lines of evidence suggest that intentional binding probably derives from predictive mechanisms of action control and is based on the comparison between the predicted sensory consequences of a voluntary movement and its actual sensory consequences. First, intentional binding depends critically on the presence of voluntary movement and requires an efferent signal. When similar movements and auditory effects occur involuntarily or when transcranial magnetic stimulation (TMS) is used to insert occasional involuntary movements of the right finger at a time when the subject intends to press the button but has not yet done so, the binding effect is reversed and cause and effect are perceived as further apart in time than they actually are. Second, intentional binding requires reliable relations between actions and effects and largely depends on the degree of discrepancy between the predicted and actual sensory feedback (Moore and Haggard 2008).

Haggard suggests that the same neural mechanism that produces intentional binding of actions also produces the sense of agency we experience for our actions and that, therefore, intentional binding may be an implicit measure of the sense of agency. Indeed, studies by Sato and Yasuda (2005) show that the same factors that modulate intentional binding also modulate the sense of self-agency subjects experience for the action.

Like Wegner, Haggard proposes a matching model of the experience of agency. His findings suggest, however, that the processes through which the sense of agency is generated are much more closely linked to the processes involved in the specification and control of action than Wegner thinks. He takes the experience of agency to depend primarily on the degree of match between the sensory consequences of an action as predicted by the motor system and its actual sensory consequences rather than on a match between a prior conscious thought and an action. Yet, neither a top-down inferential approach *à la* Wegner nor a purely bottom-up approach involving only subpersonal processes is entirely satisfactory if taken in isolation. Rather than choosing between them, several authors in the field now argue for theoretical integration and a multiple-aspects approach to the problem (Bayne and Pacherie 2007; Gallagher 2007; Pacherie 2008; Synofzik, Vosgerau, and Newen 2008).

5.5 Knowledge of actions and intentions

It is commonly held that whereas our knowledge of the intentions and actions of others involves inferring their mental states from their observed behavior, we have direct knowledge of our own actions and intentions without having to rely on observation and inference. This supposed asymmetry gives rise to a skeptical worry concerning the very possibility of knowledge of others' intentions and actions. If the process through which we make mental attributions to others is one of theoretical inference, where we observe their behavior and infer the mental state thought to be its causal antecedent, then it seems in principle possible that the theory upon which the inferences are based is incorrect and therefore that any given attribution of a mental state to others could be false.

This way of conceiving of the problem of other minds is a consequence of a Cartesian picture of the mind and its relation to bodily behavior. According to this picture, what confer intentional properties to behavior are its inner mental accompaniments and causes. In other words, nothing intrinsic distinguishes a mere bodily happening from a piece of intentional behavior; the difference is one of causal antecedents. Since internal mental causes can't be directly observed, they must be inferred, thus leaving open the possibility that the inference be incorrect. In this respect, versions of the causal theory of actions that take actions to be bodily movements with a distinctive mental cause are still very much in the grip of the Cartesian picture.

Alternatively, it can be argued that behavior and mentality are much more integrated than the Cartesian picture suggests and that the actions and intentions of others can be, at least to some extent, available to experience in their own right, rather than having to be inferred on the basis of behavioral proxies. This alternative view rests on three complementary claims: (1) that intentional bodily behavior has distinctive intrinsic characteristics, (2) that we are perceptually sensitive to these characteristics, and (3) that the internal representations we form when observing intentional behavior are similar to those we form when performing intentional behavior.

A large body of empirical evidence now exists in favor of these three claims. Intentional behavior has been shown to have distinctive observable properties, a distinctive kinematics, and a dynamics that bears systematic relations to features of the situation in a way that non-intentional behavior does not. There is also ample empirical evidence that we are perceptually attuned to these unique characteristics of intentional behavior. Perceptual sensitivity to human motion is already present in infants aged between 3 and 5 months (Bertenthal, Proffit, and Cutting 1984) and seems therefore to be innate or to develop very early. Habituation studies also indicate that infants are sensitive to the goal-directed structure of certain actions by the time they are 5–6 months of age (Woodward 2005). There is also extensive evidence that adult subjects can quickly and reliably recognize movement patterns of walking, cycling, climbing, dancing, etc., from kinematic information alone (Johansson 1973).

Recent neurological studies have yielded a set of important results on mirroring processes. In a series of single-neuron recording experiments on macaque monkeys designed to investigate the functional properties of neurons in area F5, Rizzolatti and his colleagues discovered so-called mirror neurons, i.e., sensorimotor neurons that fire both during the execution of purposeful, goal-related actions by the monkey and when the monkey observes similar actions performed by another agent (Fogassi and Gallese 2002; Rizzolatti and Craighero 2004). In addition, a large body of neuroimaging experiments have investigated the neural networks engaged during action generation and during action observation in humans, revealing the existence of an important overlap in the cerebral areas activated in these two conditions (for reviews, see Grèzes and Decety 2001; Jeannerod 2006). These results have been interpreted as support for the existence of a process of motor simulation or motor resonance whereby the observation of an action activates in the observer an internal representation of the action that matches the representation of the action activated in the brain of the performer. By linking self and other through a unique framework of shared representations of action, mirror systems would allow one to directly understand the actions of others. The nature and extent of the understanding of others that mirroring processes can provide has given rise to an intense debate, with some theorists seeing them as the fundamental neural basis of human social cognition (e.g., Gallese 2007), while others hold more deflationary views (e.g., Jacob 2008).

5.6   Conclusion

In the last decades, philosophers have developed sophisticated conceptual frameworks for thinking about the psychological structures of action. During the same period, empirical investigations have led to a better understanding of motor cognition. Integrating these complementary insights yields the prospects of a more comprehensive picture of action from deliberation and planning down to motor execution. This integrative approach still needs to proceed further. Philosophers haven't yet fully assessed the implications of empirical findings on action preparation and control processes for their views of the nature of intentional action. Conversely, neuroscientists have only recently started investigating how and where the brain stores distal intentions (Haynes *et al.* 2007). Recent controversies on free will and conscious agency also suggest that progress on these issues may depend on further collaborative efforts by philosophers and scientists. Finally, it remains to be seen how much of social cognition has its neural bases in mirroring processes. Here, one promising new area of investigation is joint action and the cognitive and neural processes that support it (Sebanz, Bekkering, and Knoblich 2006).

Further reading

Jeannerod, M. (2006). *Motor Cognition*. Oxford University Press. A stimulating and up-to-date synthesis of work on motor cognition encompassing neuropsychology, neurophysiology, philosophy, neuroimaging, comparative neurobiology, and clinical studies by a foremost researcher in this new interdisciplinary field.

Mele, A. R. (ed.) (1997). *The Philosophy of Action*. Oxford University Press. A selection of some of the most influential essays on the major contemporary issues in the philosophy of action. The introductory essay by A. Mele provides a clear guide to the current debates.

Moya, C. J. (1990). *The Philosophy of Action: An Introduction*. Cambridge: Polity Press. A clear and concise introduction to the philosophy of action, accessible to readers without special philosophical training.

Pockett, S., Banks, W. P., and Gallagher, S. (eds.) (2006). *Does Consciousness Cause Behavior? An Investigation of the Nature of Volition*. Cambridge, MA: MIT Press. This multidisciplinary collection continues the debate over whether consciousness causes behavior or plays no functional role in it, approaching the question from both empirical and theoretical perspectives. Contributors also examine the effect recent psychological and neuroscientific research could have on legal, social, and moral judgments of responsibility and blame.

Rizzolatti, G. and Sinigaglia, C. (2007). *Mirrors in the Brain: How Our Minds Share Actions, Emotions, and Experience*. Oxford University Press. Jointly written by one of the discoverers of mirror neurons and a philosopher, this very readable book provides a systematic overview of mirror neurons and investigates the role of mirroring processes in action understanding, imitation, language, and the sharing of emotions.

Roessler, J. and Eilan, N. (eds.) (2003). *Agency and Self-Awareness*. Oxford University Press. A collection of essays by philosophers, psychologists, neuropsychologists, and neuroscientists on consciousness of action, its role in the control of intentional action, and its contribution to self-awareness.

Sebanz, N. and W. Prinz (eds.) (2006). *Disorders of Volition*. Cambridge, MA: MIT Press. In this collection of essays, philosophers, psychologists, neuroscientists, and psychiatrists seek to advance our understanding of the processes supporting voluntary action by addressing the will and its pathologies from both theoretical and empirical perspectives.

References

Anscombe, G. E. M. (1963). *Intention* (2nd edn.). Ithaca, NY: Cornell University Press.

Bach, K. (1978). A representational theory of action, *Philosophical Studies* 34: 361–79.

Bayne, T. (2006). Phenomenology and the feeling of doing: Wegner on the conscious will, in S. Pockett, W. P. Banks, and S. Gallagher (eds.), *Does*

Consciousness Cause Behavior? An Investigation of the Nature of Volition (pp. 169–85). Cambridge, MA: MIT Press.

Bayne, T. and Pacherie, E. (2007). Narrators and comparators: The architecture of agentive self-awareness, *Synthese* 159: 475–91.

Bertenthal, B. I., Proffitt, D. R., and Cutting, J. E. (1984). Infant sensitivity to figural coherence in biomechanical motions, *Journal of Experimental Child Psychology* 37: 213–30.

Blakemore, S.-J., Wolpert, D. M., and Frith, C. D. (1999). Spatiotemporal prediction modulates the perception of self-produced stimuli, *Journal of Cognitive Neuroscience* 11: 551–9.

Brand, M. (1984). *Intending and Acting*. Cambridge, MA: MIT Press.

Bratman, M. E. (1987). *Intentions, Plans, and Practical Reason*. Cambridge, MA: Harvard University Press.

Davidson, D. (1980). *Essays on Actions and Events*. Oxford: Clarendon Press.

Fogassi, L. and Gallese, V. (2002). The neural correlates of action understanding in non-human primates, in M. I. Stamenov and V. Gallese (eds.), *Mirror Neurons and the Evolution of Brain and Language* (pp. 13–35). Amsterdam: John Benjamins.

Frith, C. D., Blakemore, S.-J., and Wolpert, D. M. (2000). Abnormalities in the awareness and control of action, *Philosophical Transactions of the Royal Society of London B* 355: 1771–88.

Gallagher, S. (2007). The natural philosophy of agency, *Philosophy Compass* 2: 347–57.

Gallese, V. (2007). Before and below "theory of mind": Embodied simulation and the neural correlates of social cognition, *Philosophical Transactions of the Royal Society of London B* 362: 659–69.

Goldman, A. (1970). *A Theory of Human Action*. Englewood Cliffs, NJ: Prentice-Hall.

Grèzes, J. and Decety, J. (2001). Functional anatomy of execution, mental simulation, observation and verb generation of actions: a meta-analysis, *Human Brain Mapping* 12: 1–19.

Haggard, P. and Clark, S. (2003). Intentional action: Conscious experience and neural prediction, *Consciousness and Cognition* 12: 695–707.

Haggard, P., Clark, S., and Kalogeras, J. (2002). Voluntary action and conscious awareness, *Nature Neuroscience* 5: 382–5.

Haynes, J.-D., Sakai, K., Rees, G., Gilbert, S., Frith, C., and Passingham, R. E. (2007). Reading hidden intentions in the human brain, *Current Biology* 17, 323–8.

Heilman, K. M. and Rothi L. J. G. (1993). Apraxia, in K. M. Heilman and E. Valenstein (eds.), *Clinical Neuropsychology* (pp. 141–163, 3rd edn.). Oxford University Press.

Hornsby, J. (1980). *Actions*. London: Routledge and Kegan Paul.

Israel, D., Perry, J., and Tutiya, S. (1993). Executions, motivations and accomplishments, *Philosophical Review* 102: 515–40.

Jacob, P. (2008). What do mirror neurons contribute to human social cognition? *Mind and Language* 23: 190–223.

Jeannerod, M. (1997). *The Cognitive Neuroscience of Action.* Oxford: Blackwell.
(2006). *Motor Cognition.* Oxford University Press.

Johansson, G. (1973). Visual perception of biological motion and a model for its analysis, *Perception and Psychophysics* 14: 201–11.

Lashley, K. S. (1951). The problem of serial order in behavior, in L. A. Jeffress (ed.), *Cerebral Mechanisms in Behavior* (pp. 112–36). New York: Wiley.

Lhermitte, F. (1983). Utilization behavior and its relation to lesions of the frontal lobes, *Brain* 106: 237–55.

Libet, B. (1985). Unconscious cerebral initiative and the role of conscious will in voluntary action, *Behavioral and Brain Sciences* 8: 529–66.

Mele, A. R. (1992). *Springs of Action.* Oxford University Press.
(2002). Action, in L. Nadel (ed.), *Encyclopedia of Cognitive Science* (pp. 20–23). London: MacMillan.
(2003). *Motivation and Agency.* Oxford University Press.

Moore, J. and Haggard, P. (2008). Awareness of action: Inference and prediction, *Consciousness and Cognition* 17: 136–44.

Pacherie, E. (2008). The phenomenology of action: A conceptual framework, *Cognition* 107: 179–217.

Perenin, M. T. and Vighetto, A. (1988). Optic ataxia: A specific disruption in visuomotor mechanisms. I: Different aspects of the deficit in reaching for objects, *Brain* 111: 643–74.

Rizzolatti, G. and Craighero, L. (2004). The mirror-neuron system, *Annual Review of Neuroscience* 27: 169–92.

Rossetti, Y., Vighetto, A., and Pisella, L. (2003). Optic ataxia revisited: Immediate motor control versus visually guided action, *Experimental Brain Research* 153: 171–9.

Sato, A. and Yasuda, A. (2005). Illusion of sense of self-agency: Discrepancy between the predicted and actual sensory consequences of actions modulates the sense of self-agency, but not the sense of ownership, *Cognition* 94: 241–55.

Searle, J. R. 1983. *Intentionality.* Cambridge University Press.

Sebanz, N., Bekkering, H., and Knoblich, G. (2006). Joint action: Bodies and minds moving together, *Trends in Cognitive Science* 10: 70–6.

Sherrington, C. S. (1947). *The Integrative Action of the Nervous System.* New Haven: Yale University Press.

Synofzik, M., Vosgerau, G., and Newen, A. (2008). Beyond the comparator model: A multifactorial two step account of agency, *Consciousness and Cognition* 17: 411–24.

Taylor, C. (1964). *The Explanation of Behaviour.* London: Routledge and Kegan Paul.

Von Holst, E. and Mittelstaedt, H. (1950). Das Reafferenz Prinzip: Wechselwirkungen zwischen Zentralnervensystem und Peripherie, *Naturwissenschaften* 37: 464–76.

Wegner, D. M. (2002). *The Illusion of Conscious Will.* Cambridge, MA: MIT Press.

Wegner, D. M. and Wheatley, T. (1999). Apparent mental causation: Sources of the experience of will, *American Psychology* 54: 480–92.

Woodward, A. L. (2005). Infants' understanding of the actions involved in joint attention, in N. Eilan, C. Hoerl, T. McCormack, and J. Roessler (eds.), *Joint Attention, Communication, and Other Minds* (pp. 85–109). Oxford University Press.

6 Human learning and memory

Charan Ranganath, Laura A. Libby, and Ling Wong

Many of us have experienced the frustration of forgetting where we put the car keys or "blanking" on a person's name or phone number. Such experiences are not only annoying, but they illustrate how much we depend on memory for almost every act of daily living. The goal of this chapter is to provide a brief introduction to the modern science of memory and present some significant issues in the field.

6.1 Different approaches to the study of human memory

The scientific study of memory can be traced back at least to the work of Hermann Ebbinghaus (1885), who studied his own ability to learn lists of nonsense syllables. Ebbinghaus made several important discoveries, but perhaps his greatest contribution was the development of techniques to study memory processes experimentally. In his experiments, he examined memory for lists of stimuli, and to this day, list-learning paradigms remain the standard for how most scientists study memory. Another key development in the field came from Frederick Bartlett (1932), who studied memory for meaningful, complex material such as literary passages. Bartlett's findings suggested that remembering is not simply a verbatim replay of a past event. Instead, it is an "imaginative construction" by which we take bits of recovered experience and reconstruct what might have happened, often filling in the blanks with knowledge-based inferences. A third major breakthrough in the study of memory came from Brenda Milner's pioneering research on amnesic patients (Scoville and Milner 1957) such as Henry Molaison (also known as "H.M."). Milner demonstrated that damage to certain areas of the brain could selectively impair the formation of new memories for events, while sparing the ability to develop new knowledge and skills in other cognitive domains (Milner 1972). These findings paved the way for neuroscience research designed to investigate the roles of different brain areas in specific memory processes.

Our research is supported by National Institute of Mental Health Grants R01MH068721 and R01MH083734 (C.R.). The content is solely the responsibility of the authors and does not necessarily represent the official views of the National Institute of Mental Health or the National Institutes of Health.

The contributions of Ebbinghaus, Bartlett, and Milner represent three general traditions of memory research: one aimed at understanding the characteristics of veridical memory, one aimed at examining constructive and inferential processes that can both facilitate and distort memory, and one aimed at using neurobehavioral data to suggest fundamental differences between different kinds of memory processes or representations. Each approach has revealed important insights into how memory works, and this chapter will draw upon each approach in characterizing the functional organization of human memory.

6.2   Short-term vs. long-term memory

One of the most significant questions in memory research has been whether there is a fundamental difference between the retention of information across short delays (on the order of a few seconds) versus long delays (minutes, days, or longer). For instance, William James (1890) proposed a distinction between "primary memory," consisting of previous experiences that remain active in consciousness, and "secondary memory," consisting of events that have faded from consciousness but can be subsequently recovered. James' introspective definition implied that there should be fundamental limits on the amount of information that can be maintained in primary memory. Consistent with this idea, Miller (1956) reviewed results from a variety of paradigms which converged on the idea that there is a limit of 7 ± 2 items that can be kept in mind at any given time. Critically, this memory capacity could be circumvented by "recoding" information based on prior knowledge. For instance, the letters string "USAFBICIAKGB" could be easily maintained as four "chunks" (USA, FBI, CIA, KGB) rather than twelve letters. More recent proposals suggest that working memory capacity limits may be approximately three to four chunks (Cowan 1997). The finding that pre-existing knowledge can be used to circumvent capacity limits demonstrates that primary memory is not simply a buffer for incoming sensory information. Instead, primary memory may represent the activated portion of secondary memory, a point we will revisit below.

In the 1950s and 1960s, several researchers developed models which expanded on the primary/secondary memory distinction. In general, these models (which have been collectively referred to as the 'modal model'; Murdock 1974) proposed that information that is active could be held in a capacity-limited short-term store (short-term memory, or STM), and that the act of processing this information in STM would result in the development of a memory trace that could be accessed even after long delays (long-term memory, or LTM). Although not all dual-store models proposed that short- and long-term stores were supported by different brain regions (e.g., Atkinson and Shiffrin

1968), accumulating evidence seemed to support this conclusion. Some of this work focused on serial position effects in verbal learning. Specifically, the likelihood of recalling a word from a previously studied list is increased for words at the beginning (primacy) and end (recency) of the list. Whereas some manipulations disproportionately impact the primacy effect and recall of middle-list items (e.g., presentation rate), others disproportionately affect the recency effect (e.g., lag between end of list and recall test). Intuitively, it would seem sensible to assume that primacy and middle-item memory is an index of LTM, whereas recency is additionally influenced by processes that support STM (e.g., phonological rehearsal). In fact, more recent studies have shown that the magnitude of the primacy effect is actually influenced by rehearsal (Tan and Ward 2000), and that robust recency effects can be observed even when phonological rehearsal is not feasible (see Howard and Kahana 1999 for review). Indeed, the factors influencing primacy and recency effects remain controversial. Some suggest that these effects can largely be accounted for by a single store (Sederberg, Howard, and Kahana 2008), whereas others suggest that a temporary activation buffer (akin to the idea proposed by Hebb 1949) additionally contributes to recency (Davelaar *et al.* 2005).

Studies of patients with amnesia have also been cited as evidence for the idea that STM and LTM rely on different brain structures. Amnesic patients often have damage to the medial temporal lobe (MTL) region of the brain (although damage to other brain areas can also cause amnesia). Despite their severe impairments in the ability to retain new memories for events, amnesics can still exhibit intact attention and concentration, carry on a conversation, and hold in mind instructions to perform many complex tasks (e.g., Milner, Corkin, and Teuber 1968). These findings were interpreted as evidence that amnesic patients have a deficit in the long-term store, but an intact short-term store. Consistent with this idea, studies suggest that amnesic patients with severe LTM deficits can have intact immediate memory for simple visual stimuli or shapes (Cave and Squire 1992), and even the gist of lengthy, complex stories (Baddeley and Wilson 2002). Such observations suggest that amnesic patients can successfully retain information about simple or overlearned materials (e.g., words, digits, etc.) across short delays.

More recent studies which have examined memory for novel, complex stimuli or relationships between stimuli have found that STM for these materials is impaired in amnesia. For instance, amnesic patients with MTL damage demonstrated significant impairments at retention of novel faces (Nichols *et al.* 2006), allocentric spatial information (Hartley *et al.* 2007), object–location associations (Hannula, Tranel, and Cohen 2006; Olson *et al.* 2006), and arbitrary face–scene associations (Hannula *et al.* 2006) across even short delays of a few seconds. Consistent with the amnesia evidence, functional magnetic resonance imaging (fMRI) studies of healthy participants have shown activation in the MTL during short-term maintenance of novel scenes (Stern *et al.* 2001) and faces (Ranganath and D'Esposito 2001). These findings have led to a growing consensus that the brain structures that are impaired in amnesia may support memory at both short and long delays.

Just as amnesic patients have been argued to have a selective deficit in LTM, other patients have been reported to have a selective STM disorder (Warrington and Shallice 1969). These patients have severe impairments in phonological STM capacity, and yet exhibit intact LTM for meaningful words (Shallice and Warrington 1970; Warrington, Logue, and Pratt 1971), which led to the initial conclusion that STM can be impaired without affecting LTM. This conclusion is problematic, however, because the types of tasks/measures used to assess STM and LTM differ in a number of ways. In the digit span task typically used to assess phonological STM, one must immediately recall a short sequence of spoken digits in the correct order. In a typical LTM task, one must learn a list of meaningful words, and recall performance is assessed across multiple learning trials. Thus, one of the many differences between typical STM and LTM measures is that the former tend to use meaningless digits and the latter tend to use meaningful words. This raises the question of whether STM patients truly have an STM deficit or whether they have a more general deficit in encoding information that cannot be processed semantically. Recent studies suggest that the latter explanation is correct, as patients with phonological STM deficits exhibit severely impaired LTM for auditorily presented, meaningless nonwords (e.g., Baddeley, Papagno, and Vallar 1988). Thus, the overall pattern of results suggests that these patients do not have selective STM deficits, but have deficiencies in STM *and* LTM for phonological materials that lack a pre-existing semantic representation.

Although the idea that STM and LTM are fully independent has not withstood close scrutiny, the initial reports of neuropsychological and functional double dissociations between STM and LTM were highly influential. These findings, along with other results, contributed to the eventual rejection of the modal model. What followed was a conceptual schism in memory research, with one tradition focusing on exploring the processes that support STM (see section 6.3 below) and another focusing on exploring the relationship between short-term processing and LTM performance (see section 6.4 below).

6.3 Working memory

With the rejection of the modal model, researchers began to ask new questions, such as how information in memory is used in the service of text and discourse comprehension, reasoning, problem solving, and skill learning. To address these questions, Baddeley and Hitch (1974) proposed a model that conceptualized STM not as a static store but rather as the outcome of several dynamic or "working" processes. Their *working memory* (WM) model moved the field forward in several ways. What is particularly notable about the model is that it proved to be remarkably prescient in light of subsequent evidence from cognitive neuroscience.

One of the innovative aspects of the Baddeley model was that it proposed a fundamental difference between the retention of phonological information, via the "phonological loop," and retention of visual information, via the "visuospatial sketchpad." Consistent with this proposal, neuroimaging studies have consistently reported dissociations between the brain regions that are active during maintenance or manipulation of visual versus verbal information (Smith *et al.* 1998). Second, the model proposed that the mechanisms for short-term retention are essentially similar to mechanisms for perception and action. For instance, the phonological loop was proposed to consist of two components, a phonological store and an articulatory control process, which can support covert (subvocal) rehearsal. Consistent with this idea, fMRI studies have shown that areas involved in phonological processing and articulatory control show increased activity during working memory tasks (Smith *et al.* 1998). More generally, studies have revealed a remarkable degree of overlap between neural systems for perception and action, and regions involved in the maintenance of perceptual information or preparation of a response (Ranganath and D'Esposito 2005; Postle 2006).

A third innovation of the WM model was that it proposed a separation between short-term storage (or "maintenance") and the manipulation of information in the service of task goals. That is, in the original model, two slave systems (the phonological loop and visuospatial sketchpad) were proposed to mediate maintenance, whereas a different component, the central executive, was proposed to mediate the selection, inhibition, and manipulation of information in working memory. Supporting evidence for this idea has come from studies of the prefrontal cortex, an area in the frontal lobes that lies anterior to the motor and premotor cortex and is thought to play a role in the control of both perception and action (see Figure 6.1). Damage to the prefrontal cortex results in poor performance on tasks that require planning, inhibition of prepotent responses, or manipulation of information. However, prefrontal damage minimally affects working memory capacity (as measured by digit span), and animals with prefrontal lesions can show relatively normal abilities to retain information across short delays in the absence of distracting stimuli (D'Esposito and Postle 1999).

Although the original Baddeley and Hitch (1974) model provided important insights into the nature of short-term storage and manipulation processes, many findings, particularly from fMRI studies, have suggested the existence of mechanisms for short-term retention of a range of materials that extend well beyond the phonological and visuospatial domains (Postle 2006). To deal with the temporary retention of other materials, and the problem of integration of information across modalities, Baddeley (2000) added a new component to

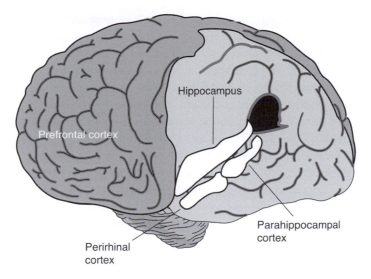

Figure 6.1 Relative locations of the prefrontal cortex and medial temporal lobes. Note that a section of the brain has been cut away to reveal the relative locations of structures in the medial temporal lobes.

the model, termed the "episodic buffer." At present, this component is less specified than other components of the model.

An alternative theoretical approach advocated by some researchers is that information "in" working memory might consist of the activated contents of LTM (e.g., Cowan 1997; Ruchkin *et al.* 2003; Postle 2006; Ranganath 2006; Jonides *et al.* 2008). According to this view, mechanisms for attentional selection play a role in the activation of representations, and consequently the limits of attentional focus constrain STM capacity (Cowan 1997). Consistent with this idea, brain imaging studies suggest that activity in the posterior parietal cortex – a critical region for goal-directed attentional selection – is correlated with STM capacity limits (Todd and Marois 2004). In many respects, this view is compatible with many of the important ideas originally proposed by Baddeley, but is also more general because it proposes that working memory reflects the temporary activation of conceptual, perceptual, and action representations in the service of task goals. Put another way, there may not be a dedicated neural system for working memory. Instead working memory processes may "arise through the coordinated recruitment, via attention, of brain systems that have evolved to accomplish sensory-, representation-, and action-related functions" (Postle 2006).

6.4 Memory encoding and retrieval processes

Following the demise of the modal model, several researchers began to investigate the effects of processes that are engaged during encoding and retrieval.

This shift was initiated in part by the levels of processing framework (Craik and Lockhart 1972), which proposed that memory is a byproduct of a series of processes that support perception and comprehension of a stimulus. According to this framework, the memorability of a stimulus should depend on the degree to which it was analyzed at different levels during initial learning (i.e., the processes engaged during encoding). For instance, Craik and Tulving (1975) compared the effects of encoding words from a list (e.g., "shark") at either the orthographic ("Does it contain an 's'?"), phonological ("Does it rhyme with 'park'?"), or semantic ("Is it a type of fish?") levels. According to the levels of processing framework, these *encoding* operations could be considered as varying along a continuum of elaboration or "depth of processing." Consistent with this idea, memory performance was worst for words encoded in the orthographic condition, in-between for the phonological condition, and best for the semantic condition.

The levels of processing framework had a lasting influence on the field by demonstrating the importance of the way in which information is processed during encoding. Unfortunately, the framework was often criticized because it was difficult to lay out clear principles for what qualifies as deep vs. shallow processing. One way around this problem has been to assume that elaboration benefits memory because it results in a more distinctive memory trace or that it allows new information to be integrated within existing organized knowledge structures (e.g., Hunt and Einstein 1981). A more serious challenge for the levels of processing framework came from studies demonstrating that encoding factors alone do not determine subsequent memory performance, and that the more critical relationship may be between encoding processes and cues available during the time of retrieval. For instance, Tulving and Thomson (1973) proposed the encoding specificity principle, suggesting that the outcome of a memory retrieval operation relies not on the depth of encoding, but on the interaction between a retrieval cue and the memory trace that was formed during encoding. As evidence for this idea, they demonstrated that if two weakly related items were studied together, one of these items would serve as an effective cue for retrieving the other – even compared to a retrieval cue that is highly related to, but was not studied with, the study item. In a similar vein, Morris, Bransford, and Franks (1977) proposed that successful memory depends on whether the method of encoding suits the conditions under which the information will later be retrieved, a theory known as "transfer appropriate processing." In a clever study, they investigated the effects of phonological vs. semantic processing of words on subsequent memory performance on a standard item recognition test (as done by Craik and Tulving 1975) and also on a "rhyme recognition" test. On the rhyme test, people had to decide if a test word rhymed with a particular word that was studied. For instance, if participants studied the word "regal," one question might be "Did you study a word that rhymed with 'eagle'?" Morris and his colleagues replicated the finding that item recognition was superior for semantically encoded words than for phonologically encoded words, but they showed that on the rhyme recognition test memory was superior for phonologically encoded words than for semantically encoded words. Collectively, the findings from these studies indicate that successful memory performance depends not only on how information is encoded, but also on interactions between encoding and retrieval processes.

Other findings have demonstrated that being in a particular context (in terms of location, mental, and emotional state, etc.) can facilitate memory for events that occurred in a similar context.[1] For instance, recall is facilitated if one is in the same room (Smith 1979), in the same emotional state (Bower 1981), or in the same intoxicated state (Goodwin *et al.* 1969) during study and test. These findings suggest that, although many studies examine memory for specific items, people naturally tend to associate the item with a particular contextual state, and that is why reinstantiating the study context facilitates memory for the associated items. On a practical note, the data suggest that, when searching for something that was lost, the common practice of "retracing one's steps" may be quite helpful.

6.5   Forgetting

The previous section reviewed research on encoding or retrieval processes which can contribute to successful remembering. A related and controversial issue is the question of what causes forgetting. Obviously, no one would dispute that total failure of encoding would result in a failure to subsequently remember an item (e.g., if you could not hear what someone was saying you would be unlikely to remember what she or he said). However, forgetting can occur even for information that was adequately processed at encoding. Since the initial research of Ebbinghaus (1885), it has been known that most of the forgetting that takes place occurs within forty-eight hours of the learning episode.

In general, consolidation theory and interference theory are the most popular accounts of forgetting. Consolidation theory (Müller and Pilzecker 1900) proposes that, after encoding, there is a period of time (e.g., the first twenty-four to forty-eight hours) that is required for the memory to become stabilized.

---

[1] It should be noted that context-dependent benefits are primarily evident in recall tasks, in which one must generate the sought-after information. In contrast, reinstating a past context does not help as much in recognition tests. This is thought to be because in a recall test one must reconstruct the past context in order to generate the items (e.g., recalling where you put your keys), whereas in a recognition test, the item is presented (e.g., seeing your keys on the table) so the retrieval context is not as useful. Thus, if one is taking an essay test, it might make sense to try to reinstantiate the context in which the information was learned, but this would be less helpful for a multiple choice test.

Interference theory (McGeoch 1932), in contrast, proposes that forgetting may reflect a failure to *find* a memory ("retrieval failure") due to competition from information learned before ("proactive interference") or after ("retroactive interference") the event. In their strongest versions, consolidation theory and interference theory can be seen as conflicting, as the former might suggest if an item is forgotten, it can never be recovered, whereas the latter might suggest that memories may be "lost" and subsequently found. However, the two theories can be viewed as complementary: Consolidation theory does well at explaining the time course of forgetting and is consistent with a wealth of evidence suggesting that changes in the strength of connections between neurons ("synaptic plasticity") depend on changes in protein synthesis that occur during a critical period after initial learning (Morris *et al.* 2003). However, consolidation theory does not make strong predictions about which memories will eventually survive and which will be lost. Interference theory, in contrast, does not make strong predictions about the time course of forgetting, but it does make predictions about which memories will be more or less vulnerable. Specifically, interference theory predicts that the likelihood of forgetting a piece of information will be influenced by the extent to which other learned information overlaps in content or context (Gardiner, Craik, and Birtwistle 1972). Given the different areas of emphasis of the two theories, some combination of consolidation and interference theory may be needed to account for forgetting in real-life situations (Bower 2000).

6.6 Distinctions between putative memory systems or processes

Since the seminal findings of Milner and her students, neuroscience has played an increasingly important role in helping researchers understand how memory processes might be organized. The most extensively researched distinction to emerge from this work is the distinction between *declarative* and *procedural* memory. The first evidence for this distinction came from studies showing that H.M. and other amnesic patients could acquire new visuomotor skills despite their severe amnesia for recent events (including the events during which the skills were acquired). For instance, patient H.M. showed steady improvement in his ability to trace figures with visual feedback from a mirror (Milner *et al.* 1968). Another study by Warrington and Weiskrantz (1968) demonstrated that previous exposure to a picture or word improved the subsequent ability to perceptually recognize that stimulus. This effect, now known as *repetition priming*, was observed in amnesic patients, demonstrating another domain where a capacity for new learning is spared in amnesia.

Building on this work, Cohen and Squire (1980) demonstrated that amnesic patients could learn to read mirror-reversed word triplets with training, indicating intact acquisition of a cognitive skill. However, they also found that controls were faster at reading repeated triplets relative to novel triplets, and this facilitation was reduced for amnesic participants. To explain these results, along with previous studies of skill learning in amnesia, Cohen and Squire proposed that, "Whether a task can or cannot be learned in amnesia seems to depend on the nature of the information...demanded by the task." They argued that amnesia might be conceptualized as a deficit in *declarative memory* (which facilitates the report of specific material), whereas *procedural memory* (which supports the performance of operations and procedures) might be spared. H.M., for example, was unable to remember having previously performed the mirror-reversal word task – a task that he practiced daily for a period of weeks – but his accuracy on that task improved significantly across training sessions. Put another way, the distinction between declarative and procedural memory can be thought of as the difference between "knowing that" and "knowing how."

Squire and Zola-Morgan (1991) subsequently expanded the declarative/procedural distinction, by proposing that declarative memory represented a collection of abilities dependent on the "medial temporal lobe (MTL) memory system," an anatomically connected set of structures that includes the entorhinal, perirhinal and parahippocampal cortices, and the hippocampus (see Figure 6.1). According to their model, these structures mediated acquisition of new memories for facts and events in a manner that could support conscious recollection. The MTL memory system was proposed to play a temporary role in the storage of new declarative memories, whereas more remote memories could be accessed without the involvement of this system. They also proposed that *nondeclarative memory*, a collection of abilities including skill/habit learning ("procedural memory"), priming, and classical conditioning, does not depend on the MTL memory system. Squire and Zola-Morgan's proposal paralleled the distinction between *explicit and implicit memory* put forth by Graf and Schacter (1985). That is, in humans, measures of declarative memory are typically thought to require explicit (conscious) access to a memory for a past event, whereas nondeclarative memory has been associated with learning that can be expressed implicitly (in a nonconscious manner). Support for these distinctions has come from studies demonstrating that patients with amnesia can show normal levels of performance on trial-and-error-based learning tasks that do not require explicit memory (Squire and Knowlton 2000). However, as described below, there is some evidence suggesting that the MTL may be necessary for some kinds of implicit learning effects (Chun and Phelps 2000; Ryan *et al.* 2000), and that new semantic information may be acquired and accessed explicitly, even with severe MTL damage (Vargha-Khadem *et al.* 1997; Bayley *et al.* 2008).

In contrast to the definition of declarative memory, which treats memories for events and facts in a similar manner, Tulving (1985) argued that memory for past events, or *episodic memory*, can be distinguished from memory for facts, or *semantic memory*. Tulving proposed that episodic memory retrieval involves conscious re-experiencing of an event (i.e., "remembering"), whereas semantic memory retrieval involves awareness of information independent of personal experience (i.e., "knowing"). For instance, one might be able to retrieve an autobiographical memory for a personal experience as an episodic memory ("I remember how I felt on my eighteenth birthday") or as a semantic memory ("I know that I celebrated my eighteenth birthday in San Jose"). Tulving's proposal was not extensively specified at the neuroanatomical level, but several researchers have since argued that episodic memory formation and retrieval depend on the hippocampus (Nadel and Moscovitch 1997; Aggleton and Brown 1999), whereas the perirhinal cortex, a neocortical region that projects to the hippocampus (and is part of the putative MTL memory system), may be necessary and sufficient to support the acquisition of new semantic knowledge. The strongest support for this proposal came from studies of people who had experienced relatively specific damage to the hippocampus early in life (Vargha-Khadem *et al.* 1997). These individuals, like many amnesic patients, had difficulties orienting to time, remembering recent events, and remembering spatial information. Despite their severe episodic memory deficits, these patients were able to acquire a great deal of semantic knowledge, and even graduate high school. It has been argued that these patients were able to acquire semantic knowledge because the perirhinal cortex was relatively intact, whereas this region was lesioned in severely amnesic patients such as H.M. (Corkin *et al.* 1997).

Another idea that bears some similarity to the episodic/semantic distinction is that between *recollection* and *familiarity* (Yonelinas 2002). This delineation originally arose from models that were proposed to account for experimental dissociations between performance on tests of item recognition and free recall or associative recognition tests (e.g., Atkinson and Juola 1974; Mandler 1980). Many of these "dual-process" models argue that recognition memory is based on both assessment of the familiarity strength of a given item and recollection of information associated with that item. The recollection/familiarity distinction is similar to the episodic/semantic distinction described above, in that recollection can be seen as an expression of episodic memory, whereas familiarity could be viewed as a measure of the fluency or strength of semantic memory representations (Yonelinas 2002). Dual-process theories can additionally be used to quantitatively model the contributions of these processes to recognition performance. For instance, according to one model (Yonelinas 2002), familiarity may be a signal-detection process, whereas recollection may be a threshold process. According to this view, some degree of familiarity will be elicited by *every* item (old or new), whereas recollection will only occur for some items.

The theoretical distinction between recollection and familiarity has led to significant insights into the functional organization of the MTL. For instance, a number of studies (e.g., Yonelinas *et al.* 2002; Tsivilis *et al.* 2008) have demonstrated that patients with relatively selective hippocampal damage or dysfunction can show striking recollection impairments and relative sparing of familiarity-based recognition. Converging evidence has come from a study of recognition memory in rats with hippocampal lesions (Fortin, Wright, and Eichenbaum 2004). By using techniques to manipulate the extent to which the rats would adopt a liberal or conservative response criterion and analyzing the data using the same mathematical model used to estimate recollection and familiarity in humans, these researchers found that hippocampal lesions significantly reduced the recollection component of recognition while sparing familiarity. Consistent with the lesion data, fMRI results have also shown that hippocampal activation is increased during processing of items that are recollected compared to items that are recognized on the basis of familiarity or those that were incorrectly endorsed as new (Diana, Yonelinas, and Ranganath 2007). In contrast, activation in the perirhinal cortex (a different MTL region) is correlated with familiarity and typically does not change further for recollected items.

It is notable that many of the distinctions described above (implicit/explicit, episodic/semantic, recollection/familiarity) are based at least in part on sub-jective experience. An alternative approach has been to distinguish between the types of *information* that support memory performance. For instance, building on the procedural/declarative distinction proposed by Cohen and Squire (1980), Cohen and Eichenbaum (1993) proposed the *relational mem-ory* theory. According to this account, the MTL, particularly the hippocam-pus, mediates memory for relationships between items. This account suggests that patients with hippocampal damage can learn specific pieces of informa-tion and access this information in a rigid manner. However, these patients should be unable to use previously learned information in novel contexts or remember arbitrary associations between items that co-occurred in a particular context.

Given the plethora of distinctions that has been proposed so far, one might conclude that we are quite far from characterizing the neural and functional organization of memory processes. However, there is general agreement on the idea that MTL damage only affects certain forms of learning and memory, while sparing basic reinforcement-learning mechanisms, repetition priming, and classical conditioning. There is also a great deal of overlap among pro-posed models to explain the neural basis of explicit/declarative memory and the functional organization of the MTL. For instance, many models stress the idea that there is functional heterogeneity in the MTL, such that the perirhi-nal cortex supports familiarity-based memory for specific items whereas the hippocampus supports recollection of relationships amongst items and the context in which they were previously encountered (Eichenbaum, Yonelinas, and Ranganath 2007).

6.7   Inferential and attributional processes in memory

In his classic monograph, *Remembering: A Study in Experimental and Social Psychology*, Frederic Bartlett (1932) concluded that, "remembering appears to be far more decisively an affair of construction rather than one of mere reproduction." Bartlett argued that it is over-simplistic to assume that remembering solely reflects recovery of a memory "trace" that constitutes the entire event and carries with it an explicit temporal tag. Instead, he proposed that over the course of experience, we come to acquire organized knowledge structures called schemas, and that schemas are often used to make reconstructive inferences during memory retrieval. For example, imagine if you read the following sentence: "Debbie and Rachel were having a conversation, but they were interrupted when the waiter asked to take their order." Later on, you might remember that Debbie and Rachel were having a conversation at a restaurant. Although the sentence did not actually state that they were at a restaurant, this would be a reasonable inference given that their conversation was interrupted by a waiter. Consistent with Bartlett's proposal, numerous studies have empirically demonstrated that activating schemas can increase the incidence of reconstructive inferences (e.g., Bransford and Johnson 1972).

In addition to knowledge-based inferences, attributional processes also play a key role in the reconstruction of a memory. For instance, in a classic study by Loftus and Palmer (1974), participants watched a video of a car accident. One group of subjects was later asked, "About how fast were the cars going when they *smashed* into each other?" In a subsequent memory test, about one third of these subjects erroneously stated that there was broken glass in the video, suggesting that participants might have misattributed associations with the word "smashed" to memory for the accident. Another now classic example of misattribution is the "Deese/Roediger/McDermott" or "DRM" paradigm (Deese 1959; Roediger and McDermott 1995), in which participants learn lists of words, all of which are highly associated with a critical word that is not in the list. For example, a list might consist of words like "bed," "rest," and "awake," all of which are related to a critical word "sleep," which was not on this list. In this paradigm, participants spontaneously recall the critical word as often as they recall words that were actually on the list. The DRM effect is remarkably robust, and participants are quite confident in remembering the critical words, even though they were not on the list. This effect can be considered a type of attribution error, because recall of a critical word indicates that the participant successfully remembered the *gist* of the list items, but misattributed this as evidence that the item was on the list. Consistent with this idea, patients with amnesia (who obviously have difficulty learning new information) often do not show false recall or false recognition of critical items (Schacter *et al.* 1998).

To explain attributional processes in memory, Marcia Johnson and her colleagues proposed the *source monitoring framework*, which frames the process of remembering in terms of attributing conscious experience to particular sources. According to source monitoring framework (Johnson, Hashtroudi, and Lindsay 1993, p. 3), "people do not typically directly retrieve an abstract tag or label that specifies a memory's source, rather, activated memory records are evaluated and attributed to particular sources through decision processes performed during remembering." A critical proposal of the framework is that, on average, the conscious experience of recalling memories from different sources will have different characteristics. For instance, your memory for a news story would likely include more visual detail if you saw the story on TV than it would if you had heard it on the radio. Consistent with this proposal, fMRI studies have shown that activity during recollection is sensitive to the type of informational content that is recovered. For instance, recollection of auditory information is associated with activation of the auditory cortex, whereas recollection of visual information is associated with activation of high-level visual cortical areas (e.g., Nyberg *et al.* 2000; Wheeler and Buckner 2004). Other work has demonstrated even more specificity, such that recall of a previously learned face is associated with increased activation in areas of the brain that are preferentially involved in face perception, whereas recall of houses is associated with activation in areas of the brain that are preferentially involved in processing of landmark information (Ranganath *et al.* 2004).

6.8 Concluding remarks

This chapter has provided a synopsis of several key questions in the field of memory research. Although the field is far from knowing all the answers, we are reaching a point when we can ask more ambitious and interesting questions. Indeed, much as vision science has benefited from the interchange of ideas between visual neuroscientists and psychophysicists, the science of memory is seeing more and more theoretical advances resulting from the exchange of ideas between psychologists and neuroscientists (e.g., Eichenbaum *et al.* 2007; Jonides *et al.* 2008). This trend is likely to continue in the coming years as researchers develop models that can even better explain both the mind and brain of human memory.

Further reading

Byrne, J. H. (2009). *Concise Learning and Memory: The Editor's Selection*. San Diego: Academic Press. An edited volume that consists of thorough reviews of many important topics in learning and memory ranging from cognitive psychology down to cellular neuroscience.

Neath, I. and Surprenant, A. M. (2003). *Human Memory*. Belmont, CA: Thomson Wadsworth. A thorough textbook on the cognitive psychology of memory.

Rosler, F., Ranganath, C., Roder, B., and Roiner, K. (eds.) (2009). *Neuroimaging of Human Memory: Linking Cognitive Processes to Neural Systems*. New York: Oxford University Press. An edited volume consisting of tutorial reviews on functional imaging of human memory in several domains and more generally about the relationship between neural and cognitive theories of human memory processes.

Tulving, E. and Craik, F. I. (eds.) (2000). *Oxford Handbook of Memory*. New York: Oxford University Press. Although slightly outdated, this book (edited by two of the most important researchers in the field) provides an extensive overview of the cognitive psychology of memory.

References

Aggleton, J. P. and Brown, M. W. (1999). Episodic memory, amnesia, and the hippocampal-anterior thalamic axis, *Behavioral and Brain Sciences* 22: 425–44.

Atkinson, R. C. and Juola, J. F. (1974). Search and decision processes in recognition memory, in D. H. Krantz, R. C. Atkinson, R. D. Luce, and P. Suppes (eds.), *Contemporary Developments in Mathematical Psychology*, vol. 1: *Learning, Memory, and Thinking* (pp. 101–46). San Francisco: Freeman.

Atkinson, R. and Shiffrin, R. (1968). Human memory: A proposed system and its control processes, in K. Spence and J. Spence (eds.), *The Psychology of Learning and Motivation* (vol. 2, pp. 89–105). New York: Academic Press.

Baddeley, A. (2000). The episodic buffer: A new component of working memory? *Trends in Cognitive Sciences* 4: 417–23.

Baddeley, A. and Hitch, G. J. (1974). Working memory, in G. Bower (ed.), *Recent Advances in Learning and Motivation* (vol. 8, pp. 47–90). New York: Academic Press.

Baddeley, A., Papagno, C., and Vallar, G. (1988). When long-term learning depends on short-term storage, *Journal of Memory and Language* 27: 586–95.

Baddeley, A. and Wilson, B. A. (2002). Prose recall and amnesia: Implications for the structure of working memory, *Neuropsychologia* 40: 1737–43.

Bartlett, F. C. (1932). *Remembering: A Study in Experimental and Social Psychology*. New York: MacMillan.

Bayley, P. J., O'Reilly R. C., Curran, T., and Squire, L. R. (2008). New semantic learning in patients with large medial temporal lobe lesions, *Hippocampus* 18: 575–83.

Bower, G. H. (1981). Mood and memory, *The American Psychologist* 36: 129–48.

(2000). A brief history of memory research, in E. Tulving and F. I. Craik (eds.), *The Oxford Handbook of Memory* (pp. 3–32). New York: Oxford University Press.

Bransford, J. D. and Johnson, M. K. (1972). Contextual prerequisites for under-standing: Some investigations of comprehension and recall, *Journal of Verbal Learning and Verbal Behavior* 11: 717–26.

Cave, C. B. and Squire, L. R. (1992). Intact verbal and nonverbal short-term memory following damage to the human hippocampus, *Hippocampus* 2: 151–63.

Chun, M. M. and Phelps, E. A. (2000). Memory deficits for implicit contextual information in amnesic subjects with hippocampal damage, *Nature Neuroscience* 2: 844–7.

Cohen, N. J. and Eichenbaum, H. (1993). *Memory, Amnesia, and the Hippocampal System*. Cambridge, MA: MIT Press.

Cohen, N. J. and Squire, L. R. (1980). Preserved learning and retention of pattern-analyzing skill in amnesia: Dissociation of knowing how and knowing that, *Science* 210: 207–10.

Corkin, S., Amaral, D. G., González, G., Johnson, K. A., and Heyman, B. T. (1997). H. M.'s medial temporal lobe lesion: findings from magnetic resonance imaging, *The Journal of Neuroscience* 17: 3964–79.

Cowan, N. (1997). *Attention and Memory*. New York: Oxford University Press.

Craik, F. I. and Lockhart, R. (1972). Levels of processing: A framework for memory research, *Journal of Verbal Learning and Verbal Behavior* 11: 671–84.

Craik, F. I. and Tulving, E. (1975). Depth of processing and the retention of words in episodic memory, *Journal of Experimental Psychology: General* 104: 268–94.

D'Esposito, M. and Postle, B. R. (1999). The dependence of span and delayed-response performance on prefrontal cortex, *Neuropsychologia* 37: 1303–15.

Davelaar, E. J., Goshen-Gottstein, Y., Ashkenazi, A., Haarmann, H. J., and Usher, M. (2005). The demise of short-term memory revisited: Empirical and computational investigations of recency effects, *Psychological Review* 112: 3–42.

Deese, J. (1959). On the prediction of occurrence of particular verbal intrusions in immediate recall, *Journal of Experimental Psychology* 58: 17–22.

Diana, R. A., Yonelinas, A. P., and Ranganath, C. (2007). Imaging recollection and familiarity in the medial temporal lobe: A three-component model, *Trends in Cognitive Sciences* 11: 379–86.

Ebbinghaus, H. (1885). Memory: A contribution to experimental psychology. http://psy.ed.asu.edu/~classics/Ebbinghaus/index.htm.

Eichenbaum, H., Yonelinas, A. P., and Ranganath, C. (2007). The medial temporal lobe and recognition memory, *Annual Review of Neuroscience* 30: 123–52.

Fortin, N. J., Wright, S. P., and Eichenbaum, H. (2004). Recollection-like memory retrieval in rats is dependent on the hippocampus, *Nature* 431: 188–91.

Gardiner, J., Craik, F. I., and Birtwistle, J. (1972). Retrieval cues and release from proactive inhibition, *Journal of Verbal Learning and Verbal Behavior* 11: 778–83.

Goodwin, D. W., Powell, B., Bremer, D., Hoine, H., and Stern, J. (1969). Alcohol and recall: State-dependent effects in man, *Science* 163: 1358–60.

Graf, P. and Schacter, D. L. (1985). Implicit and explicit memory for new associations in normal and amnesic subjects, *Journal of Experimental Psychology: Learning, Memory, and Cognition* 11: 501–18.

Hannula, D. E., Tranel, D., and Cohen, N. J. (2006). The long and the short of it: Relational memory impairments in amnesia, even at short lags, *The Journal of Neuroscience* 26: 8352–9.

Hartley, T., Bird, C. M., Chan, D. *et al.* (2007). The hippocampus is required for short-term topographical memory in humans, *Hippocampus* 17: 34–48.

Hebb, D. O. (1949). *Organization of Behavior: A Neuropsychological Theory.* New York: John Wiley and Sons.

Howard, M. W. and Kahana, M. J. (1999). Contextual variability and serial position effects in free recall, *Journal of Experimental Psychology: Learning, Memory, and Cognition* 25: 923–41.

Hunt, R. R. and Einstein, G. O. (1981). Relational and item-specific information in memory, *Journal of Verbal Learning and Behavior* 20: 497–514.

James, W. (1890). *Principles of Psychology.* New York: Holt.

Johnson, M. K., Hashtroudi, S., and Lindsay, D. S. (1993). Source monitoring, *Psychological Bulletin* 114: 3–28.

Jonides, J., Lewis, R. L., Nee, D. E. *et al.* (2008). The mind and brain of short-term memory, *Annual Review of Psychology* 59: 193–224.

Loftus, E. F. and Palmer, J. C. (1974). Reconstruction of automobile destruction: An example of interaction between language and memory, *Journal of Verbal Learning and Verbal Behavior* 13: 585–9.

Mandler, G. (1980). Recognizing: The judgment of previous occurrence, *Psychological Review* 87: 252–71.

McGeoch, J. A. (1932). Forgetting and the law of disuse, *Psychological Review* 39: 352–70.

Miller, G. A. (1956). The magical number seven, plus or minus two: Some limits on our capacity for processing information, *Psychological Review* 63: 81–97.

Milner, B. (1972). Disorders of learning and memory after temporal lobe lesions in man, *Congress of Neurological Surgeons* 19: 421–46.

Milner, B., Corkin, S., and Teuber, H.-L. (1968). Further analysis of the hippocampal anmesic syndrome: 14 year follow-up study of H.M, *Neuropsychologia* 6: 215–34.

Morris, C. D., Bransford, J. D., and Franks, J. J. (1977). Levels of processing versus transfer appropriate processing, *Journal of Verbal Learning and Verbal Behavior* 16: 519–33.

Morris, R. G., Moser, E. I., Reidel, G. *et al.* (2003). Elements of a neurobiological theory of the hippocampus: The role of activity-dependent synaptic plasticity in memory, *Philosophical Transactions: Biological Sciences* 358: 773–86.

Müller, G. E. and Pilzecker, A. (1900). Experimentelle Beiträge zur Lehre vom Gedächtnis, *Zeitschrift für Psychologie, Ergänzungsband* 1: 1–300.

Murdock, B. B. (1974). *Human Memory: Theory and Practice.* Hillsdale, NJ: Lawrence Erlbaum.

Nadel, L. and Moscovitch, M. (1997). Memory consolidation, retrograde amnesia and the hippocampal complex, *Current Opinion in Neurobiology* 7: 217–27.

Nichols, E. A., Kao, Y. C., Verfaellie, M., and Gabrieli, J. D. (2006). Working memory and long-term memory for faces: Evidence from fMRI and global amnesia for involvement of the medial temporal lobes, *Hippocampus* 16: 604–16.

Nyberg, L., Habib, R., McIntosh, A. R., and Tulving, E. (2000). Reactivation of encoding-related brain activity during memory retrieval, *Proceedings of the National Acadademy of Sciences of the United States of America* 97: 11120–4.

Olson, I. R., Page, K., Moore, K. S., Chatterjee, A., and Verfaellie, M. (2006). Working memory for conjunctions relies on the medial temporal lobe, *The Journal of Neuroscience* 26: 4596–4601.

Postle, B. R. (2006). Working memory as an emergent property of the mind and brain, *Neuroscience* 139: 23–38.

Ranganath, C. (2006). Working memory for visual objects: Complementary roles of inferior temporal, medial temporal, and prefrontal cortex, *Neuroscience* 139: 277–89.

Ranganath, C., Cohen, M. X., Dam. C., and D'Esposito, M. (2004). Inferior temporal, prefrontal, and hippocampal contributions to visual working memory maintenance and associative memory retrieval, *The Journal of Neuroscience* 24: 3917–25.

Ranganath, C. and D'Esposito, M. (2001). Medial temporal lobe activity associated with active maintenance of novel information, *Neuron* 31: 865–73.

(2005). Directing the mind's eye: Prefrontal, inferior and medial temporal mechanisms for visual working memory, *Current Opinion in Neurobiology* 15: 175–82.

Roediger, H. L. and McDermott, K. B. (1995). Creating false memories: Remembering words not presented in lists, *Journal of Experimental Psychology: Learning, Memory, and Cognition* 21: 803–14.

Ruchkin, D. S., Grafman, J., Cameron, K., and Berndt, R. S. (2003). Working memory retention systems: A state of activated long-term memory, *The Behavioral and Brain Sciences* 26: 709–28; discussion 728–77.

Ryan, J. D., Althoff, R. R., Whitlow, S., and Cohen, N. J. (2000). Amnesia is a deficit in relational memory, *Psychological Science* 11: 454–61.

Schacter, D. L., Verfaellie, M., Anes, M. D., and Racine, C. (1998). When true recognition suppresses false recognition: Evidence from amnesic patients, *Journal of Cognitive Neuroscience* 10: 668–79.

Scoville, W. B. and Milner, B. (1957). Loss of recent memory after bilateral hippocampal lesions, *Journal of Neurology, Neurosurgery, and Psychiatry* 20: 11–21.

Sederberg, P. B., Howard, M. W., and Kahana M. J. (2008). A context-based theory of recency and contiguity in free recall, *Psychological Review* 115: 893–912.

Shallice, T. and Warrington, E. K. (1970). Independent functioning of verbal memory stores: A neuropsychological study, *The Quarterly Journal of Experimental Psychology. A: Human Experimental Psychology* 22: 261–73.

Smith, E. E., Jonides, J., Marshuetz, C., and Koeppe, R. A. (1998). Components of verbal working memory: Evidence from neuroimaging, *Proceedings of the National Academy of Sciences of the United States of America* 95: 876–82.

Smith, S. M. (1979). Remembering in and out of context, *Journal of Experimental Psychology: Learning, Memory, and Cognition* 5: 460–71.

Squire, L. R. and Knowlton, B. J. (2000). The medial temporal lobe, the hippocampus, and the memory systems of the brain, in M. S. Gazzaniga (ed.), *The New Cognitive Neurosciences* (pp. 765–79). Cambridge, MA: MIT Press.

Squire, L. R. and Zola-Morgan, S. (1991). The medial temporal lobe memory system, *Science* 253: 1380–6.

Stern, C. E., Sherman, S. J., Kirchhoff, B. A., and Hasselmo, M. E. (2001). Medial temporal and prefrontal contributions to working memory tasks with novel and familiar stimuli, *Hippocampus* 11: 337–46.

Tan, L. and G. Ward (2000). A recency-based account of the primacy effect in free recall, *Journal of Experimental Psychology: Learning, Memory, and Cognition* 26: 1589–1625.

Todd, J. J. and Marois, R. (2004). Capacity limit of visual short-term memory in human posterior parietal cortex, *Nature* 428: 751–4.

Tsivilis, D., Vann, S. D., Denby, C. *et al.* (2008). A disproportionate role for the fornix and mammillary bodies in recall versus recognition memory, *Nature Neuroscience* 11: 834–42.

Tulving, E. (1985). Memory and consciousness, *Canadian Psychology* 26: 1–12.

Tulving, E. and Thomson, D. M. (1973). Encoding specificity and retrieval processes in episodic memory, *Psychological Review* 80: 352–73.

Vargha-Khadem, F., Gadian, D. G., Watkins, K. E., Connelly, A., Van Paesschen, W., and Mishkin, M. (1997). Differential effects of early hippocampal pathology on episodic and semantic memory, *Science* 277: 376–80.

Warrington, E. K., Logue, V., and Pratt, R. T. (1971). The anatomical localisation of selective impairment of auditory-verbal short-term memory, *Neuropsychologia* 9: 377–87.

Warrington, E. K. and Shallice, T. (1969). The selective impairment of auditory verbal short term memory, *Brain* 92: 885–96.

Warrington, E. K. and Weiskrantz, L. (1968). New method of testing long-term retention with special reference to amnesic patients, *Nature* 217: 972–4.

Wheeler, M. E. and Buckner, R. L. (2004). Functional-anatomic correlates of remembering and knowing, *Neuroimage* 21: 1337–49.

Yonelinas, A. P. (2002). The nature of recollection and familiarity: A review of 30 years of research, *Journal of Memory and Language* 46: 441–517.

Yonelinas, A. P., Kroll, N. E., Quamme, M. M. *et al.* (2002). Effects of extensive temporal lobe damage or mild hypoxia on recollection and familiarity, *Nature Neuroscience* 5: 1236–41.

7 Reasoning and decision making

Mike Oaksford, Nick Chater, and Neil Stewart

In this chapter, we introduce some recent developments in the areas of human reasoning and decision making. We focus on the how people use given information to make inferences concerning new information (i.e., reasoning) or to decide what to do (i.e., decision making). The fields of reasoning and decision making are both large, and we will be selective. In particular, in our discussion of reasoning, we shall focus on theories of how people reason with conditionals, i.e., theories of the nature of the linkage between given and inferred information. Regarding decision making, we focus on decision-under-risk, using problems which are explicitly described in linguistic or symbolic terms.

7.1 Reasoning

Perhaps the fundamental question in the psychology of reasoning is: do people reason correctly (Wason 1960; Wason and Johnson-Laird 1972)? Answering this question requires relating data on how people *do* reason to a normative theory of how they *should* reason. The normative theory typically adopted in the field is deductive logic. To be rational is, on this view, to be logical.

We focus in this chapter on experimental work on human *deductive* reasoning as opposed to *inductive* reasoning. There are various ways of marking this distinction. Perhaps the most fundamental is that in a deductive argument, if the premises are the true, the conclusion must be true. In an inductive argument, the premises merely make the conclusion plausible or probable. Thus, an argument from observing specific white swans to the conclusion *all swans are white* is inductive – here, because it is entirely possible that later counterexamples (e.g., black swans) exist. That is, the conclusion can be defeated by further information and so the argument is *defeasible*. Second, inductive reasoning relies on content (Goodman 1954). For example, suppose a long-term Königsberg resident notes that all swans observed so far have lived in Königsberg. The observer is unlikely to confidently conclude that *all swans live in Königsberg*. The difference depends on content: color, but not geographical location, are properties likely to be shared by all members of

Nick Chater was supported by a Senior Research Fellowship from the Leverhulme Trust.

a species. By contrast, defeasibility and the effect of content do not affect deductive validity. However, they do affect how people reason deductively.

The standard logic of the conditional, *if. . . then*, has been assumed to provide the normative standard in much of the experimental work on human deductive reasoning. In standard logic, the meaning of logical terms (*if p then q, p or q, p and q*) is given by a truth function, mapping all possible truth value assignments to the constituent propositions (*p, q*) to a truth value. The conditional is true, if and only if *p*, the antecedent, is false or *q*, the consequent, is true; otherwise it is false. That is, the conditional is only false where *p* is true and *q* is false. This is the *material implication* semantics of the conditional. This semantics licenses a variety of formal (i.e., content-independent) rules of inference. Despite the existence of a variety of formal rules that logically can be derived involving the conditional, the psychology of reasoning has typically concentrated its research effort on only two: the conditional syllogisms, *modus ponens* (MP) and *modus tollens* (MT). For these rules of inference, if the premises (above the line) are true ("¬" = not), then the conclusion (below the line) must be true, i.e., they are logically *valid*:

MP $\dfrac{p \rightarrow q, \, p}{\therefore q}$ MT $\dfrac{p \rightarrow q, \, \neg q}{\therefore \neg p}$

In psychological reasoning experiments these valid rules of inference are usually paired with two logical fallacies, *denying the antecedent* (DA) and *affirming the consequent* (AC):

DA $\dfrac{p \rightarrow q, \, \neg p}{\therefore \neg q}$ AC $\dfrac{p \rightarrow q, \, q}{\therefore p}$

Over the last fifty years, the question of the quality of people's deductive reasoning has been pursued using a number of experimental paradigms. The three paradigms that have been most studied are the Wason selection task (Wason 1968), quantified syllogistic reasoning (Johnson-Laird and Steedman 1978), and conditional inference (Taplin 1971). In each case, standard deductive logic makes precise predictions about people's performance.

Wason's selection task can be illustrated like this. Consider four birds. Of two of them you know only their species; one is a swan and one is a crow. Of the other two you know only their color; one is white and one is black. The question a participant must address is which birds must be examined in order to confirm or disconfirm that *all swans are white*. The logical form of this claim is *All(x)(Swan(x) → White(x))*, i.e., a universally quantified conditional, which is only false if one finds a black swan. The question of which birds to look at has a determinate logical answer if it is assumed that the domain of *x* is restricted to just the four birds under consideration. Only the swan and the black bird could falsify the claim in this restricted domain, and so only these birds must be examined. However, in experimental versions of this task using letters and numbers, people tend not to give the logical answer. For example, given the conditional, *if there is an A on a one side of a card, then there is a 2 on the other*, people mainly ask to see the reverse of the *A* and the *2* cards (Wason 1968). That is, rather than attempting to falsify the hypothesis, people appear to choose evidence that might confirm it, by revealing a card with an *A* on one side and a *2* on the other. This behavior has been labeled *confirmation bias*.

Quantified syllogistic reasoning involves the logical quantifiers, *All P are Q*, *Some P are Q*, *No P are Q*, and *Some P are not Q* (capital *P*s and *Q*s are used to distinguish these *predicates* from the *propositional* variables used in describing the conditional syllogisms). A quantified syllogism involves two of these statements as premises connected by a *middle term* (*R*), for example

> *Some P are R*
> *All R are Q*
> _____
> ∴ *Some P are Q*

This is a logically *valid* syllogism. The *All* statement has the same conditional logical form as in the swan example. The end terms (*P*, *Q*) and the middle term can assume four configurations (called *figures*) in the premises:

Some P are R	*Some P are R*	*Some R are P*	*Some R are P*
All R are Q	*All Q are R*	*All R are Q*	*All Q are R*

For each figure, there are 16 possible combinations of quantifiers (4 options for the first and second premises), yielding 64 possible syllogisms (or 512, if all 8 possible conclusions are also considered). If people responded logically in tasks where they are asked whether the conclusion follows logically from the premises, they should endorse the valid syllogisms and not endorse the invalid syllogisms. However, people show systematically graded behavior, i.e., they reliably endorse certain valid syllogisms more than others. Moreover, they also endorse invalid syllogisms over which they also show systematically graded behavior.

In conditional inference tasks, participants are given the two valid inference rules (MP and MT) and the two fallacies (DA and AC), and are asked which they wish to endorse. If they are reasoning logically, they will endorse the valid inferences but not the fallacies. However, people typically select MP more than MT. Moreover, they also select DA and AC but select AC more than DA and occasionally select more AC than MT (Schroyens and Schaeken 2003). *Content* also matters. For example, people endorse the MP inference more for a conditional such as, *if the apple is ripe, then it will fall from the tree*, than for the conditional, *if John studies hard, then he will do well in the test* (Cummins 1995). Furthermore, the difference can be directly located in the differential *defeasibility* of these two conditionals. It appears, for example, much easier for people to generate scenarios in which John will not do well in the test (e.g., he is depressed, he has a low IQ . . . etc.) than ones in which the ripe apple remains forever stuck to the tree. As we pointed out above, defeasibility and effects of content are normally considered properties of inductive, rather than deductive inference.

In summary, the three experimental paradigms (conditional inference, the selection task, and syllogistic reasoning) that have been the main focus of empirical research in the psychology of reasoning reveal considerable deviations from logical expectations. The currently most active area of research is on conditional inference. This is because over the last ten years or so there have been considerable theoretical and methodological advances in this area. Some are shared with other inferential modes but they can be best exemplified in conditional inference. Moreover, it is unequivocally agreed both in philosophical logic (e.g., Bennett 2003) and in experimental psychology (e.g., Evans and Over 2004) that the conditional is the core of human inference.

The response to apparently illogical responses in these tasks is to appeal to cognitive limitations and/or the nature of people's mental representations of these arguments. So, on a *mental logic* view (e.g., Rips 1994), people tend to draw the MT inference less than MP because they only have the MP rule of inference (see above) in their mental logic. Consequently, they must draw the MT inference using a *suppositional* strategy (they suppose the denial of the conclusion and show that this leads to a contradiction). This strategy is more cognitively demanding, and so fewer participants complete it. On the *mental models* account, people have no mental inference rules but rather construct a mental representation of the possibilities allowed by a conditional over which they draw inferences. These possibilities relate directly to the truth conditions of the conditional: they are representations of the states of affairs in the world that are not ruled out assuming the conditional is true. Moreover, because of working memory limitations, they do not mentally represent all of these possibilities:

$$p \quad q$$
$$\cdots \tag{1}$$

(1) shows the *initial* mental model for the conditional. It shows just the possibility that p is true and q is true but misses out the false antecedent possibilities ($\neg p \ q$ and $\neg p \ \neg q$), which are also true instances of the conditional. (1) allows MP, because the categorical premise, p, matches an item in the model which suggests it "goes with" q, the conclusion of MP. However, this model does not match the categorical premise, $\neg q$, of the MT inference. (1) needs to be *fleshed out* with the false antecedent truth table cases for a match to be found for $\neg q$, which suggests it "goes with" $\neg p$. This extra mental operation makes the MT inference harder and so fewer people endorse it.

Yet how could such an error-prone reasoning system have evolved? How could it lead to successful behavior in the real world? Over the last ten years or so alternative accounts of human reasoning based on probability theory have been proposed which may address these questions. Moreover, they directly address the fact that inductive properties like content dependence and defeasibility arise, even when people are presumed to be solving deductive reasoning tasks. For example, *birds fly* could be interpreted to mean that the conditional probability that something flies, given that it is a bird, is high (say, .95) (i.e., $P(fly(x)|bird(x)) = .95$), and this is consistent with the probability that something flies, given that it is a bird *and* an ostrich, being zero or close to zero (i.e., $P(fly(x)|bird(x),ostrich(x)) \approx 0$).

The source of these probability judgments is world knowledge (Oaksford and Chater 2007). In truly deductive inference, people should ignore their prior knowledge of the specific content of the premises. Stanovich and West (2000) note that people find this difficult, calling it "the fundamental computational bias." Different theories take different approaches to addressing this bias. They vary from making adjustments to a theory designed to account for standard logical inference, as in mental models (Johnson-Laird and Byrne 2002), to rejecting standard logic as the appropriate normative standard for these psychological tasks, as in the probabilistic approach (Oaksford and Chater 2007).

Recently, researchers have begun quantitatively to compare models of reasoning using a "model-fitting" approach – building mathematical accounts of different models and testing how closely the predictions of these models fit the empirical data. This approach has been used in the selection task (Oaksford and Chater 2003a; Klauer, Stahl, and Erdfelder 2007), syllogistic reasoning (Klauer, Musch, and Naumer 2000), and conditional inference (Oaksford and Chater 2003b; Oaksford, Chater, and Larkin 2000; Oberauer 2006; Schroyens and Schaeken 2003).

How have accounts of conditional reasoning responded to the apparent influence of content and defeasibility? The mental logic approach does not address the issue directly, and it has been suggested that such influences arise from non-deductive reasoning mechanisms (e.g., Rips 1994, 2001). Mental model theory addresses these issues directly. Johnson-Laird and Byrne (2002) argue that mental models of conditionals can be modulated by prior knowledge that rules out or rules in various truth-functional possibilities. They call this process *semantic and pragmatic modulation*. The process of semantic and pragmatic modulation may even lead to the representation of possibilities that falsify the conditional, i.e., the $p \neg q$ model. For example, they argue that a conditional such as, *if there is gravity (which there is), then your apples may fall* induces the following mental models:

$$p \quad q$$
$$p \quad \neg q \tag{2}$$

The false antecedent possibilities are not considered because gravity is always present but on any given occasion the apples may or may not fall. Notice that the modal "may" here is represented simply by listing both consequents as possible, which appears radically oversimplified from the standpoint of conventional logic. Johnson-Laird and Byrne (2002) discuss no less than ten possible interpretations of the conditional by showing how the ten different models they specify may capture the intended meanings of various examples that differ in content (see Johnson-Laird and Byrne 2002, p. 667, table 4). Each of these ten different models licenses different patterns of inference.

Johnson-Laird and Byrne (2002) relate their ten interpretations to specific examples that motivate the interpretations. Frequently, this involves the inclusion of *modal* terms like *possibly* or *may* in the consequent (*q*) clause that linguistically marks the fact that the consequent *may* not occur given the antecedent. This suggests that the surface form of the conditional can trigger the appropriate interpretation. This may directly involve accessing information from pragmatic world knowledge rather than indicating that such a search for a counterexample (e.g., a case where the apple does not fall) would be successful (see Schroyens and Schaeken 2003 for an alternative viewpoint). One problem for this account is that it appeals directly to semantic and pragmatic intuitions in order to generate predictions, and, indeed, the underlying mental models representations serve as a notation for describing these intuitions, rather than constraining them.

New probabilistic approaches to conditional inference directly address defeasibility and effects of problem content by starting from a different normative theory of conditionals. The key idea is that the probability of a conditional, *if p then q*, is the conditional probability, $P(q|p)$. In probability logic (Adams 1998), $P(q|p)$ is given by the subjective interpretation provided by the *Ramsey Test*. As Bennett (2003, p. 53) says:

> The best definition we have [of conditional probability] is the one provided by the Ramsey test: your conditional probability for *q* given *p* is the probability for *q* that results from adding $P(p) = 1$ to your belief system and conservatively adjusting to make room for it.

Recent evidence shows that people do regard the probability of a conditional to be the conditional probability (Evans, Handley, and Over 2003; Oberauer and Wilhlem 2003; Over *et al.* 2003). For example, Evans *et al.* (2003) assessed people's probabilistic interpretations of conditional rules and their contrapositives (*if ¬q then ¬p*). They tested three possibilities: first, that the probability of a conditional is $1 - P(p, ¬q)$ (i.e., 1 minus the probability of finding a falsifying case), as material implication predicts; second, that the probability of a conditional is $P(q|p)$, as predicted by the conditional probability account; and third, that the probability of the conditional is the joint probability, $P(p,q)$ (the conjunction interpretation). According to material implication, conditionals and their contrapositives should be endorsed equally because they are logically equivalent. Consequently, there should be a strong correlation between ratings of how likely the conditional and its contrapositive are to be true. However, according to the conditional probability account, $P(q|p)$ and $P(\neg p|\neg q)$ can differ considerably and would not be expected to reveal a perfect correlation.

Evans *et al.* (2003) varied $P(q|p)$, $P(\neg q|p)$, and $P(\neg p)$ by describing the distribution of cards in packs of varying sizes. For example, given a conditional *if the card is yellow then it has a circle printed on it*, participants were told that there are four yellow circles, one yellow diamond, sixteen red circles, and sixteen red diamonds (Oaksford *et al.* (2000) used similar manipulations). So $P(q|p) = .8$, $P(\neg q|p) = .2$, and $P(\neg p) = 32/37$. On material implication, ratings of $P(if\ the\ card\ is\ yellow\ then\ it\ has\ a\ circle\ printed\ on\ it)$ should increase with increases in $P(\neg p)$, since the conditional is true if the antecedent is false; according to conditional probability, they should be independent of $P(\neg p)$; and according to the conjunction interpretation, they should decrease with increases in $P(\neg p)$, because $\neg p$ implies that the conjunction is false. The evidence supported the conditional probability interpretation, with some evidence for a joint probability interpretation.

Over *et al.* (2003) replicated these findings for everyday conditionals which were pre-tested for $P(p)$ and $P(q)$, as in Oaksford, Chater, and Grainger (1999) and Oaksford *et al.* (2000, experiment 3). While replicating the effect of conditional probability, in contrast to Evans *et al.* (2003), they found that the conjunctive interpretation was rarely adopted by participants. Consequently, the conjunctive interpretation is probably an artifact of unrealistic stimuli (Oberauer and Wilhelm 2003).

The results seem to confirm that the probability of the conditional equals the conditional probability, i.e., $P(p \rightarrow q) = P(q|p)$, as Adams' (1998) account of the probability conditional requires. However, it is the implications for inference of this change in normative focus that are of fundamental importance to the psychology of reasoning. Via the Ramsey test, the probability conditional reveals the total dependence of conditional inference on prior world knowledge. Most recent work has attempted to integrate these insights into a psychological theory of conditional reasoning. We have already looked at the mental model approach (Johnson-Laird and Byrne 2002). We now look at the other approaches that have been suggested.

Perhaps the most direct approach has been taken by Oaksford, Chater, and Larkin (2000; Oaksford and Chater 2007). They have proposed a computational-level account of conditional inference as dynamic belief updating. So if a high probability is assigned to *if x is a bird, x flies*, then on acquiring the new information that *Tweety is a bird*, one's degree of belief in *Tweety flies* should be revised to one's degree of belief in *Tweety flies given Tweety is a bird*, i.e., one's degree of belief in the conditional. So using P_0 to indicate *prior* degree of belief and P_1 to indicate *posterior* degree of belief, then:

$$P_1(q) = P_0(q|p), \quad \text{when } P_1(p) = 1. \tag{3}$$

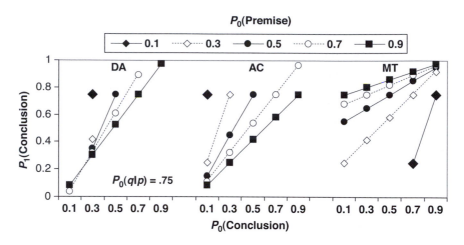

Figure 7.1 The behavior of Oaksford *et al.*'s (2000) conditional probability model, showing how the posterior probability of the conclusion (P_1(Conclusion)) varies as a function of the prior probability of the conclusion (P_0(Conclusion)) and the prior probability of the categorical premise (P_0(Premise)) for DA, AC, and MT with P_1 (Premise) = 1.

Thus, according to this account, the probability with which someone should endorse the MP inference is the conditional probability. This is the approach taken in Oaksford *et al.* (2000).

However, as Oaksford and Chater (2007) point out, there is a problem with extending this account to MT, DA, and AC (Sober 2002). The appropriate conditional probabilities for the categorical premise of these inferences to conditionalize on are $P(\neg p|\neg q)$, $P(\neg q|\neg p)$, and $P(p|q)$ respectively. But the premises of MT and the fallacies do not entail values for these conditional probabilities (Sober 2002; Sobel 2004; Wagner 2004). Oaksford *et al.* (2000) suggested that people had prior knowledge of the marginals, $P(p)$ and $P(q)$, which together with $P(q|p)$ do entail appropriate values (see Wagner 2004 for a similar approach). Thus, letting $a = P_0(q|p)$, $b = P_0(p)$, and $c = P_0(q)$:

MP $P_1(q) = P_0(q|p) = a$ (4)

DA $P_1(\neg q) = P_0(\neg q|\neg p) = \dfrac{1 - c - (1 - a)b}{1 - b}$ (5)

AC $P_1(p) = P_0(p|q) = \dfrac{ab}{c}$ (6)

MT $P_1(\neg p) = P_0(\neg p|\neg q) = \dfrac{1 - c - (1 - a)b}{1 - c}$ (7)

Equations (4)–(7) show the posterior probabilities of the conclusion of each inference assuming the posterior probability of the categorical premise is 1. As can be seen in Figure 7.1, this account provides a close fit with the empirical data.

In summary, recently the psychology of reasoning, and the psychology of conditional reasoning in particular, has shifted its focus away from the old debates about whether rule-based mental logic approaches or mental models provided the best account of human inference. The emergence of computational-level models framed in terms of probability theory rather than standard logic has fundamentally changed the questions being asked. The questions are now whether or how to incorporate these new insights. Should we view the probability conditional as a wholesale replacement for the standard logic-based mental models approach? How does world knowledge modulate reasoning and/or provide probability information?

7.2 Decision making

Whereas reasoning concerns how people use given information to derive new information, the study of decision making concerns how people's beliefs and values determine their choices. As we have seen, in the context of reasoning, there is fundamental debate concerning even the most basic elements of a normative framework against which human performance should be compared – for example, whether the framework should be logical (e.g., Johnson-Laird and Byrne 1991; Rips 1994) or probabilistic (Oaksford and Chater 2007). By contrast, expected utility theory is fairly widely assumed to be the appropriate normative theory to determine how, in principle, people ought to make decisions.

Expected utility theory works by assuming that each outcome, i, of a choice can be assigned a probability, $\Pr(i)$, and a utility, $U(i)$, and that the utility of an uncertain choice (e.g., a lottery ticket or, more generally, any action whose consequences are uncertain) is

$$\sum \Pr(i)\,U(i) \qquad (8)$$

That is, the expected utility of a choice is the sum of the utilities, $U(i)$, of the possible outcomes, each weighted by its probability $\Pr(i)$ given that choice. Expected utility theory recommends the choice with the maximum expected utility.

This normative account is breathtakingly simple, but hides what may be enormous practical complexities – both in estimating probabilities and establishing what people's utilities are. Thus, when faced with a practical personal decision (e.g., whether to take a new job, which house to buy, whether or whom to marry), decision theory is not easy to apply because the possible consequences of each choice are extremely complex, their probabilities ill-defined, and moreover, we often have little idea what preferences we have, even if the outcomes were definite. Thus, one difficulty with expected utility theory is practicability in relation to many real-world decisions. Nonetheless, where probabilities and utilities can be estimated with reasonable accuracy, expected utility is a powerful normative framework.

Can expected utility theory be used as an explanation not merely for how agents *should* behave, but of how agents actually *do* behave? Rational choice theory, which provides a foundation for explanation in microeconomics and sociology (e.g., Elster 1986), as well as perception and motor control (Körding and Wolpert 2006), animal learning (Courville, Daw, and Touretzky 2006), and behavioral ecology (Krebs and Davies 1996), assumes that it does. This style of explanation involves inferring the probabilities and utilities that agents possess, and using expected utility theory to infer their choices according to those probabilities and utilities. Typically, there is no specific commitment concerning whether or how the relevant probabilities and utilities are represented – instead, the assumption is that preferences and subjective probabilities are "revealed" by patterns of observed choices. Indeed, given fairly natural consistency assumptions concerning how people choose, it can be shown that the observed pattern of choices can be represented in terms of expected utility – (i.e., appropriate utilities and subjective probabilities can be inferred; Savage 1954), with no commitment to their underlying psychological implementation. Indeed, this type of result can sometimes be used as reassurance that the expected utility framework is appropriate, even in complex real-world decisions, where people are unable explicitly to estimate probabilities or utilities.

As with the study of reasoning, the descriptive study of how people make decisions has taken the normative perspective as its starting point and aimed to test experimentally how far normative assumptions hold good. In a typical experiment, outcomes are made as clear as possible. For example, people may choose between monetary gambles with known probabilities or between gambles and fixed amounts of money. A wide range of systematic departures from the norms of expected utility are observed in such experiments, as demonstrated by the remarkable research program initiated by Kahneman, Tversky, and their colleagues (e.g., Kahneman, Slovic, and Tversky 1982; Kahneman and Tversky 2000). For example, people can be induced to make different decisions, depending on how the problem is "framed." Thus, if a person is given £10 at the outset and told they must choose between a gamble, with a 50 percent chance of keeping the £10 and a 50 percent chance of losing it all, or giving back £5 for certain, they tend to prefer to take the risk. But if they are given no initial stake, but asked whether they prefer a 50–50 chance of £10 or a certain £5, they tend to play safe. Yet, from a formal point of view these choices are identical; the only difference is that in one case the choice is framed in terms of losses (where people tend to be risk-seeking), rather than gains (where they tend to be risk-averse).

Expected utility theory cannot account for framing effects of this type. From a normative point of view, only the formal structure of the problem should matter; the way in which it is described should be irrelevant. Indeed, expected

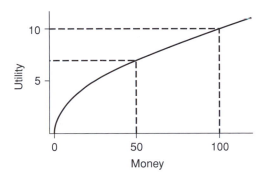

Figure 7.2 The utility function in conventional expected utility theory. The utility function is usually assumed to have a convex shape, as shown, although this is not an essential part of the theory. A concave utility function implies that the utility of, say, £50 is greater than the average utility of £0 and £100. This implies risk aversion, since risky options involve such averaging of good and poor outcomes. Note that expected utility theory applies to overall wealth, rather than directly to the outcomes of the gambles. If the gambles are small in relation to overall wealth, this implies that the utility curve is fairly flat, and hence that risk average should be small. The high levels of risk aversion shown in laboratory experiments are difficult to reconcile with expected utility theory (Rabin 2000).

utility theory cannot well account for the more basic fact that people are not risk-neutral (i.e., neutral between gambles with the same expected monetary value) for small stakes (Rabin 2000). This is because, from the standpoint of expected utility theory, people ought to evaluate the possible outcomes of a gamble in "global" terms – i.e., in relation to the impact on their life overall. Hence, if a person has an initial wealth of £10,000, then the gambles above amount to choosing between, on the one hand, a 50–50 chance of ending up with a wealth of £10,010 or £10,000, and, on the other, a certain wealth of £10,005 (see Figure 7.2).

One reaction to this type of clash between human behavior and rational norms is the observation that the human behavior is error-prone – and hence, where this is true, expected utility will be inadequate as a *descriptive* theory of choice. A natural follow-up to this, though, is to attempt to modify the normative theory so that it provides a better fit with the empirical data. A wide range of proposals of this sort have been put forward, including prospect theory (Kahneman and Tversky 1979). Indeed, prospect theory, which is by far the most influential framework, was deliberately conceived as an attempt to find the minimal modifications of expected utility theory that would describe human choice behavior (Kahneman 2000).

In essence, prospect theory modifies expected utility theory in three main ways. First, monetary outcomes are considered in isolation, rather than aggregated as part of total wealth. This fits with the wider observation that people

(a)   (b)

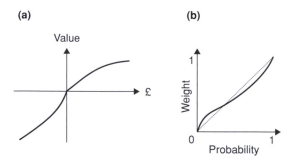

Figure 7.3 The value function (a) and "decision weights" (b) in prospect theory. Decision weights are presumed to be systematically distorted with respect to "true" probabilities in an inverse-S shape (for comparison, the non-distorted function is shown as a dotted line).

view different amounts of money (or indeed goals, quantities, or events of any kind) one by one, rather than forming a view of an integrated whole. This observation is the core of Thaler's (1985) "mental accounting" theory of how people make real-world financial decisions.

Second, prospect theory assumes that while the value function (i.e., relating money to subjective value) for positive gains is concave (i.e., negatively accelerating, indicating risk aversion in an expected utility framework), the value function for losses is convex (i.e., positively accelerating; see Figure 7.3a). This implies that the marginal extra pain for an additional unit of loss (e.g., each extra pound or dollar lost) decreases with the size of the loss. Thus, people are risk-seeking when a gamble is framed in terms of losses, but risk-averse when it is framed in terms of gains, as we noted above. Moreover, the value function is steeper for losses than for gains, which captures the fact that most people are averse to gambles with a 50 percent chance of winning £10, and a 50 percent chance of losing £10 (Kahneman and Tversky 1979). This phenomenon, *loss aversion*, has been used to explain a wide range of real-world phenomena, including the status quo bias (losing one thing and gaining another tends to seem unappealing, because the loss is particularly salient; Samuelson and Zeckhauser 1988) and the equity premium puzzle (share returns may be "unreasonably" high relative to fixed interest bonds, because people dislike falls in stock prices more than they like the equivalent gains; Benartzi and Thaler 1995).

The final key modification of expected utility theory is that prospect theory assumes that people operate with a distorted representation of probability (Figure 7.3b). They overestimate probabilities near zero, and underestimate probabilities near 1, so that the relation between probability, $p(i)$, and the "decision weights," $w(i)$, which are assumed to determine people's choices, is represented by an inverse-S shape. According to prospect theory, this

Table 7.1 **The four-fold pattern of risky choice**

	Small probability	High probability
Gain	Certain 50p vs. 1/2000 probability of £1,000. Choose gamble (risk seeking).	Certain £500 vs. 1/2 probability of £1,000. Choose certainty (risk aversion).
Loss	Certain −50p vs. 1/2000 probability of −£1,000. Choose certainty (risk aversion).	Certain −£500 vs. 1/2 probability of −£1,000. Choose gamble (risk seeking).

distortion can explain the so-called "four-fold pattern" of risky decision making – that is, the observation that for small probabilities risk-preferences reverse both for gains and losses (Table 7.1). Thus, while people are normally risk-averse for gains, they still play lotteries. According to prospect theory, this is because they drastically overestimate the small probability of winning. Similarly, while people are normally risk-seeking for losses, they still buy insurance. According to prospect theory, this is because they drastically overestimate the small probability of needing to claim on that insurance.

The machinery of prospect theory integrates values and decision weights to assign a value to each gamble (where this is any choice with an uncertain outcome), just as in expected utility theory, so that the value of a risky option is

$$\sum w\,(i)\,v\,(i) \tag{9}$$

where $w(i)$ is the decision weight (i.e., distorted probability) for outcome i, and $v(i)$ is the value of that outcome. Thus, the value of a risky option is the sum of the products of the subjective value of each possible outcome and the subjective "weight" (distorted probability) assigned to each outcome. Prospect theory and other variants of expected utility theory hold with the assumption that people represent value and probability on some kind of absolute internal scale and that they integrate these values by summing the product of weight and value over possible outcomes, to obtain the value of each gamble. Two recent psychological theories, however, set aside the structure of expected utility theory; instead of seeking to modify normative considerations, they attempt to trace the consequences of assumptions about the cognitive system.

One recent approach (Brandstätter, Gigerenzer, and Hertwig 2006) focuses on processing limitations, and on the consequences of assuming that the cognitive system is unable to integrate different pieces of information and that people can focus on only one piece of information at a time. This assumption is controversial. In perceptual judgments (e.g., concerning the identity of a phoneme, or the depth of a surface), many theories explicitly assume (linear) integration between different sources of information (Schrater and Kersten 2000). In a probabilistic framework, this corresponds, roughly, to adding logs of the strength of evidence provided by each cue. Many models of higher-level judgment have assumed that information is also integrated, typically linearly (e.g., Hammond 1996). However, Gigerenzer and colleagues (e.g., Gigerenzer and Goldstein 1996) have influentially argued that high-level judgments – most famously, concerning the larger of pairs of German cities – do not involve integration. Instead judgment is assumed to involve considering cues, one at a time. If a cue determines which city is likely to be larger, that city is selected; if not, a further cue is chosen, and the process is repeated. There has been considerable, and ongoing, controversy concerning the circumstances under which integration does or does not occur in the context of judgment (Hogarth and Karelaia 2005).

Brandstätter, Gigerenzer, and Hertwig's (2006) innovation is to show that a non-integrative model can make inroads into understanding how people make risky decisions – a situation which has been viewed as involving a trade-off between "risk" and "return" almost by definition. Their model, the priority heuristic, recommends the following procedure: For gambles which contain only gains (or £0), consider features of the gambles in the order: minimum gain, probability of minimum gain, maximum gain. If gains differ by at least $\frac{1}{10}$ of the maximum gain (or, for comparison of probabilities, if probabilities differ by at least $\frac{1}{10}$), choose the gamble which is "best" on that feature (defined in the obvious way). Otherwise, move to the next feature in the list, and repeat.

To see how this works, consider the gambles illustration of the "four-fold pattern" of risky choice, described by Kahneman and Tversky (1979), in Table 7.1. For the high-probability gamble over gains, the minimum gain for the certain outcome is £500, but the minimum gain for the risky gamble is £0. This difference is far more than $\frac{1}{10}$ of the maximum gain, £1,000. Hence, the safe option is preferred. By contrast, for the low-probability gamble, the difference between the minimum gains for the options is just 50p, which is much less than $\frac{1}{10}$ of the maximum gain of £1,000. Hence, this feature is abandoned, and we switch to probability of minimum gain. This is clearly higher for a certain gamble, as there is only one outcome, which is by definition the minimum. The risky gamble, with the smaller probability of minimum gain, is therefore preferred. Thus, we have risk-seeking behavior with small probabilities of large gains (and hence an explanation of why people buy lottery tickets).

Brandstätter, Gigerenzer, and Hertwig propose a modification of the heuristic for gambles containing just losses, where "gain" is replaced by "loss" throughout, so that the feature order is: minimum loss, probability of minimum loss, maximum loss. If gains differ by at least $\frac{1}{10}$ of the maximum loss (or probabilities differ by at least $\frac{1}{10}$), choose the gamble which is "best" on that feature (defined in the obvious way). Otherwise, move to the next feature in the list, and repeat. Tracing through the argument described above for the "loss" gambles in Table 7.1 yields the conclusion that people should appear risk-seeking for losses, except where there is a small probability of a large loss; here people will again be risk-averse (e.g., they will buy insurance).

The priority heuristic model does, however, make some extremely strong and counterintuitive predictions – for example, that if the minimum gains differ sufficiently, then all other features of the gambles (including the probability of obtaining those gains) will have no impact on choice. In extreme cases, this seems implausible. For example, a certain 11p should be preferred to a .999999 probability of £1 (and otherwise £0). Brandstätter, Gigerenzer, and Hertwig (2006) restrict their account, however, to cases for which the expected values of the gambles are roughly comparable; where they are not, the gamble with the obviously higher expected value is chosen, and the priority heuristic is not invoked.

Another recent approach to risk decision making, starting from cognitive principles rather than a normative economic account, is Decision by Sampling (DbS; Stewart, Chater, and Brown 2006). This viewpoint assumes that people have no underlying internal "scales" for utility or probability. Nonetheless, it turns out to be possible to reconstruct something analogous to the value and decision weight functions from prospect theory. If people assess the gut feel of a magnitude in relation to prior examples, the statistical distribution of such magnitudes is likely to be important. Other things being equal, this distribution will provide an estimate of the probabilities of different comparison items being considered in particular judgments. Thus, if small sums of money are much more commonly encountered than large sums of money, then it is much more likely that people will consider small sums of money as comparison items, other things being equal. Therefore, the difference in "gut" feel between £5 and £50 will be much greater than that between £1,005 and £1,050 because sampling an item in the first interval (so that the lower and upper items will be assigned different ranks) is much more likely than sampling an item in the second. More generally, the attractiveness of an option, according to DbS, is determined by its rank in the set of comparison items. Hence, its typical attractiveness (across many sampling contexts) can be estimated by its rank position in a statistical sample of occurrences of the relevant magnitude. Figure 7.4a shows a sample of "positive" sums of money – credits into accounts from a high street bank. Plotting monetary value against rank (Figure 7.4b) then produces a concave function, reminiscent of those in utility theory and prospect theory. Thus, the "gut" attractiveness of a sum of money is, on average, a diminishing function of amount. The similar analysis for losses (using bank account debits as a proxy) yields a convex function of value against losses, as in prospect theory (Figure 7.4c). Moreover, for losses, the statistical distribution is more skewed toward small items, which has the consequence that ranks change more rapidly for small values for losses than

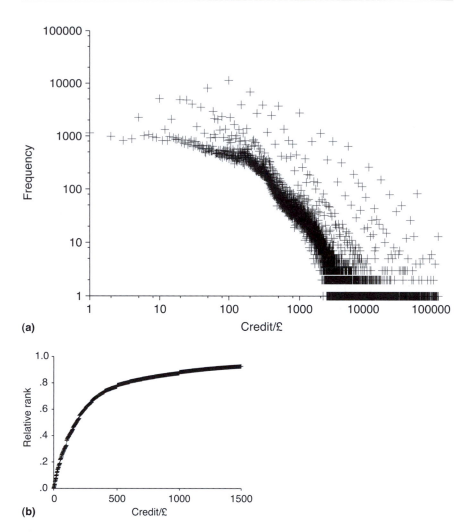

(a)

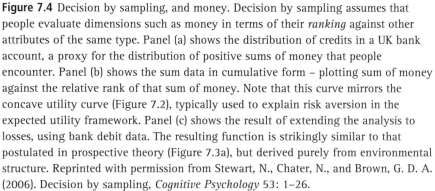

(b)

Figure 7.4 Decision by sampling, and money. Decision by sampling assumes that people evaluate dimensions such as money in terms of their *ranking* against other attributes of the same type. Panel (a) shows the distribution of credits in a UK bank account, a proxy for the distribution of positive sums of money that people encounter. Panel (b) shows the sum data in cumulative form – plotting sum of money against the relative rank of that sum of money. Note that this curve mirrors the concave utility curve (Figure 7.2), typically used to explain risk aversion in the expected utility framework. Panel (c) shows the result of extending the analysis to losses, using bank debit data. The resulting function is strikingly similar to that postulated in prospective theory (Figure 7.3a), but derived purely from environmental structure. Reprinted with permission from Stewart, N., Chater, N., and Brown, G. D. A. (2006). Decision by sampling, *Cognitive Psychology* 53: 1–26.

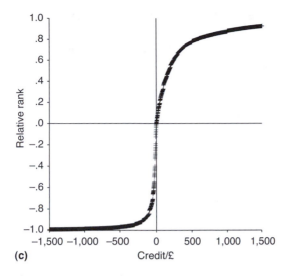

(c)

Figure 7.4 (*continued*)

for gains. This corresponds to a steeper value curve for losses and gains, and hence captures loss aversion. Indeed, the curve for both gains and losses is strikingly reminiscent of that postulated in prospect theory.

7.3   Concluding comments

In both reasoning and decision making, there is a certain air of paradox in human performance (Oaksford and Chater 1998). Human common-sense reasoning is far more sophisticated than any current artificial intelligence models can capture; yet people's performance on, for example, simple conditional inference, while perhaps explicable in probabilistic terms, is by no means effortless and noise-free. Similarly, in decision making, it appears that "low-level" repeated decision making may be carried out effectively. But perhaps this situation is not entirely paradoxical. It may be that human reasoning and decision making function best in the context of highly adapted cognitive processes such as basic learning, deploying world knowledge, or perceptuo-motor control. Indeed, what is striking about human cognition is the ability to handle, even to a limited extent, reasoning and decision making in novel, hypothetical, verbally stated scenarios, for which our past experience and evolutionary history may have provided us with only minimal preparation.

Further reading

Adler, J. E. and Rips, L. J. (2008). *Reasoning*. Cambridge University Press. A collection of summaries and classic papers in the field.

Baron, J. (2008). *Thinking and Deciding* (4th edn.). Cambridge University Press. A classic textbook, but thoroughly updated.

Braine, M. D. S. and O'Brien, D. P. (1998). *Mental Logic*. London: Taylor and Francis. An edited collection of papers on the mental logic theory.

Evans, J. St. B. T. (2007). *Hypothetical Thinking*. Brighton: Psychology Press. An exhaustive review of the psychology of reasoning and how the "suppositional" theory can explain it.

Evans, J. St. B. T. and Over, D. E. (2004). *If*. Oxford University Press. An extended account of how different logical analyses of the conditional bear on explaining the experimental data on conditional reasoning.

Gigerenzer, G. and Selten, R. (2001). *Bounded Rationality: The Adaptive Toolbox*. Cambridge, MA: MIT Press. An interdisciplinary collection on boundedly rational models of decision making.

Johnson-Laird, P. N. (2006). *How We Reason*. Oxford University Press. The most recent instantiation of how the mental models theory accounts for the experimental data on human reasoning.

Kahneman, D. and Tversky, A. (eds.) (2000). *Choices, Frames and Values*. Cambridge University Press. A classic collection on the heuristics and biases approach to decision making.

Oaksford, M. and Chater, N. (2007). *Bayesian Rationality*. Oxford University Press. An account of the conceptual underpinnings of the probabilistic approach and of how it explains the experimental data on human reasoning.

References

Adams, E. W. (1998). *A Primer of Probability Logic*. Stanford: CLSI Publications.

Benartzi, S. and Thaler, R. H. (1995). Myopic loss aversion and the equity premium puzzle, *Quarterly Journal of Economics* 110: 73–92.

Bennett, J. (2003). *A Philosophical Guide to Conditionals*. Oxford University Press.

Brandstätter, E., Gigerenzer, G., and Hertwig, R. (2006). The priority heuristic: Making choices without trade-offs, *Psychological Review* 113: 409–32.

Courville, A. C., Daw, N. D., and Touretzky, D. S. (2006). Bayesian theories of conditioning in a changing world, *Trends in Cognitive Sciences* 10: 294–300.

Cummins, D. D. (1995). Naïve theories and causal deduction, *Memory and Cognition* 23: 646–58.

Elster, J. (ed.) (1986). *Rational Choice*. Oxford: Basil Blackwell.

Evans, J. St. B. T., Handley, S. H., and Over, D. E. (2003). Conditionals and conditional probability. *Journal of Experimental Psychology: Learning, Memory and Cognition* 29: 321–55.

Evans, J. St. B. T. and Over, D. E. (2004). *If*. Oxford University Press.

Gigerenzer, G. and Goldstein, D. (1996). Reasoning the fast and frugal way: Models of bounded rationality, *Psychological Review* 103: 650–69.

Goodman, N. (1954). *Fact, Fiction, and Forecast*. London: The Athlone Press.

Hammond, K. R. (1996). *Human Judgment and Social Policy: Irreducible Uncertainty, Inevitable Error, Unavoidable Injustice.* Oxford University Press.

Hogarth, R. M. and Karelaia, N. (2005). Simple models for multi-attribute choice with many alternatives: When it does and does not pay to face trade-offs with binary attributes, *Management Science* 51: 1860–72.

Jeffrey, R. (1965). *The Logic of Decision.* New York: McGraw Hill.

Johnson-Laird, P. N. and Byrne, R. M. J. (1991). *Deduction.* Hillsdale, NJ: Lawrence Erlbaum.

(2002). Conditionals: A theory of meaning, pragmatics, and inference, *Psychological Review* 109: 646–78.

Johnson-Laird, P. N. and Steedman, M. (1978). The psychology of syllogisms, *Cognitive Psychology* 10: 64–99.

Kahneman, D. (2000). Preface, in D. Kahneman and A. Tversky (eds.), *Choices, Values and Frames* (pp. ix–xvii). New York: Cambridge University Press and the Russell Sage Foundation.

Kahneman, D., Slovic, P., and Tversky, A. (eds.) (1982). *Judgment under Uncertainty: Heuristics and Biases.* New York: Cambridge University Press.

Kahneman, D. and Tversky, A. (1979). Prospect theory: An analysis of decisions under risk, *Econometrica* 47: 313–27.

(eds.) (2000). *Choices, Values and Frames.* New York: Cambridge University Press and the Russell Sage Foundation.

Klauer, K. C., Musch, J., and Naumer, B. (2000). On belief bias in syllogistic reasoning, *Psychological Review* 107: 852–84.

Klauer, K. C., Stahl, C., and Erdfelder, E. (2007). The abstract selection task: New data and an almost comprehensive model, *Journal of Experimental Psychology: Learning, Memory and Cognition* 33: 680–703.

Körding, K. P. and Wolpert, D. M. (2006). Bayesian decision theory in sensorimotor control, *Trends in Cognitive Sciences* 10: 319–26.

Krebs, J. R. and Davies, N. (eds.) (1996). *Behavioural Ecology: An Evolutionary Approach* (4th edn.). Oxford: Blackwell.

Oaksford, M. and Chater, N. (1998). *Rationality in an Uncertain World.* Hove, UK: Psychology Press.

(2003a). Optimal data selection: Revision, review and re-evaluation, *Psychonomic Bulletin and Review* 10: 289–318.

(2003b). Conditional probability and the cognitive science of conditional reasoning, *Mind and Language* 18: 359–79.

(2007). *Bayesian Rationality: The Probabilistic Approach to Human Reasoning.* Oxford University Press.

Oaksford, M., Chater, N., and Grainger, B. (1999). Probabilistic effects in data selection, *Thinking and Reasoning* 5: 193–244.

Oaksford, M., Chater, N., and Larkin, J. (2000). Probabilities and polarity biases in conditional inference, *Journal of Experimental Psychology: Learning, Memory and Cognition* 26: 883–9.

Oberauer, K. (2006). Reasoning with conditionals: A test of formal models of four theories, *Cognitive Psychology* 53: 238–83.

Oberauer, K. and Wilhelm, O. (2003). The meaning(s) of conditionals: Conditional probabilities, mental models and personal utilities, *Journal of Experimental Psychology: Learning, Memory and Cognition* 29: 680–739.

Over, D. E., Hadjichristidis, C., Evans, J., St. B. T., Handley, S. J., and Sloman, S. A. (2003). The probability of conditionals: The psychological evidence, *Mind & Language* 18: 340–58.

Rabin, M. (2000). Diminishing marginal utility of wealth cannot explain risk aversion. In D. Kahneman and A. Tversky (eds.), *Choices, Values, and Frames* (pp. 202–8). New York: Cambridge University Press.

Rips, L. J. (1994). *The Psychology of Proof.* Cambridge, MA: MIT Press.

  (2001). Two kinds of reasoning, *Psychological Science* 12: 129–34.

Samuelson, W. F. and Zeckhauser, R. J. (1988). Status quo bias in decision making, *Journal of Risk and Uncertainty* 1: 7–59.

Savage, L. J. (1954). *The Foundations of Statistics.* New York: Wiley.

Schrater, P. R. and Kersten, D. (2000). How optimal depth cue integration depends on the task, *International Journal of Computer Vision* 40: 71–89.

Schroyens, W. and Schaeken, W. (2003). A critique of Oaksford, Chater and Larkin's (2000) conditional probability model of conditional reasoning, *Journal of Experimental Psychology: Learning, Memory and Cognition* 29: 140–9.

Sobel, J. H. (2004). *Probable Modus Ponens and Modus Tollens and Updating on Uncertain Evidence.* Unpublished manuscript, Department of Philosophy, University of Toronto, Scarborough.

Sober, E. (2002). Intelligent design and probability reasoning, *International Journal for Philosophy of Religion* 52: 65–80.

Stanovich, K. E. and West, R. F. (2000). Individual differences in reasoning: Implications for the rationality debate? *Behavioral and Brain Sciences* 23: 645–65.

Stewart, N., Chater, N., and Brown, G. D. A. (2006). Decision by sampling, *Cognitive Psychology* 53: 1–26.

Taplin, J. E. (1971). Reasoning with conditional sentences, *Journal of Verbal Learning and Verbal Behavior* 10: 219–25.

Thaler, R. (1985). Mental accounting and consumer choice, *Marketing Science* 4: 199–214.

Wagner, C. G. (2004). Modus tollens probabilized, *British Journal for Philosophy of Science* 55: 747–53.

Wason, P. C. (1960). On the failure to eliminate hypotheses in a conceptual task, *Quarterly Journal of Experimental Psychology* 12: 129–40.

  (1968). Reasoning about a rule, *Quarterly Journal of Experimental Psychology* 20: 273–81.

Wason, P. C. and Johnson-Laird, P. N. (1972). *Psychology of Reasoning: Structure and Content.* London: Batsford.

8 Concepts

Gregory L. Murphy and Aaron B. Hoffman

8.1 What are concepts?

Everyday experience is replete with novelty. We continually encounter new objects – both novel examples of familiar categories and completely new kinds of things. Every event is different in some way from previous events; each object is different in some way from every other. However, this novelty does not baffle us, because nearly every object and experience is also similar in some way to our past experiences, and we can draw on those experiences to understand new situations. *Concepts* are the representations that allow us to do this. They represent our knowledge of classes of entities (*categories*), which we then use to understand new things. Indeed, we are so good at using concepts that we seldom think that this pork chop is completely novel, that we have never seen that car passing by, or that the squirrel in our neighbor's yard is a new one to us.

Psychologists have primarily studied concepts of objects rather than events, situations, or more abstract entities like personalities or aesthetic categories. This is because objects are a particularly important part of our knowledge and are relatively easy to study experimentally. And, as in many areas of experimental psychology, researchers have often studied simplified concepts and tasks to gain experimental control and to discover basic processes of concept learning. Whether this strategy has been successful is controversial. Indeed, differences in methodology and interests have combined to create two very different strands of research on concepts. One strand focuses on learning of artificial categories, generally using mathematical models to represent the learning process. It is influenced by basic research on learning, such as classical conditioning. This research often uses categories specifically constructed to test alternative learning theories and is not particularly interested in whether those categories correspond to everyday concepts like cats or computers. The second strand focuses on real-world concepts, often investigating the effects of higher-level knowledge and issues derived from philosophy and cognitive science more generally. This strand often has a developmental focus.

We thank Bob Colner for helpful comments on a draft. Writing of this chapter was supported by NIMH grants MH41704 to GLM and MH73267 to ABH.

It is not really possible to integrate these two strands of research, because their points of intersection are few. However, both tell us something important about how concepts are learned and represented, and we will attempt to review both. Indeed, it seems likely that further progress in a comprehensive theory of concepts will be made when researchers from each strand begin to take more seriously the issues and results of the other. The difficulty is that very different accounts of concepts are assumed by these two approaches (see Murphy 2005), which suggests that (at least) one of them must be wrong, or that the notion of "concept" is not a unitary one. Perhaps both of these are true.

In the next section we briefly review basic findings of the psychology of concepts that are the basis for both strands. Then we discuss formal models of category learning and conclusions from that research. Transitioning toward the second strand, the subsequent section discusses how higher-level knowledge influences the category-learning task, suggesting that a broader approach may be required. Finally, we move completely to the second strand and review work on conceptual development, essentialism, and knowledge effects.

8.2   Classical vs. prototype concepts

The modern psychology of concepts began with the work of Eleanor Rosch in the 1970s (most notably Rosch 1975; Rosch and Mervis 1975; Rosch *et al.* 1976). Her work was responding to a tradition in psychology and philosophy, called the *classical view* by Smith and Medin (1981), that assumed that concepts could be represented by a set of properties or *features* that picked out a category of objects. Thus, all category members would have those properties, and nonmembers would not. This tradition led to a rich set of psychological questions, including how people identified the critical features, and how learning a category depended on variables such as the number of features and their relations (Bruner, Goodnow, and Austin 1956). However, Rosch questioned the assumptions of this entire approach, arguing that many categories could not be *defined* by features common to all category members.

The work of Rosch and many others to overturn the classical view has been reviewed in many places and will not be detailed here (see Murphy 2002; Smith and Medin 1981). Two basic phenomena arose from this work that are essential to understanding all later work on concepts and categorization. The first was the finding of unclear category membership. For most categories, it is possible to find items that are not clearly in or out of the category – not only do people disagree with each other about the category membership of such items, individuals disagree with themselves when tested at different times (McCloskey and Glucksberg 1978). This uncertainty seems incompatible with the idea that categories are well defined.

The second phenomenon was typicality effects: Some items are "better" category members than others. For example, a robin is considered a more typical bird than a swan. But the classical view predicts that no category member should be better than any other. Objects should either belong to a category or not. Furthermore, typicality turns out to predict many behaviors related to categories, such as classification and induction. As items become less typical, their category membership becomes less clear, and people may become uncertain about how to classify them. For example, a tall, four-legged piece of furniture with a large seat and no back would be at best an atypical chair; and at the same time, some people might classify it as a bar stool rather than a chair. Hampton (1995) documented the relation between typicality and unclear membership in detail.

Rosch (1975) explained these results in terms of a *prototype* model of concepts, in which a concept was represented not by defining features but by typical features. Some properties of a concept are very common, and others less so. The more of the common features that an object possesses, the more typical it is of the concept. Rosch and Mervis (1975) provided experimental evidence for this view.

However, later research has shown that other accounts of conceptual representations are possible. The main competitor has been *exemplar models* of concepts, which state that people remember specific instances or exemplars and use these to generalize to new instances (Medin and Schaffer 1978). For example, if you remember a number of items that have been called "chairs," and then you encountered that backless seat described above, you would find it not very similar to many of the examples of chairs in your memory. And it is somewhat similar to examples of stools that you remember. Depending on the degree of similarity to these exemplars, you might call the object a stool or a chair, or possibly be indecisive between the two – i.e., the item would have unclear category membership. Note that the exemplar view agrees with Rosch's claim that there are no defining features of a category, and that typicality is related to category uncertainty. Both rely on the notion of *similarity* to a category representation, but differ in assumptions about the underlying representation of the concept – whether it contains properties common to category members or specific exemplars.

Much effort has been spent in attempting to decide between prototype and exemplar models of concepts. In the typical experiment, people learn two concepts by repeatedly viewing and classifying instances. Then different models of their performance are applied to their learning rate, the errors made on each item, and sometimes to special test items. As a general summary, in many experiments of artificial category learning, exemplar theories predict the results better. However, there are also a number of phenomena that exemplar models do not appear to explain, such as generalizations made about an entire category (Ross, Perkins, and Tenpenny 1990) or the hierarchical structure of categories (animal, mammal, dog, terrier; see Murphy 2002: ch. 7). Furthermore, some have argued that experimental settings in which the same exemplars are presented over and over are exactly the conditions in which one would expect people to memorize exemplars, and such circumstances may not always be present in everyday life. See Smith and Minda (1998) and Nosofsky and Johansen (2000) for a detailed analysis of the exemplar–prototype issue, and Murphy (2002) for more background.

One reason that the debate between prototypes and exemplar models has continued is that prototype models seem most compatible with work from the second strand of concept research (reviewed later), which investigates higher-level knowledge. This is because one's knowledge about the world is generally stated in terms of entire classes (e.g., all living things must breathe or perform gas exchange of some kind) rather than in terms of encountered exemplars (my pet squirrel breathes). Many researchers have gone on to investigate specific topics of interest without necessarily committing to either the prototype or exemplar view, so progress can be made in understanding other aspects of concepts even without agreement on this basic issue. The next section discusses prominent models of category learning from both perspectives.

8.3 Formal models

We have described in broad strokes the core theories in the psychology of concepts. But there are formal versions of these theories that spell out what is meant by *prototypes* or *exemplars*. Computational models make specific predictions about how often a person will make errors, how fast they can respond, what type of information they use when making a response, and how long it will take to learn a novel category. Applying a model to human categorization data – response times (RTs), classification responses, or error rates – typically involves "fitting" free parameters in the model to the data. That is, the researcher will adjust the variables in the model so that the model behaves as closely to human behavior as possible. Each model's *goodness of fit* to the experimental data is used to determine which one is best.

8.3.1 Models of classification

We begin with Medin and Schaffer's (1978) *context model* (CM), the first formalization of exemplar theory, to provide a sense for how computational models in categorization research work. Imagine a universe of items that differ in three ways – large or small, blue or yellow, and triangle or square. The features blue and yellow, or large and small, are said to compose the *dimensions* of color and size, respectively.

The model calculates similarity between category items by scoring matches and mismatches along dimensions. Whereas matches are scored as 1, mismatches are given a value between 0 and 1. The exact value (i.e., how much the mismatch reduces similarity) is a parameter and can change depending on the learner or the particular dimension. Another way to think about the value of a mismatch is in terms of how important a dimension is for people's classifications. In the CM, these mismatch values are low when there is an important mismatch that reduces overall similarity.

As a concrete example, we calculate the similarity between a large blue square and a small yellow square, assuming that the decision weights are 0.5, 0.25, and 0.25 for the three dimensions, respectively. The first two dimensions mismatch, so they contribute 0.5 and 0.25 to the similarity calculation, and the last dimension matches, so it contributes a 1.0. According to the CM, the values are multiplied, yielding a similarity of: $0.5 \times 0.25 \times 1.0 = 0.125$. Because of the multiplication, two or three mismatching values can lower similarity greatly. In general, exemplar models weigh close similarity among exemplars heavily, and moderate similarity does not count for much.

Similarity calculations provide the basis for determining whether a person is likely to classify an item, call it X, into one or another category. To do so, one calculates the similarity between X and each exemplar in Categories A and B. Similarities are summed, producing an overall similarity between X and Category A (Sim$A$) and between X and Category B (Sim$B$). Finally, the model uses a choice rule – a weighing of evidence – to calculate the probability a person will classify an X into Category A:

$$P(A|X) = \mathrm{Sim}\,A/(\mathrm{Sim}\,A + \mathrm{Sim}\,B).$$

That is, the probability of choosing Category A given X is the similarity to Category A compared to the similarity to all categories (in this case Categories A and B).

This choice rule can also be used by formalizations of prototype theory, with similarity calculations made between a test item and category prototypes (lists of features characterizing each category).

Despite formal differences, exemplar and prototype models can be difficult to distinguish using empirical data. Proponents of each have succeeded in designing clever experiments demonstrating how one or the other model provides a superior fit to human classification data. While there are notable exceptions, the exemplar model generally seems to do the best in accounting for category-learning experiments.

Although prototype theorists acknowledge that people may memorize exemplars, they argue that exemplars will become the basis of category representations only under conditions typically found in experiments, when categories contain few members or when the same exemplars are viewed repeatedly. To demonstrate this, Minda and Smith (2001) taught subjects categories of bugs. In one category a bug might have had a short body, round head, green eyes and long legs, whereas one in the opposite category might have had a long body, oval head, red eyes and short legs. They examined the effect of varying the number of category exemplars (10 vs. 30) and stimulus dimensions (four vs. eight). They found that increasing either factor improved the fit of the prototype model to subjects' data, and thus revived the idea that people may abstract prototypes when categories are large or contain many features.

Such findings have led to *mixture models* that involve both prototype extraction and exemplar learning (e.g., Smith and Minda 2000). The processes are mixed with varying proportions controlled by free parameters. Such models can account for any mixture of prototype and exemplar learning behavior. Although these models might be viewed as having too much flexibility to make strong predictions, it seems likely that people are also flexible in how they learn categories.

One limitation of the early exemplar, prototype, and mixture models is that they describe classification only at a fixed level of performance. They do not explain how classification unfolds over time, how exemplars are stored, how decision weights are learned, or how the category label becomes linked to a concept. Although these models still motivate research, they cannot explain why humans adopt a prototype or exemplar strategy or how they discover a concept's distinguishing features.

8.3.2   Process models

Some categorization models are not fixed-performance models; they describe the category-learning process itself, explaining classification performance over the course of learning rather than at the endpoint. In so doing, they attempt to explain how decision weights arise, or how categorizers learn that certain exemplars become associated to the other category. Thus, process models attempt to explain category learning in more detail than fixed-performance models described earlier.

Kruschke's (1992) attention learning covering map, ALCOVE, is a successful process model. It combines exemplar representations and similarity calculations with a network-learning algorithm known as backpropagation. Networks are systems of connections that vary in their strength or *weights* (see Chapters 3 and 12). ALCOVE learns to associate exemplars to category labels by updating those association weights. A high association weight means that an exemplar is closely linked to a category label, whereas a low association weight means that the network is less certain about an exemplar's category membership. ALCOVE also uses *attention weights*, which function much like the decision weights described earlier in the CM by altering the influence that particular dimensions have on the network's classification decisions. The network learns to "attend" to the most informative dimensions by adjusting its attention weights. As such, ALCOVE improves on earlier exemplar models, where associations between exemplar and category are input directly by the modeler, and decision weights are selected so that the model's classification behavior closely matches the human's. By contrast, ALCOVE's exemplar associations and attention weights are learned by gradient descent on error during learning. In other words, it changes weights to reduce classification errors by the greatest amount. The updating of ALCOVE's association and attention weights makes specific predictions about how humans might attend to the stimulus while learning.

The rule-plus-exception model, or RULEX (Nosofsky, Palmeri, and McKinley 1994), is another process model, based on the premise that people are attempting to learn rules that determine categories. (Unlike the classical view, RULEX does not assume that categories necessarily can be learned by such rules.) Beginning with the simplest hypothesis, it searches for the category's necessary and sufficient features by looking for a single dimension rule to classify a set of exemplars perfectly. If this fails (i.e., the model continues to make classification errors), it tries a different single dimension, and then multiple dimensions. Hypothesis testing continues in search of a perfect rule. If none is found, it uses imperfect rules and memorizes exceptions (and hence is a mixed model as well). RULEX can account for fundamental classification-learning phenomena, including typicality effects and effects of category complexity (Nosofsky et al. 1994). Its success comes from its inherent flexibility as a mixed model, in that it can both test rules and memorize exemplars.

The popularity of mixture models of different kinds reflects a growing assumption that multiple processes operate during classification learning (Ashby *et al.* 1998; Erickson and Kruschke 1998; Nosofsky, Clark, and Shin 1989). Nevertheless, many resist models of increasing complexity in favor of simpler theories, arguing that mixed models can account for any data without making strong predictions in advance. It seems likely that mixed models will become more successful when they are better able to explain when the different component processes are used, i.e., exactly what determines the mixture.

Love, Medin, and Gureckis' (2004) SUSTAIN model is an example of a single-process network model that behaves at first as if it is learning simple rules, increasing the complexity of its internal representation of the category as needed. SUSTAIN belongs to a class of models known as *clustering algorithms*, which gradually build mental clusters of objects as they are exposed to new items. Each cluster corresponds to a concept or subconcept, and each is associated to a category name. (Multiple clusters may be associated to the same name.) Even though SUSTAIN is a single-process model, it has a surprising amount of flexibility. It starts off with the smallest number of clusters (one) and adds clusters when the existing ones fail to classify a new item correctly. Thus, its representations change based on the experienced category structure. It can act like a prototype-based model if the category structure allows it or like an exemplar model (with many clusters) if the category structure requires it.

8.3.3   New sources of data

The complexity and sophistication of categorization models forces researchers to search for new sources of data. By adjusting parameters, flexible models can provide a good fit to almost any pattern of classification data. A mixture model, for example, can mimic any combination of prototype abstraction and exemplar memorization, and SUSTAIN can adjust how readily it forms new clusters. This is why finding other sources of data, besides classification responses, has become increasingly important to discriminate the models. For example, Nosofsky and Palmeri (1997) measured subjects' RTs as they repeatedly classified 12 colored squares into 2 categories. The experiment involved 1,800 trials which learners completed over the course of five days. They developed a model to not only account for average RTs but also for the rate at which those RTs decreased with practice.

Rehder and Hoffman (2005) provided a new source of data to evaluate models of category learning, namely, eye fixations. By measuring which stimulus dimensions people fixated during learning, they were able to estimate the attention that people gave to different dimensions, thereby evaluating models that make predictions about attention (e.g., ALCOVE and prototype models). When people are hypothesis testing, they tend to focus on the dimensions that are in their hypothesis. When people are learning exemplars, they tend to look at all the dimensions of a stimulus. It is likely that measures such as eye fixations, RTs, and learning curves will form an important part of future work evaluating different models.

8.3.4   Objections and limitations

Models of category learning have not been very extendable to different uses of concepts. For example, concepts allow us not only to identify classes of objects, but they can also be combined to form new concepts. You may not have heard of a *shoe magnet* (because we just invented it) but you may have some idea of what it might be. It is difficult to see how exemplar models, as currently formulated, can explain what a shoe magnet is, if it isn't the intersection of shoes and magnets (Murphy 1988).

Further limitations stem from using artificial concepts with little connection to previously acquired ones. This makes modeling easier, by removing factors that are difficult to represent formally. But as a result, most models ignore the influence of other concepts on learning. Nonetheless, considerable research has investigated the influence of prior knowledge on learning, as we review next.

8.4 Influences of knowledge

Most experiments that investigate basic learning processes are part of the first strand of concept research; they use artificially constructed categories that do not make contact with known concepts. The assumption is that this kind of learning is present in all concept acquisition, but it might be masked by particular things that people know. Therefore, it is methodologically purest to study learning with "neutral" stimuli such as geometric figures, dot patterns, cartoon-like animals, and so on in simple situations where category learning is the only task. That assumption does not deny that people may use their prior knowledge about the world to help learn new concepts or that people's goals influence how a concept is acquired. What the first strand of concept research does seem to assume, however, is that the same basic learning processes are involved and that findings in artificial category learning will still be found in more realistic settings. There is reason to question this assumption.

Experiments in the second strand of research have looked at the use of prior knowledge by comparing the learning of categories that make contact with existing knowledge to the learning of formally identical categories that do not. For example, Murphy and Allopenna (1994) compared categories constructed from three different kinds of features. One set of categories was made up of typographical symbols like !, #, and %. Another set of categories was made up of English phrases, like "eats meat" and "made in Norway," but these phrases were unrelated to one another. A third set was made up of the same phrases, but in each category, the phrases combined to describe a coherent kind of object. For example, features like "eats meat," "has sharp teeth," and "lives alone" were properties of one category that could be thought of as a predator. A contrast category had properties of prey, such as "eats plants," "has flat teeth," and "lives in groups." Murphy and Allopenna found that the first two types of categories were equally difficult to learn. Using English phrases did not make category learning any easier than the arbitrary typographical symbols, so mere meaningfulness of the features did not seem very important. But the final type was much easier to learn. When the phrases could be linked together by a common theme, people apparently identified that theme and then used it to guide further learning of the category. Later research has shown that such effects are powerful, finding that even if a minority of a concept's features are connected by a common theme, category learning still benefits (Kaplan and Murphy 2000).

This work is significant in helping to explain how it is that people learn concepts so quickly in everyday life. In many experiments, category learning is slow and often not completed by the end of the experiment. Yet, children learn thousands of new concepts without explicit study. One reason may be that most unknown concepts in life are often related to already-known concepts, either by being similar to them (e.g., if you know *lion* and *cat*, *panther* is not very different) or by being related to more general knowledge (e.g., basic knowledge of biology can help one understand a new animal).

A theoretically critical question about knowledge effects is whether basic findings with artificial categories are replicated when concepts are related to prior knowledge. In some cases, they are not. For example, in a classic study, Wattenmaker *et al.* (1986) compared two different kinds of category structures – those that are *linearly separable* vs. those that are not. Linearly separable categories can be learned by an additive combination of their properties, as in most prototype theories. That is, a learner can learn which features are typical of a category, and make classification decisions based on how many of those features it possesses. Nonlinearly separable categories do not necessarily have typical features, and, therefore, one must learn specific feature configurations, or memorize exemplars. For example, young children might learn that mammals tend to have four legs, fur, walk, and so on. But dolphins and whales do not have enough of such features, and so the category of mammals cannot be represented by such a list.

Linear separability is a purely formal aspect of category structures, and much research has shown that it does not consistently influence category-learning difficulty (which turns out to be consistent with exemplar theory, for reasons beyond the scope of this discussion). But Wattenmaker *et al.* showed that one could vary the *content* of the category to make learning one or the other kind of structure harder. That is, sometimes the category's meaning suggested that the configuration of features was relevant, and sometimes not. Nonlinearly separable categories were easier to learn in the former case but linearly separable categories were easier in the latter. Another basic finding is that categories are typically harder to learn when they involve a disjunction of features (e.g., tall-OR-blond) then when they involve a conjunction of features (tall-AND-blond). Pazzani (1991) showed that prior knowledge could change the relative ease of learning disjunctive and conjunctive categories.

In both these cases, formal models of category learning (including versions of prototype and exemplar theories) could not account for the results. Either a given structure is easy to learn or it is difficult – formal models cannot change their processing based on the content of the category. Such findings have not had the effect that one might expect, of causing researchers to drop their purely formal models or to attempt to expand them to encompass these knowledge effects. Instead, they have encouraged the split between what we are calling the two strands of concept research. That is, (most) researchers with formal models continue to study the detailed learning process with artificial materials, and (most) researchers interested in prior knowledge have examined knowledge effects without developing a detailed model of the learning process. However, there are some signs that this situation is slowly improving, as computational models that include both artificial category learning and knowledge effects have recently been constructed (Heit and Bott 2000; Rehder and Murphy 2003).

Another important issue in recent research concerns the concept-learning task itself. In most experiments, people are placed into an overt category-learning situation and are instructed to learn one or (most often) two categories, by repeatedly classifying examples. However, in many cases, people may encounter category members while doing something else. Ross (1997) found that when people encountered examples as part of a problem-solving task, the concepts they formed were dependent on the processing they did to solve the problem. People learned different things about the same items, depending on how they were used in the task. Yamauchi and Markman (1998) gave people a different learning task, feature inference. Subjects viewed a partial exemplar with its category name provided, and they had to decide which of two properties it had. Other subjects viewed whole exemplars and had to decide which of two category names it had (the usual task). Although both groups learned the categories, the feature inference group learned more of the properties, and they also did not restrict their attention to properties that discriminated the two categories. The category-learning group tended to learn the critical features that distinguished the categories but did not learn other properties as well. Most models of category learning predict the latter result, because they were designed to explain the typical classification task. But when concepts are acquired in some other way, their assumptions may not be correct (see Markman and Ross 2003 for a review).

One computational model that attempts to account for some of these results is Rogers and McClelland's (2004) *parallel distributed processing* (PDP) model of people's knowledge of the world, or *semantic cognition*, as they call it. It does so by representing properties and names in a large associative network. When the model experiences a yellow singing canary with wings, the relevant properties (yellow, singing, has wings) and name (canary) are activated within the network, and the model learns to associate them to one another. In this model, there is no single concept that represents birds or shirts or parties. Instead, knowledge of the world is the set of associations among properties, out of which conceptual behavior arises.

To give a simplified idea of how this complex model works, imagine that you saw something with wings fly past your window. The properties of wings and flying would be activated in your semantic network, giving rise to other features associated with the ones you observed, such as feathers, living in nest, having a beak, and so on. Names related to those features such as *bird* or *pigeon* might also be activated. Thus, you could classify the object and make inferences about its other features through the learned associations.

What is intriguing about this approach is that it says your inference about these features is not done by an overt classification. That is, you did not say, "Hmmm, that must be a bird, and so I imagine that it has feathers, lives in a nest..." You do not explicitly represent a concept of birds – the concept of birds emerges out of all the associations you have learned. Rogers and McClelland's approach is difficult to compare to the other models of concepts we have been discussing because it focuses on different phenomena. It does not address the mass of data on category learning, for example, but looks at knowledge effects and the effect of dementia on one's knowledge of the world, which most categorization models do not. Perhaps future development of each approach will result in models that explain both kinds of data.

8.5   Conceptual development

Conceptual development concerns the origins and changes in concepts from birth through adulthood. Much research in this domain has come from the second strand, focusing on real-world concepts and their interaction with the things that the child knows. One reason for this is that children cannot do the category-learning experiments that adults are subjected to. But perhaps the strongest reason is that the second strand speaks more to central issues in cognitive development than do experiments on learning artificial rules or exemplar memorization.

At the youngest ages tested, infants appear to form concepts and use information from past experiences with objects to understand new objects. Because of their lack of behavioral control, this has been shown primarily through measures of looking and attending. For example, if one shows an infant pictures of cats, it will look at them avidly. After a while, if one gives the infant the chance to look at a new cat or a new dog, the infant will prefer the dog (Quinn, Eimas, and Rosenkrantz 1993). Since both pictures are new, this preference suggests that the infant has noted that the cat is similar to and the dog is different from the previous stimuli. That is, the infant has generalized from experienced category members to a new member.

This kind of evidence is somewhat indirect, and the infant cannot tell us exactly what it is thinking, and in particular whether it conceives of the cats as forming a coherent category. Some have suggested that the infant's ability to discriminate images of cats and dogs does not represent true conceptual ability, but only perceptual-motor learning (e.g., Mandler 2004). This view is primarily a matter of skepticism about infants' abilities, as direct evidence for it is not very strong. Nonetheless, one cannot be sure just what the infant is thinking about the pictures of the cats, and whether its knowledge could serve some conceptual function other than directing attention.

One basic function of concepts is induction. If you know that cats like tuna, then you can infer that a new cat you have met will like tuna, even absent any experience with that cat's taste preferences. Baldwin, Markman, and Melartin (1993) reasoned that if children can draw such inferences, then they have one of the main functions that concepts subserve. Although they could not test the youngest infants tested in the looking tasks (3- and 4-month-olds), they were able to study children as young as 9 months. In a clever experiment, they exposed the children to novel toys that had a surprising property (e.g., making a sound or coming apart unexpectedly). Then they gave the children a clearly different exemplar of the same category and videotaped their behavior. Children who had seen the surprising property of the toy attempted to repeat it in the new exemplar (e.g., they tried to make the sound); those who had not, did not. Thus, the children expected this new item to have a property that was not directly visible, based on their prior experience with the category. That is, they showed true conceptual behavior, and not just changes in their visual attention as a skeptical view would have predicted.

In summary, children seem to have conceptual abilities as young as we can measure them. Unfortunately, it is not possible to measure every conceptual ability at every age. However, there is little specific reason to doubt that even very young children can form concepts. Of course, they lack experience (that they will later gain) with many categories of objects, and they also lack the understanding of many aspects of the world that are necessary to form accurate concepts. But these deficiencies do not seem to reflect a problem with concept learning. Indeed, researchers have suggested that infants' knowledge about the physical world (gravity, solidity of objects, and so on) may begin as a set of event categories that represent expected kinds of outcomes (e.g., when something is knocked off the table, it falls to the ground; Baillargeon 1998). Moreover, aspects of vocabulary learning can be attributed to processes of conceptual development (Gelman and Byrnes 1991). Thus, concept formation may be essential to infants' learning and communicating about the world they live in, rather than being a later developing process.

Another important topic of research in conceptual development concerns how children's concepts reflect their beliefs about the world around them. Children's concepts of animals reflect what they believe about biological kinds; their concepts of actions reflect their understanding of social conventions and psychological processes; and their concepts of substances and elements reflect their understanding of chemical–physical structure. For this reason, studies of children's concepts of some domain are often carried out by researchers who are more interested in the domain itself (e.g., children's understanding of biology or social relations) than in concepts.

An important theme in this work is *psychological essentialism*. Medin and Ortony (1989) argued that people believe that there is an invisible, underlying essence or causal mechanism that is common to all category members and that is responsible for their superficial properties. Claims of actual essentialism have been largely rejected in the sciences, but nonetheless, people tend to believe that every dog has something inside that makes it a dog.

There has been considerable interest in whether children believe in essences. One notable test of this idea was performed by Keil (1989). He used a transformation paradigm in which animals and objects began as one kind of thing and then were changed to be more like something else. For example, children were shown pictures of a raccoon that was dyed, operated on, and generally mistreated until it had the superficial properties of a skunk. Keil found that both children and adults, after the age of 4, agreed that the animal was still a raccoon. Even though it looked (and smelled) exactly like a skunk, subjects agreed that its category could not be changed by such operations. Presumably, this reflects that the raccoon's essence is an internal property, which cannot be changed by dyeing and other superficial transformations. Similarly, Gelman and Wellman (1991) found that if a pig were raised by cows, eating and living like a cow, children believed it would still be a pig and would have pig parts.

Not everything has an essence. Keil discovered that performing "operations" on artifacts did actually change their identity, both for adults and children. Thus, people are not simply averse to entities changing their identities, but they view some changes as impossible because the object's essence is not affected.

Belief in an essence is one way to explain the belief in category-based induction. Why should we expect two dogs to have the same heart structure or the same gut enzymes? What permits generalization from one category member to another? If the category members share an essence, then they have a common mechanism that can give rise to the shared properties. For example, perhaps genetic structure leads to a particular heart morphology. There has been much interest in children's use of categories in induction, largely spurred by Ellen Markman and Susan Gelman's work (reviewed in Markman 1989).

In an early study, Gelman and Markman contrasted perceptual similarity with category membership as the basis for induction. For example, they might tell a child that a depicted bird (flamingo) feeds its babies bugs, and a depicted bat feeds its babies milk. Then they were asked about another bird that looked much like the bat (and nothing like the flamingo). Children generally said that this bird also fed its babies bugs, like the other, dissimilar bird. Thus, category membership overrode perceptual similarity in making the induction. However, Gelman, and Markman also showed that similarity is still important, as induction became stronger when the perceptual similarity between category members increased. There has recently arisen a debate about how much children's induction relies on perceptual similarity, with some authors arguing that it is more dependent on similarity and less on category membership or shared essence (Sloutsky and Fisher 2004). The debate is not yet settled, but it does not seem that the evidence yet overturns the basic finding that category membership confers a belief in induction above and beyond any perceptual factors. However, induction probably *should* be based on both perceptual and conceptual factors, and it is possible that development consists to some degree of learning to coordinate those two sources.

8.6   Conclusions about knowledge effects

The research programs discussed in sections 8.4 and 8.5 are diverse, but they are consistent in exposing limitations of the traditional category-learning paradigm. In ordinary learning, we usually do not encounter exemplar after exemplar of a category over and over for minutes at a time. Sometimes encounters are separated by weeks or months. We usually do not label all these objects and have those labels immediately corrected by someone else if we make an error. If a teacher is available, this person will often describe or attempt to define the category, rather than simply providing feedback on our labeling, and for children, such verbal interaction can greatly aid learning (e.g., Mervis 1987; Waxman, Shipley, and Shepperson 1991). Often people *interact* with the objects they classify, as Ross (1997) noted in his work, rather than simply labeling. Perhaps they use the new tool they have just encountered or play with the new kind of dog or eat the new food. And new concepts usually are not totally isolated from the things we know about the world. Perhaps they are new animals, and we already know many animals and know much about biology in general. Or they are a new form of technology, based on physical principles, functions, and user interfaces of older technological devices.

A major challenge for future research will be to discover more about how concepts are learned under more realistic situations and to integrate this with what has been learned from constrained experimental settings. In some cases, the learning process and representations formed must be rather different from the traditional case. If one only sees four exemplars of an object, spread across two years, one cannot very easily extract a prototype of that category. If one is told verbal information about that entire category, then this might be used to classify future members; but this would be prototype information rather than a memory for an individual exemplar. Thus, the traditional distinctions between different theories of concepts may have to be broken down in order to provide a complete explanation. Or, we will have to explain how it is that bits and pieces of different kinds of information (a few facts one has been told, memory of two exemplars, knowledge of the domain in general) are combined in order to produce conceptual behavior. That goal is still far from being achieved.

8.7   Conclusions

Much has been learned about the psychology of concepts over the past decades, but this does not mean that agreement has been reached about exactly how concepts are represented. Progress has been in the form of an accumulation of important phenomena, the better understanding of specific issues and problems, and an increasing recognition that this domain is an extremely rich and complex one, and that the psychology of concepts will likely be correspondingly complex. There is no single type of concept or single way of learning and representing concepts. Indeed, it is remarkable that almost every study that has looked at individuals (rather than averaging over groups) has found that people differ in how they learn (e.g., Malt 1989; Smith, Murray, and Minda 1997). More and more often, formal models of category learning are turning to mixtures of different processes, with the hope that they can predict when one form of learning (rule testing, prototype extraction, exemplar learning) is preferred. Thus, it seems likely that progress in understanding concepts will not come about through the rejection of possibilities and the field settling down to a single agreed-upon model, but that progress will involve the inclusion of diverse forms of learning and representation, with a better understanding of when each one is used and how these different forms are coordinated.

We have suggested that there are currently two very different strands of research that investigate concepts, one focusing on formal aspects of categories and studying artificial category-learning, the other focusing on the content of concepts and how learning and judgment interact with prior knowledge. Clearly, there must be further integration of these two strands before we can say that we have a coherent idea of how concepts are formed. That goal is still far off, but at least some investigators are working to combine the two.

Further reading

Reviews of the field

Ahn, W., Goldstone, R. L., Love, B. C., Markman, A. B., and Wolff, P. (eds.) (2005). *Categorization Inside and Outside the Lab: Essays in Honor of Douglas Medin.* Washington, DC: APA. An interesting collection of articles from a cross-section of the field.

Ashby, F. G. and Maddox, W. T. (2005). Human category learning, *Annual Review of Psychology* 56, 149–78. There are relatively few reviews or book-length collections of what we have called the first strand of research, the experiments and models with artificial categories. This is one exception, with a focus on neuropsychological data.

Markman, A. B. (1999). *Knowledge Representation.* Mahwah, NJ: Lawrence Erlbaum. Provides a detailed analysis of the mental representation of features, prototypes, and exemplars, among other things.

Murphy, G. L. (2002). *The Big Book of Concepts.* Cambridge, MA: MIT Press. The most extensive recent review of the field.

Smith, E. E. and Medin, D. L. (1981). *Categories and Concepts*. Cambridge, MA: Harvard University Press. An earlier book that is still worth reading for its analysis of the classical view and early prototype theory.

Development and breakdown

Carey, S. (2009). *The Origin of Concepts*. Oxford University Press. A true tour de force. It focuses primarily on higher-level concepts (such as number), making an important contribution to understanding the interaction of innate and learned influences.

Gelman, S. A. (2003). *The Essential Child: Origins of Essentialism in Everyday Thought*. Oxford University Press. Gelman discusses her work on psychological essentialism and how it influences concept and word learning.

Keil, F. C. (1989). *Concepts, Kinds, and Cognitive Development*. Cambridge, MA: MIT.

Markman, E. M. (1989). *Categorization and Naming in Children: Problems of Induction*. Cambridge, MA: MIT Press. Although the Keil and Markman books are a bit dated, they are thoughtful, well-written, and still useful as introductions to basic issues of the development of concepts.

Rogers, T. T. and McClelland, J. L. (2004). *Semantic Cognition: A Parallel Distributed Processing Approach*. Cambridge, MA: MIT Press. A detailed description of their model and data on how knowledge is acquired in childhood and declines with brain damage.

References

Ashby, F. G., Alfonso-Reese, L. A., Turken, A. U., and Waldron, E. M. (1998). A neuropsychological theory of multiple systems in category learning, *Psychological Review* 105: 442–81.

Baillargeon, R. (1998). Infants' understanding of the physical world, in M. Sabourin, F. Craik, and M. Robert (eds.), *Advances in Psychological Science*, vol. 2: *Biological and Cognitive Aspects* (pp. 503–29). London: Psychology Press.

Baldwin, D. A., Markman, E. M., and Melartin, R. L. (1993). Infants' ability to draw inferences about nonobvious object properties: Evidence from exploratory play, *Child Development* 64: 711–28.

Bruner, J. S., Goodnow, J. J., and Austin, G. A. (1956). *A Study of Thinking*. New York: Wiley.

Erickson, M. A. and Kruschke, J. K. (1998). Rules and exemplars in category learning, *Journal of Experimental Psychology: General* 127: 107–40.

Gelman, S. A. and Byrnes, J. P. (eds.) (1991). *Perspectives on Language and Thought: Interrelations in Development*. Cambridge University Press.

Gelman, S. A. and Wellman, H. M. (1991). Insides and essences: Early understandings of the non-obvious, *Cognition* 38: 213–44.

Hampton, J. A. (1995). Testing the prototype theory of concepts, *Journal of Memory and Language* 34: 686–708.

Heit, E. and Bott, L. (2000). Knowledge selection in category learning, in D. L. Medin (ed.), *Psychology of Learning and Motivation* (pp. 163–99). San Diego: Academic Press.

Kaplan, A. S. and Murphy, G. L. (2000). Category learning with minimal prior knowledge, *Journal of Experimental Psychology: Learning, Memory, and Cognition* 26: 829–46.

Keil, F. C. (1989). *Concepts, Kinds, and Cognitive Development*. Cambridge, MA: MIT Press.

Kruschke, J. K. (1992). ALCOVE: An exemplar-based connectionist model of category learning, *Psychological Review* 99: 22–44.

Love, B. C., Medin, D. L., and Gureckis, T. M. (2004). SUSTAIN: A network model of category learning, *Psychological Review* 111: 309–32.

Malt, B. C. (1989). An on-line investigation of prototype and exemplar strategies in classification, *Journal of Experimental Psychology: Learning, Memory, and Cognition* 15: 539–55.

Mandler, J. M. (2004). *The Foundations of Mind: Origins of Conceptual Thought*. Oxford University Press.

Markman, A. B. and Ross, B. H. (2003). Category use and category learning, *Psychological Bulletin* 129: 592–613.

Markman, E. M. (1989). *Categorization and Naming in Children: Problems of Induction*. Cambridge, MA: MIT Press.

McCloskey, M. E. and Glucksberg, S. (1978). Natural categories: Well defined or fuzzy sets? *Memory & Cognition* 6: 462–72.

Medin, D. L. and Ortony, A. (1989). Psychological essentialism, in S. Vosniadou and A. Ortony (eds.), *Similarity and Analogical Reasoning* (pp. 179–95). Cambridge University Press.

Medin, D. L. and Schaffer, M. M. (1978). Context theory of classification learning, *Psychological Review* 85: 207–38.

Mervis, C. B. (1987). Child-basic object categories and early lexical development, in U. Neisser (ed.), *Concepts and Conceptual Development: Ecological and Intellectual Factors in Categorization* (pp. 201–33). Cambridge University Press.

Minda, J. P. and Smith, J. D. (2001). Prototypes in category learning: The effects of category size, category structure, and stimulus complexity, *Journal of Experimental Psychology: Learning, Memory, and Cognition* 27: 775–99.

Murphy, G. L. (1988). Comprehending complex concepts, *Cognitive Science* 12: 529–62.

   (2002). *The Big Book of Concepts*. Cambridge, MA: MIT Press.

   (2005). The study of concepts inside and outside the lab: Medin vs. Medin, in W. Ahn, R. L. Goldstone, B. C. Love, A. B. Markman, and P. Wolff (eds.), *Categorization Inside and Outside the Lab: Essays in Honor of Douglas Medin* (pp. 179–95). Washington, DC: APA.

Murphy, G. L. and Allopenna, P. D. (1994). The locus of knowledge effects in concept learning, *Journal of Experimental Psychology: Learning, Memory, and Cognition* 20: 904–19.

Nosofsky, R. M., Clark, S. E., and Shin, H. J. (1989). Rules and exemplars in categorization, identification, and recognition, *Journal of Experimental Psychology: Learning Memory and Cognition* 15: 282–304.

Nosofsky, R. M. and Johansen, M. K. (2000). Exemplar-based accounts of "multiple-system" phenomena in perceptual categorization, *Psychonomic Bulletin & Review* 7: 375–402.

Nosofsky, R. M. and Palmeri, T. J. (1997). An exemplar-based random walk model of speeded categorization, *Psychological Review* 104: 266–300.

Nosofsky, R. M., Palmeri, T. J., and McKinley, S. C. (1994). Rule-plus-exception model of classification learning, *Psychological Review* 101: 53–79.

Pazzani, M. J. (1991). Influence of prior knowledge on concept acquisition: Experimental and computational results, *Journal of Experimental Psychology: Learning, Memory, and Cognition*, 17: 416–32.

Quinn, P. C., Eimas, P. D., and Rosenkrantz, S. L. (1993). Evidence for representations of perceptually similar natural categories by 3-month-old and 4-month-old infants, *Perception* 22: 463–75.

Rehder, B. and Hoffman, A. B. (2005). Eyetracking and selective attention in category learning, *Cognitive Psychology* 51: 1–41.

Rehder, B. and Murphy, G. L. (2003). A knowledge-resonance (KRES) model of knowledge-based category learning, *Psychonomic Bulletin & Review* 10: 759–84.

Rogers, T. T. and McClelland, J. L. (2004). *Semantic Cognition: A Parallel Distributed Processing Approach*. Cambridge, MA: MIT Press.

Rosch, E. (1975). Cognitive representations of semantic categories, *Journal of Experimental Psychology: General* 104: 192–233.

Rosch, E. and Mervis, C. B. (1975). Family resemblance: Studies in the internal structure of categories, *Cognitive Psychology* 7: 573–605.

Rosch, E., Mervis, C. B., Gray, W., Johnson, D., and Boyes-Braem, P. (1976). Basic objects in natural categories, *Cognitive Psychology* 8: 382–439.

Ross, B. H. (1997). The use of categories affects classification, *Journal of Memory and Language* 37: 240–67.

Ross, B. H., Perkins, S. J., and Tenpenny, P. L. (1990). Reminding-based category learning, *Cognitive Psychology* 22: 460–92.

Sloutsky, V. M. and Fisher, A. V. (2004). When development and learning decrease memory, *Psychological Science* 15: 553–8.

Smith, E. E. and Medin, D. L. (1981). *Categories and Concepts*. Cambridge, MA: Harvard University Press.

Smith, J. D. and Minda, J. P. (1998). Prototypes in the mist: The early epochs of category learning, *Journal of Experimental Psychology: Learning, Memory, and Cognition* 24: 1411–36.

(2000). Thirty categorization results in search of a model, *Journal of Experimental Psychology: Learning, Memory, and Cognition* 26: 3–27.

Smith, J. D., Murray, M. J., Jr., and Minda, J. P. (1997). Straight talk about linear separability, *Journal of Experimental Psychology: Learning, Memory, and Cognition* 23: 659–80.

Wattenmaker, W. D., Dewey, G. I., Murphy, T. D., and Medin, D. L. (1986). Linear separability and concept learning: Context, relational properties, and concept naturalness, *Cognitive Psychology* 18: 158–94.

Waxman, S. R., Shipley, E. F., and Shepperson, B. (1991). Establishing new subcategories: The role of category labels and existing knowledge, *Child Development* 62: 127–38.

Yamauchi, T. and Markman, A. B. (1998). Category learning by inference and categorization, *Journal of Memory and Language* 39: 124–48.

9 Language

Ray Jackendoff

Within cognitive science, language is often set apart (as it is in the present volume) from perception, action, learning, memory, concepts, and reasoning. Yet language is intertwined with all of them. Language perception is a kind of perception; language production is a kind of action. Vocabulary and grammar are learned and stored in long-term memory. As novel utterances are perceived or produced, they are built up in working memory. Concepts are most often studied in the context of word meanings; reasoning is most often studied in the context of inferring one sentence from another.

What makes the study of language different from these other areas of cognitive science is its emphasis on the details of the mental structures deployed in the course of language processing. An entire discipline and methodology, linguistics, is devoted to these structures. The present chapter attempts to integrate linguistic theory with more general concerns of cognitive science.

9.1 Language systems: uses and acquisition

Unlike other communication systems in the natural world, language is a combinatorial system that can express an unlimited number of different messages on the basis of a finite vocabulary. Combinatorially constructed signals do appear in the communication systems of certain primates, birds and cetaceans, but, so far as is known, the messages conveyed are quite limited in character (Hauser 1996). By contrast, the rich combinatoriality of linguistic utterances reflects rich combinatoriality in the messages the utterances convey. Human languages can be used to talk about the weather, the war, philosophy, physics, myth, gossip, and fixing the sink; they can be used to inform, inquire, instruct, command, promise, amuse, seduce, or terrorize. Language is also used as a medium of conscious thought: most humans (at least among the literate) are aware of their thinking primarily through the "stream of consciousness," which is experienced as verbal imagery.

In the context of cognitive science, language is best thought of as a cognitive system within an individual's brain that relates certain aspects of thought to acoustic signals (or, in signed languages, motions of hands and face; in the interests of space we ignore written languages here). In order for a group of individuals to communicate intelligibly, they must have sufficiently similar language systems in their brains. From this point of view, the "English language" is an idealization over the systems in the brains of a community of mutually intelligible speakers. For many purposes, it is convenient to assume that speakers' systems are homogeneous. For other purposes, it is important to recognize differences among speakers, dividing them by dialect (another convenience) or individual idiolect, each corresponding to a slightly different system in speakers' brains. In particular, in studying language acquisition, it is commonplace to treat children as having partially developed systems that deviate in some respects from that of the surrounding community.

Children's acquisition of language has been a central issue in linguistics and psycholinguistics for nearly fifty years. All normal children become fluent speakers of the language(s) spoken in their environment. Given the complexity of linguistic structure, and given the inability of the entire community of trained linguists to describe this structure over a period of decades, it is a major puzzle how children manage to master one or more languages within a few years. The literature calls this puzzle the *poverty of the stimulus*. It has led to the hypothesis that children have an innate predisposition to structure linguistic input in a fashion conducive to discovering the principles of the language(s) they are hearing. The theoretical term for this predisposition is *universal grammar* (UG).

The character of UG has been among the most contentious issues in linguistics for over four decades. There have been many different theories of UG, even by its most outstanding proponent, Noam Chomsky (compare Chomsky 1965, 1981, 1995). In contrast, many researchers claim that there is *no* poverty of the stimulus – that language is entirely learnable from the input – and that little if anything is special about language acquisition (e.g., Elman *et al.* 1996; Tomasello 2003; Bybee and McClelland 2005).

An important demonstration that language is *not* entirely learned from the input comes from two cases in which children have created languages *de novo*. (1) Deaf children whose parents do not use sign language often create a system called Home Sign (Goldin-Meadow 2003). Although Home Signs (every child's is different, of course) are rudimentary by the standards of normal languages, they still display many of the lexical, grammatical, and semantic properties of human languages, and they go well beyond any animal communication system in their expressive range. Notably, the parents are invariably less fluent than their children, showing that the system is genuinely the child's creation. (2) The founding of schools for the deaf in Nicaragua in the middle 1980s created a community of deaf children, none of whom had previously been exposed to a signed language. An indigenous sign language quickly emerged, created by the children. Since then, younger generations of speakers have increased its complexity, sophistication, and fluency, to the extent that

Nicaraguan Sign Language is now regarded as a fairly standard sign language (Kegl, Senghas, and Coppola 1999).

These cases vividly demonstrate that there is something to language acquisition beyond statistical correlation of inputs. The question is not *whether* there is a predisposition to acquire language, but *what* this predisposition consists of. To the extent that it can be subsumed under other cognitive capacities, that is all to the better; but we should not expect that every aspect of language is susceptible to such analysis. This is an empirical issue, not an ideological one (as it has unfortunately often been treated).

9.2   Linguistic structure

In order to appreciate the sophistication of the child's achievement in acquiring language, it is useful to examine all the structure associated with a very simple fragment of English such as the phrase *those purple cows*.

(1) Working memory encoding of *those purple cows*

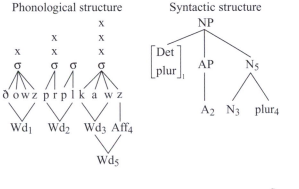

(1) differs somewhat from the way linguistic structure is often presented. It explicitly divides the structure of the phrase into three major domains: phonological (sound) structure, syntactic (grammatical) structure, and semantic (meaning) structure. Phonological structure represents the phrase as a sequence of speech segments or phonemes, here notated in terms of a phonetic alphabet. More explicitly, each segment is encoded in terms of vocal tract configurations: free vs. restricted air flow through the vocal tract (roughly vowel vs. consonant), tongue position, whether the vocal cords are vibrating, the lips are rounded, or the nasal passage is open. The speech segments are collected into syllables (notated by σ). The relative stress on syllables is encoded in

terms of a *metrical grid* of "x"s above the syllables: more "x"s above a syllable indicates higher stress. Not notated in (1) is the intonation contour, which
will partly depend on the phrase's context.

Segments are also grouped in terms of *morphophonology*, notated below
the sequence of segments. This divides the sequence into phonological words
and affixes, which in turn correlate with syntactic and semantic structure.
The correlations are notated in (1) by means of subscripts; for example, the
phonological sequence /prpl/ is coindexed with the Adjective (A) in syntactic
structure and with PURPLE in semantic structure. Morphophonological grouping is distinct from syllabic grouping because they do not always match. For
example, the final *z* in (1) is part of the syllable /kawz/, but morphologically
it is an independent affix, coindexed with plurality in syntax and semantics.

The syntactic structure is a tree structure of the familiar sort, with one
exception. It has always been customary to notate syntactic structures with
words at the bottom, as in (2).

(2)

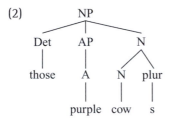

The notation in (1) clarifies which aspects of the structure belong to which
component. It is a phonological fact, not a syntactic fact, that a certain word
is pronounced /prpl/, and a semantic fact that this word denotes a certain
color. The only syntactic aspect of the word is its being an adjective. These
properties of the word are therefore encoded in the appropriate structures and
linked together with a subscript.

One other aspect of the syntactic structure bears mention: the plural suffix
is attached to the noun under a noun node. Such syntactic structure within a
word is its *morphosyntax*, by contrast with *phrasal* syntax, the organization
above the word level.

Syntactic tree structures and their associated phonology are often abbrevi-
ated as a labeled bracketing, e.g., (3).

(3) [$_{NP}$ [$_{Det}$ those] [$_{AP}$ [$_A$ purple]] [$_N$ [$_N$ cow] [$_{plur}$ s]]]

The semantic structure calls for somewhat more commentary. The notations
COW and PURPLE are stand-ins for the concepts 'cow' and 'purple', however
these are mentally encoded. The property PURPLE is embedded as a modifier
of the object COW. The resulting constituent is the meaning of the phrase
purple cow. Plurality is encoded as a function whose argument is the type of

object being pluralized; the output of the function denotes an aggregate made up of such objects. Finally, the determiner *those* designates this aggregate as being pointed out or having been previously referred to; this is notated in semantic structure by DEM ('demonstrative').

This version of semantic structure is based on the approach of *conceptual semantics* (Jackendoff 1983, 1990, 2002); there are many other proposals in the literature for every aspect of this structure (e.g., Heim and Kratzer 1998 for formal semantics, Langacker 1987 for cognitive grammar). For instance, standard logic would represent COW and PURPLE as conjoined predicates, and plurality as some sort of quantifier. In many of the approaches, plurality is a deeply embedded affix in the syntactic structure but the outermost operator in semantic/conceptual structure. Such mismatches in hierarchical organization between syntax and semantics are not atypical. We will return to this issue in section 9.3.

The semantic structure in (1) should be the same for translations of *those purple cows* into any other language, whatever syntactic and phonological structures happen to be correlated with it. Minor nuances of difference may arise: another language's color system may not partition the primary colors the same as English does, or the concept 'cow' may carry different cultural connotations. Nevertheless, the basic structural organization of the semantics remains intact from language to language, and to the extent that translation is accurate, semantic structure is preserved.

(1) implicitly represents a claim that speaking, perceiving, or thinking the phrase *those purple cows* involves constructing this structure in working memory. The exact notation in (1) is not crucial. What *is* crucial is that the brain must make distinctions corresponding to those in (1). In phonological structure, for instance, each segment must be distinguished from every other possible segment in the language; the segments must be arranged linearly; they must be grouped into syllables which are associated with relative stress; the segments must also be grouped into morphological units, in turn grouped into morphological words such as *cows*. Each of the morphophonological units must also be correlated with units of syntactic and semantic structure; this relation parallels the notion of *binding* in neuroscience. Similar distinctions must be made in syntactic and semantic structure. All these distinctions may be made in the same part of the brain, or they may be distributed throughout the brain (or, say, in different parts of Broca's and Wernicke's areas; Hagoort 2005) – an issue for which there is no space in the present chapter.

If the phrase *those purple cows* is used to draw a hearer's attention to cows in the visual environment, the semantic structure undergoes further linking to mental representations that instantiate the viewer's understanding of the scene. Such linkings allow us to talk about what we see (hence, in the philosophical sense, language comes to be *about* something). More generally, semantic structure is language's gateway to perception, reasoning, inference, and the formulation of action.

The division of linguistic structure into phonological, syntactic, and semantic domains leads to a paradoxical observation about so-called conscious thought. As mentioned earlier, we often experience our thought in terms of verbal imagery, the Joycean stream of consciousness. Thought itself – computation in terms of semantic structure – is supposed to be independent of language: it is preserved by translation. Yet the phenomenology is of thinking *in English* (or whatever language). The stream of consciousness has all the characteristics of phonological structure: it has sequenced phonemes grouped into syllables and words, with stress and intonation. By contrast, syntactic structure is not directly present to awareness: experience does not come labeled with categories such as noun and verb. Still less does experience display the organization that any of the various theories of meaning attribute to semantic structure; for example, one does not *experience* plurality as an outermost logical operator. Moreover, unlike meaning, verbal imagery is not invariant regardless of what language one "is thinking in." These observations lead to the surprising hypothesis that the "qualia" associated with conscious thought are primarily phonological rather than semantic – contrary to practically all extant theories of consciousness, which tend to focus on visual awareness (see Jackendoff 1987, 2007a, 2012).

The deep concern with the interlocking details of linguistic structure is what distinguishes the investigation of language from other subdisciplines of cognitive science. Complex structure certainly exists in other cognitive domains. In vision, viewers structure the visual field into grouped configurations of objects, each of which is built of hierarchically configured parts. Each part has its own color and texture, and the parts of animate objects may also have their own independent motion. Similarly, episodic memory is supposed to encode particular events in one's experience; such events must be structured in terms of the spatial, temporal, and social status of their various characters and the interactions among them. However, there is no robust tradition of studying the mental structures involved in vision and episodic memory, as there is in language. This is one reason why the concerns of linguistics often seem distant from the rest of cognitive science.

9.3   Theories of linguistic combinatoriality in syntax and semantics

If the phrase *those purple cows* is novel, i.e., it has not been stored in memory as a unit, how is it constructed from parts that *are* stored in memory?

Clearly the word *cow* is stored in memory. It involves a pronunciation linked with a meaning and the syntactic feature *Noun* (plus, in a language like Spanish, grammatical gender). This could be notated as (4): a coindexed triple of phonological, syntactic, and semantic structure (binding indices are random numbers).

(4) Long-term memory encoding of *cow*

Phonological structure	Syntactic structure	Semantic structure
kaw_3	N_3	COW_3

Some words will also contain sociolinguistic annotations, for example formal vs. informal register (e.g., *colleague* and *isn't* vs. *buddy* and *ain't*). A bilingual speaker must also have annotations that indicate which language the word belongs to. Some words lack one of these components. *Ouch* and *phooey* have phonology and meaning but do not participate in syntactic combination, hence lack syntactic features. The *it* in *it's snowing* and the *of* in *a picture of Bill* have no semantic content and just serve as grammatical glue; thus they have phonology and syntax but no semantic structure.

However, a store of words is not enough: a mechanism is necessary for combining stored pieces into phrases. There have been two major lines of approach. The first, inspired in part by neural modeling and the behavior of semantic memory, tends to judge the success of analyses by their ability to identify statistical regularities in texts (e.g., Landauer *et al.*'s 2007 *latent semantic analysis*) or to predict the next word of a sentence, given some finite preceding context (e.g., connectionist models such as Elman 1990; MacDonald and Christiansen 2002; Tabor and Tanenhaus 1999).

The implicit theory of language behind such models is that well-formed language is characterized by the statistical distribution of word sequencing. Indeed, statistics of word sequencing are symptoms of grammatical structure and meaning relations, and much language processing and language learning is mediated by priming relations among semantic associates. But these associations do not *constitute* grammatical structure or meaning. Theories of language understanding based on statistical relations among words shed no light on *interpretation*. How could a language processor predict, say, the sixth word in the next clause, and what good would such predictions do in understanding the sentence? We have known since Chomsky (1957) that sequential dependencies among words in a sentence are not sufficient to determine understanding or even grammaticality. For instance, in (5), the italicized verb is *like* rather than *likes* because of the presence of *does*, fourteen words away; and we would have no difficulty making the distance longer.

(5) Does the little boy in the yellow hat who Mary described as a genius *like* ice cream?

What is significant is not the distance in *words*; it is the distance in *noun phrases* – the fact that *does* is one noun phrase away from *like*. This relation is not captured in any theory of combinatoriality that does not explicitly recognize hierarchical constituent structure of the sort in (1).

The second major line of approach to linguistic combinatoriality, embracing a wide range of theories, is specifically built around the combinatorial properties of linguistic structure. The most influential such theory is *generative grammar* (Chomsky 1965, 1981, 1995). It treats combinatoriality in terms of a set of freely generative rules that build syntactic structures algorithmically; the terminal nodes of these structures are morphemes, complete with their phonological and semantic structures. These structures are then distorted by a sequence of operations, originally called *transformations* (Chomsky 1957, 1965) and later (1981 and on) called *Move*. The output of a sequence of these restructurings is "spelled out" in terms of phonological structure. Further restructurings result in a syntactic structure, *logical form*, from which semantic structure can be read off directly. Because semantic structure does not correspond one-to-one with surface syntactic form, logical form differs considerably from surface syntax. The operations deriving it are termed "covert" – inaccessible to awareness.

The particulars of this theory have mutated considerably over forty years. However, three important features have remained intact throughout, in large part inherited from traditional grammar and from generative grammar's roots in mathematical logic (e.g., Carnap 1939). First, the combinatorial properties of language arise from syntactic structure; phonology and semantics are "interpretive." Second, the formalization is in terms of *derivations*: algorithmic sequences of operations. Third, there is a strict distinction between rules of grammar, responsible for combinatoriality, and lexical items, which are passive "riders" in the derivation of syntactic structures.

Generative grammar's detailed formalization and explicitly mentalistic outlook on language (section 9.1) has led to an explosion in research on linguistic structure, language processing, and language acquisition. Yet the theory is difficult to integrate cleanly into the rest of cognitive science. Language perception proceeds from sound to meaning; language production proceeds from meaning to sound. Generative grammar, however, proceeds algorithmically outward from syntax to both meaning and sound. (6) illustrates the contrast.

(6) a. **Directionality of language perception**

   Phonological structure $\longrightarrow$ Syntactic structure $\longrightarrow$ Semantic structure

   b. **Directionality of language production**

   Phonological structure $\longleftarrow$ Syntactic structure $\longleftarrow$ Semantic structure

   c. **Directionality in generative grammar derivations**

   Phonological structure $\longleftarrow$ Syntactic structure $\longrightarrow$ Semantic structure

This difference is often rationalized by saying that the formal ordering of derivations is meant as a "metaphorical" description of linguistic "competence" and has little if anything to do with the temporal course of processing in "performance" (Chomsky 1965); the role of formal grammatical derivations in actual language processing is deliberately left inexplicit. For this reason, many researchers in psycholinguistics have abandoned generative grammar as a theoretical grounding for experimental investigation.

Another intuitive difficulty with generative grammar comes from deriving semantic combinatoriality from syntax. It does offer an attractive account of the active–passive relation, where a passive sentence such as *The bear was chased by the wolf* is derived from a syntactic underlying form (or "deep structure") with word order more like the active, *the wolf chased the bear.* Similarly, it accounts nicely for the "understood" position of *what* as direct object of *see* in *What did you see?*, in that *what* is moved to the front from an underlying object position. Many other well-known constructions submit insightfully to such treatment.

However, to be consistent, this approach requires every aspect of meaning that is not overt in the words of the sentence to nevertheless be present in syntax, covertly. A traditional example concerns scope of quantification, where the quantifiers in (7a) "raise" to the positions where they would be represented in quantificational logic, yielding (7b) and (7c) as alternative covert logical forms.

(7) a. Every professor spoke an obscure language.
   b. every professor$_i$ [an obscure language$_j$ [t_i spoke t_j]]
      [cf. $\forall x \, \exists y (x$ spoke $y)$]
   c. an obscure language$_j$ [every professor$_i$ [t_i spoke t_j]]
      [cf. $\exists y \, \forall x (x$ spoke $y)$]

However, some constructions have quantificational interpretations but no overt quantifier that can "raise." For instance, (8) has the same interpretations as (7a), yet a syntactic derivation along the lines of (7b, c) is inevitably artificial.

(8) Professor after professor spoke an obscure language.

   A different problem arises with the Rodgers and Hart lyric in (9a, b).

(9) a. It seems we stood and talked like this before. We looked at each other in the same way then.
   b. But I can't remember where or when.

(9b) is understood along the lines of "... where or when we stood and talked like this and looked at each other in the same way as now." The generative approach requires this structure covertly in syntax (cf. Merchant 2001). However, it proves tricky to find a notion of *syntactic* identity in terms of which ellipted material can be deleted: there can be no single clause following *where or when* in (9b) that is identical with the two full sentences (9a) that precede it. Moreover, it is unlikely that a speaker processing (9b) actually understands the sentence by reconstructing a full syntactic structure for the ellipsis.

A wide variety of such cases (e.g., Culicover and Jackendoff 2005) suggest that not all semantic combinatoriality is a product of syntactic combinatoriality. Rather, semantic structure has its own combinatorial principles, correlated only in part with syntactic structure. In this light, much of the complexity and abstractness of mainstream generative syntax can be seen as a result of forcing covert syntax into isomorphism with the structure of meaning. Once we acknowledge that the correlation is not exact, the syntax can be far closer to the simpler structures standardly assumed in psycholinguistic research – as well as in many non-mainstream combinatorial theories of syntax, e.g., *head-driven phrase structure grammar* (Pollard and Sag 1994).

Another strain of linguistic theory, *cognitive grammar* (Langacker 1987; Lakoff 1987; also *functional grammar*, Givón 1995) makes the converse claim: all linguistic form is driven by semantic structure. This claim has considerable justice, since syntactic structure functions to express the semantic relations among the words in a sentence, and since differences in word order often (but not always) convey differences in meaning. Yet the claim is overdrawn. No semantic difference is conveyed by the fact that English verbs go after the subject while Japanese verbs go at the end of the clause, nor by the fact that in French, Spanish, and Italian, direct object pronouns go before the verb instead of after it like other direct objects. These are purely syntactic facts. The proper conclusion is that there is a correlation but not an isomorphism between syntactic and semantic structure.

Viewing phonological, syntactic, and semantic structure as independent correlated systems – rather than all derived from syntax – is consonant with the organization of nonlinguistic parts of the brain. The visual system utilizes many brain areas, each devoted to particular aspects of visual perception, yet all correlated in producing understanding of the visual field. Moreover, the connection between vision and language can also be understood in terms of a partial correlation of semantic structure and high-level visual representations.

9.4   The words–rules continuum

Return to the traditional assumption that the "atoms" of linguistic structure – and therefore the pieces stored in long-term memory – are words or morphemes. Several independent lines of investigation (e.g., cognitive grammar, Langacker 1987; *emergent grammar*, Hopper 1987; *construction grammar*, Goldberg 1995; *parallel architecture*, Jackendoff 2002) have questioned this assumption. For instance, alongside their knowledge of words, English speakers know an enormous number of idioms: pieces of linguistic structure larger than words that are entrenched in memory and in many cases carry their own meaning. Many idioms have normal syntax conforming to general rules: *kick the bucket* is a verb phrase, *son of a gun* is a noun phrase, *down in the dumps* is a prepositional phrase, *the jig is up* is a sentence, and so on. A few have anomalous syntax, e.g., *by and large, for the most part, day in day out.* Many idioms have open positions (or variables) that must be filled by other material: e.g., *take X for granted* requires a noun phrase between its two parts. Some idioms have both anomalous syntax and open positions, such as *Far be it from X to Y*, where *X* is a noun phrase (usually a pronoun), and *Y* is a verb phrase.

We also find oddball forms such as (10).

(10) a. *PP with NP!*   Off with his head! Into the closet with you!

    b. *How about X?*   How about a cup of coffee? How about we have a talk?

    c. *NP and S*   One more beer and I'm leaving. One more step and I shoot!

    d. *the more S, the more S*   The more I eat, the fatter I get.

Each of these carries its own idiosyncratic meaning, not attributable to any of the individual words. Still other cases look syntactically like normal verb phrases, but have idiomatic meanings:

(11) a. He sang/drank/laughed his head off.
      ([$_{VP}$ V his head off] = 'V excessively')

    b. Bill belched/lurched/laughed his way out of the meeting.
      ([$_{VP}$ V his way PP] = 'go PP while/by V-ing')

    c. Sara drank/sang/laughed the whole afternoon away.
      ([$_{VP}$ V NP away] = 'spend amount of time V-ing')

    d. The trolley squealed/rumbled around the corner.
      ([$_{VP}$ V PP] = 'go PP, inducing V-ing sound')

Constructions like (10) and (11) are the motivation behind construction grammar (Fillmore, Kay, and O'Connor 1988; Goldberg 1995), which claims that much (or even all) of syntactic structure is built out of such *meaningful constructions*. Aspects of construction grammar have been adopted within other frameworks as well.

This range of phenomena leads to the conclusion that human memory must store linguistic expressions of all sizes, from individual words to full idiomatic sentences such as *The jig is up*. These expressions fall along a continuum of generality: words and idioms are fully specified, while the meaningful constructions have variables that can be filled out productively.

At the extreme of productivity are principles such as the structure of the English verb phrase, which can be stored in memory as a "treelet" along the lines of (12a). It consists entirely of variables and lacks any special meaning.

(12) a.   VP   (alternatively, [$_{VP}$ V (NP) (PP)])

                V   (NP) (PP)

       b.   VP → V (NP) (PP)

(12a) does the same formal work as the traditional phrase structure rule (12b), but it is not meant as an algorithmic step in a derivation. Rather, it is a piece of stored structure that can form part of larger structures constructed in working memory. There is then no strict distinction between words and grammatical rules: they lie along a continuum of stored structures, with idioms and meaningful constructions in between.

   This notation for rules of grammar can be used to state a word's contextual restrictions. For example, the fact that the verb *devour* is transitive can be encoded as shown in (13).

(13) Long-term memory encoding of *devour*

Phonological structure	Syntactic structure	Semantic structure
dəvawr$_4$	[$_{VP}$ V$_4$ NP$_5$]	X DEVOUR$_4$ Y_5

(13) stipulates that the verb pronounced *devour* occurs within a transitive VP. The verb's direct object is a variable, to be filled in by a noun phrase; it is linked to a position in the semantics of the thing that gets devoured. Thus (13) is a very restricted rule that applies to the behavior of this single verb, further illustrating the word–rule continuum.

   In this approach, the combinatorial character of sentences arises by "clipping together" pieces of stored structure at shared nodes. There is no particular algorithmic order for constructing sentences: they may be built from the top down, the bottom up, or any combination. Alternatively, one can check the well-formedness of a tree by making sure that every part of it conforms to one of the treelets in the lexicon. The formal operation of "clipping" pieces of structure, *unification* (Shieber 1986), is the fundamental combinatorial operation in head-driven phrase structure grammar, construction grammar, lexical-functional grammar (Bresnan 2001), and parallel architecture (Jackendoff 2002). It is compatible with serial, parallel, top-down, or bottom-up computation.

   Unification-based grammars lend themselves directly to theories of sentence processing. Suppose an utterance begins with the word *the*, which is listed in the lexicon as a determiner (14).

(14) Det

       the

Det is the initial node in the stored treelet for the structure of a noun phrase, (15a), which can therefore be clipped onto (14) to form (15b) in working memory.

(15) a.

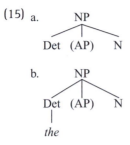

b.

Since this NP is at the beginning of the utterance, it can be clipped into treelet (16a), which provides a position for an initial NP, yielding tree (16b) in working memory.

(16) a.

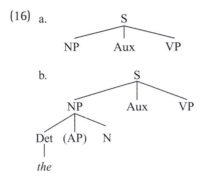

b.

In other words, just the single word *the* can lead to the setting up of grammatical expectations by constructing a tree from the bottom left, going upward and to the right. Further words in the sentence, say ... *green monkey will eat...,* may be attached on the basis of the top-down structure anticipated in (16). Alternatively, they may disconfirm this structure, as in *The more I read, the less I understand* – in which case the treelet for the meaningful construction in (10d) may jump in.

Summing up, the regular rules of grammar, like words, idioms, and meaningful constructions, are pieces of structure stored in long-term memory. They are retrieved into working memory and used in the construction of structure in exactly the same way as words are.

9.5   Regular and irregular morphology

A debate of over twenty years' standing concerns the distinction between regular and irregular morphological forms in language. For example, the English regular past tense is formed by adding (phonological) *-d, -t,* or *-əd* to a verb stem, depending on the final sound of the verb: *judged* (*-d*), *talked* (*-t*), or *guarded* (*-əd*). However, about 180 verbs have past tenses not formed this way. Some leave the stem alone (*put*, not *putted*), some change the vowel (*fell*, not *falled*), some change the vowel and add an ending (*kept*, not *keeped*), and some are quite irregular altogether (*caught* not *catched*, *went* not *goed*).

Classical generative phonology (e.g., Chomsky and Halle 1968) treated all these forms as generated productively from the verb stem plus a past tense morpheme; the irregular forms were seen as special principles of "spell-out" and morphophonology. A competing connectionist paradigm (Rumelhart and McClelland 1986) claims that there is no regular rule, and that both regular and irregular forms are to be treated in terms of statistical association with similar forms. Pinker and associates (Pinker 1999) compromise: the regular forms are produced by a productive rule and the irregular forms arise through statistical association. Much experimentation has been devoted to determining whether different processes are needed for regulars and irregulars, or whether a single associationist process is sufficient. At issue is how speakers form the past tense of unfamiliar words. Everyone agrees that if a word sounds like other irregular verbs, speakers tend to form its past tense by analogy: the past tense of a putative verb *tring* might be *trang*, parallel to *sing/sang* and *ring/rang*. The question is how speakers deal with new verbs that don't sound like any other verb, say the putative verb *flarb*, and come up with the form *flarbed*.

The problem takes on a different perspective under the view that productive rules of grammar are stored structures. The "rule" for the regular past tense can be notated as (17), a lexical entry that, like other lexical entries, has phonological, syntactic, and semantic parts. However, its phonological and syntactic parts are subword structures, i.e., morphological.

(17) Long-term memory encoding of the English regular past tense

Phonological structure	Syntactic structure	Semantic structure
X_8-[$_{Aff}$ d/t/əd]$_7$	[$_V$ V$_8$-Tense$_7$]	[PAST$_7$ (Y_8)]

The phonological part says this is a suffix pronounced *d/t/əd*. The syntactic part says it is a tense, attached to a verb. The semantic part says this affix means the past tense of the verb. The contextual restrictions (indexed 8) are entirely parallel to those for a transitive verb like *devour* (13). The difference lies only in the item's category (affix rather than verb) and the required context (a verb rather than a noun phrase). Thus, just as a transitive verb can be combined with any direct object, (17) can be combined with any verb; this is what makes it a regular affix.

By contrast, an irregular past tense such as *caught* is encoded as (18).

(18) Long-term memory encoding of *caught*

Phonological structure	Syntactic structure	Semantic structure
$kɔt_9$	$[_V V–Tense]_9$	$[PAST (CATCH)]_9$

This is a stipulated combination of verb and past tense, corresponding to a unitary piece of phonology. Thus, just as the meaning of the idiom *kick the bucket* cannot be predicted from its syntactic parts, the phonological form of *caught* cannot be predicted from its syntactic parts, and so it has to be stored in memory.

The upshot is that the distinction between regular and irregular inflections parallels the distinction between transitive verbs and transitive idioms. All are encoded in the same format; they differ only in whether they deal with phrasal or morphological combination, and in whether they have open variables (transitive verbs and regular past do, transitive idioms and irregular past tenses do not). This is a sort of "dual-process" model, but the two processes are fundamentally of the same sort. Moreover, since free combinatoriality is necessary for combining verbs with their direct objects, there can be no objection to using the same combinatorial machinery for combining regular past tense with verb stems.

9.6 Sentence processing

Most experimental work on sentence processing concerns speech perception; there is a robust tradition in production as well. A major issue has been the respective roles of syntax, semantics, and external context in establishing the structure of an understood sentence. Here is where matters now stand.

To understand a sentence, one must identify the words being spoken. Although a hearer may anticipate the speaker's next words, the primary cues are phonological: matching the heard input with the phonological structure of known words. One's knowledge of words may be used to "fill in" a noisy input: in the *phoneme restoration effect* (Warren 1970), one hears, say, *design* instead of a presented *de*ign*, where the * is a burst of extraneous noise. (This parallels seeing unified visual objects despite partial occlusion.) Hearers can use visual cues from the speaker's lip and tongue conformation to help establish phonological input; this *McGurk effect* (Massaro 1997) is completely unconscious and results, paradoxically, in perceived *sound*.

The time it takes to identify a word is inversely proportional to the word's frequency in speech (Oldfield and Wingfield 1965), as might be expected from theories of Hebbian learning. When a word is morphophonologically composite, say *cows* or *attributed*, retrieval speed often depends on the frequency of the stem (with some caveats; see Pinker 1999, p. 303, n. 11). Furthermore, a word accessed in the mental lexicon primes semantically related items, so that they are more quickly retrieved for a brief period thereafter: hearing *doctor* speeds up subsequent identification of *nurse*.

When a phonological word is accessed, *all* of its possible meanings are active and they prime related items, regardless of which meaning is contextually appropriate. For instance, in the sentence *The spies will bug your room*, the word *bug* speeds up identification of the word *insect* on the basis of its other meaning (Tanenhaus, Leiman, and Seidenberg 1979; Swinney 1979). This stands to reason: the processor has no way to verify which meaning is appropriate before identifying both. This shows that sentence processing must from the outset involve some parallel processing.

A further question is whether syntactic structure is constructed one possible structure at a time, or whether parallel possibilities are constructed in competition until all but one is extinguished. The former hypothesis gains plausibility from so-called *garden-path* sentences such as the infamous (19).

(19) The horse raced past the barn fell. (= 'The horse that was raced past the barn fell.')

Many speakers cannot interpret (19) as indicated in the paraphrase. Evidently, interpreting *raced* as a simple past tense verb is irresistible, so one doesn't consider the correct alternative that it is a passive participle. Similarly, consider (20).

(20) a. John knew the answer to the physics problem by heart.
     b. John knew the answer to the physics problem was easy.

In (20b), *the answer* is the subject of a subordinate clause; it is more difficult to parse than (20a), where *the answer* is the direct object of *knew*. Examples like this suggest (e.g., Frazier 1987) that the syntactic processor considers one possible structure first – on syntactic grounds alone – then, if it is unacceptable, tries another. In (19), the disconfirming information comes too late for a reanalysis, so the correct reading cannot be accessed.

Two lines of evidence militate against this approach. First, the choices of syntactic analysis are highly dependent on the relative frequency of particular words in different constructions. Thus a great deal of processing is word-driven (MacDonald, Perlmutter, and Seidenberg 1994). Second, interpretation can be biased in the course of processing by *visual* input. For instance, (21a) has two possible continuations (21b, c), corresponding to different syntactic structures.

(21) a. Put the apple on the...
     b. Put the apple on the towel.   [towel is where the apple should end]
     c. Put the apple on the towel in the cup.   [towel is where the apple is]

Tanenhaus *et al.* (1995) show through use of eye-tracking that subjects hearing (21a) immediately start scanning the visual environment to determine whether there is one apple or there are multiple apples, one of which is on the towel. Thus both parses are under consideration, and the choice is being guided by visual information.

The conclusion from such studies (and many others) is that sentence perception is incremental and opportunistic (Marslen-Wilson and Tyler 1987; Cutler and Clifton 1999). Information relevant to understanding is drawn from any available source – phonological, syntactic, or semantic – whenever it is available. As in lexical access, multiple candidate structures are constructed in competition, and all but one are eventually extinguished. Furthermore, processing involves not only feedforward from phonology to syntax to semantics (and eventually to vision), but also feedback from semantics (and even vision) to syntax and phonology, so the outcome of processing is a complete set of structures along the lines of (1) in working memory.

The view of grammar as stored knowledge of structures makes such a treatment of processing quite natural. Just as words are retrieved promiscuously from long-term memory, so are the "treelets" that are used to compose syntactic structure and the pieces of meaning that compose sentence meanings. This leads to a tight relation between "competence" grammar and processing: the "competence" grammar characterizes the pieces of structure and the relations among them that are deployed in the course of perception and production (Jackendoff 2002, 2007b).

9.7   What is special about language?

Perhaps the most enduringly fascinating issue in the study of language is why humans have language and other animals do not. What is special about the human brain (and body) that supports the learning and even the creation of language? To what extent do these differences arise from developments in the hominid line that have nothing per se to do with language? In approaching these questions, it is useful to distinguish four kinds of properties.

Class 1 consists of characteristics of language that have required no changes from the ancestral genome. Examples would be the lungs and the basic auditory system, which appear essentially unchanged from primate prototypes. Following the discussion of the previous section, many aspects of language processing, such as its incremental and opportunistic character, seem common to many cognitive faculties, for instance the visual system.

Class 2 characteristics are innovations in the human lineage that are essential to language or language acquisition but that serve purposes more general than language. Examples might be voluntary breath control, pointing for drawing attention, the capacity for detailed imitation of others' actions, and fully developed Theory of Mind (the ability to conceptualize the beliefs and intentions of others, including their beliefs about one's own beliefs and intentions) (Povinelli 2000; Tomasello *et al.* 2005).

Class 3 characteristics are unique to humans, are used exclusively for language or language acquisition, and result from some alterations or specialization of pre-existing primate structures or capacities. A clear example would be the shape of the human vocal tract and the neural structures for controlling it in speech.

Class 4 consists of aspects of language that require something altogether new and unprecedented in the primate lineage.

Classes 1 and 2 are what Hauser, Chomsky, and Fitch (2002) call the *broad faculty of language*; Class 4 is their *narrow faculty of language*. It is not clear where Class 3 falls according to their criteria (see Jackendoff and Pinker 2005). On evolutionary grounds, one would prefer a theory of language that puts as little as possible in Classes 3 and 4, so that it takes less work for evolution to arrive at the human language capacity. Those who think language is purely a cultural phenomenon (e.g., Tomasello 2003; Bybee and McClelland 2005) are in effect claiming that Classes 3 and 4 are empty. Deacon (1997) and Arbib (2005) think the only thing specific to language is the capacity for symbolic use of sound and/or gesture; Classes 3 and 4 are otherwise empty. Hauser *et al.* (2002) hypothesize that the capacity for recursion is the only inhabitant of Class 4, and they speculate that even this may be adapted from other recursive capacities in the brain, that is, it belongs in Class 3.

Pinker and Jackendoff (2005) examine the components of the language capacity in some detail and come to a different assessment. In particular, the recursion-only hypothesis does not address the cognitive roots of the lexicon, where all the features specific to particular languages are coded. These features include the phonological structure of words, which is digitized as a sequence of discrete segments, each of which codes a vocal tract configuration. This differs from the structure of vocal signals in other species, including those of our closest relatives. Hence these features seem to belong to Class 3 or 4, requiring some special innovation in our species.

Lexical entries also include syntactic features such as *transitive verb*, illustrated in (13) above, which determine possibilities for syntactic combinatoriality. There are no nouns, verbs, prepositions, agreement markers, or case markers in any other cognitive capacity. These syntactic aspects of the lexicon are cognitively useful only if there are syntactic trees to insert them into. Hence these are specifically syntactic features, and by definition belong to Class 4.

In the parallel architecture suggested above, semantic structure is the product of a combinatorial capacity that is independent of syntax. This allows the possibility that thought was highly structured in our prelinguistic ancestors – they just couldn't express it. Combinatorial thought could serve as a crucial preadaptation for evolution of combinatorial expression. Evidence from apes (Köhler 1927; Hauser 2000; Povinelli 2000) suggests that they indeed have combinatorial thought in domains such as spatial and social cognition, doubtless not as rich as humans', but able to serve as a substrate from which linguistic expression could have evolved.

Thus what appears special about human language is the existence of phonological and syntactic representations, plus the ability to use these to voluntarily code and express thought. The jury is still out on whether, given these ways of structuring inputs, any further special learning mechanisms are necessary (Culicover and Nowak 2003).

Another question to ask is whether analogues exist elsewhere in human or animal cognition for the lexicon, which is a huge store of associations of phonological, syntactic, and semantic structure. One possibility is our vast knowledge of artifacts and how to use them, which correlates visual and motor representations; another is the vast number of associations between the appearance of foods and their tastes. That is, the ability to learn extensive cross-modal associations is not specific to language. What *is* special is again the formats linked by these associations, specifically phonological and syntactic structures.

The overarching issue, of course, is how these differences are instantiated in the detailed architecture of the brain, how they come to be established in the brain by the human genome, and what evolutionary steps led to their presence. The current debate is lively but as yet inconclusive.

Further reading

On the organization of the language faculty

Jackendoff, R. (2002). *Foundations of Language.* Oxford University Press.

On language processing

Brown, C. and Hagoort, P. (eds.) (1999). *The Neurocognition of Language.* Oxford University Press.
Gaskell, G. (ed.) (2007). *The Oxford Handbook of Psycholinguistics.* Oxford University Press.

On language acquisition

Foley, C. and Lust, B. (eds.) (2004). *First Language Acquisition: The Essential Readings.* Malden, MA: Blackwell.

On aphasia

Hillis, A. (ed.) (2002). *The Handbook of Adult Language Disorders*. Hove, UK: Psychology Press.

On the evolution of language

Christiansen, M. and Kirby, S. (eds.) (2003). *Language Evolution*. New York: Oxford University Press.

Fitch, W. T. (2010). *The Evolution of Language*. Cambridge University Press.

References

Arbib, M. (2005). From monkey-like action recognition to human language: An evolutionary framework for neurolinguistics, *Behavioral and Brain Sciences* 28: 105–24.

Bresnan, J. (2001). *Lexical-Functional Syntax*. Oxford: Blackwell.

Bybee, J. and McClelland, J. (2005). Alternatives to the combinatorial paradigm of linguistic theory based on domain general principles of human cognition, *The Linguistic Review* 22: 381–410.

Carnap, R. (1939). *Foundations of Logic and Mathematics*. University of Chicago Press.

Chomsky, N. (1957). *Syntactic Structures*. The Hague: Mouton.

(1965). *Aspects of the Theory of Syntax*. Cambridge, MA: MIT Press.

(1981). *Lectures on Government and Binding*. Dordrecht: Kluwer.

(1995). *The Minimalist Program*. Cambridge, MA: MIT Press.

Chomsky, N. and Halle, M. (1968). *The Sound Pattern of English*. New York: Harper & Row.

Culicover, P. and Jackendoff, R. (2005). *Simpler Syntax*. Oxford University Press.

Culicover, P. and Nowak, A. (2003). *Dynamical Syntax*. Oxford University Press.

Cutler, A. and Clifton, C. (1999). Comprehending spoken language: A blueprint of the listener, in C. Brown and P. Hagoort (eds.), *The Neurocognition of Language* (pp. 123–66). Oxford University Press.

Deacon, T. (1997). *The Symbolic Species*. New York: Norton.

Elman, J. (1990). Finding structure in time, *Cognitive Science* 14: 179–211.

Elman, J., Bates, E., Johnson, M., Karmiloff-Smith, A., Parisi, D., and Plunkett, K. (1996). *Rethinking Innateness*. Cambridge, MA: MIT Press.

Fillmore, C., Kay, P., and O'Connor, M. C. (1988). Regularity and idiomaticity in grammatical constructions: The case of *let alone*, *Language* 64: 501–38.

Frazier, L. (1987). Theories of sentence processing, in J. Garfield (ed.), *Modularity in Knowledge Representation and Natural-Language Understanding* (pp. 291–308). Cambridge, MA: MIT Press.

Givón, T. (1995). *Functionalism and Grammar*. Philadelphia: John Benjamins.

Goldberg, A. (1995). *Constructions*. University of Chicago Press.

Goldin-Meadow, S. (2003). *The Resilience of Language*. New York: Psychology Press.

Hagoort, P. (2005). On Broca, brain, and binding: A new framework, *Trends in Cognitive Sciences* 9: 416–23.

Hauser, M. (1996). *The Evolution of Communication*. Cambridge, MA: MIT Press.
    (2000). *Wild Minds: What Animals Really Think*. New York: Henry Holt.

Hauser, M., Chomsky, N., and Fitch, W. T. (2002). The faculty of language: What is it, who has it, and how did it evolve? *Science* 298: 1569–79.

Heim, I. and Kratzer, A. (1998). *Semantics in Generative Grammar*. Oxford: Blackwell.

Hopper, P. (1987). Emergent grammar, *Berkeley Linguistics Society* 13: 139–57.

Jackendoff, R. (1983). *Semantics and Cognition*. Cambridge, MA: MIT Press.
    (1987). *Consciousness and the Computational Mind*. Cambridge, MA: MIT Press.
    (1990). *Semantic Structures*. Cambridge, MA: MIT Press.
    (2002). *Foundations of Language*. Oxford University Press.
    (2007a). *Language, Consciousness, Culture*. Cambridge, MA: MIT Press.
    (2007b). A Parallel Architecture perspective on language processing, *Brain Research* 1146: 2–22.
    (2012). *A User's Guide to Thought and Meaning*. Oxford University Press.

Jackendoff, R. and Pinker, S. (2005). The nature of the language faculty and its implications for the evolution of the language capacity, *Cognition* 97: 211–25.

Kegl, J., Senghas, A., and Coppola, M. (1999). Creations through contact: Sign language emergence and sign language change in Nicaragua, in M. DeGraff (ed.), *Language Creation and Language Change* (pp. 179–237). Cambridge, MA: MIT Press.

Köhler, W. (1927). *The Mentality of Apes*. London: Kegan Paul.

Lakoff, G. (1987). *Women, Fire, and Dangerous Things*. University of Chicago Press.

Landauer, T., McNamara, D., Dennis, S., and Kintsch, W. (eds.) (2007). *Handbook of Latent Semantic Analysis*. Hillsdale, NJ: Lawrence Erlbaum.

Langacker, R. (1987). *Foundations of Cognitive Grammar*. Stanford University Press.

MacDonald, M. C., and Christiansen, M. (2002). Reassessing working memory, *Psychological Review* 109: 35–54.

MacDonald, M. C., Pearlmutter, N. J., and Seidenberg, M. S. (1994). Lexical nature of syntactic ambiguity resolution, *Psychological Review* 101: 676–703.

Marslen-Wilson, W. and Tyler, L. (1987). Against modularity, in J. Garfield (ed.), *Modularity in Knowledge Representation and Natural-Language Understanding* (pp. 37–62). Cambridge, MA: MIT Press.

Massaro, D. (1997). *Perceiving Talking Faces*. Cambridge, MA: MIT Press.

Merchant, J. (2001). *The Syntax of Silence*. Oxford University Press.

Oldfield, R. C., and Wingfield, A. (1965). Response latencies in naming objects, *Quarterly Journal of Experimental Psychology* 17: 273–81.

Pinker, S. (1999). *Words and Rules*. New York: Basic Books.

Pinker, S. and Jackendoff, R. (2005). The faculty of language: What's special about it? *Cognition* 95: 201–36.

Pollard, C. and Sag, I. (1994). *Head-Driven Phrase Structure Grammar*. University of Chicago Press.

Povinelli, D. (2000). *Folk Physics for Apes*. Oxford University Press.

Rumelhart, D. and McClelland, J. (1986). On learning the past tense of English verbs, in J. McClelland, D. Rumelhart, and the PDP Research Group, *Parallel Distributed Processing* (vol. 2: pp. 216–71). Cambridge, MA: MIT Press.

Shieber, S. (1986). *An Introduction to Unification-Based Approaches to Grammar*. Stanford, CA: CSLI Publications.

Swinney, D. (1979). Lexical access during sentence comprehension, *Journal of Verbal Learning and Verbal Behavior* 18: 645–59.

Tabor, W. and Tanenhaus, M. (1999). Dynamical models of sentence processing, *Cognitive Science* 23: 491–515.

Tanenhaus, M., Leiman, J., and Seidenberg, M. (1979). Evidence for multiple states in the processing of ambiguous words in syntactic contexts, *Journal of Verbal Learning and Verbal Behavior* 18: 427–40.

Tanenhaus, M., Spivey-Knowlton, M., Eberhard, K., and Sedivy, J. (1995). Integration of visual and linguistic information in spoken language comprehension, *Science* 268: 1632–4.

Tomasello, M. (2003). *Constructing a Language*. Cambridge, MA: Harvard University Press.

Tomasello, M., Carpenter, M., Call, J., Behne, T., and Moll, H. (2005). Understanding and sharing intentions: The origins of cultural cognition, *Behavioral and Brain Sciences* 28: 675–91.

Warren, R. M. (1970). Perceptual restoration of missing speech sounds, *Science* 167: 392–3.

10 Emotion

Jesse Prinz

Emotions are a central topic of inquiry within cognitive science, and it is easy to see why. Emotions provide us with information that matters to survival, and they contribute to evaluation and decision making. Emotions interact with core cognitive systems such as attention and memory, and they play a crucial role in guiding action. Emotions also color human experience in profound ways. Some emotions we actively seek, and others we actively avoid. Without emotions we would be very different creatures. Recognizing this fact, there have been vigorous efforts to understand the nature of emotions in recent years, and those efforts have deepened our understanding considerably. In this chapter I review some important themes in contemporary emotion science. I will divide the chapter into three main sections corresponding to the causes, constituents, and effects of emotion. These are the most foundational issues in emotion research. In the final section I will briefly survey some other topics, such as the role of emotions in reasoning and the relative contributions of biology and culture.

10.1 Causes of emotions

10.1.1 Cognitive causes

Much of the work on emotion focuses on the conditions that bring them about. Research into this question has been important for understanding what emotions are because it helps us see what their function is in human life. Emotions are not random mental events, like spasms of the mind. They respond in systematic and predicable ways to various elicitors. Emotions can also, to some degree, be distinguished by their causes; different emotions are caused by different things.

It is useful to distinguish two kinds of emotional causes: cognitive and non-cognitive. The term "cognitive" is somewhat thorny, because it can be defined in different ways by different researchers. Intuitively, cognitive events can be understood in terms of the pre-theoretical umbrella term "thoughts." Thoughts are mental episodes that require the use of concepts. Thoughts may be unbidden or automatic, but they are not merely copies of the stimuli that impinge on our senses. They go beyond mere sensations and present the world as being a certain way. Thoughts can occur through processes of deliberation and can be affected, in many cases at least, by reasoning. In discussing the cognitive causes of emotions, I mean to be discussing cases in which emotions are caused by thoughts.

It is widely recognized that thoughts can cause emotions. But what kinds of thought can have this effect? Many thoughts (the thought that snow is white or that 3 is prime, for example) have little impact on most people. The thoughts that elicit emotions tend to be evaluative thoughts: thoughts that assess things in a way that reflects our attitudes towards them. For example, one may have no emotion in response to the thought that a kitchen knife is sharp, but emotions will likely follow the thought that a knife is dangerous. The concept of danger characterizes the world in a way that bears directly on well-being. Many emotion researchers use the term "appraisal" to denote evaluations of this kind (Arnold 1960). An appraisal can be defined as a thought representing an organism–environment relationship that bears on well-being (Lazarus 1991). The thought that I am in danger represents the world as posing a threat to me.

It is well documented that appraisals affect our emotions. For example, Lazarus and Alfert (1964) conducted studies in which different narratives were used to accompany the same film clip. The narratives promoted different appraisals of events within the film clip, and were found to affect the resulting emotions. In another study, Smith and Lazarus (1993) gave participants vignettes and varied the content to manipulate appraisals and again found emotional effects. For example, if participants are invited to construe an event as a loss, they might feel sad, and if they hear about doing something offensive or wrong, they might feel angry.

Lazarus and Smith argue that coarse-grained appraisals, such as "I am in danger" or "there has been a loss," do not necessarily occur in that form during emotion elicitation. Rather, such appraisals are a theoretician's summary of a *set* of "molecular" appraisals that actually take place. On their view, there are several appraisal dimensions that underlie every emotion. For example, we ask ourselves, is this situation important to our goals? Is it goal-congruent or incongruent? Who deserves blame or credit? What coping strategies are available to me? What expectation should I form for the outcome? Different answers to these questions correspond to different emotions. For example, happiness is goal-congruent, anger involves placing blame on another person, and fear involves coping strategies such as flight. Despite these differences, Smith and Lazarus claim that all emotions are alike insofar as they derive from the same basic dimensions of evaluation. This is called a *dimensional appraisal theory*, and there are several closely related variants in the literature (see Roseman, Spindel, and Jose 1990 for a review).

Most dimensional appraisal theories believe that molecular appraisals can occur automatically and unconsciously. It is sometimes suggested that these appraisals can vary in their degree of cognitive sophistication. For example, Scherer, who calls molecular appraisals "Stimulus evaluation checks," has developed an account distinguished by two interesting claims. He argues that molecular appraisals take place in a fixed sequence and that for each appraisal there can be both primitive and cognitively elaborated variants. For example, a novelty check can involve matching the perceivable features of events against perceptual memories or reflection on whether an event is unprecedented in its significance.

Dimensional appraisal theories are not universally accepted. For example, some researchers think that emotions are elicited by thoughts such as "I am in danger" or "I have been wronged" rather than molecular appraisals. The research on molecular appraisals is designed to show that changing thoughts at this fine-grained scale can influence our emotions (a shift from other-blame to self-blame, for example, can make a shift from anger to guilt). But it may be that these cognitive changes influence emotions only by affecting our coarse-grained appraisals. That would mean that molecular appraisals can influence our emotions but are not an essential aspect of emotion elicitation. Indeed, some dimensional appraisal theorists may agree, treating the molecular appraisals as part of the semantic analysis of emotion terms rather than as components of a process model (see, for example, Ortony, Clore, and Collins 1988).

Molecular or coarse-grained, many psychologists assume that cognitive states in some form are necessary for emotion elicitation. But some researchers believe that emotions can have non-cognitive causes as well.

10.1.2   Non-cognitive causes

The most obvious non-cognitive elicitors of emotions are perceptual states. For example, a foul smell can cause disgust, a sudden loss of support can cause fear, tickling can cause amusement, and seeing someone cry can cause sadness.

It might be assumed that perceptual states cause emotions by affecting our appraisals. For example, if you see someone punching another person, you may respond with fear if you think you are in danger next, and rage if you think the victim was undeserving. If the event is a boxing match, you may experience neither of these things, and the emotion you have (jubilation or sadness) will depend on whether the person throwing the punch is the boxer you are rooting for. Perception often requires interpretation before an emotion arises. But in many cases, it's less plausible that perception requires thought in order to elicit emotions. For example, when there is a loud sudden sound, the resulting startle response (which is arguably an emotion) is so rapid and so lawfully triggered by such stimuli that it would seem gratuitous to postulate an intervening thought.

More direct evidence for emotion induction without cognition comes from neuroscience. Among the brain regions that can initiate an emotional response is the amygdala, an almond-shaped collection of nuclei buried deep in the temporal lobe. The amygdala is an ancient brain structure – a part of the limbic system – with homologues in reptiles (Laberge *et al.* 2006). The amygdala is itself too primitive to harbor cognitive states; its nuclei are more involved in regulating structures that control bodily responses. Cognitive states can cause emotions *via* the amygdala, because it is connected to structures in the frontal cortex that are among our most evolutionarily advanced. But amygdala responses can also be triggered by non-cognitive structures, including both cortical and subcortical perception pathways (LeDoux 1996). The subcortical pathways make the point most dramatically. The thalamus is connected to the amygdala via the superior colliculus, and it receives information from sensory transducers, such as the optic nerve. Thus, visual information that has not yet reached the neocortex, where visual object recognition takes place, can be sent on to the amygdala. This may be what happens when we have a sudden fear response to, say, a coiled rope, mistaking it, at first fleeting glance, for a snake. By the time the brain is able to visually categorize the rope, we know, cognitively speaking, that we are not in any danger, but we are already experiencing fear.

Thus, there is good reason to think that emotions can be triggered by even very simple perceptual inputs. Indeed, emotions can even be triggered in cases where we do not cognitively grasp that there is a meaningful relationship between what we perceive and how we feel. For example, emotions can be affected by music (Blood *et al.* 1999), by weather (Palinkas and Houseal 2000), and exercise (Roth 1989). Even more obviously, emotions can be affected by directly changing the chemistry of the brain, as when we take drugs that affect the autonomic nervous system or drink alcohol. It is also well established that we can alter our emotions by changing expressive behaviors. The effect of facial expressions has been known for some time (Laird 1974), and can occur even when we are aware of the fact that we are making expressions that have emotional significance (Strack, Martin, and Stepper 1988; Zajonc, Murphy, and Inglehart 1989). An inadvertent smile can lift our spirits. Typically, we wouldn't say that these elicitors give us a *reason* for the emotions they cause. Alcohol does not *justify* jubilation, frowning does not *warrant* sadness, and exposure to light does not provide a *rationale* for happiness. These things are causes, rather than reasons. That does not mean they are arbitrary. Evolution may have programmed us to feel elated when we exercise as a way of rewarding an activity that is good for our health. Good weather may make us happy because happiness is an emotion that leads to exploratory behavior (see below), and it is easier to explore in good weather. Music may make us sad when it resembles the sound of crying (such as the opening of Mozart's

Requiem), because we are evolved to have an immediate empathetic response to the distress calls of conspecifics. Facial feedback may work as a way of calibrating emotions in groups: if I automatically mimic your expressions and thereby feel the expressed emotion, I will come to share the emotions you are feeling. In these ways, automatic, non-cognitive processes can generate contextually appropriate emotions even when we lack cognitive insight into the reasons for having those emotions.

Some theorists reject this interpretation, arguing that the examples here involve *unconscious* cognitive appraisals rather than non-cognitive causes. This alternative proposal can be challenged by noting that evolutionary pressure promotes the emergence of emotional responses that arise immediately upon perceiving stimuli that have great relevance for survival. Cognitive intermediaries would slow down vital reactions, such as freezing after a sudden noise.

10.2   Constituents of emotions

As we have just seen, both perceptions and thoughts can cause emotions to arise. But, if these are the causes, what are the things that get caused? What exactly is an emotion itself?

One possibility is that an emotion is not an entity distinct from its causes. Perhaps the mental states that bring emotions about also constitute the emotions. This possibility has most frequently been defended by proponents of what I will call "pure cognitive theories of emotion." According to cognitive theories, emotions necessarily involve cognitions, such as appraisal judgments. Among such cognitive theories, we can distinguish the pure and the impure. A pure cognitive theory is one that identifies emotions with a judgment (or thought, or construal, etc.) and nothing more. For example, anger might consist in the judgment that I have been wronged (or the entertaining of such a thought, or a construal of some event as an affront against me or those I care about). Such theories are not uncommon in philosophy. Contemporary defenders include Solomon (1976) and Nussbaum (2001). Pure cognitive theorists can make little sense of the idea that emotions are caused by evaluative cognitions and constituted by something else. They collapse cause and constituent, and argue that emotions are identical to the kinds of mental states that were described in section 10.1.1 above.

Pure cognitive theories face an obvious objection, however. Emotions do not seem like ordinary judgments. To use a popular metaphor, they seem hot rather than cold. We can judge that snow is white with cool indifference. But when we angrily judge that we have been wronged, we are anything but indifferent. If emotions were merely judgments, thoughts, or construals, their heat would be difficult to explain. Faced with this objection, cognitive theorists can choose between four strategies of response. One option is to dig in one's heels. Perhaps the heat of emotions is not a component of the emotion, but an effect. Some cognitive theorists argue that the characteristic emotional feeling, such as the lump in the throat sensation that occurs when we are sad, are contingent consequences of emotions rather than component parts (Solomon 1976). When we say, "I feel sad" in reference to such feelings, we mean "I feel the feelings that sadness tends to bring about," not "I feel sadness itself." A second strategy is to argue that emotions are constituted by judgments that are special in some way. They are hot judgments. But it's not clear what would make a judgment hot, if it were not supplemented by something other than a judgment. A third strategy is to capture the heat of emotions by appeal to cognitive capacities, but not just the capacity to judge or construe. For example, one might say an emotion is an evaluative judgment combined with certain patterns of attention, problem solving, and memory. As we will see in the next section, different emotions are associated with different information-processing styles. It might be argued that these cognitive differences can explain why emotions seem unlike ordinary judgments without abandoning the view that emotions are fundamentally and purely cognitive. For example, fear might be more than a thought that I am in danger; it might also include compulsive attention to the threat I am facing and compulsive attention to possible means of escape.

The preceding three strategies show ways in which a cognitive theorist could account for the fact that emotions seem hot without abandoning the conjecture that emotions are constituted wholly by cognitive states and processes. An alternative strategy for accommodating heat is to adopt an *impure* cognitive theory. On impure theories, emotions have both a cognitive component and a non-cognitive component.

What are non-cognitive correlates of emotion? Here, answers vary. On some impure cognitive theories, there is just one kind of non-cognitive component: physiological arousal (Schacter and Singer 1962). On other theories, there are two components, which distinguish positive and negative emotions; Spinoza (1677, 1992), for example, says every emotion comprises both a judgment and either pleasure or pain. Some theories integrate both of these kinds of non-cognitive states. For example, some "circumplex" models conceive emotions as points in a multidimensional space whose dimensions are the degree of arousal and the valence, which spans from intensely positive to intensely negative (Russell 1980). On some circumplex theories, emotions integrate a point in this non-cognitive space with a cognitive interpretation (Barrett 2006). In contrast to circumplex theories, it is sometimes argued that arousal is not the only physiological dimension that can contribute to our emotions. It may be the case that different discrete emotions can be further distinguished by musculoskeletal responses, specific patterns of activity in visceral organs, and changes in levels of neurotransmitters (Damasio *et al.* 2000).

Levenson, Ekman, and Friesen (1990) argue that different emotions correspond to distinctive bodily patterns, though they admit that no single physiological measure can distinguish emotions (see also Cacioppo *et al.* 2000, for a somewhat skeptical review). These body patterns are not believed to be arbitrary; rather, they correspond to the preparations for behaviors that suit the emotion they subserve. Fear, for example, is associated with bodily states that facilitate freezing (constriction of the blood vessels), or fleeing (blood flow to the extremities), whereas anger is associated with preparation for fighting (blood flow to the hands, and bearing of canine teeth). This link between body and action has led some researchers to say that each emotion has its own "action tendency," a behavioral disposition underwritten by systematic physiological changes. Some impure cognitive theorists say that emotions include both appraisals and action tendencies (Arnold 1960; Frijda 1986; see also Ekman 1999).

Impure cognitive theories raise the possibility that emotional cognitions and emotional feelings can come apart. The non-cognitive feeling component might have a different time-course than the cognition. On some appraisal theories, for example, it is suggested that a series of appraisal judgments initiates the emotional state, and then a feeling state follows as a result. The feeling state can outlast the cognitions.

Once non-cognitive states are introduced as constituents of emotions, there are several possible answers one can give to the question, What constitutes an emotion? One answer is to say that an emotion is constituted by the joint occurrence of cognitive and non-cognitive components (thoughts and feelings), and, once either subsides, the emotion is gone. The second possibility is to say that emotions are constituted by non-cognitive states alone, but insist that those states count as emotions if and only if they are caused by the right kinds of cognitions. By analogy, Gordon (1987) has suggested that we think of sunburns. Sunburns do not contain the sun as a component part – they are located on the skin – but a burn counts as a sunburn if and only if it is caused by the sun. Likewise, fear might be equated with a particular feeling state that was caused by judgments about being in danger. On this kind of theory, emotions necessarily have cognitive antecedents, but they do not necessarily have cognitive components. The feeling of fear can linger after the judgment stops, and the feeling still counts as fear when that happens, on such a view. Some appraisal theorists in psychology may implicitly endorse a view of this kind (cf. Lazarus 1991).

Once non-cognitive states are accepted as constituents of emotions there is also a further option. One could opt for a non-cognitive theory of emotion. On such an account, cognitive states are neither constituents of emotions nor necessary precursors; emotions are purely non-cognitive. For example, consider the circumplex theories, which were mentioned above. According to two-dimensional circumplex theories, emotions are points in arousal–valence space. One can combine this idea with a cognitive theory and argue that emotions involve arousal, valence, and an interpretation of that arousal–valence compound. This would allow for the possibility of distinct emotions that are alike in arousal and valence, but different in meaning (say terror and rage, for example). But one could also have a circumplex theory without a cognitive component, and say that emotions are nothing more than a combination of arousal and valence (Russell 1980). A fully developed version of a circumplex theory would have to say something more about what these two dimensions are. For example, does arousal just include activity in the autonomic nervous system? Is it restricted to sympathetic autonomic responses (those that cause excitation in our visceral organs) or does it also include parasympathetic responses (those that cause inhibition)? Is it the actual bodily states that matter or merely the experience of arousal? There are also questions about valence. Does this just refer to a range of feelings, which spans from pleasant to unpleasant? Or does it refer to something more behavioral, like a disposition to approach or avoid? (See Prinz 2004 for discussion and Solomon 2003, who uses ambiguities in the term "valence" to raise doubts about use of that construct in theories of emotion.)

The circumplex model implies that emotion space is continuous, rather that categorical or discrete. Emotions differ from each other by degrees along shared dimensions, and between any two labeled points there might be a third. Other pure non-cognitive theories reject this assumption and insist that different emotions (or each family of emotions) may have qualitatively distinct non-cognitive components, such as distinctive physiological patterns. As noted above, no single physiological dimension can be used to differentiate the emotions, but some emotions may have physiological components that are not shared by others. Fear, for example, often involves the erection of hair follicles and sadness involves a characteristic lump in the throat. Some emotions may also be distinguished by facial expressions (Ekman 1993). This raises the possibility that each emotion can be identified with a unique pattern of bodily change that includes expressive behaviors, arousal, and other states.

Given such somatic differences, one option for the non-cognitive theorist is to equate each emotion with a range of characteristic somatic states. That option implies that emotions are bodily states, rather than mental states. Another more popular option is to equate emotions with *sensations* of bodily states. This view was most influentially advanced by William James (1884), but was simultaneously put forward by Carl Lange (1885) and has contemporary supporters (Damasio 1994; Prinz 2004).

James suggests that the bodily sensations that constitute our emotions are always consciously experienced. Emotions on his view are feelings; they are feelings of bodily change. This view accords with an aspect of vernacular usage. The term "feeling" in English is often used to refer to emotions, though it is more inclusive and also includes non-emotional experiences – most typically somatic in nature. Languages that lack a word for emotions typically do have a word similar in extension to "feelings" (Wierzbicka 1999). Others claim that emotions need not occur consciously, and are, hence, not always felt. Even some followers of James make this claim. They say that emotions are sensations of the body, but like sensory states quite generally, they can occur below the conscious threshold (Prinz 2004). This view is consistent with the claim that when emotions are conscious, they are feelings. Thus it preserves the vernacular link between emotions and feelings, albeit less completely than James' account. Pure cognitive theorists reject both views and ague that feelings are never identical to emotions; they are concomitant states.

In sum, we have seen that there are several possible candidates for the constituents of emotions: cognitive states, such as appraisals, levels of arousal, emotional valence, perceptions of bodily change, action tendencies, or some combination of these. Much energy in emotion research goes into debating which of these elements really constitute our emotions, and which merely come along for the ride. Defenders of cognitive theories argue on empirical grounds that cognitions are regularly involved in emotional states (Smith and Lazarus 1993). On conceptual grounds they argue we would not count a state as, say, anger if it were not accompanied by a judgment that someone had been wronged (Solomon 1976; Lazarus 1984). It is also argued, on conceptual grounds, that emotions are *intentional* mental states (they are *about* things), and it is not clear how a non-cognitive state can be intentional; we don't say that twinges and pangs are *about* anything (Pitcher 1965; Solomon 1976). Non-cognitive theories are empirically defended by arguing that as a matter of fact emotions can arise without cognitions, as the evidence cited in the section on non-cognitive causes would suggest (Zajonc 1984). It is also observed that the brain areas that are most active during emotional episodes include structures that are involved in body perception (Damasio *et al.* 2000) and body regulation (Critchley, Mathias, and Dolan 2001). These structures include the somatosensory cortex, the insula, and both anterior and posterior cingulate cortex. Impure cognitive theorists might counter that there are often also activations in areas that associate cognitive and non-cognitive states, such as the temporal pole, ventromedial prefrontal cortex, and orbitofrontal cortex (for a review, see Phan *et al.* 2002). Pure cognitive theorists would counter that somatic brain activations reflect the effects of our emotions, and not the emotions themselves.

Deciding between competing theories has proven difficult because the key empirical data are often compatible with multiple interpretations and theoretical arguments often depend on conceptual intuitions that vary from theorist to theorist (must my anger always include a judgment that I have been wronged?). It has also been suggested that different emotions may have different components (Griffiths 1997). Notice, however, that informative emotion research can continue in the absence of a settled theory. Most theories agree that cognitions, bodily sensations, and valenced feelings occur during emotional episodes much of the time. And these phenomena can be studied without deciding which are essential to emotions, which are constitutive, and which are simply contingent concomitants.

10.3   Effects of emotions

10.3.1   Behavioral effects

Once an emotion has been initiated, it can have a variety of different effects. Understanding these is important for understanding the functions that emotions serve. Emotions influence both behavior and cognitive processes. We can consider these in turn.

Behavioral effects have already been touched on in discussing somatic theories of emotion and emotional action tendencies. It is widely recognized that different discrete emotions are associated with different behaviors. Anger is associated with aggression, disgust with rejection, fear with flight/fight/freezing responses, sadness with lethargy, shame with self-concealment, guilt with reparation, and so on. It may be difficult to link some emotions with specific behaviors (e.g., hope, pride, aesthetic pleasure, confusion, nostalgia, and so on). It may be that some named emotions can impact behavior in a variety of different ways, and it may also turn out that some emotions are not associated with highly specific biologically prepared behavioral responses. But it is plausible that every emotion has some behavioral impact.

One way to capture this is to divide emotions into two broad classes: negative and positive. In addition to the specific effects that a given emotion can have, negative emotions, as a class, tend to have certain broad behavioral effects in common, and likewise for positive emotions. Let's start with the negative.

Negative emotions include fear, sadness, anger, disgust, guilt, and shame. Generally speaking, negative emotions are associated with behavioral inhibition, withdrawal, and avoidance. Let's look at these three effects in turn. Inhibition refers to a suppression or interruption of a current activity. Gray (1991) suggests that negative emotions engage a behavioral inhibition system (associated with the septohippocampal system in the brain). Behaviorally this can involve highly stereotyped behavioral programs such as freezing or more generalized tendencies to cease or desist.

Withdrawal refers to movements that increase distance between an agent and an emotionally evocative stimulus or situation. The agent can move her body away from the stimulus or move the stimulus away from the body.

Research suggests that negative emotions spontaneously elicit withdrawal dispositions. For example, Chen and Bargh (1999) asked participants to rate words as positive or negative by either pulling or pushing on a joystick. Participants who had to pull the joystick toward themselves to indicate negative words were slower than participants who were instructed to push the joystick away. It might be noticed that one of the paradigmatic negative emotions, anger, often involves approach, rather than withdrawal. Anger promotes aggression, and aggression usually requires physical contact. But notice that some people withdraw from those who enrage them, and some forms of anger (like sullen brooding or stewing) do not involve contact. Notice, too, that aggressive forms of approach have the effect of suppressing the offending object. People try to beat off or eradicate those who trespass against them. And, physically speaking, aggressive responses are often more like pushing away than pulling toward. So the end result of aggression is a kind of withdrawal, broadly construed.

Avoidance, though often used as a synonym for withdrawal, might be better regarded as a more enduring tendency to resist contact with a stimulus known to elicit negative emotions. Consider, for example, Damasio, Tranel, and Damasio's (1991) "somatic marker hypothesis," according to which we make decisions by anticipating the emotional consequences of an action under consideration. In testing this hypothesis, Damasio *et al.* show that people avoid risky strategies – such as gambling on decks of cards that have high costs – when and only when negative emotions become linked to such strategies. Individuals who are unable to assign negative emotions to risky decks because of damage to ventromedial prefrontal cortex continue to play those decks despite net losses.

Whereas negative emotions promote inhibition, withdrawal, and avoidance, positive emotions seem to promote behavioral activation, approach, and continuation. Gray (1991) associates positive emotions with the dopaminergic behavioral activation system in the brain. Dopamine is associated with increased energy. Positive emotions promote various forms of approach behavior, including helping (Isen and Levin 1972) and exploration (Fredrickson 1998). In the Chen and Bargh (1999) study, participants who pulled a joystick toward them to indicate positive words were faster than subjects who were instructed to push the joystick away. In the nervous system positive feelings and approach may involve somewhat different circuitry, as suggested by lesion studies in rats, which can show signs of liking in the absence of wanting (Berridge 1996). But the studies just cited show that liking and wanting (positive feelings and approach) are normally linked. Positive emotions are also normally linked to behavioral continuation. If an activity is hedonically rewarding, we will work to sustain it or repeat it. Some forms of addiction work this way, and, of course, this is a basic aspect of behavioral conditioning through positive reinforcement.

10.3.2   Cognitive effects

Turn now from behavior to cognition. As we have seen, thoughts can induce emotions and some emotion theorists claim that emotions have judgments as component parts. Regardless of whether one endorses a cognitive theory, in this sense, it is clear that emotions can influence our cognitive states. These effects can be divided into two kinds: emotions can influence what we think about and they can influence how we think.

First, consider how emotions influence the contents of our thoughts. As an example, consider the fact that people who are depressed often form negative self-appraisals. It turns out that some of these appraisals may actually be more accurate than appraisals made in more favorable emotional states. The term "depressive realism" refers to the fact that people who are depressed may be more accurate than others in assessing their abilities and relative standing in a group (Alloy and Abrahamson 1988). Positive emotions, in contrast, are associated with the "self-serving bias," a tendency to see one's self as more capable than one actually is. Another example of how emotions influence thought contents can be found in the domain of moral psychology. Studies show a link between emotion and moral judgments (reviewed in Prinz 2007). Among these findings, it has been shown that hypnotic induction of disgust can increase a person's assessment of how wrong certain actions are (Wheatly and Haidt 2005). Likewise, anger can increase people's judgments about how much an individual should be punished (Lerner, Goldberg, and Tetlock 1998).

Emotions can influence information processing along a number of dimensions. There can be effects on memory, attention, problem solving, and perception. One well-studied pair of memory effects is emotion-congruent encoding and recall (Bower 1981). Emotion-congruent *encoding* refers to the fact that people will more readily encode information that is consistent with a current emotion or mood. If a person is happy, positive aspects of the current situation are more likely to be stored. Emotion-congruent *recall* refers to the fact that people have an easier time recalling an emotionally charged event when in a similar emotional state.

Emotions can affect attention in highly specific ways. The effects of fear on attention have been particularly well studied. For example, Öhman, Flykt, and Esteves (2001) found scary stimuli (spiders and snakes) were detected in an array of photographs faster than innocuous objects (flowers and mushrooms). The effect was magnified for people with phobias. Fear may be more likely to interact with attention than some other emotions because fear alerts us to dangers. It is advantageous to attend to a potential threat and to monitor it.

Emotions can also have selective effects on problem solving. Positive emotions are believed to increase our capacity for solving problems in creative ways. Isen, Daubman, and Nowicki (1987) used silly films (television bloopers) and small gifts to induce positive affect. They then gave participants a problem used to test for creativity: find a way to affix a candle to a cork board so that it does not drip on the floor using a box of thumbtacks as the only tool. The trick is to see that the box itself can be used: pin the candle to the box and the box to the board, and there will be no dripping on the floor. Participants in the funny film condition and gift condition did better than control groups.

Positive emotions can also have an impact on perception. It is well established that people are better at recognizing members of their in-group as compared to out-groups. Johnson and Fredrickson (2005) found that, after positive emotion induction, white participants had an easier time recognizing black faces. Perception can also be affected by negative emotions. For example, Bouhuys, Bloem, and Groothuis (1995) found that sad music caused people to perceive emotionally ambiguous faces as more sad in comparison to a control group, and to perceive happy faces as less inviting.

The findings reviewed here are the tip of a large iceberg. Cognitive effects of emotion are being actively studied and there is a guiding principle that, just as different emotions have different facial expressions, different emotions may induce different cognitive styles.

10.4   Other topics in emotion research

This chapter has focused on the causes, constituents, and effects of our emotions. These efforts suggest a dazzling variety. Emotions can be caused by everything from subcortical sensory states to our most sophisticated cognitive ruminations. Emotions can influence both behavior and thought, including every dimension of information processing that has been investigated. Debate continues about the constituents of emotions, but it is certainly agreed that both non-cognitive and cognitive changes take place when people are in emotional states. These are the most foundational questions in emotion research, because they concern the essence of emotions, but other important questions are also actively investigated. I end with a brief survey, drawing attention to ways in which these other lines of research may depend on the issues that have been reviewed above.

One line of research explores the question of whether there are basic emotions. A basic emotion can be defined as one that is functionally basic and biologically basic. To say that an emotion is functionally basic is to say that it does not have other emotions as parts and that it is not constituted by components that are used to constitute other emotions. To say that an emotion is biologically basic is to say it is species typical and unlearned, or innate. Some authors argue that all emotions are basic, meaning that each is an innate response profile that functions independently of one's capacity to have any other (Ekman 1999). Some authors say that no emotions are basic, meaning all derive from a more primitive set of components that underlie every emotion, such as appraisal judgments (Ortony and Turner 1990). Still others say there is a basic stock of primitive emotions that combine together or get elaborated to form others (Plutchik 1980).

Research on basic emotions relates to work on emotion recognition. We can recognize some emotions by their facial expressions, and this can even be done unconsciously. It often supposed that the emotions we recognize are basic because basic emotions may have distinctive innate, facial expressions. Proponents of basic emotions often try to identify and expand their lists of basic emotions by looking for a set of cross-culturally identifiable faces. Ekman, Sorenson, and Friesen (1969) argues that there is cross-culturally robust recognition of joy, sadness, anger, disgust, surprise, and fear. Recently, various researchers have tried to expand this list to include contempt, pride, embarrassment, shame, among others. Russell (1994) critiques this research and argues that interpretation of emotional expressions is cognitively mediated.

Cultural comparison also plays a role in another area of research: the origins of emotions. Some who think that emotions are innate also offer evolutionary explanations for how they came to exist (Plutchik 1980). Others argue that emotions are socially constructed, meaning that emotions are attained through cultural learning and are not necessarily shared across groups (Harré 1986). Defenders of appraisal theories can argue that cultures introduce novel emotions by inculcating culturally specific patterns of appraisal or by applying the same universal appraisals to events that are appraised differently in other social settings. It may turn out that some emotions are evolved and others are constructed, in which case emotions may not constitute a natural kind (Griffiths 1997).

Quite a different line of research explores the roles of emotions in reasoning. Historically, emotions have been regarded as irrational forces that interfere with reasoning. As already noted, however, emotions contribute to cognitive styles in systematic ways and, sometimes, to our advantage. Recall that positive emotions can make us more creative (Isen *et al.* 1987) and negative emotions can make us more accurate (Alloy and Abrahamson 1988). There is currently an interest in how we use emotions online to make decisions, and one popular view is that we sometimes decide what to do by anticipating the emotional consequences. Recall that sometimes people make riskier decisions when emotions are impaired (Damasio *et al.* 1991). On cognitive theories of emotion, it is no surprise that emotions influence reasoning, since they comprise judgments. Non-cognitive theorists argue that emotions influence reasoning by giving rise to gut feelings, rather than judgments.

There is also extensive research on individual differences in emotions, coping strategies, and psychopathology (for a review, see Rottenberg and Johnson 2007). People differ in their degree of emotionality and the degree to which they experience emotions and to which they can describe what they experience. Poor capacity to express emotions is called alexithymia. Some people also experience pathological levels of specific emotions, such an anxiety, which can be regarded as excessive or inappropriate worry. The capacity to respond to emotions that might otherwise interfere with life depends on coping strategies, which can be improved using cognitive behavioral therapy (CBT). Talk therapy can also be used to identify unconscious causes of pathological emotions and offer strategies for reconstruing life events in more positive ways. Talk therapy and CBT are especially likely to work in cases where emotions are elicited by cognitive appraisals. In cases where emotions have non-cognitive causes, pharmaceutical interventions may be more effective. These are active questions in clinical research but also relate quite clearly to questions at the heart of this chapter.

10.5   Conclusion

This chapter reviewed recent research on the emotions with an emphasis on their causes, constituents, and effects. One major dispute that emerged is between cognitive theories, which emphasize the role of appraisal judgments in emotions, and non-cognitive theories, which propose that emotions can arise in the absence of cognition. This debate has ramifications for other research questions, including the question of whether emotions can be culturally constructed, whether some emotions are basic, the ways in which emotions influence reasoning, and the strategies available for treating emotional pathologies.

Further reading

Damasio, A. R. (1999). *The Feeling of What Happens: Body and Emotion in the Making of Consciousness.* New York: Harcourt Brace and Company. An accessible review of emotion systems in the brain, and their relation to body and self.

Ekman, P. and Davidson, R. J. (eds.) (1994). *The Nature of Emotion: Fundamental Questions.* Oxford University Press. A great overview of core questions in emotion research and competing answers.

Frank, R. H. (1988). *Passions within Reason: The Strategic Role of the Emotions.* New York: Norton. Emotions and reasoning from the perspective of evolutionary theory and economics.

Jenkins, J. M., Oatley, K., and Stein, N. L. (eds.) (1998). *Human Emotions: A Reader.* Oxford: Blackwell. A collection of classic readings on emotion research, from Darwin to the present.

Manstead, A. S. R., Frijda, N. H., and Fischer, A. H. (eds.) (2004). *Feelings and Emotions*. New York: Cambridge University Press. Essays by some of the most influential figures in recent psychology of the emotions.

Mesquita, B. and Frijda, N. H. (1992). Cultural variations in emotions: A review, *Psychological Bulletin* 112: 179–204. A handy review of research on cultural similarities and differences in emotion.

Prinz, J. J. (2004). *Gut Reactions: A Perceptual Theory of Emotions*. New York: Oxford University Press. Provides an overview of emotion research, and defends a non-cognitive Jamesian theory.

Scherer, K., Schorr, A., and Johnstone, T. (eds.) (2001). *Appraisal Processes in Emotion: Theory, Methods, Research*. Oxford University Press. An excellent anthology of recent cognitive approaches to emotions in psychology.

Solomon, R. C. (2004). *Thinking about Feeling: Contemporary Philosophers on Emotions*. Oxford University Press. Essays by some of the most influential figures in recent philosophy of the emotions.

References

Alloy, L. and Abrahamson, L. (1988). Depressive realism, in L. B. Alloy (ed.), *Cognitive Processes in Depression* (pp. 441–85). New York: Guilford Press.

Arnold, M. B. (1960). *Emotion and Personality*. New York: Columbia University Press.

Barrett, L. F. (2006). Emotions as natural kinds? *Perspectives on Psychological Science* 1: 28–58.

Berridge, K. C. (1996). Food reward: Brain substrates of wanting and liking, *Neuroscience and Biobehavioral Reviews* 20: 1–25.

Blood, A. J., Zatorre, R. J., Bermudez, P., and Evans, A. C. (1999). Emotional responses to pleasant and unpleasant music correlate with activity in paralimbic brain regions, *Nature Neuroscience* 2: 382–7.

Bouhuys, A. L., Bloem, G. M., and Groothuis, T. G. G. (1995). Induction of depressed and elated mood by music influences the perception of facial emotional expressions in healthy subjects, *Journal of Affective Disorders* 33: 215–26.

Bower, G. H. (1981). Mood and memory, *American Psychologist* 36: 129–48.

Cacioppo, J., Berntson, G., Larson, J., Poechlmann, K., and Ito, T. (2000). The psychophysiology of emotion, in M. Lewis and J. Haviland-Jones (eds.), *Handbook of Emotions* (2nd edn., pp. 173–91). New York: Guilford Press.

Chen, M. and Bargh, J. A. (1999). Nonconscious approach and avoidance behavioral consequences of the automatic evaluation effect, *Personality and Social Psychology Bulletin* 25: 215–24.

Critchley, H. D., Mathias, C. J., and Dolan, R. J. (2001). Neural correlates of first and second-order representation of bodily states, *Nature Neuroscience* 4: 207–12.

Damasio, A. R. (1994). *Descartes' Error: Emotion, Reason, and the Human Brain*. New York: Gossett/Putnam.

Damasio, A. R., Grabowski, T. J., Bechara, A. *et al.* (2000). Subcortical and cortical brain activity during the feeling of self-generated emotions, *Nature Neuroscience* 3: 1049–56.

Damasio, A. R., Tranel, D., and Damasio, H. (1991). Somatic markers and the guidance of behavior: Theory and preliminary testing, in H. S. Levin, H. M. Eisenberg, and A. L. Benton (eds.), *Frontal Lobe Function and Dysfunction* (pp. 217–29). New York: Oxford University Press.

Ekman, P. (1993). Facial expression and emotion, *American Psychologist* 48: 384–92.

  (1999). Basic emotions, in T. Dalgleish and T. Power (eds.), *The Handbook of Cognition and Emotion* (pp. 45–60). New York: John Wiley and Sons.

Ekman, P., Sorenson, E. R., and Friesen. W. V. (1969). Pan-cultural elements in facial displays of emotions, *Science* 164: 86–8.

Fredrickson, B. L. (1998). What good are positive emotions? *Review of General Psychology* 2: 300–19.

Frijda, N. H. (1986). *The Emotions.* Cambridge University Press.

Gordon, R. (1987). *The Structure of Emotions.* Cambridge University Press.

Gray, J. A. (1991). The neuropsychology of temperament, in J. Strelau and A. Angleitner (eds.), *Explorations in Temperament* (pp. 105–28). New York: Plenum Press.

Griffiths, P. E. (1997). *What Emotions Really Are.* University of Chicago Press.

Harré, R. (1986). The social constructivist viewpoint, in R. Harré (ed.), *The Social Construction of Emotions* (pp. 2–14). Oxford: Blackwell.

Isen, A. M., Daubman, K. A., and Nowicki, G. P. (1987). Positive affect facilitates creative problem solving, *Journal of Personality and Social Psychology* 52: 1122–31.

Isen, A. M. and Levin, P. F. (1972). Effect of feeling good on helping: Cookies and kindness, *Journal of Personality and Social Psychology* 21: 384–8.

James, W. (1884). What is an Emotion? *Mind* 9: 188–205.

Johnson, K. J. and Fredrickson, B. L. (2005). We all look the same to me: Positive emotions eliminate the own-race bias in face recognition, *Psychological Science* 16: 875–81.

Laberge, F., Mühlenbrock-Lenter, S., Grunwald, W., and Roth, G. (2006). Evolution of the amygdala: New insights from studies in amphibians, *Brain, Behavior and Evolution* 67: 177–87.

Laird, J. D. (1974). Self-attribution of emotion: The effects of expressive behavior on the quality of emotional experience, *Journal of Personality and Social Psychology* 29: 475–86.

Lange, C. G. (1885). *Om sindsbevaegelser: et psyko-fysiologisk studie.* Kjbenhavn: Jacob Lunds. Reprinted (1922) in *The Emotions*, C. G. Lange and W. James (eds.), I. A. Haupt (trans.). Baltimore: Williams and Wilkins Company.

Lazarus, R. S. (1984). On the primacy of cognition, *American Psychologist* 39: 124–9.

  (1991). *Emotion and Adaptation.* New York: Oxford University Press.

Lazarus, R. S. and Alfert, E. (1964). Short-circuiting of threat by experimentally altering cognitive appraisal, *Journal of Abnormal and Social Psychology* 69: 195–205.

LeDoux, J. E. (1996). *The Emotional Brain*. New York: Simon & Schuster.

Lerner, J., Goldberg, J., and Tetlock, P. E. (1998). Sober second thought: The effects of accountability, anger, and authoritarianism on attributions of responsibility, *Personality and Social Psychology Bulletin* 24: 563–74.

Levenson, R. W., Ekman, P., and Friesen, W. V. (1990). Voluntary facial action generates emotion-specific autonomic nervous system activity, *Psychophysiology* 27: 363–84.

Nussbaum, M. C. (2001). *Upheavals of Thought: The Intelligence of the Emotions*. Cambridge University Press.

Öhman, A., Flykt, A., and Esteves, F. (2001). Emotion drives attention: Detecting the snake in the grass, *Journal of Experimental Psychology: General* 130: 466–78.

Ortony, A., Clore, G. L., and Collins, A. (1988). *The Cognitive Structure of Emotions*. Cambridge University Press.

Ortony, A. and Turner, W. (1990). What's basic about basic emotions? *Psychological Review* 97: 315–31.

Palinkas, L. A. and Houseal, M. (2000). Stages of change in mood and behavior during a winter in Antarctica, *Environment and Behavior* 32: 128–41.

Phan, K. L., Wager, T. D., Taylor, S. F., and Liberzon, I. (2002). Functional neuroanatomy of emotion: A meta-analysis of emotion activation studies in PET and fMRI, *NeuroImage* 16: 331–48.

Pitcher, G. (1965). Emotion, *Mind* 74: 324–46.

Plutchik, R. (1980). *Emotion: A Psychoevolutionary Synthesis*. New York: Harper & Row.

Prinz, J. J. (2004). *Gut Reactions: A Perceptual Theory of Emotions*. New York: Oxford University Press.

   (2007). *The Emotional Construction of Morals*. Oxford University Press.

Roseman, I. J., Spindel, M. S., and Jose, P. E. (1990). Appraisals of emotion-eliciting events: Testing a theory of discrete emotions, *Journal of Personality and Social Psychology* 59: 899–915.

Roth, D. L. (1989). Acute emotional and psychophysiological effects of aerobic exercise, *Psychophysiology* 26: 593–602.

Rottenberg, J. and Johnson, S. L. (eds.) (2007). *Emotion and Psychopathology: Bridging Affective and Clinical Science*. Washington, D.C.: APA Books.

Russell, J. A. (1980). A circumplex model of affect, *Journal of Personality and Social Psychology* 39: 1169–78.

   (1994). Is there universal recognition of emotion from facial expression? A review of cross-cultural studies, *Psychological Bulletin* 115: 102–41.

Schachter, S. and Singer, J. (1962). Cognitive, social, and physiological determinants of emotional state, *Psychological Review* 69: 379–99.

Smith, C. A. and Lazarus, R. S. (1993). Appraisal components, core relational themes, and the emotions, *Cognition and Emotion* 7: 233–69.

Solomon, R. C. (1976). *The Passions*. New York: Doubleday.

Solomon, R. C. (2003). Against valence, in R. C. Solomon, *Not Passion's Slave*. New York/Oxford: Oxford University Press.

Spinoza, Benedict De (1677/1994). *Ethics*, in *A Spinoza reader*, ed. and trans. E. Curley. Princeton University Press.

Strack, F., Martin, L., and Stepper, S. (1988). Inhibiting and facilitating conditions of the human smile: A nonobtrusive test of the facial feedback hypothesis, *Journal of Personality and Social Psychology* 54: 768–77.

Wheatley, T. and Haidt, J. (2005). Hypnotically induced disgust makes moral judgments more severe, *Psychological Science* 16: 780–4.

Wierzbicka, A. (1999). *Emotions across Languages and Cultures: Diversity and Universals*. Cambridge University Press.

Zajonc, R. B. (1984). On the primacy of affect, *American Psychologist* 39: 117–23.

Zajonc, R. B., Murphy, S. T., and Inglehart, M. (1989). Feeling and facial efference: Implications for the vascular theory of emotion, *Psychological Review* 96: 395–416.

11 Consciousness

William G. Lycan

In 1989, the *Dictionary of Behavioral Science* defined "conscious or consciousness" as

1. Referring to the property of being aware or knowing. 2. Characterizing a
person who is aware. 3. Pertaining to the ability to react to stimulation in the
environment. 4. Pertaining to that which is observable by introspection.
5. (psychoanalysis) The upper part of the topographic structure where rational
processes can take place. (Wolman 1989, p. 72)

In the same year, the *Macmillan Dictionary of Psychology* offered this entry
for "consciousness":

[T]he having of perceptions, thoughts, and feelings; awareness. The term is
impossible to define except in terms that are unintelligible without a grasp of
what consciousness means. Many fall into the trap of equating consciousness
with self-consciousness – to be conscious it is only necessary to be aware of the
external world. Consciousness is a fascinating but elusive phenomenon: it is
impossible to specify what it is, what it does, or why it evolved. Nothing worth
reading has been written on it. (Sutherland 1989, p. 90)

Have matters improved? No subsequent reference work has thus disparaged
the entire literature without further comment,[1] but characterizations of "the"
explanandum in question are still a grab-bag.

Most psychologists regard consciousness as awareness. Unfortunately, the
concept of awareness is no less ambiguous... [A]wareness signifies, perceptual
awareness, introspective awareness, reflective awareness, subliminal awareness,
self-awareness, awareness of awareness, and so on. (K. Rao in the *Encyclopedia
of Psychology* 1994, p. 302)

1. Of or relating to the function of the mind through which one is aware of
mental experiences such as perceptions, thoughts, emotions, and wishes...

---

[1] Though some lingering pessimism is expressed in the 1999 *Companion to Cognitive Science*:
"Mentality is information processing... [I]ntelligent information processing is what
cognitive science studies. What does this have to do with consciousness? The answer is
nothing, unless consciousness is thought or found to be involved in information processing
in the systems, such as humans, that are conscious" (Bechtel and Graham 1999, pp. 178–9).

2. Awake, alert, and aware of what is happening in the immediate vicinity; not in a state of sleep, trance, or coma. 3. Aware of and giving due weight to something, as in *Are you conscious of the need for action? Or I am not at all clothes-conscious . . .* [T]he normal mental condition of the waking state of humans, characterized by the experience of perceptions, thoughts, feelings, awareness of the external world, and often in humans (but not necessarily in other animals) self-awareness. (Colman's *Dictionary of Psychology* 2001, p. 160)

There is a puzzle here. "Consciousness" is supposed to be "fascinating but elusive," mysterious, "impossible to define," and the like. Philosophers, especially, have made a very big deal of it: "Without consciousness the mind–body problem would be much less interesting. With consciousness it seems hopeless" (Nagel 1974, p. 166). But nothing in the passages quoted above suggests any great mystery. The "normal waking state" is whatever it is, neurophysiologically. And *insofar as* "consciousness" means only "the ability to react to stimulation in the environment" or "being aware" or "the having of perceptions," and "to be conscious it is only necessary to be aware of the external world," the phenomenon is not elusive, mysterious, or impossible to define. It is just perceiving, by one sense modality or another, and some human perceptual systems are fairly well (though of course not perfectly) understood.

11.1   Facets of consciousness

But in fact, there is a large multiplicity of topics besides sense perception that have been investigated under the heading of "consciousness studies," and they are strikingly diverse: empirical questions of accessibility, attention, and reportability; intentions and the control of voluntary action; various temporal anomalies, in which subjects seem to become aware of events before those events have happened (color phi, the cutaneous rabbit, etc.); the Binding Problem(s), e.g., of how the brain synthesizes information from different sense modalities into a unified experience; the development of the *self* concept; deficits and neglects; the possession of information without awareness of that information (blindsight, semantic etc. priming, agnosias with "covert knowledge," neglect ditto; see below); issues of unity and identity as in split-brain subjects; unexpected failures such as change blindness.

If there is any unifying theme here, Rao (following Natsoulas 1978) had it right: Each of the items on our scattered list is at least loosely about *awareness*. But Rao was wrong to call the concept of awareness ambiguous. His and our profusion of awarenesses is not a multiplicity of meanings of the term, but only that of awareness' objects, i.e., of the widely disparate things of which we can be aware: physical objects in the environment, parts of our own bodies, our own mental states, our awarenesses themselves, and perhaps more.[2]

If there were a solid motif, it might have attracted competing theories of the common phenomenon. But not so. As we shall see, though many scientists and philosophers have offered theories "of consciousness," the theories have respectively been directed toward quite specific and disparate explananda. Some of those are empirical and tractable to a degree. Others are almost purely philosophical and unilluminated by science. Often, some have been conflated with each other, which has not helped at all.

Here are some issues of "consciousness" that have recently concerned cognitive scientists. (Necessarily, my list is selective, and it is biased in favor of issues that interest philosophers.)

11.1.1   Attention and its relation to awareness and experience

William James (1890) famously held that we consciously experience all and only those stimuli that we attend to. Interestingly, there is evidence that some attentional processing does not produce conscious awareness (Kentridge, Heywood, and Weiskrantz 1999), so even if attention is necessary for consciousness it is not sufficient. It would be hard to decide empirically whether attention is necessary, because experiments would have to distinguish between complete lack of attention and merely a very low level of attention. (But see Mack and Rock 1998.)

There is an issue of how early or late in perceptual processing attention can affect what gets consciously perceived. The evidence is equivocal; some studies seem to support "early selection" while others seem to support "late" or even post-perceptual selection. Lavie and Tsal (1994) argue that this is because there is no such single processing stage; rather, attention affects perceptual processing earlier or later depending on level of perceptual load.

11.1.2   Information without awareness

There are many different sorts of case in which a subject is shown to have and use sensory information while unaware of possessing any such information. Perhaps the most dramatic of these is that of blindsight (Weiskrantz 1986). Patients with damage to striate cortex (V1) experience large blind spots. When stimuli are presented to their blind fields, they report seeing nothing; yet for some of those subjects, if they are asked to guess direction, motion, rudimentary shape or color, they do far better than chance, still with no awareness that their answers are anything but guesses. And there is semantic priming: if

---

[2] It would be pleasant to think that the concept "aware of" is familiar and unproblematic as well as unambiguous, but it is not unproblematic; see Dretske (2006).

a word or set of words is presented to the blind field, its meaning is likely to influence subjects' guesses on relevant topics.

There are several different theories of what is going on in blindsight. Some skeptical or deflationary theories (e.g., that blindsight is only degraded normal vision and subjects are just too cautious in reporting) have been fairly decisively refuted (Stoerig and Cowey 1995). Blindsight might be a failure of introspection, but the damage is in a specifically visual area, and in any case why would introspection fail so selectively? More plausibly, Milner and Goodale (1995) have suggested on the basis of independent evidence from brain-damaged patients that there are really two visual systems, one associated with the ventral cortical stream and one with the dorsal; it is the former that normally leads to visual awareness and reportability, while the latter is responsible for more primitive "online" visuomotor control. A possible explanation of blindsight, then, is that although the patient's ventral system is impaired, her or his dorsal system continues to deliver information despite the patient's scotoma.

11.1.3   Inattentional blindness and change blindness

Surprisingly, we fail to notice even large and obtrusive events that happen right before our eyes, if we are not narrowly attending to the relevant sectors of our visual fields (Mack and Rock 1998; Simons and Chabris 1999). The phenomenon is held to be specifically attentional, rather than a matter of eye movement or foveating. The extraordinary eye-tracking experiments recorded in Grimes (1996) (also Littman and Becklen 1976; Lavie 2006) have shown that subjects were blind even to what they foveated. Rensink, O'Regan, and Clark (1997) showed that if a photographic image is shown and followed after a "flicker" or brief blank interval by an altered version of the same image, subjects will usually not notice the change, even when it is fairly dramatic and even when the two images continue to alternate for a while. Typically, when a subject does finally notice the change or is shown it in slow motion, she or he is astonished at having missed it until then.

What morals should be drawn from these blindnesses? First, that the focus of ordinary perceptual attention at a moment is much narrower than we would commonsensically suppose. Second, that even if attention is not strictly required for awareness, lack of it can produce dramatic lack of awareness. Third, that a thing's being smack in front of our eyes is no guarantee that we will see it (but for dissent on this point, see Dretske 2006). A fourth moral is often alleged: that there is a "grand illusion" of introspection (see below).

11.1.4   "Filling in"

Everyone has a blind spot in each eye, because of there being no photoreceptors where the optic nerve leaves the retina. But no one notices this unless it is called to her or his attention in a fairly special, nearly experimental setup. Moreover, as James (1890) said, there are ubiquitous if tiny gaps in our experience – eye blinks, occlusions of objects by other objects, minute lapses of attention – yet we feel no gaps; our experience seems to us smooth and continuous. It is tempting to infer that the brain somehow "fills in" the gaps.

But what could this "filling in" be? Does the brain create extra representations to paper over the gaps between actual perceptual representations? Dennett (1991) resists that computationally expensive suggestion. First, he rightly distinguishes between not perceiving X and perceiving not-X; that we do not perceive things in our blind spots does not entail or even suggest that we would perceive nothingness there. Second, it is plausible to think that the brain employs "etc." or "more of the same" representations that extrapolate from a few actually represented items to suggest a whole field of such items without any more of them being individually represented (think of Warhol's mosaic of Marilyn Monroes).

Yet there are more complicated and startling cases of apparent "filling in" that do not seem to yield to either of those deflationary explanations; see especially Ramachandran and Gregory (1991) and Ramachandran and Blakeslee (1998). For example, the latter presented subjects with an array of yellow doughnut shapes. If one of the doughnut holes falls within a subject's blind spot, the subject will see a yellow *disk* among the doughnuts; indeed, it will "pop out." In some way yet to be explained, the doughnut hole has been filled in with yellow in particular.

11.1.5   The "grand illusion" issue

It seems to us that our visual fields are fairly rich in detail, as if we were watching a movie, or at least that at any given moment, we see a lot in front of us. But inattentional blindness, change blindness and the various "filling in" phenomena can be taken to show that although the richness and detail are there in front of us in the world, they are not in our actual perceptions; we perceive a lot less than we seem to ourselves to do. This is a "grand illusion," as it is called by Thompson, Pessoa, and Noë (2000). If that is correct, it would show that *introspection* is unexpectedly fallible in a striking way. (But Noë (2000) argues against this, maintaining that in fact it does not seem to us that our visual fields are fairly rich in detail.)

11.1.6   The temporal anomalies

There are well-known paradoxical cases in which we seem to become aware of a stimulus before it actually occurs. For example, "color phi" (Kolers and von Grunau 1976) is a startling twist on the familiar "phi" or "marquee" illusion, in which lights arranged in a fixed line light up one at a time in rapid succession and an observer seems to see a single light that moves along the line. In color phi, two adjacent lights of different colors are flashed in quick succession – say, first red and then green – and as in the noncolor case the observer seems to see a single moving light. But subjects uniformly report that the light changed from red to green as it moved, i.e., "the" light seemed to turn green before the green bulb came on! Cf. also the "cutaneous rabbit" (Geldard and Sherrick 1972).

Some theorists have gone so far as to take these mysterious goings-on as evidence of mind/body dualism, the idea being that the mind learns something before anything in the brain could learn that thing. (Notice that to account for the phenomena, an immaterial mind would have to be not only immaterial but precognitive in the paranormal sense of the term.) But a naturalistic explanation has been offered by Dennett (1991) and Dennett and Kinsbourne (1992).

11.1.7   Intentions, agency, and control of behavior

It is natural to think that our deliberate actions proceed from our conscious decisions. But Libet (1985) claimed to have shown that some voluntary motor actions are initiated in the brain before the agent decides to perform them. It had been known for some years that voluntary actions are preceded by the onset of a "readiness potential" in the brain. Libet's subjects were asked to decide to perform a simple action (such as raising a hand) and to signal the moment of their decision. When they did so, the decision did not occur until about 300 milliseconds after the readiness potential did. It seems, then, that the action was initiated prior to any conscious mentation on the agent's part.

Libet's methodology and experimental techniques have been subjected to intense scrutiny on each of several points (see Chapter 5), but his basic findings have held up well. In his experiments, the conscious decision to act is prefigured preconsciously. It is as if the decision is itself made unconsciously and the subject only later becomes aware of it. That is a bit eerie, but notice that nothing follows straightway about freedom of the will. In particular, that a decision is not a conscious one does not show that the action did not properly result from it, that the action was not the agent's own, or that it was not up to the agent whether to perform the action. Nonetheless, Wegner (2002) argues on the basis of his own experiments that the experience of free will is an illusion.

11.1.8   Unities and disunities

Normal consciousness displays a number of unities, synchronic and diachronic. We "bind" separate detections of position, shape, color, texture, and temperature into the perception of a single physical object such as a cup of coffee in our hand. We sense our own bodies as unitary physical objects. We experience change as such, i.e., first one thing and then another but in a single perception. These things and more need explaining (Dainton 2000; Bayne and Chalmers 2003; Tye 2003). And there are corresponding pathological disunities. For example, psychotics misidentify their own verbal thoughts as alien voices speaking to them; neurology patients may be alienated from their own limbs, perceiving them (horribly) as loose body parts of someone else's. And of course there is MPD (now Dissociative Identity Disorder), in which what looks like a single person displays multiple distinct personalities or identities at different times, each with its own characteristic behavior pattern and autobiography and sometimes some actually different physiology.

But in some ways the most extraordinary disunity of consciousness is that found in commissurotomized (split-brain) patients. Their everyday behavior is surprisingly normal. But under laboratory conditions in which different inputs are fed selectively to the different hemispheres, the patients seem to exhibit two streams of consciousness (Sperry 1968); each hemisphere perceives and knows things the other does not. For example, a subject's left hemisphere may see a picture of a live chicken and verbally report seeing a chicken, while the right hemisphere sees only a bottle and may reach for the bottle and a glass. In a few cases, a patient's left and right hands have frustratedly struggled with each other.

Nagel (1971) considered five hypotheses: (1) Only the left hemisphere is a conscious mind; the right hemisphere is a mere automaton. (2) There is mentation in right hemisphere, but it is not integrated into a mind. (3) There are two minds, one in each hemisphere. (4) There is only one mind, but it is dissociated mind. (5) There is ordinarily one normal mind, but the experimental conditions cause temporary fission. (Notice that each of these extrapolates to the normal human being: e.g., if (3) is true and a split-brain patient has two minds, one in the left hemisphere and one in the right, should we not infer that you now have two minds, one in each hemisphere, or maybe even that "you" are really two people locked up in one body?) Each theory has had its supporters. For additional discussion, see Marks (1981).

The perceptual examples in this section have all involved vision, rather than hearing, smell, taste, or touch. That bias reflects the literature, but is unfortunate: If a phenomenon is exhibited by vision but not for another sense modality, that would be an important constraint on explaining the phenomenon.

Some of the topics and issues that have gone under the heading of "consciousness" are straightforwardly empirical. Some are more abstractly theoretical. Some, as we have seen, are in between. Some are outright philosophical and conceptual: Philosophers (and a few psychologists as well) have tended to think of "consciousness" in the same mental breath as "phenomenal character," "qualia," "subjectivity," "the phenomenal/qualitative feel of our experience," and the like. Those issues will be addressed in section 11.3.

11.2 "State" consciousness

A theoretical and only mildly philosophical question is that of *state/event consciousness*. A mental state of a subject, or an event occurring within the subject, is a "conscious" state or event as opposed to an unconscious, pre-conscious or subconscious one if, and only if, the subject is directly aware of being in the state/hosting the event; cf. "a conscious memory," "a conscious decision." (That is a stipulative definition, needed because the phrase "conscious state" has been used in several quite different senses, as, e.g., by Dretske (1993, 1995) and Block (1995); failure to keep these senses separate has led to much confusion.) That direct access we have to the internal qualitative character of our experience is privileged; you are aware of your own experience in a way in which others cannot be aware of your experience. Yet this is true of only some of your mental states; of others you are entirely unaware, either because you simply do not notice them, or because (like motives) they are very difficult to introspect, or because (like language-processing states) they are structurally inaccessible to introspection. In virtue of what, then, is a mental state a conscious one in this sense?

The leading theories here are the *higher-order* (HO) theories, according to which the state/event in question is itself the object of one of the subject's mental representations.[3]

HO theories come in two types: the Lockean *inner sense* or *higher-order perception* (HOP) view offered by Armstrong (1968, 1981) and Lycan (1987, 1996), and the *higher-order thought* (HOT) theory defended by Rosenthal (1993, 1997) (see also Gennaro 1996). According to HOP, the higher-order representing of the target state is done quasi-perceptually, by a set of internal monitors or attention mechanisms, that scan other mental/brain states. On this view, introspective awareness is much like internal perception, and (like any mode of perception) gives its subject a unique and partial perspective on what she or he is perceiving.

Baars' (1988) *global workspace* theory is a close relative of HOP, since he identifies conscious activity with that which takes place under the "spotlight" of attention, in a "workspace" in which the incoming outputs of many parallel

---

[3] Competing views include Dennett's (1969) *volume control* hypothesis, subsequently defended by Hill (1987, 1991), and the *intermediate level* theory proposed by Jackendoff (1987) and developed by Prinz (2005, 2007). HO theories have occasionally been taken to be more ambitious, as attempts to explain not only state consciousness but "phenomenal consciousness" in a sense to be addressed in section 11.3 below (Carruthers 2004; Byrne 2004). On that understanding they have a wider field of competitors, such as "FOR" theories of phenomenal consciousness.

processes are broadcast widely throughout the system, access to the workspace being governed by the attention mechanisms. But Baars' own emphasis is on the broadcasting, which constitutes the integrative function of consciousness (cf. Dehaene and Naccache 2001).

HOT theorists resist the perceptual model, and maintain that merely having a thought about the first-order state will suffice for consciousness, provided that the thought arose from the state itself without benefit of (person-level) inference. HOT has two obvious advantages over HOP: It does not require the higher-order representations to be in any way perception-like, and in particular it posits no special scanning or monitoring mechanism. But it has several disadvantages as well. For example, it does not explain our voluntary control over which of our own mental states we attend to. (You can concentrate on your visual field as such, then decide to focus on a particular patch of phenomenal red, then shift your attention to the upper left quadrant of the field, then ask yourself what you are smelling at the moment, etc., and you can do those things at will, with a remarkable degree of facility and precision. All that activity feels unmistakably like scanning and monitoring rather than just thinking.) Also, since thought is conceptual, it requires the subject to mobilize concepts that small children and higher animals probably do not have.[4]

It is usually thought by HO proponents that for a state to be a conscious one is for it to be represented by *another* of the subject's mental states. But, following Brentano (1874), a number of theorists have maintained that the higher-order content in virtue of which a conscious state is conscious is not that of a separate and distinct state, but is intrinsic to the original state itself (Gennaro 1996, 2004; Natsoulas 1996; Kriegel 2003; Van Gulick 2004, 2006). Van Gulick offers a *higher-order global state* (HOGS) theory designed to capture that idea; on his view, the first-order state is "recruited" into a complex global state that constitutes the subject's "conscious self-awareness" at a time; indeed, it is incorporated into that higher-order global state as a component. Van Gulick (2004) argues that this view has several advantages over both HOP and HOT.

HO theories face one chief objection. Some philosophers, such as Shoemaker (1994), have complained that HO theories leave introspective beliefs too fallible and actually underrate the privileged access we have to our own mental states. An internal monitor, or whatever device produces a higher-order thought, works only contingently; it might produce a false representation. But the objectors contend that our awareness of our own mental states is either infallible or in any case not as readily fallible as would be the contingent operation of a mechanism. Neander (1998) offers an especially incisive version of the objection: Since the relevant representation could be a false positive, it could seem to you introspectively that you were in agonizing,

---

[4] Lycan (2004) defends HOP as against HOT; Rosenthal (2004) replies.

unbearable pain, when in fact you were in no pain whatever. Does that even make sense?[5]

HOP and HOT theorists have assumed that the relevant higher-order representation is an actual, occurrent psychological state. That assumption has been challenged by Carruthers (2000, 2004), who proposes that a first-order state may be conscious in virtue merely of being disposed to give rise (noninferentially) to a higher-order thought. What grounds the disposition, Carruthers suggests, is that the target state is held in short-term memory, and is thereby available to thought. The dispositional theory inherits the advantages of HOT noted above.

11.3   Purely philosophical issues

An important division within matters of "consciousness" is that of "how does" questions from "how possibly" questions: "How does a human subject/brain accomplish such-and-such a task?" vs. "How could a mere information-processing system possibly have properties of this remarkable sort?" or "How could this refractory mental phenomenon possibly be explained by any existing sort of theory?" or even "How is this mental phenomenon physically possible at all?"

Cognitive or brain scientists sometimes introduce their papers by reference to one or another notorious "how possibly" question, and even voice that question in a tone of awed respect, but then proceed to announce that what we need is more information-processing models, or more neuroscience, ignoring the theoretical obstacle that drives the "how possibly" question, the obstacle that makes the relevant capacity seem impossible.[6]

For example, all too often it is suggested that advances in cognitive neuroscience will solve Thomas Nagel's (1974) and Frank Jackson's (1982) conceptual problem of "knowing what it's like." Nagel and Jackson contend that no amount of scientific, third-person information about a bat or a fellow human being would suffice to predict or explain what it is like for that subject to experience such-and-such a type of sensation; hence, they infer, there is an irreducible, intrinsically perspectival kind of phenomenal knowledge that precisely cannot be revealed by science of any kind. Nagel's and Jackson's respective *Knowledge Arguments* for this radical thesis are purely philosophical; they contain no premises that depend on scientific fact. Now, either the arguments are unsound or they are sound. If they are unsound, then so far as has been shown, there is no such irreducible knowledge, and neither science nor anything else is needed to produce it. But if the arguments are

---

[5] Lycan (1998) tries, not very effectually, to answer Neander.
[6] This theme has also been emphasized, and well documented, by Block (1995) and by Chalmers (1996).

sound, they show that no amount of science could possibly help to produce the special phenomenal knowledge. And in particular, note that no "new" post-Newtonian science, such as quantum physics or chaos theory or nonlinear dynamics, could. Either way, neither neuroscience nor any other science is pertinent. (More on the knowledge argument below.)

The further topics and issues that philosophers have debated under the heading of "consciousness" form a category that is fairly separate from the concerns catalogued in the previous two sections. As noted above, philosophers often use "consciousness" to refer to the "phenomenal." At least four separate problems fall into this category (though Chalmers 1996 conflates them under the label "the hard problem"). They are a daunting array.

Theories "of consciousness" have been offered by cognitive scientists (Mandler 1985; Jackendoff 1987; Baars 1988; Johnson-Laird 1988; Shallice 1988a, 1988b; Schacter 1989; Kosslyn and Koenig 1992; Humphrey 1992), and by neuroscientists (Edelman 1989, 1992; Crick and Koch 1990; Crick 1994; Tononi 2004). As we have seen, philosophers have put forward others, notably the HO theories and Dennett's (1991) *multiple drafts* theory. But a key thing to grasp about all of these is that not one of them even addresses any of the four problems of phenomenal experience. To say that is not pejorative, and in particular it is no criticism of any of the theories. Their creators did not really aim them at any of the philosophical problems, though they may have paid lip service as noted above. Others, particularly the philosophers, have invoked some of the theories in crafting solutions to the four problems, but only in ancillary roles.

As Chalmers (1996) has emphasized, no one should claim that problems of phenomenal experience have been solved by any purely cognitive or neuroscientific theory. But neither can such theories fairly be criticized for failing to illuminate problems of phenomenal experience. And many of them have been so criticized, e.g., by Chalmers (1996) (also, Block 1993, and Goldman 1993). HOP and HOT, in particular, are very explicitly theories of *awareness* and of privileged access, not theories of *qualia* or of *subjectivity* or of "what it's like," to name several different aspects of "phenomenal experience." Here are the four problems.

11.3.1   Sensory qualities

Sensory qualities ("qualia" in the strict sense)[7] are the first-order qualitative features of which we are aware in sensory experience: colors, pitches, smells, textures. It is important to see that such perceptions may be illusory and the properties unreal. If you are hallucinating pink rats, there are no real rats

---

[7] The technical term "qualia" has been used in diverse loose ways. The present sense is that of Lewis (1929) and Goodman (1951).

and likewise no pink things in your actual environment, but nonetheless you are experiencing some pinkness. When you are aware of a green after-image, what exactly is it that has the green color? For that matter, when you are (veridically) seeing a ripe banana, there is a corresponding yellow patch in your visual field. What ontological account is to be given of the yellowness of that patch (which might be as it is even if the banana were not real)? Bertrand Russell took it to be obvious, in need of no argument at all, that the bearers of such phenomenal color properties are nonphysical individuals, "sense data" as he called them; for impressive argument in addition, see Jackson (1977).

Psychology and neuroscience can have no truck with nonphysical or immaterial things, and materialist philosophers want none of them either. But there is a nasty problem. Suppose that while you are experiencing the after-image, there is in reality no green physical object in your environment. Suppose also that there is no green physical object in your brain. But there is a green *something* before you, Russellian sense-datum or not. If there is no green physical object outside your head and no green physical object inside your head, it follows that the green something is a nonphysical object. So much for materialism; it seems that the green thing might as well be a sense-datum after all. (This is a problem that only a philosopher could love.)

The leading attempt to carry us between the horns of this dilemma is what has come to be called the *representational* theory of the sensory qualities: When you see a (real) ripe banana and there is a corresponding yellow patch in your visual field, the yellowness "of" the patch is, like the banana itself, a representatum, an intentional object of the experience. The experience represents the banana and it represents the yellowness *of the banana*, and the latter yellowness is all the yellowness that is involved; there is no mental patch that is itself yellow. If you were only hallucinating a banana, the unreal banana would still be a representatum, but now only a nonexistent intentional object; and so would be its yellowness. The yellowness would be as it is even though the banana were not real. Likewise, when you experience a green after-image, you visually represent a colored spot in real physical space, and the greenness is the represented spot's represented color.

Here is how the representationalist eludes the Russellian dilemma: Notice that each of its horns assumes that the green "something" is an *actual* thing (else we could not derive the unwanted conclusion that there actually exists a nonphysical green thing). The representational theory affords a third alternative, by supposing that sensory qualities are merely *intentional contents* of sensory states, properties of intentional objects, represented properties of representata. Of course it is characteristic of intentional contents, such as the pink rats, that they and their colors may or may not actually exist. Your visual system quite often portrays, alleges something green. But, vision being not entirely reliable, on a given occasion the green thing may or may not actually exist.

Suppose Ned is seeing a real Granny Smith apple in good light, and it looks green to him. He is visually representing the actual greenness of the apple, and veridically so. But suppose Ted is experiencing a green after-image as a result of seeing a red flash bulb go off. According to the representational theory, that is for Ted to be visually representing a filmy green blob located at such-and-such a spot in the room. The representation has a truth-condition involving greenness.

There visually appears to Ned to be a green apple; there visually appears to Ted to be a green blob. Ned's apple is real and so is its greenness, but Ted's blob is unreal, merely an intentional object, and so is its greenness. The greenness is the color of an illusory, nonexistent thing.

Note that to suppose that because the object of awareness is green, there must be something green about the representing experience itself, would be an instance of a common fallacy: that of confusing the object of awareness with the awareness, the being aware, itself. All too often psychologists or philosophers tacitly and fallaciously infer properties of one from those of the other. More generally, we tend to conflate properties of a represent*ing* with those of the represent*ed*. E.g., from the fact that we experience visual images that are in some sense pictorial rather than sentence- or formula-like, it does not follow (though it might still be true) that there is anything else pictorial about the relevant representations themselves.

11.3.2   Perspectivalness

The second problem is the intrinsic perspectivalness, point-of-view-iness, and/or first-personishness of experience, as discussed by Gunderson (1970), Nagel (1974), and others. In one way or another, our experience of our own mental states requires the adopting of a very special point of view; our experience of our external environment, though invariably from a point of view, is not perspectival in the same, deeper way.

The best hope here is offered by HO theories of state consciousness, especially HOP. If introspection is the operation of an internal scanner or monitor that produces representations of your first-order mental states themselves, those representations will be selective and perspectival as all representations are, especially if they are made of concepts peculiar to the monitoring device. Ways of representing one and the same thing can differ so strikingly from each other as to convince us falsely that different things are represented. For example, seeing an event and hearing the same event may be nothing alike. And introspecting what is in fact a neural event is not a bit like seeing that same event as from outside one's head, using mirrors. Your introspective device deploys very distinctive concepts of its own. These features of the introspector combine, the HOP theorist can maintain, to explain the intrinsic perspectivalness of the mental: The mental *as such* is the neural, not as such, but as viewed from the unique introspective perspective.

An alternative but not incompatible explanation suggested by Loar (1990) and Papineau (2002) is that we are acquainted with our own mental states under distinctively phenomenal concepts. Such concepts are unique in that they neither need nor have the descriptive backings that attend ordinary concepts. As before, the mental *in propria persona* is the neural, but a subject represents her or his own mental states in a uniquely unmediated way. Phenomenal concepts are said to be "purely recognitional" concepts; they classify sensations and other mental states without bearing any analytic or otherwise a priori connections to other concepts easily expressible in natural language, and without dependence on the subject's existing beliefs about the mental state in question. And, practically speaking, to have the concept one must oneself have experienced the mental state in question.

It is in part because we have concepts of this sort that we are able to conceive of having a sensation of *this* kind without the sensation's playing its usual causal role, without its representing what it usually represents, without its being physical at all, etc. For the same reason, we are able to conceive of there being a body that is just like ours and in exactly similar circumstances but that is not giving rise to a sensation of *this* kind. From our ability to conceive these things mind/body dualism is sometimes fallaciously inferred.

11.3.3   Funny facts

The third problem is the existence of funny facts and/or special phenomenal knowledge as allegedly revealed by the knowledge arguments mentioned above. Jackson (1982) offers the now familiar example of Mary, the brilliant color scientist trapped in an entirely black-and-white laboratory. (Even she herself is painted black and white.) Working through her internet connection and various black-and-white monitors, she becomes scientifically omniscient as regards the physics and chemistry of color, the neurophysiology of color vision, and every other conceivably relevant scientific fact; we may even suppose that she becomes scientifically omniscient, period. Yet when she is finally released from her captivity and ventures into the outside world, she sees colors themselves for the first time, and she thereby learns something, viz., she learns what it is like to see red and many of the other colors. That is, she learns what it is like to experience *subjective* or phenomenal redness, never mind the actual colors of the physical objects she encounters (which, scientifically, she already knew).

And so she has acquired information that is – by hypothesis – outside the whole domain of science. It is intrinsically subjective phenomenal information, and what she has learned seems to be an intrinsically perspectival *fact*, that eludes all of science. According to materialist theories of mind, no fact about the mind is anything but a neurophysiological or otherwise scientific or "objective" fact; so it would follow that materialism is false.

A number of responses are available to the materialist. One (Dennett 1991) is ruthlessly to insist that if Mary really did know *all* the scientific/"objective" facts, she would after all know what it is like to see red. A second is to grant that Mary would learn something but to hold that her acquisition is, not a fact, but a mere ability, a knowing-*how* (Nemirow 1990; Lewis 1990) or a mere acquaintance (Conee 1994).

But the most popular response is to maintain that although Mary does learn a fact, she does so only in a very fine-grained sense of "fact," not in that of a new chunky fact in the world. Learning and knowledge are representation-dependent: You can know that water is spilling without knowing that H_2O molecules are moving; if I am amnesic I can know that WGL is a philosopher of mind without knowing that I myself am a philosopher of mind. In such cases, I know one and the same chunky fact under one way of representing it but not under a different one. Similarly, Mary is newly able not only to go into the brain state that constitutes seeing red, but to represent it in a dramatically new way, introspectively. She now knows that seeing red is like... *this*. This thin-fact approach is trenchantly criticized by Levine (2001).

11.3.4   The explanatory gap

The last problem is the *explanatory gap* called to our attention by Levine (1983, 1993): Even if God were to assure us that materialism is true and that such-and-such a conscious experience is strictly identical with a firing of certain neural fibers, we would still lack an explanation of why those fiber firings feel to their subjects in the distinctive way they do. Indeed, to Levine it seems "arbitrary" that they do.

As before, Dennett (1991) denies that there is any such gap in principle. But notice that if there is, it is not confined to consciousness in any sense or even to mind; there are many kinds of intrinsically perspectival (fine-grained) facts that cannot be explained. Suppose an opthalmologist explains why WGL is nearsighted. That does nothing to explain why *I* am nearsighted; nor could anyone or anything explain that – unless, of course, one *first* conceded the identity of me with WGL.

11.4   Conclusion

Brian Smith once said of computation that it "is a *site*, not a subject-matter." By comparison, "consciousness" is a flea market. We can at least broadly distinguish empirical from philosophical issues, and cognitive scientists are making some progress on the former. The latter will remain a battleground.

Further reading

Baars, B. J., Banks, W. P., and Newman, J. B. (eds.) (2003). *Essential Sources in the Scientific Study of Consciousness*. Cambridge, MA: MIT Press. Comprehensive; a very large range of classic and newer material.

Block, N. J., Flanagan, O., and Güzeldere, G. (eds.) (1997). *The Nature of Consciousness*. Cambridge, MA: Bradford Books/MIT Press. Philosophers' writings on "state" consciousness and the problems of phenomenal experience.

Chalmers, D. (1996). *The Conscious Mind*. Oxford University Press. A complex argument against materialism based on the problems of phenomenal experience.

Davies, M. and Humphreys, G. (eds.) (1993). *Consciousness*. Oxford: Basil Blackwell. A grab bag.

Dennett, D. C. (1991). *Consciousness Explained*. Boston: Little, Brown & Co. Offers a repressively deflationary view.

Smith, Q. and Jokic, A. (eds.) (2003). *Consciousness: New Philosophical Perspectives*. Oxford University Press. New philosophical essays.

Velmans, M. and Schneider, S. (eds.) (2007). *The Blackwell Companion to Consciousness*. Oxford: Blackwell Publishing. An excellent reference work.

Zelazo, P. D., Moscovitch, M., and Thompson, E. (eds.) (2007). *The Cambridge Handbook of Consciousness*. Cambridge University Press. Speculative papers by cognitive and neuroscientists.

References

Armstrong, D. M. (1968). *A Materialist Theory of the Mind*. London: Routledge and Kegan Paul.

(1981). What is consciousness?, in *The Nature of Mind and Other Essays* (pp. 55–67). Ithaca, NY: Cornell University Press.

Baars, B. J. (1988). *A Cognitive Theory of Consciousness*. Cambridge University Press.

Bayne, T. and Chalmers, D. (2003). What is the unity of consciousness?, in A. Cleermans (ed.), *The Unity of Consciousness: Binding, Integration, Dissociation* (pp. 23–58). Oxford University Press.

Bechtel, W. and Graham, G. (eds.) (1999). *A Companion to Cognitive Science*. Oxford: Blackwell.

Block, N. J. (1993). Review of D. C. Dennett, *Consciousness Explained, Journal of Philosophy* 90: 181–93.

(1995). On a confusion about a function of consciousness, *Behavioral and Brain Sciences* 18: 227–47.

Brentano, F. (1874). *Psychologie vom Empirischen Standpunkt.* Leipzig: Duncker & Humblot.

Byrne, A. (2004). What phenomenal consciousness is like, in R. J. Gennaro (ed.), *Higher-Order Theories of Consciousness* (pp. 203–25). Philadelphia, PA: John Benjamins.

Carruthers, P. (2000). *Phenomenal Consciousness.* Cambridge University Press.

(2004). HOP over FOR HOT theory, in R. Gennaro (ed.), *Higher-Order Theories of Consciousness* (pp. 115–35). Philadelphia, PA: John Benjamins.

Chalmers, D. (1996). *The Conscious Mind.* Oxford University Press.

Colman, A. M. (ed.) (2001). *Dictionary of Psychology.* Oxford University Press.

Conee, E. (1994). Phenomenal knowledge, *Australasian Journal of Philosophy* 72: 136–50.

Crick, F. (1994). *The Astonishing Hypothesis.* New York: Scribner's.

Crick, F. and Koch, C. (1990). Towards a neurobiological theory of consciousness, *Seminars in the Neurosciences* 2: 263–75.

Dainton, B. (2000). *Stream of Consciousness: Unity and Continuity in Experience.* London: Routledge.

Dehaene, S. and Naccache, L. (2001). Towards a cognitive neuroscience of consciousness: Basic evidence and a workspace framework, *Cognition* 79: 1–37.

Dennett, D. C. 1969. *Content and Consciousness.* London: Routledge and Kegan Paul.

(1991). *Consciousness Explained.* Boston: Little, Brown & Co.

Dennett, D. C. and Kinsbourne, M. (1992). Time and the observer: The where and when of consciousness in the brain, *Behavioral and Brain Sciences* 15: 183–247.

Dretske, F. (1993). Conscious experience, *Mind* 102: 263–83; reprinted in N. J. Block, O. Flanagan, and G. Güzeldere (eds.), *The Nature of Consciousness.* Cambridge, MA: Bradford Books/MIT Press.

(1995). *Naturalizing the Mind.* Cambridge, MA: Bradford Books/MIT Press.

(2006). Perception without awareness, in T. S. Gendler and J. Hawthorne (eds.), *Perceptual Experience* (pp. 147–80). Oxford University Press.

Edelman, G. (1989). *The Remembered Present: A Biological Theory of Consciousness.* New York: Basic Books.

(1992). *Bright Air, Brilliant Fire.* New York: Basic Books.

Geldard, F. A. and Sherrick, C. E. (1972). The cutaneous "rabbit": A perceptual illusion, *Science* 178: 178–9.

Gennaro, R. (1996). *Consciousness and Self-Consciousness.* Philadelphia, PA: John Benjamins.

(ed.) (2004). *Higher-Order Theories of Consciousness.* Philadelphia, PA: John Benjamins.

Goldman, A. I. (1993). Consciousness, folk psychology, and cognitive science, *Consciousness and Cognition* 2: 364–82.

Goodman, N. (1951). *The Structure of Appearance.* Cambridge, MA: Harvard University Press.

Grimes, J. (1996). On the failure to detect changes in scenes across saccades, in K. Akins (ed.), *Perception: Vancouver Studies in Cognitive Science* (vol. 5, pp. 89–110). Oxford University Press.

Gunderson, K. (1970). Asymmetries and mind–body perplexities, in M. Radner and S. Winokur (eds.), *Minnesota Studies in the Philosophy of Science* (vol. 4, pp. 273–309). Minneapolis: University of Minnesota Press.

Hill, C. S. (1987). Introspective awareness of sensations, *Topoi* 6: 9–22.

(1991). *Sensations*. Cambridge University Press.

Humphrey, N. (1992). *A History of the Mind: Evolution and the Birth of Consciousness*. New York: Simon & Schuster.

Jackendoff, R. (1987). *Consciousness and the Computational Mind*. Cambridge, MA: MIT Press.

Jackson, F. (1977). *Perception*. Cambridge University Press.

(1982). Epiphenomenal qualia, *Philosophical Quarterly* 32: 127–36.

James, W. (1890). *The Principles of Psychology*. London: Macmillan.

Johnson-Laird, P. N. (1988). A computational analysis of consciousness, in A. J. Marcel and E. Bisiach (eds.), *Consciousness in Contemporary Science* (pp. 357–68). New York: Clarendon Press/Oxford University Press.

Kentridge, R. W., Heywood, C. A., and Weiskrantz, L. (1999). Attention without awareness in blindsight, *Proceedings of the Royal Society of London Series B* 266: 1805–11.

Kolers, P. A. and von Grunau, M. (1976). Shape and color in apparent motion, *Vision Research* 16: 329–35.

Kosslyn, S. and Koenig, O. (1992). *Wet Mind: The New Cognitive Neuroscience*. Glencoe, IL: Free Press.

Kriegel, U. (2003). Consciousness as intransitive self-consciousness: Two views and an argument, *Canadian Journal of Philosophy* 33: 103–32.

Lavie, N. (2006). The role of perceptual load in visual awareness, *Brain Research* 1080: 91–100.

Lavie, N. and Tsal, Y. (1994). Perceptual load as a major determinant of the locus of selection in visual attention, *Perception and Psychophysics* 56: 183–97.

Levine, J. (1983). Materialism and qualia: The explanatory gap, *Pacific Philosophical Quarterly* 64: 354–61.

(1993). On leaving out what it's like, in M. Davies and G. Humphreys (eds.), *Consciousness* (pp. 121–36). Oxford: Blackwell.

2001. *Purple Haze*. Oxford University Press.

Lewis, C. I. (1929). *Mind and the World Order*. New York: C. Scribners Sons.

Lewis, D. K. (1990). What experience teaches, in W. G. Lycan (ed.), *Mind and Cognition* (pp. 499–519). Oxford: Blackwell.

Libet, B. (1985). Unconscious cerebral initiative and the role of conscious will in voluntary action, *Behavioral and Brain Sciences* 8: 529–39.

Littman, D. and Becklen, R. (1976). Selective looking with minimal eye movements, *Perception and Psychophysics* 20: 77–9.

Loar, B. (1990). Phenomenal states, in J. E. Tomberlin (ed.), *Philosophical Perspectives*, vol. 4: *Action Theory and Philosophy of Mind* (pp. 81–108). Atascadero, CA: Ridgeview Publishing.

Lycan, W. G. (1987). *Consciousness*. Cambridge, MA: Bradford Books/MIT Press.

(1996). *Consciousness and Experience*. Cambridge, MA: Bradford Books/MIT Press.

(1998). In defense of the representational theory of qualia (replies to Neander, Rey and Tye), in J. E. Tomberlin (ed.), *Philosophical Perspectives*, vol. 12: *Language, Mind, and Ontology* (pp. 479–87). Atascadero, CA: Ridgeview Publishing.

(2004). The superiority of HOP to HOT, in R. Gennaro (ed.), *Higher-Order Theories of Consciousness* (pp. 93–113). Philadelphia, PA: John Benjamins.

Mack, A. and Rock, I. (1998). *Inattentional Blindness*. Cambridge, MA: MIT Press.

Mandler, G. (1985). *Cognitive Psychology*. Hillsdale, NJ: Lawrence Erlbaum.

Marks, C. E. (1981). *Commissurotomy, Consciousness and the Unity of Mind*. Montgomery, VT: Bradford Books.

Milner, A. D. and Goodale, M. A. (1995). *The Visual Brain in Action*. Oxford University Press.

Nagel, T. (1971). Brain bisection and the unity of consciousness, *Synthese* 22: 396–413.

(1974). What is it like to be a bat? *Philosophical Review* 83: 435–50.

Natsoulas, T. (1978). Consciousness, *American Psychologist* 33: 906–14.

(1996). The case for intrinsic theory: II. An examination of a conception of consciousness$_4$ as intrinsic, necessary, and concomitant, *Journal of Mind and Behavior* 17: 369–90.

Neander, K. (1998). The division of phenomenal labor: A problem for representational theories of consciousness, in J. E. Tomberlin (ed.), *Philosophical Perspectives*, vol. 12: *Language, Mind, and Ontology* (pp. 411–34). Atascadero, CA: Ridgeview Publishing.

Nemirow, L. (1990). Physicalism and the cognitive role of acquaintance, in W. G. Lycan (ed.), *Mind and Cognition* (pp. 490–9). Oxford: Blackwell.

Noë, A. (2002). Is the visual world a grand illusion?, in A. Noë (ed.), *Is the Visual World a Grand Illusion?* (pp. 1–12). Thorverton, UK: Imprint Academic.

(2004). *Action in Perception*. Cambridge, MA: MIT Press.

Papineau, D. (2002). *Thinking about Consciousness*. Oxford University Press.

Prinz, J. (2005). A neurofunctional theory of consciousness, in A. Brook and K. Akins (eds.), *Cognition and the Brain: The Philosophy and Neuroscience Movement* (pp. 381–96). Cambridge University Press.

(2007). *The Conscious Brain*. New York: Oxford University Press.

Ramachandran, V. S. and Blakeslee, S. (1998). *Phantoms in the Brain*. London: Fourth Estate.

Ramachandran, V. S. and Gregory, R. L. (1991). Perceptual filling in of artificially induced scotomas in human vision, *Nature* 350: 699–702.

Rao, K. (1994). Consciousness, in R. J. Corsini (ed.), *Encyclopedia of Psychology* (2nd edn., vol. 1, pp. 302–6). Hoboken, NJ: Wiley.

Rensink, R. A., O'Regan, J. K., and Clark, J. J. (1997). To see or not to see: The need for attention to perceive changes in scenes, *Psychological Science* 8: 368–73.

Rosenthal, D. (1993). Thinking that one thinks, in M. Davies and G. Humphreys (eds.), *Consciousness* (pp. 197–223). Oxford: Blackwell.

(1997). A theory of consciousness, in N. J. Block, O. Flanagan, and G. Güzeldere (eds.), *The Nature of Consciousness* (pp. 729–53). Cambridge, MA: Bradford Books/MIT Press.

(2004). Varieties of higher-order theory, in R. Gennaro (ed.), *Higher-Order Theories of Consciousness* (pp. 17–44). Philadelphia, PA: John Benjamins.

Schacter, D. L. (1989). On the relation between memory and consciousness: Dissociable interactions and conscious experience, in H. Roediger and F. Craik (eds.), *Varieties of Memory and Consciousness: Essays in Honour of Endel Tulving* (pp. 355–89). Hillsdale, NJ: Lawrence Erlbaum.

Shallice, T. (1988a). *From Neuropsychology to Mental Structure*. Cambridge University Press.

(1988b). Information-processing models of consciousness: Possibilities and problems, in A. J. Marcel and E. Bisiach (eds.), *Consciousness in Contemporary Science* (pp. 305–33). New York: Clarendon Press/Oxford University Press.

Shoemaker, S. (1994). Self-knowledge and "inner sense". Lecture II: The broad perceptual model, *Philosophy and Phenomenological Research* 54: 271–90.

Simons, D. J. and Chabris, C. F. (1999). Gorillas in our midst: Sustained inattentional blindness for dynamic events, *Perception* 28: 1059–74.

Sperry, R. (1968). Hemisphere disconnection and unity in conscious awareness, *American Psychologist* 23: 723–33.

Stoerig, P. and Cowey, A. (1995). Visual perception and phenomenal consciousness, *Behavioral Brain Research* 71: 147–56.

Sutherland, N. S. (ed.) (1989). *Macmillan Dictionary of Psychology*. London: Macmillan.

Thompson, E., Pessoa, L., and Noë, A. (2000). Beyond the grand illusion: What change blindness really teaches us about vision, *Visual Cognition* 7: 93–106.

Tononi, G. (2004). An information integration theory of consciousness, *BMC Neuroscience* 5: 42.

Tye, M. (2003). *Consciousness and Persons: Unity and Identity*. Cambridge, MA: Bradford Books/MIT Press.

Van Gulick, R. (2004). Higher-order global states (HOGS): An alternative higher-order model of consciousness, in R. Gennaro (ed.), *Higher-Order Theories of Consciousness* (pp. 67–92). Philadelphia, PA: John Benjamins.

(2006). Mirror-mirror, is that all?, in U. Kriegel and K. Williford (eds.), *Self-Representational Approaches to Consciousness* (pp. 11–39). Cambridge, MA: Bradford Books/MIT Press.

Wegner, D. (2002). *The Illusion of Conscious Will.* Cambridge, MA: MIT Press.

Weiskrantz, L. (1986). *Blindsight: A Case Study and Implications.* Oxford University Press.

Wolman, B. B. (ed.) (1989). *Dictionary of Behavioral Science.* San Diego, CA: Academic Press.

Part III

Research programs

12 Cognitive neuroscience

Dominic Standage and Thomas Trappenberg

12.1 Introduction

The field of cognitive neuroscience addresses the question *How does the brain think?* Although simplistic, this short definition captures the primary characteristics of the field. The word *how* addresses the physical mechanisms underlying our thought processes, the word *brain* stresses that our explanations must be rooted in structures and functions of the brain, and the word *think* addresses the high-level, systemic nature of the processes under study. By its common usage, thinking refers to things like problem solving, decision making, and the recall of personal memories.

To cognitive neuroscientists, providing a mechanistic account of cognitive phenomena means linking experimental results obtained at the levels of neuroscience and behavior. Crucially, these mechanisms must be rooted in brain function. We may interpolate between physiological and behavioral data at a number of levels of abstraction, but in all cases, the mechanisms proposed must have structural or functional correlates with the brain. Below, we describe a number of approaches to this research goal. In all cases, our usage of the term *mechanism* refers to brain-related processes. Our examples show that methods in cognitive neuroscience make different assumptions and focus on different levels of abstraction, but they all have this fundamental trait in common. Most examples in this chapter reflect our computational background, but other approaches fall under the umbrella of cognitive neuroscience if they mechanistically link cognitive function and brain activity.

Despite much recent interest and the popularization of several prominent methods, cognitive neuroscience is not as new as one might think. The term *cognitive neuroscience* was coined in the late 1970s, but the field has its origins in the work of philosophers and psychologists considering the "mind–brain" problem. The first cognitive neuroscientist was arguably Franz Joseph Gall, who believed that the human brain was compartmentalized according to psychological function. Around 1800, Gall proposed that personality traits were localized in the cortex and that the most active locations, reflecting a person's dominant personality traits, should grow to be the most prominent. His doctrine of phrenology claimed that the growth of these cortical "organs" leads to bumps on the skull, so that a person's personality could be determined by the shape of his or her head. With the benefit of hindsight, phrenology seems at best quaint and at worst absurd, but it may represent the first attempt to address the physical underpinnings of behavior.

Cognitive neuroscience may be roughly divided into four subfields: clinical studies of neurological patients, non-invasive brain imaging methods, electrophysiology, and computational modeling. The first of these approaches is by far the oldest. Perhaps the best example of early lesion studies of cognitive phenomena comes from the work of neurologist Paul Broca in 1861. Broca discovered a clinical patient who could make only one verbal sound, but whose language comprehension was unaffected. Following the patient's death, damage was found to his left frontal-parietal lobe, now known as Broca's area. Several years later, neurologist Carl Wernicke discovered a stroke victim who made grammatically well-formed utterances that were seemingly devoid of meaningful content. After the patient's death, a lesion was discovered along the border of his parietal and temporal lobes, now known as Wernicke's area. Together, these clinical cases showed that the cognitive phenomenon of language was mediated by locally specific cortical regions, contributing to different aspects of speech generation and comprehension.

Lesion studies have provided a wealth of scientific data showing the cortical and subcortical localization of various aspects of cognitive phenomena. Clinical methods face several challenges, however, including the requirement of patients with similar lesions. Slight differences in the location of brain lesions can lead to major differences in cognitive performance. More recently, neuroimaging techniques have provided a powerful means of studying the respective functions of brain structures, including electroencephalogram (EEG) recordings, positron emission tomography (PET), and functional magnetic resonance imaging (fMRI). The non-invasiveness of these methods enables researchers to record brain activity in healthy, behaving human subjects. Electrophysiological methods, such as single- and multi-electrode recordings, provide much higher resolution, albeit with nonhuman animal subjects. Clearly, these approaches are highly complementary.

In particular, fMRI has made a huge impact in cognitive neuroscience in recent years, where the blood oxygen level dependent (BOLD) signal reveals brain structures correlated with the performance of cognitive tasks. Note the reference here to measurements of brain activity and behavior. Without data, there can be no cognitive neuroscience. On their own, though, data are not enough. We must have a theory to link brain activity with behavioral measurements. In the case of fMRI, the BOLD signal tells us that a region of the brain contributes to a cognitive function, but *how* does this region contribute to that function? Computational models are a powerful way to address this question. These models are mathematical descriptions of brain systems, programmed on a computer. Here, a mathematical description is necessary to

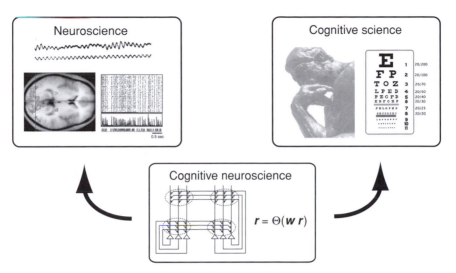

Figure 12.1 Cognitive neuroscience links activity in the brain with cognitive function.

make quantifiable hypotheses, as interactions between subsystems can lead to complex and sometimes unexpected system behavior. The role of models in identifying the causal relationship between brain activity and behavior is the central theme of this chapter and is depicted in Figure 12.1.

We have chosen three cognitive phenomena for discussion: episodic memory, decision making, and category learning. We believe these three phenomena exemplify different challenges to cognitive neuroscientists and their methods, facilitating discussion of a wide spectrum of computational, cognitive research. We also believe they provide a well-rounded chronological and historical perspective. Episodic memory has been the subject of research interest for the longest of the three, but is arguably the most poorly understood. Research on decision theory in many ways exemplifies current computational cognitive methods, and research on category learning exemplifies a budding research area within the computational, cognitive community. Episodic memory is poorly understood for good reasons, and we discuss this cognitive phenomenon first to illustrate the sorts of challenges faced by cognitive neuroscientists. We believe that decision theory is in many ways more tractable, both experimentally and computationally. This belief in no way suggests that episodic memory is "too hard" or that research methods in this field are misguided. Decision-making processes simply provide a more direct example of how computational methods can link physiology and behavior. Finally, cortical models of category learning provide an example of an exciting, rapidly expanding field. This field is by no means new, but is receiving long-overdue interest and recognition.

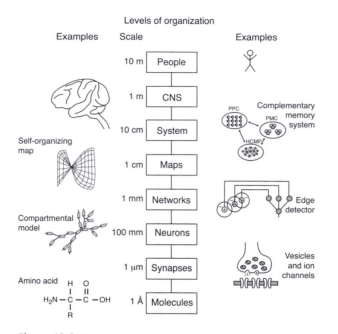

Figure 12.2 Structural scales of the brain and behavior. From *Fundamentals of Cognitive Neuroscience*, 2nd edn., by Thomas Trappenberg (2009), fig. 1.2, p. 4. By permission of Oxford University Press.

12.2   Computational modeling of cognitive phenomena

Before presenting some examples of cognitive neuroscience research, we introduce some of our methods. We have stated that the aim of cognitive neuroscience is to bridge brain activity and cognitive function with structural or mechanistic properties of the brain. As computationalists, our approach is to devise models that touch both sides of this gap. Our models of behavior must therefore be grounded in structures or activity found in the brain. A challenge raised by this requirement stems from the many scales of these structures and the mechanisms they generate. Of course, this challenge facilitates methodological flexibility and diversity, and may rightly be considered a strength of the field. A range of structural scales is depicted in Figure 12.2 where examples span the molecular and personal levels. With this dilemma in mind, on which level should we describe the brain? A subatomic level is probably too detailed, but what about the neural level? Should our models address intracellular mechanisms?

The answer is that it depends on what we are studying and how we study it. While molecular effects can have direct consequences on behavior, we do not expect a single neuron to assume full responsibility for a behavioral phenomenon. Such a scenario would defy stability in neural information

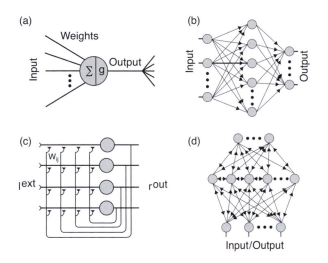

Figure 12.3 (a): In each node in a neural network, output is a function of the sum of weighted inputs. (b), (c), (d): Feedforward, recurrent, and bidirectional architectures respectively.

processing. We discuss several approaches to modeling in cognitive neuroscience at different levels of abstraction. There are trade-offs in these cases. For instance, we can record brain activity in nonhuman animals with neural resolution, but our interpretation of their behavior is highly constrained. Alternatively, the behavior of human subjects is much easier to assess, but resolution of data such as fMRI is lower. Finding an appropriate level of abstraction is a fundamental challenge to scientific enquiry. A theory must be simple enough to provide insight and constrained enough to make verifiable predictions. Cognitive neuroscience is consequently found in many forms, linking many levels of structure in the brain with the behavior of organisms.

In the following, we focus on abstractions underlying so-called *neural network* models. Models under this umbrella have long addressed behavioral data and have evolved into descriptions of brain structures and activity. We refer to the basic units in these models as nodes, as these units are not representative of neurons per se. As depicted in Figure 12.3a, each node receives input from potentially many sources, where each input channel has its own strength or *weight*. All inputs are multiplied by the weight of their respective channels and then summed together. The net input is run through a function (g in the figure) determining the output of the node.

If a node doesn't represent a neuron, what does it represent? As a mathematical construct, it can represent a lot of things. The most common interpretation in the present context is that it represents a *Hebbian cell assembly*, a collection of neurons involved at a specific stage of a cognitive task. The output of the node represents the population activity or *rate* of the neurons in the assembly.

Later, we show a case where the rate represents the average spike frequency of a neuron within the population, but often, individual neurons in an assembly exhibit very different response characteristics, so the node only represents the population average. In these cases, the global activity of collections of nodes may be more appropriately compared to larger-scale brain activity such as that revealed by fMRI.

Clearly, the computational abilities of nodes are very limited, but they can be very powerful in combination. Examples of neural network architectures are shown in Figure 12.3. In Figure 12.3b, activity is fed from left to right in a multi-layer *feedforward* network. These networks are often called multi-layer perceptrons and have been widely used in the connectionist movement in cognitive science, also known as parallel distributed processing (PDP). The fundamental difference between connectionist neural networks and those in cognitive neuroscience is that structural and/or mechanistic correlates with the brain are required of the latter. Their realization is left unspecified in PDP architectures. For example, the backpropagation algorithm (Rumelhart and McClelland 1986) is a common method to establish weight values in neural networks like the one in Figure 12.3b. Such an algorithm is a practical way to specify weights to achieve many tasks, but only the final weights may be assigned biological meaning. That is, the final weights allow the network to behave in a biologically plausible manner, but the learning algorithm is biologically unrealistic. Additionally, connectionist models usually employ finely tuned, task-specific architectures, while a major trend in cognitive neuroscience models is to capture more general brain mechanisms and relate them to specific tasks. Feedforward architectures certainly have functional relevance to brain processes, but they represent just one of many architectures found in the brain.

A network architecture we discuss at length is shown in Figure 12.3c. In this *recurrent* network, the output from each node is fed back as input to all other nodes in the network[1]. Recurrent networks are formally dynamic systems and their behavior is well understood mathematically. For instance, recurrent networks can function as fast-learning, content addressable memory systems, where the network retrieves learned patterns from partial or noisy versions of these patterns. These memories are believed to be crucial to several forms of information processing in the brain, notably episodic memory. Recurrent networks dominate much of the discussion in this chapter.

Finally, we believe networks that model general brain functions are likely to be of a more general type. For instance, we expect the same type of network to mediate learning in sensory and association cortices. An example of such a general architecture is provided by Figure 12.3d. We believe this architecture captures one of the brain's fundamental information-processing principles,

---

[1] Feedback activity between nodes in the same neural substrate should not be confused with the backpropagation of error signals mentioned above.

as discussed in section 12.5. As shown in the figure, this network has a hierarchical structure with bidirectional flow of information. The dynamic between bottom-up and top-down processing is an essential component of a number of cognitive phenomena and a major *modus operandi* of the brain. Through this and related mechanisms, we learn to represent the likelihood that sensory information matches learned expectations of the world, facilitating a flexible representational and predictive framework.

12.3   Episodic memory

Before considering episodic memory, or the memory of personal experience, we first consider memory formation at the (subcognitive) level of neurons and synapses. It is widely believed that memory is accomplished by the change in strength of synapses, or *synaptic plasticity*. Moreover, plasticity is believed to be activity-dependent. Consider two neurons A and B, where A synapses onto B. When A contributes to firing B, the synapse from A to B increases in strength. When B fires without A's help, the synapse decreases in strength. This principle was first proposed by the great neuropsychologist Donald Hebb (1949) and has long been established experimentally.

12.3.1   The SPM hypothesis and the need for models

While Hebbian plasticity is near-universally accepted as a fundamental learning mechanism, direct evidence is a difficult proposition. Martin, Grimwood, and Morris (2000) suggest several criteria for establishing the synaptic plasticity and memory (SPM) hypothesis. If an animal displays memory for some experience, synaptic change should be detectable. If so, then imposing these changes without the actual experience should lead to the same memory. Conversely, preventing the synapses from changing should prevent the memory from being formed. These are very difficult criteria to establish experimentally, not least because of the immense difficulty in identifying the synapses participating in learned representations, the difficulty of measuring these synapses individually, and the complicated time scales and stages of learning and plasticity. Some studies show compelling evidence in support of the SPM hypothesis, but the difficulty of providing direct evidence for this theory is foreboding of the sorts of challenges facing more cognitive-level research and highlights the usefulness of computational methods. Models allow us to explore the system-level consequences of more detailed experimental observations. For example, neural network models of memory have long used Hebbian rules to demonstrate the SPM hypothesis. We come back to this point briefly in section 12.5.

Moving from the level of neurons and synapses to the level of systems of neuronal networks is a huge step up. What would constitute a definitive test of a theory about episodic memory? We'd need to precisely identify the brain structures responsible for representations of personal experience and monitor these representations as they progress through a series of transformations. Theories abound as to the structures and representational forms involved, but identification of specific networks, neurons, and synapses within these macroscopic structures is an unenviable task.

There is overwhelming evidence that multiple brain structures are involved in the encoding and recall of episodic memories. Some of these structures support sustained activity for short periods, some support rapid encoding of representations over an intermediate-length period, some are believed to transfer these representations to structures responsible for more long-term encoding, and some are believed to compare expected representations with incoming neural activity. Within networks of networks of networks, where each network contains (at least) millions of neurons and billions of synapses, and where each synapse is associated with multiple learning states, we must identify and measure individual synapses before and after some experience, showing how they move through a series of states and how these states contribute to neural activity within each network.

Even if we ignore the overwhelming technical challenges to our definitive test, current technologies addressing this level of resolution are invasive, so we do not expect volunteers. We must turn instead to nonhuman animal subjects, raising another major challenge to cognitive neuroscience methods. Episodic memory involves the mental "reliving" of some part of a subject's personal history, an extremely difficult phenomenon to assess nonverbally. The current approach to experiments on nonhuman animals is to demonstrate *episodic-like* memory. That is, to show that an animal remembers *what* happened, *where* it happened, and *when* it happened, the three qualities generally regarded as essential to episodic memory. Many of these experiments are brilliantly designed and very convincing, but nonetheless, there is no direct way to assess whether an animal is mentally reliving a previous experience. In this case, if you accept the three criteria, you are free to interpret experimental results within the scope of this assumption.

12.3.2   Computational models of episodic memory

Now look at a modeling approach. Arguably, the first computational cognitive neuroscience model belongs to David Marr (1971). Marr was less concerned with episodic memory per se than with the function of the hippocampus more generally, but the two have been inextricably linked since Scoville and Milner's report of the memory deficits of patient H.M. in 1957. Following bilateral removal of his hippocampus and nearby cortical structures, H.M. was unable to form new experiential memories, despite being able to learn new motor skills. Marr's hippocampal model exemplifies computational cognitive neuroscience because it provides an anatomically grounded, mechanistic explanation of these and other behavioral data.

The basic network structure underlying these models is shown in Figure 12.3c. Each node is connected to all other nodes, and the strength of the connection between any two nodes is a function of their states, as proposed by Hebb and described at the beginning of this section. During a learning phase, nodes are "clamped" to values that represent internal representations of external events. This clamping may be equated with the response of the hippocampus to cortical input. During a retrieval phase, recurrent networks such as Marr's have an important property known as attractor dynamics. Given a noisy version of a state from the training set, the original state is retrieved by summing the input arriving at each node via all connections in the network. That is, the network can be cued by partial or noisy input to retrieve previous states. This ability is referred to as pattern completion and is a form of *autoassociative* memory, so called because the memory is associated with itself. In more cognitive terms, the model recalls its experience following exposure to single events, essential properties of episodic memory.

To Marr, hippocampal subfield CA3 was reminiscent of a recurrent architecture because of the unusually high density of collateral interactions between neurons in this region. In addition to proposing a role for the extensive collateral interactions of CA3 neurons, Marr was aware of the sparseness of neural activity in the dentate gyrus (DG), a hippocampal region providing input to CA3. He hypothesized that sparse representations (fewer active neurons) in DG reduce the overlap between representations entering CA3, allowing rapid encoding. The importance of this hypothesis cannot be overstated. Computationally, overlapping patterns are suited to slow extraction of central tendencies, such as the learning of object categories or motor skills. Conversely, the extraction of statistical regularities must be *avoided* in a structure that learns specific, individual patterns, such as those representing specific, personal experiences. In brief, overlap between representations leads to competition between them in the recall process. By reducing overlap, Marr's DG allowed CA3 to perform one-shot learning, a requirement of episodic memory.

12.3.3   Hippocampal models in the tradition of Marr

A thorough account of hippocampal modeling in the tradition of Marr would fill this entire volume, but we believe the basic model of Alvarez and Squire (1994) captures the dominant theory of the most important hippocampal data. A crucial aspect of these data concerns cortical memory consolidation. Above, we briefly mentioned patient H.M. and his inability to form new experiential memories following removal of his hippocampus. This *anterograde* amnesia

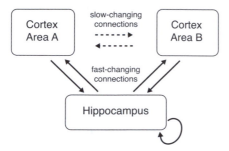

Figure 12.4 The hippocampal model of Alvarez and Squire (1994).

is common to many hippocampal patients, though H.M.'s case is certainly extreme. H.M. also exhibited a *graded retrograde* amnesia. Among his experiences before surgery, he was less likely to remember events occurring closer to the time of excision. His memories of events more than around two years before surgery appeared to be unaffected. Like anterograde amnesia, graded retrograde amnesia is common to many hippocampal patients. This phenomenon suggests that memories are stored in the hippocampus for an intermediate period, but are ultimately encoded in neocortex.

In Alvarez and Squire's model, shown in Figure 12.4, the hippocampus plays the role of a rapid learner, serving to consolidate cortical memories. Under this general framework, the hippocampus responds to a unique configuration of cortical activity with a unique internal representation. Because cortical–hippocampal pathways are bidirectional, this representation serves as a key or index to the cortical activity that created it. Upon presentation of a subset of the original cortical activity, the key is retrieved by the pattern completion abilities of recurrent networks, as in Marr's model. The key reactivates the full cortical representation and thereby the memory. With repeated activation of the hippocampal key and consequent reactivation of the composite cortical pattern, cortical representations gradually learn to activate each other and eventually no longer need the hippocampus as intermediary. Learning is achieved by a simple Hebbian rule, where changes in weight depend on the correlation between the firing rates of the nodes they connect. The rule simply uses a higher learning rate with the hippocampal weights than the cortical weights. In summary, the fast-learning hippocampus serves memory consolidation in the slower-learning cortex.

We have noted that, in general, the purpose of nonhuman animal experiments in cognitive neuroscience is to allow researchers to invasively study brain activity in behaving subjects. Most of these data reflect activity at the level of neurons, but the models described here do not provide this level of resolution. Spatial constraints prevent us from discussing so-called *spiking neuron models* of the hippocampus and episodic memory, but suffice to say, these models offer cellular resolution because each node may be equated with a single neuron. As such, their output may be directly compared with intra-cellular recordings from behaving nonhuman animal subjects. These models embody different sets of assumptions than the models we have discussed and provide a powerful means of bridging high resolution activity and structure with behavioral data.

12.4 Dynamic neural field models and decision making

Our discussion of episodic memory highlights many of the challenges faced by cognitive neuroscientists and the importance of memory systems to the understanding of brain function. Next, we introduce dynamic neural field (DNF) models. These basic models capture fundamental characteristics of neural organization, describing both neural and behavioral data. To demonstrate these important characteristics, we show how a DNF model captures basic neural response properties, comparing output from the model with *tuning curves* in cat visual cortex. We then discuss the model in the context of perceptual choice, showing how it explains neural responses in monkey inferior temporal cortex (IT). We also demonstrate the model in a closely related decision-making task, where the strength of visual evidence is easily controlled and psychophysical measurements such as reaction times and response accuracy are easily determined. The model captures many details of neural activity in monkey lateral intraparietal cortex (LIP) and corresponding psychometric functions.

12.4.1 Dynamic neural field models and tuning curves

To understand DNF models, consider again a recurrent network where each node is connected to all other nodes, depicted in Figure 12.3c. In Marr's model, we considered a cognitive task in which connection weights where determined by Hebbian learning. Here, our nodes have the same structure and function, but the weight between any two nodes is solely a function of the distance between them. Consider the nodes in Figure 12.5a. The weight from node 3 to node 2 is the same as the weight from node 3 to node 4 because the distance between them is the same. Similarly, the weight from 3 to 1 is the same as the weight from 3 to 5. This arrangement holds for the connections emanating from any node, so the weight from 2 to 1 is the same as the weight from 2 to 3 and so on. Furthermore, the same weights hold for any node-centric perspective. For instance, the weight from 1 to 4 is the same as the weight from 2 to 5.

For this illustrative case, we use Gaussian weights, depicted in Figure 12.5b. This connectivity may be genetically encoded in some structures, but can also result from Hebbian learning. This arrangement initially renders all weights

(a)

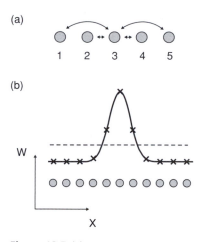

(b)

Figure 12.5 (a) A dynamic neural field model is a recurrent network (Figure 12.3c) where weights depend on the distance between nodes. (b) Subtracting a constant from a Gaussian function of this distance provides negative (inhibitory) weights below the dashed line.

positive, approaching 0 with increasing distance between nodes. With all positive weights, we have no competition because all nodes excite one another, leading to an explosion of network activity. We therefore include a global, activity-dependent inhibition by subtracting a constant value from all weights, creating negative (inhibitory) weights. These weights are represented in the figure by values below the dashed line. The inhibition mimics the activity of a pool of inhibitory neurons. The resulting network allows nodes to support each other locally and inhibit each other distally.

Now we look at some physiological data. Figure 12.6a shows data from the experiments of Henry, Dreher, and Bishop (1974). These data show electrophysiological recordings from a neuron in cat primary visual cortex (V1) while moving line segments are shown to the cat at different orientations. This neuron is maximally responsive to horizontal lines, responding with decreasing activity as the stimulus deviates from this preferred orientation. The neuron's

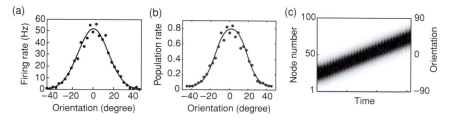

Figure 12.6 Tuning curves of cortical neurons are explained by a dynamic neural field model.

response to specific feature values is called its *tuning curve*. In this case, the tuning curve is approximately Gaussian.

Now look at Figure 12.6c. In the surface plot, the x-axis shows time and the y-axis shows the position of 100 nodes in the model. Node activity is shown on a gray scale, where dark areas depict high-rate activity. Over time, we provide inputs centered on a succession of nodes, corresponding to the presentation of line segments with orientations from -45 to 45 degrees. Consider node 50, maximally responsive to an orientation of 0 degrees (shown on the right). Initially, the stimulus does not evoke a noticeable response from node 50, evidenced by the white (low) activity at this location in the network. With different orientations over time, node 50 becomes more active and then decreases it response again, as shown in Figure 12.6b. This figure is remarkably similar to the electrophysiological recordings shown to the left in Figure 12.6a. For this reason, DNF models are a dominant model of cortical hypercolumns (Hansel and Sompolinsky 1998).

12.4.2   Perceptual choice

We now apply the above model to a more cognitive task, that of perceptual choice. Perceptual choice is a decision-making process. We routinely make decisions based on sensory data, much of which may be uncertain or may conflict with other sources of information such as our memories and expectations. We weigh up all these sources and decide accordingly. The two crucial aspects of models of perceptual choice are that a decision is made by accumulating evidence over time and that this evidence is uncertain.

Historically, two types of models have been discussed in the literature: accumulator models and diffusion models. With accumulator models, evidence for stimuli accumulates over time and a decision is reached when evidence for a particular stimulus exceeds a threshold, or when a response is required and the stimulus with the greatest sub-threshold evidence is chosen. With diffusion models, it is not the absolute evidence that is accumulated, but the difference between the evidence for each stimulus. Traditional models of perceptual choice provide a good example of cognitive science methods because they make useful predictions about behavior, but they do not come under the umbrella of cognitive *neuro*science because they are not concerned with the biological mechanisms underlying their implementation. With a DNF model, evidence for competing stimuli is modeled by inputs to the network, demonstrated by the tuning curves above. Competition is provided by mutual inhibition between active regions of the network, where the first region to reach a threshold level of activity corresponds to the perceptual choice.

We now demonstrate a DNF model of perceptual choice. In the experiments of Chelazzi *et al.* (1993), electrophysiological recordings were made from

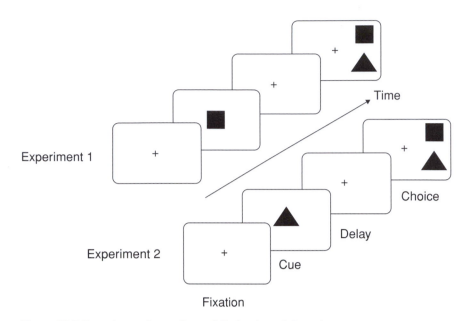

Figure 12.7 Experimental paradigm of Chelazzi *et al.* (1993).

monkey inferior temporal cortex (IT), an area correlated with higher-level visual processing. Monkeys were shown numerous images from magazines until a "good" and "poor" stimulus were identified for each of several neurons. A good stimulus is one that elicits a strong neuronal response. A poor one does not. As depicted in Figure 12.7, monkeys first fixated on a central dot on a computer screen. Subsequently, either a good or poor visual stimulus was presented for fraction of a second, depicted for simplicity by the square and the triangle respectively in Figure 12.7. After a further delay, the two images were simultaneously presented and the monkey's task was to move its eyes to the image that was previously shown.

Figure 12.8a shows the response of an IT neuron during the experiment. The left shaded area shows the time of cue presentation. When the good image is presented, the neuron responds with a pronounced increase in rate, plotted by the solid line. The poor image leads to a decrease in firing rate, plotted by the dashed line. This behavior is consistent with the DNF model, shown for this task in b. In computer simulations, presentation of the good stimulus alone leads to the high-rate response shown by the solid line in the left shaded area. Because the network implements local excitation and distal inhibition, this stimulus leads to a decrease in activity in a node that responds to a different (poor) stimulus, plotted by the dashed line.

As alluded to in section 12.2, we are now comparing the activity of a node to the response of an individual neuron, not to a population of neurons. This comparison is appropriate because the node represents a group of neurons with similar response characteristics. No single neuron in the group is solely

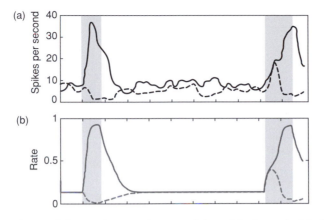

Figure 12.8 Data from Chelazzi *et al.* (1993) is shown in (a). Output from a dynamic neural field model is shown in (b). From *Fundamentals of Computational Neuroscience*, 2nd edn., by Thomas Trappenberg (2009), fig. 7.11, p. 196. By permission of Oxford University Press.

responsible for the network's response to the preferred feature, but in this case, all members exhibit similar activity.

The most stunning result by Chelazzi *et al.* is the response of the system when both the poor and the good images are presented after 3.3 seconds. If the initial cue was the good image, the neuron again responds strongly, but when the cue was the poor image, an initial increases in rate is followed by a marked decrease in activity. This effect is easily understood with the help of the DNF model. Presentation of both stimuli leads to strong initial responses by nodes selective for these inputs, shown by the solid and dashed curves in the right shaded area. We give a small bias of 1 percent to the cued image, corresponding to the memory of the cue. Mutual inhibition does the rest, as the remembered stimulus dominates processing.

12.4.3   Decision making, psychophysics, and uncertainty

Our discussion of perceptual choice has thus far centered on electrophysiological data, addressing animal behavior with neural resolution, but with very crude behavioral resolution. To provide a cognitive perspective, we need finer-grained behavioral measurements. Motion discrimination experiments provide such a tool. In a typical motion discrimination task, a display of dots is presented on screen and a fraction of the dots are repeatedly displaced at a fixed offset. This offset provides a kind of step frame animation, so the dots appear to move in the direction of displacement, typically to the left or to the right. Monkeys are trained to move their eyes in the direction of dominant movement to indicate their perceptual choice. Experimentalists manipulate the *coherence* of movement by controlling the percentage of displaced dots.

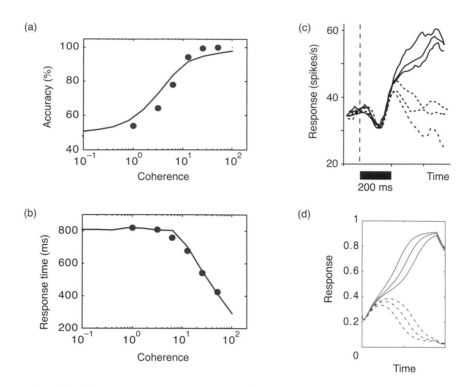

Figure 12.9 Data from Roitman and Shadlen (2002) is explained by the dynamic neural field model. (a) The *psychometric* function: dots show data, the curve shows a simulation. (b) The *chronometric* function. (c) Neural response over time for different strengths of evidence. (d) Simulations of the task in (c).

This simple manipulation allows experimentalists to finely control the strength of evidence. Recording response time and accuracy provides psychophysical measurements in response to the controlled parameter (coherence in this case).

Psychophysical measurements from Roitman and Shadlen (2002) are shown as dots in Figures 12.9a and 12.9b. These figures show the *psychometric* and *chronometric* functions respectively, depicting accuracy and reaction time as a function of the strength of evidence. At low levels of coherence, the monkey makes many errors and reaction times are long. With increasing coherence, accuracy increases and reaction times become shorter. Output from the model fits these data well (solid curves) where coherence and response time are modeled by input strength and the time to threshold respectively. Results from corresponding neural recordings in monkey LIP are shown in Figure 12.9c. These data also compare favorably with output from simulations, shown in Figure 12.9d. With increasing coherence, there is an increase in activity among neurons with a preferred response to the direction of motion (solid lines): the higher the coherence, the steeper the slope of the lines. The response of neurons preferential to other stimuli increases initially before decreasing (dashed lines): the stronger the evidence against their preferred direction, the steeper the slope of the decrease. This effect is equivalent to the competition between good and poor stimuli in the Chelazzi experiment, described above. For the interested reader, more details of the above simulations can be found in Trappenberg (2008). For a very thorough treatment of the experiments of the Shadlen group, see the biologically motivated, systems-level model of Grossberg and Pilly (2008).

As a final word on DNF models, we wish to emphasize their explanatory power at multiple levels of abstraction. In the examples above, DNF models provide mechanistic explanations for neurophysiological and behavioral data, suggesting that they capture a fundamental principle of information processing in the brain. Specifically, this principle is the competition between neural populations by mutual inhibition. Dynamic neural field theory addresses this competition continuously in space (neural tissue) and time, enabling the model to capture the real-time competition between feature values that differ along a continuum.

12.5   Hierarchical bidirectional memory

Models of episodic memory and decision making are exemplary of a vast computational literature within cognitive neuroscience, but in isolation, the models we have described thus far are limited in scope. In this section, we provide a brief overview of a set of models we believe will play a prominent role in future theories of cortex and cognitive function, returning to a generic architecture shown earlier in Figure 12.3d. At this level of abstraction, there are two main characteristics of these networks: hierarchical structure and bidirectional connectivity. Well known to anatomists, these characteristics are found in all processing pathways in the brain and are especially prominent in cortex. Hierarchical processing is required to represent the incredible complexity of the world and the concepts we use to function within it. Bidirectional processing generates expectations, essential to cope with the high-volume processing demands of even the simplest cognitive functions.

In the following, our usage of the term "representation" simply refers to neural activity. For instance, in sensory processing, neurons fire in response to things in the world, so their activity represents those very things in the brain's internal model of the world. In hierarchical neural processing, representations at low levels of a hierarchy are combined to form composite representations at the next level up. These representations are in turn combined so that higher-level constructs are represented at increasingly advanced levels of the hierarchy. For example, in visual processing, neurons in early visual cortex respond to points of light. Signals from these cells converge on neurons at

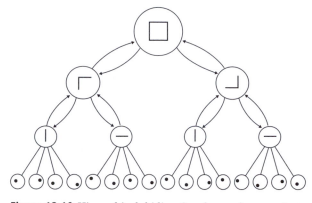

Figure 12.10 Hierarchical, bidirectional neural processing.

the next stage of processing, causing them to fire and thereby strengthening these connections by Hebbian plasticity. These cells can represent edges due to the co-appearance of points of light in natural objects. The compositional process continues such that edges are combined to form contours and so on until representations of objects are achieved. Hebbian learning facilitates this process by ensuring the same features are combined to represent the same objects as sets of features are repeatedly encountered together in the world. This fundamental, compositional process is depicted in Figure 12.10.

Described in this way, feature detection is a bottom-up process, but that is only half the story. Feedback connectivity provides top-down processing. It's well known that cortical regions are commonly reciprocally connected. That is, if an area *A* projects to area *B*, then area *B* commonly projects to *A*. It's hard to imagine this arrangement on a neuron by neuron basis, but remember, the nodes depicted in Figure 12.10 represent cell assemblies. Co-active representations at consecutive levels of a bidirectional hierarchy strengthen synapses in *both* directions, as depicted in the figure. As such, when low-level features are combined to form a composition, not only do the connections driving the composition become stronger, but the composition learns to activate the lower-level features. To us, this synergy of bottom-up and top-down processing is one of the most powerful ideas in neuroscience, explaining imagination, expectation, and perhaps most importantly, prediction.

To understand why it explains imagination, consider the square at the top. To visualize the square, we need to activate its features. In the simplified example in the figure, activating this node leads to the propagation of activity to the next level down, where the two "corner nodes" are activated. These nodes in turn propagate their activity to the nodes representing each side of the square, but they also re-excite the node above. It's as if they're saying "we're still working on your square features, but we need you to stay active to get it done." This propagation of activity continues up and down the hierarchy until representations at all levels are co-active. In short, a square, like anything else, is defined by its features, so to imagine the square, we need to activate these lower-level feature representations. You can think of this process as a kind of pattern completion, starting at the top of the hierarchy. Activation of the complete, hierarchical pattern *is* imagining the square.

To understand why hierarchical, bidirectional processing explains expectations and predictions, we turn to Stephen Grossberg's *adaptive resonance theory* (ART) (see Carpenter and Grossberg 2003). Continuing with our simplified example of visual processing, imagine that our hierarchical network has learned the square representation and that a subset of the square's features arrives at our feature detection nodes (perhaps our view of the square is partially blocked by another object). This subset of "point-of-light" nodes is enough to drive some of the "line" nodes above, which propagate activity back down to all point-of-light nodes that have consistently driven them in the past, and propagate activity back up to the "corner" nodes. Activity moving up and down the hierarchy like this is said to *resonate* as long as top-down and bottom-up representations match. That is, we see a square if our partial or noisy input provides a reasonable match with our expectations of squares. It's a beautiful idea, but there's more.

Now imagine we've been told to look out for squares. Higher cortical areas bias our top-down activity to favor square sightings, so that any square-like features are more quickly and reliably composed by virtue of this bias. In this case, top-down activity reflecting an expectation of squares is stronger than usual and the balance between top-down and bottom-up activity is dynamically adjusted. We thus more readily see squares, but only when there are squares to be seen. This stipulation may sound obvious, but it leads to an important point. Under ART, resonance breaks down when top-down expectations and bottom-up sensory information *do not* match. In this case, further network activity amounts to a search for another learned object category. If none is found (resonance is not achieved), the activity leads to the learning of a new category by Hebbian plasticity.

We believe hierarchical, bidirectional networks provide one of the most promising tools in cognitive neuroscience, with the potential to provide cortical explanations for many aspects of cognition. A recent example of work in this field is the model of George and Hawkins (2005) demonstrating these principles in a *Bayesian* framework. Such models exemplify some of the most advanced methods in machine learning. A more biologically realistic implementation of many of these foundations has been advanced by Geoffrey Hinton for many years. His networks are based on so-called Boltzmann machines or *deep belief networks*. These models have probabilistic nodes that more closely resemble the incredibly noisy processing of real neurons. While many models in this area are quite abstract, continued focus on related theo-retical and experimental research has the potential to make great strides over the coming decades.

12.6 Summary

Research in cognitive science has provided a wealth of knowledge about the underlying properties of cognitive phenomena. Related cognitive models have provided useful tools for understanding human behavior and have played an important role scientifically and in technical applications. The field of human–computer interface, for instance, has benefited immensely from behavioral modeling. In contrast, neuroscience focuses on physical mechanisms. A mechanistic understanding of the brain is essential for scientific advancements in many research areas. To give but one example, understanding the function of neuronal ion-channels is crucial to the design of drugs combating neuro-degenerative diseases. Cognitive neuroscience bridges cognitive science and neuroscience, grounding cognitive functions in the underlying mechanisms of the brain.

The brain has been assumed to be the seat of the mind since the Age of Enlightenment, and not surprisingly the boundaries between cognitive science and neuroscience are often blurry. The field of cognitive neuroscience provides many tools for understanding this relationship in more detail. Functional brain imaging methods such as EEG and fMRI are perhaps the best examples of these tools, with the power to directly measure brain activity in humans performing cognitive tasks, but we need more than just data. How are behavioral data and brain imaging data related? Theories that address this question must concisely describe these data and make testable predictions and are by no means limited to sets of mathematical equations.

Our discussion of episodic memory in section 12.3 illustrates some of the difficulties of experimental work in cognitive neuroscience. In large part, these difficulties stem from the invasiveness of current electrophysiological methods and the consequent need for nonhuman subjects. The behavior of these subjects requires interpretation, as cognitive phenomena do not typically have strong behavioral correlates and brain anatomy is far from uniform across species. Recent technological advances such as multi-voxel analysis of fMRI have great potential in this regard. The combination of this technology with the high temporal resolution of EEG provides a powerful tool for studying humans engaged in cognitive tasks. These experiments are providing a wealth of data to guide theories of the processing mechanisms of structures in the brain.

The models we have discussed make numerous assumptions, including abstractions at the levels of physiology, anatomy, and interacting dynamic systems. Without assumptions, the predictive power of a model is lost among the details of its implementation. The DNF model introduced in section 12.4 exemplifies assumptions about structure in the brain. In the implementation here, cooperation and competition within the network are implemented by short-range excitation and long-range inhibition. The model explains a remarkable variety of physiological and psychophysical data, but excitatory and inhibitory connections in the brain tend to have the opposite arrangement, i.e., local inhibition and more distal excitation. This apparent anatomical inconsistency has led to investigations of the function of individual layers in cortex, where specific roles are proposed for cell types in columnar cortical architectures. Alternatively, the *effect* of local excitation and long-range inhibition can emerge dynamically from a number of architectures. Finally, neural field models are used by some researchers to capture the effect of interacting systems in the brain, independent of the details of implementation. All three levels of enquiry are equally valuable.

In section 12.5, we briefly described an abstract, yet system-wide model of neocortex that we believe may ultimately unify theories in cognitive neuroscience. This framework offers a concrete path to the theoretical investigation of exciting experimental discoveries. The integration of experimental and theoretical methods in cognitive neuroscience is arguably still in its infancy, and interest and enthusiasm for this unified approach is rapidly growing. We believe the systematic integration of experiment and theory will lead to great advances in cognitive neuroscience in the coming decades.

Further reading

Churchland, P. S. and Sejnowski, T. J. (1992). *The Computational Brain.* Cambridge, MA: MIT Press. The first book to broadly address computational mechanisms of brain and mind. The combined expertise of the authors spans philosophy of mind and computational neuroscience, and results in a readable, thorough, and authoritative book that remains highly relevant to cognitive neuroscience.

Gazzaniga, M. S., Ivry, R. B., and Mangun, G. R. (2002). *Cognitive Neuroscience.* New York: W. W. Norton and Company. The present chapter has been mostly computational in its scope. This book provides a broader perspective on cognitive neuroscience.

Hawkins, J. and Blakeslee, S. (2004). *On Intelligence.* New York: Owl Books. Jeff Hawkins and Sandra Blakeslee provide an accessible, enjoyable account of material alluded to in section 12.5. Written for a general audience, this book beautifully captures principles of cortical information processing, offering a unified theory of cortex and a recipe for building intelligent machines.

Trappenberg, T. (2010). *Fundamentals of Computational Neuroscience* (2nd edn.). Oxford University Press. Provides more detailed explanations of modeling techniques and their interpretation and application in cognitive neuroscience.

References

Alvarez, P. and Square, L. R. (1994). Memory consolidation and the medial temporal lobe: A simple network model, *Proceedings of the National Academy of Sciences of the United States of America* 91: 7041–5.

Carpenter, G. A. and Grossberg, S. (2003). Adaptive resonance theory, in M. A. Arbib (ed.), *The Handbook of Brain Theory and Neural Networks* (2nd edn., pp. 87–90). Cambridge, MA: MIT Press.

Chelazzi, L., Miller, E. K., Duncan, J., and Desimone, R. (1993). A neural basis for visual search in inferior temporal cortex, *Nature* 363: 345–7.

George, D. and Hawkins, J. (2005). A hierarchical bayesian model of invariant pattern recognition in the visual cortex, *Proceedings of the International Joint Conference on Neural Networks (IJCNN 2005)*.

Grossberg, S. and Pilly, P. K. (2008). Temporal dynamics of decision-making during motion perception in the visual cortex, *Vision Research* 48: 1435–1473.

Hansel, D. and Sompolinsky, H. (1998). Modeling feature selectivity in local cortical circuits, in C. Koch and I. Segev (eds.), *Methods in Neural Modeling: From Ions to Networks* (2nd edn., pp. 499–568). Cambridge, MA: MIT Press.

Hebb, D. O. (1949). *The Organization of Behavior*. New York: John Wiley.

Henry, G. H., Dreher, B., and Bishop, P. O. (1974). Orientation specificity of cells in cat striate cortex, *Journal of Neurophysiology* 37: 1394–1409.

Marr, D. (1971). Simple memory: A theory of archicortex, *Philosophical Transactions of the Royal Society of London* 262: 23–81.

Martin, S. J., Grimwood, P., and Morris, R. G. M. (2000). Synaptic plasticity and memory: An evaluation of the hypothesis, *Annual Review of Neuroscience* 23: 649–711.

Roitman, J. D. and Shadlen, M. N. (2002). Response of neurons in the lateral intraparietal area during a combined visual discrimination reaction time task, *The Journal of Neuroscience* 22: 9475–89.

Rumelhart, D. E., McClelland, J. L., and the PDP Research Group (1986). *Parallel Distributed Processing: Explorations in the Microstructure of Cognition*. Cambridge, MA: MIT Press.

Scoville, W. B. and Milner, B. (1957). Loss of recent memory after bilateral hippocampal lesions, *Journal of Neurology, Neurosurgery and Psychiatry* 20: 11–21.

Trappenberg, T. (2008). Decision making and population decoding with strongly inhibitory neural field models, in D. Heinke and E. Mavritsaki (eds.), *Computational Modelling in Behavioural Neuroscience: Closing the Gap Between Neurophysiology and Behaviour* (pp. 165–86). London: Psychology Press.

(2010). *Fundamentals of Computational Neuroscience* (2nd edn.). Oxford University Press.

13 Evolutionary psychology

H. Clark Barrett

13.1 Introduction

Evolutionary psychology is the branch of the cognitive sciences that strives to unite proximate and ultimate causal explanations of why the mind has the properties it has. Evolutionary psychologists see this as an ordinary part of the more general scientific goal of explaining why humans, other animals, and all living and nonliving things have the properties they do by tracing immediate proximal causes back to more distal ones, and yet more distal ones, all the way back. What evolutionary psychology seeks to achieve is therefore akin to causal physical accounts that seek to explain why the earth as a planet has the particular properties it does. For example, a full causal explanation of the earth's current climate would need to take into account recent events (perhaps peculiar to earth) such as human modifications of the earth's surface; longer-term processes such as continental drift; properties such as the chemical composition of the earth's core, surface, and atmosphere; as well as processes general to all planets, such as the presence of solar radiation.

Similarly, explaining human minds requires considering both the immediate and long-term causal processes that build them, from processes of individual development and the nature of social and physical environments humans currently inhabit, to our general mammalian and primate heritage, to specific changes in brain and behavior that occurred since humans and chimpanzees diverged from a common ancestor. Such accounts inevitably entail merging knowledge of the materials and components of which the object is made with a historical account of how and why those particular materials got there, and an account of how everything interacts to produce what is observed now. This ambition is what gives evolutionary psychology the potential to be the most causally complete branch of the cognitive sciences. It is also, arguably, what makes evolutionary psychology one of the most controversial branches of the cognitive sciences, a target of criticism in approximate proportion to its ambitiousness.

It is difficult to argue against the goal of unifying proximate and ultimate causal explanations of why things are the way they are, because causal explanation is the goal of most science. Instead, some critics of evolutionary psychology argue that we are not in a position to make such unifications yet (nor ever will be). This extreme skepticism is unwarranted. It is certainly true that we do not yet have a complete account of the mind that joins all causal levels, from how real-time brain processes work, to how genes build them, to how evolutionary events have shaped those genes. If we did, our work would be done already. The situation in evolutionary psychology, however, is much different from fields such as string theory, which has received criticism for its untestability. The problem with string theory is that all of the predictions that it adds to conventional physics are currently untestable for technological reasons. Similarly, what some see as a virtue of evolutionary psychology – its ability to add ultimate, evolutionary explanations to cognitive science – others might argue adds nothing, because events in the past can never be observed, so (according to this argument) ultimate evolutionary hypotheses cannot be tested. However, the unobservability of past events mandates caution in inferences about the past but is not by itself a barrier to knowledge. If it were, other historical sciences such as geology, paleontology, archaeology, and history – not to mention evolutionary biology – would be impossible. The reason that we are able to make inferences about the past is that past events leave their signature in the present, including in the currently observable properties of the mind and the developmental processes that give rise to it. This renders a host of evolutionary psychological hypotheses testable.

A glance at the landscape of human psychology suggests that the areas where testable evolutionary ideas remain to be developed and explored are vastly larger than what is already known. Here I will explore how evolutionary thinking can inform the generation and testing of hypotheses in cognitive science.

13.2   Evolutionary theory, adaptationism, and the cognitivist stance

Because the goal of evolutionary psychology is to unite proximate and ultimate accounts of mental structure and mental processes, theories in evolutionary psychology can draw from virtually any branch of the biological and psychological sciences. In practice, evolutionary psychologists tend to ground their proximate theories in the computational information-processing tradition common in the cognitive sciences (see Chapters 2 and 3, this volume), and their ultimate theories in the union of population genetics and Darwinian evolutionary theory that originated in the mid twentieth century (Tooby and Cosmides 1992). However, evolutionary psychology is also compatible with virtually any subfield of the biological and psychological sciences that provides causal accounts of phenotypic and mental structure, and it is beginning to draw from subfields such as developmental genetics, evolutionary developmental biology (evo-devo), developmental systems theory, and dynamic systems theory – areas of theory in biology and psychology that examine the processes that build the structure of organisms, including their minds, during development (Barrett 2007; Bjorklund and Pellegrini 2002). In addition, there are many bodies of subtheory within evolutionary biology that serve as sources of evolutionary hypotheses about particular aspects of mind design. These include life history theory (Kaplan *et al.* 2000), optimal foraging theory (Stephens and Krebs 1986), kin selection theory (Hamilton 1964), gene–culture co-evolution theory (Boyd and Richerson 1985), and others. From the unions of proximate and ultimate theories evolutionary psychologists have used several kinds of strategy for the generation of new theories and hypotheses. The most common of these is to use a combination of prior observation (e.g., predators are a common threat to many primates) and a priori theoretical considerations (e.g., learning about predators through individual experience can be risky) to generate hypotheses about psychological adaptations (e.g., humans might possess specialized learning mechanisms for rapidly acquiring danger information from conspecifics; Barrett 2005a). Always, when possible, theorists keep in mind the particular ecological circumstances and evolutionary history of the organism under study.

The term "adaptation" refers to an aspect of an organism's phenotype whose properties have been shaped by natural selection because of the effects those properties had on individuals' fitness (survival and reproduction) in past environments. The concept of a psychological adaptation, and the criteria used to identify psychological adaptations both theoretically and empirically, are in principle the same as those used in evolutionary biology more generally. Psychological adaptations involve the processing of information and the regulation of behavior, as opposed to the strictly morphological and physiological adaptations that are more frequently studied in biology. While psychological adaptations have morphological and physiological instantiations (i.e., neurally), because their impact on fitness is primarily through the processing of information and regulation of behavior, their functions and design features are usually described in information-processing (computational, or cognitive) terms: they take informational inputs and transform them into outputs, in the service of regulating behavior (Tooby and Cosmides 1992).

13.3 Modules, domain specificity, and design features

Psychological adaptations are frequently referred to as modules. The term "module" as it is typically used by evolutionary psychologists is synonymous with "information-processing adaptation," no more and no less (Barrett and Kurzban 2006). In this regard it differs substantially from other usages of "module" which entail specific psychological properties, such as total isolation from other brain systems and lack of environmental inputs during development (e.g., Fodor 1983). Just as the concept of adaptation in biology does not entail a specific list of properties that all adaptations must share, the same is true for psychological adaptations. For example, hair follicles and livers are both adaptations – and modular – but they probably have few properties in common relevant to their specific adaptive functions (they do of course share an indefinite number of other properties, e.g., identical DNA, hugely overlapping repertoires of structural proteins, etc.). Similarly, brain adaptations regulating hunger and food-seeking behavior probably have little in common with adaptations in the visual system for detecting particular wavelengths of light.

This points to an important feature of adaptations: they are *domain specific*, meaning simply that different adaptations do different things and operate on different kinds of information. In this sense, even what are often thought of as "general-purpose" mechanisms, such as the proposed phonological loop and the visuospatial sketchpad in working memory (Repovs and Baddeley 2006) are both domain specific, in that they operate on information of a particular kind, and/or operate on information in specific ways. While domain specificity is sometimes used in a narrower sense, e.g., to refer to information content rather than format, the general biological principle of form–function fit suggests that it can apply to any dimension of an adaptation's specialized arena of operation (e.g., the domain of an eye is perceivable wavelengths of light and the domain of a fin is the hydrodynamic properties of water; Barrett and Kurzban 2006; Barrett 2009).

The term *design feature* is often used to refer to a property of an adaptation (including psychological adaptations) that has been shaped by natural selection because of its effects on fitness. The design features of an adaptation act in service of its evolved function. The causal explanation for most design features is that in past environments, there were different functional variants in the population and these differed in their effects on survival and reproduction, leading to the spread of the fitter variant, the design features of which we observe now. Concepts such as adaptation, function, and design feature are all, therefore, historical in nature: they refer to a causal chain of events that occurred in the past and that together explain the present existence and properties of the trait in question. Often, the functions and design features of adaptations are framed as solutions to adaptive problems (Tooby and Cosmides 1992), which arise when fitness-influencing genetic variation in organisms' design features appears, rendering some individuals better fitted to an aspect of the environment than other individuals (for example, better able to detect danger). Adaptive problems, in this sense, appear when relevant genetic variation appears, which is why flying is not an adaptive problem for humans.

13.3.1   The auditory looming detection mechanism as an example

These concepts can be illustrated with an example, the auditory looming detection mechanism. Many animals, including humans, exhibit specific, evolved behavioral responses to looming objects (objects that are approaching rapidly). There appear to be distinct specialized mechanisms for detecting looming objects through both vision (Schiff, Caviness, and Gibson 1962) and hearing (Neuhoff 1998; Seifritz *et al.* 2002), each of which involves specific brain areas (Seifritz *et al.* 2002). Looming detection mechanisms can be described not just in terms of the brain areas where they are instantiated but also in terms of their design features. The auditory looming object detector is sensitive to rapid increases in sound intensity, with rising intensity activating different brain areas and resulting in different behaviors (avoidance) than falling intensity (Neuhoff 1998; Seifritz *et al.* 2002). The detector exhibits a "bias": rising intensity leads to a perception of the object being closer than it actually is, but falling intensity does not. Moreover, this bias is present for harmonic tones, which can reliably indicate single sources, but not for broadband noise.

What is the ultimate explanation for these design features? Neuhoff (2001) has suggested that these are design features of an adaptation that evolved for the purpose of detecting oncoming objects and regulating behavioral responses in an adaptive fashion. Initially, one can imagine a population of animals not sensitive to approach. Mutations that altered the auditory system in a way that made it particularly sensitive to rising amplitude sounds, and that caused the hearer to attend rapidly to the source of the sound, would have increased in frequency. Guski (1992) has suggested that in these cases, selection would not necessarily have favored accuracy, per se, in the estimation of distance to the oncoming object, but rather, it would have favored the warning function of the system: alerting the individual to a possible threat as quickly as possible, and focusing attention appropriately. This potentially explains why there is a "bias" to underestimate the distance of approaching objects, but not receding ones. It also demonstrates why it is important to be precise about functional hypotheses. If selection were primarily for accuracy in distance estimations, the system would appear poorly designed. But the data are consistent with the hypothesis that selection was first and foremost for early warning.

What is the domain of this adaptation? This can be thought of in two ways. The source of selection that designed the adaptation is oncoming dangers, so one could speak of the domain as, for example, predators and other potentially dangerous moving objects. Another way of describing domains, however, is in informational terms, i.e., the properties of information that cause it to be processed by the system in question. From this perspective, the domain of the auditory looming detector would be rising sounds, and in particular, harmonic tones with rising amplitude, rather than just broadband noise. Note that sensitivity to the harmonic nature of the sound is an additional design feature that is consistent with the hypothesis that the system is adapted primarily to detect oncoming *objects*, i.e., point sources of noise rather than diffusely distributed rising sounds (thunder, ocean waves).

13.3.2   Adaptive problems and proper versus actual domains

This example points to a theoretical distinction that is critical to evolutionary psychological theories: the distinction between proper and actual domains of a psychological adaptation. Because the evolutionary process is historical in nature, it is past events that are causally responsible for the current properties of any evolved system. The design features of the auditory looming detector evolved because of the enormous set of encounters that ancestors of modern humans had with dangerous objects, leading to the selective retention of advantageous design features in the population. We can think of the evolved *function* of the looming detection system as detecting oncoming predators.

The historical nature of selection suggests that the objects that shaped the design of the looming detection system were things like leopards, hippos, and perhaps falling rocks. Modern-day automobiles and trains, because of their recent origin, are not responsible for the design of the system, which originated well before the origin of our species and is present even in nonhuman primates (though cars might have exerted a few generation's worth of selection on our recent ancestors).

Sperber (1994) introduced the terms *proper domain* and *actual domain* to capture the distinction between what an adaptation evolved to do, and what it is capable of doing. The proper domain of an adaptation refers to the set of inputs or situations that shaped the design of the system over evolutionary time, and therefore, that it was designed to process. The proper domain of the looming detection system, therefore, would be predators and other dangerous animals. However, it is an inevitable consequence of the design of any information-processing system that it will be able to process any information that meets its input criteria, even if that information is evolutionarily novel. The auditory looming detector is sensitive to any rising amplitude harmonic sound, whether it is generated by approaching dangers or not. Thus, synthesized tones generated in the lab are processed by the system, as are sounds generated by someone rapidly turning up a stereo. The actual domain refers to the set of inputs that the system is actually capable of processing, whether or not these were part of the category of inputs that shaped the evolution of the system.

13.4   The process of discovery in evolutionary psychology

Much has been written about the process of hypothesis formation and testing in evolutionary psychology, and the potential pitfalls behind it (e.g., the dangers of *post hoc* explanation). Because evolutionary psychology makes claims to special status in uniting proximate and ultimate explanation, it is worth considering exactly what the real-world process of discovery in evolutionary psychology is like.

It might be noted that in the case of the auditory looming detection system, discovery of at least some of the properties of the system preceded the development of hypotheses about the ultimate evolutionary origins of the system. In this sense, evolutionary psychology is no different from other cognitive sciences in that researchers often develop and refine proximate functionalist theories before considering ultimate accounts. For example, one could easily consider the possible benefits of early detection of oncoming point sources of sound without thinking explicitly in terms of fitness benefits in ancestral environments. This has led some critics to suggest that ultimate causal thinking is unnecessary (Buller 2005). Such critics also point to scientific advances that were made using a proximate functionalist stance in the absence of explicit evolutionary thinking, such as Harvey's discovery of blood circulation.

The notion that science proceeds strictly via a process of a priori prediction followed by falsification is an ideal that is explicitly held by many scientists, although it is not reflected in the facts about the daily practices of scientists, even ones who are successful at producing new knowledge (Godfrey-Smith 2003). Most psychological theories are not developed a priori from first principles, but rather via a back-and-forth process in which much is discovered about a phenomenon through observation, ideas are generated about possible explanations for the phenomenon, and these are refined through further tests and data collection. Scientific inference is sometimes described as abductive; that is, it seeks the best possible explanation for the available facts. In the case of auditory looming, the best available explanation for design features such as the approach bias and its restriction to harmonic tones is that they are adaptations for rapid detection of potential oncoming dangers. What makes this the best possible explanation is not a single factor but many, including the match between observations and the hypothesis, the evolutionary plausibility of the hypothesis, and the lack of others.

13.4.1   Discriminative parental solicitude as an example

Another example of how evolutionary theory along with knowledge of the specific organism under study can be used to generate hypotheses, and how abductive plausibility plays a role in evaluating research results, can be seen in Daly and Wilson's work on the so-called "Cinderella effect" (1998). One of the best-established observations in evolutionary biology is that across many social species where individuals regularly encounter genetic relatives, individuals are more prone to offer assistance and resources to relatives than to unrelated individuals (Silk 2002). This pattern evolves because of the way genes are distributed across individuals due to sexual reproduction (Hamilton 1964).

Because human social structure satisfies these conditions, Daly and Wilson predicted that humans would exhibit discriminative parental solicitude (in essence, favoritism) toward their own genetic offspring compared to the off-spring of others, and consequently, that step-parents would exhibit less solicitude toward step-children than would the genetic parents of those same children, manifesting in a greater probability of neglect and abuse by step-parents. This prediction is a prediction about the behavioral footprint of at least two types of psychological mechanisms: mechanisms for detecting genetic kin and mechanisms for regulating behavior toward them. This is a good example of how evolutionary psychological hypotheses can make predictions about observable patterns of behavior that are entailed by psychological mechanisms, even when the mechanisms themselves are not being directly studied.

Daly and Wilson provided evidence for this hypothesis from several large data sets (Daly and Wilson 1998). Buller (2005), however, suggested that the data were better accounted for by a reporting bias in which neglect by step-parents was differentially detected due to cultural suspicions about step-parents. Daly and Wilson effectively showed that reporting biases were unlikely to account for the Cinderella effect because they would require huge numbers of undetected abuse cases by genetic parents (who are overwhelmingly more frequent caretakers) in order to equal the frequency detected in the much smaller number of step-parents in a given population (Daly and Wilson 2005). However, the debate overlooked an equally important factor: the extreme plausibility of Daly and Wilson's hypothesis, from an evolutionary point of view. Given what is known about kin selection, it is unlikely that parents in any species with parental care would exhibit equal degrees of solicitude toward their own offspring and the offspring of others. Kin selection is, in this sense, a parsimonious explanation for Daly and Wilson's data.

13.4.2   The heuristic role of evolutionary theorizing, with humans as a special case

Evolutionary theories such as kin selection theory almost always play a heuristic role in the generation of hypotheses, rather than strictly narrowing down possible evolutionary outcomes to a single one. Evolutionists have often noted that while evolutionary theory does make predictions, they are context-specific, and depend on details about the taxa in question. For example, discriminative parental solicitude is only possible in organisms that can distinguish between kin and non-kin, and that regularly encounter examples of both. Many coral reef fish broadcast fertilized zygotes into the open ocean, to settle hundreds or thousands of miles away from their parents. Discriminative parental solicitude is therefore not expected in these species, nor is the ability to distinguish kin from non-kin, because closely related individuals are never encountered. This illustrates an important point: general evolutionary principles exist, but how these principles are realized depends on the facts of individual species' idiosyncratic evolutionary histories and circumstances. This is where knowledge of the human species, and our particular evolutionary history, plays a crucial role.

The context-dependence of evolutionary theorizing is important and insufficiently appreciated. It matters in the case of humans because humans are not just any animal. We are at the same time animals, vertebrates, mammals, primates, apes, and humans. That we are mammals means that we have internal fertilization and gestation, which has implications for sex differences in the degree of parental care, and therefore sex differences in mating psychology that would not be expected in taxa without such divergent degrees of parental investment. Like other primates but to a much greater degree, human offspring depend on parental care, and parents care for them for a time after birth. This means that human parents co-reside with, and care for, their own offspring and that siblings co-reside with each other, at least for a time.

These facts about humans, along with knowledge about the potential deleterious effects of inbreeding (due to the same process of shared genes that leads to kin-selected altruism), have been used to make predictions about the psychology of inbreeding avoidance in humans: that co-rearing of individuals would lead to sexual aversion between them, and that certain cues during early co-rearing, such as children's observation of younger siblings breast-feeding, would be of particular importance (Lieberman, Tooby, and Cosmides 2003). Thus, while the pathway of discovery does not always lead unidirectionally from a priori evolutionary theorizing to hypothesis formation to testing, sometimes it can. Even in these cases, however, hypothesis formation must always take into account both general evolutionary principles – such as how genetic reproduction patterns the distribution of shared genes among individuals – and specifics of the species, such as altriciality and co-residence during childhood.

13.5 Situating human psychological adaptations in phylogenetic context

The failure to consider the historical nature of the evolutionary process has led to a variety of misunderstandings about the nature of proper adaptationist theories about humans. Phylogeny refers to the evolutionary history of species, including the historical evolutionary relationships between different taxa. The evolutionary process of descent with modification from common ancestors leads to phylogenies that are branching trees, with ancestral taxa speciating and giving rise to multiple descendent taxa. As a consequence, when we trace our lineage back in time we find that we share common ancestors with other extant species: humans and chimps diverged from a common ancestral species between 6 and 10 million years ago, all primates from a common ancestor before that, all mammals from a common ancestor even farther back, and so on.

These simple facts are known to most modern scientists, but many discussions about the evolution of human psychology fail to sufficiently appreciate their implications. Perhaps the most egregious of these misunderstandings is the claim that "human nature," the explanatory target of evolutionary psychology, comprises only what is unique to humans. This is a major error, because it implies that it is possible to partition off just those features of human psychology that evolved since the human–chimp common ancestor, and that these represent "new" adaptations, while the rest remain the same. Similarly, it would be an error to claim that predation is not part of "lion nature" just because it is shared across carnivores. If one requires what is "unique" to humans to be only adaptations that have no homologs in other species, one leaves out large parts of human cognition. The process of descent with modification means not only that humans can be substantially different in many ways from our nearest evolutionary neighbors through recent genetic change, but also that the cognitive traits that we view as "uniquely" human, such as language and theory of mind, make enormous use of pre-existing design.

All of our "new" adaptations carry much that is old with them, including the majority of the genes that are involved in building them, and many millions of years of accumulated design that is still useful. It is a mistake, though a common one, to think that the only evolutionary route to the capacities underlying human cognition was to take all of the old capacities that were present in the human–chimp common ancestor, freeze them, and then add X brand new modules, each with a corresponding chunk of new genes exclusively for those modules.

To see why this is overly simplistic, consider the human face. Everyone would presumably agree that human faces and chimpanzee faces are different, and each species has a characteristic facial structure. However, humans do not possess the ancestral chimp–human face with a second, newly evolved human face "added on." Instead, modern humans and chimps both have just one face, each of which is a modified version of the face present in the common ancestor. The genes involved in making the face in both species are likely to be overwhelmingly the same genes, with some modifications, particularly in regulatory elements. The human face is uniquely adapted to the human situation, but it is not a *de novo*, wholly "new" adaptation. When we think about psychological adaptations, we should think the same way.

This is not to say that humans do not possess adaptations that are radically different from those present in chimps or the common ancestor; we probably do. We may also have a greater number of such adaptations, but even if we do, we should not think of these adaptations as arising totally *de novo*. Perhaps a better analogy would be with thinking about the evolution of new digits or limbs. Suppose humans evolved an additional finger on each hand, which improved our abilities to manipulate objects. How might this come about? Many innovations come about through alterations in regulatory genes and other elements (Carroll, Grenier, and Weatherbee 2005). In the case of a new digit, a mutation in the pathway regulating digit development could initially lead to the presence of a sixth digit. This could involve a minimal genetic change, since most of the genes involved in making the new digit would be the same ones involved in making other digits. One would therefore have a whole new piece of phenotype with few new genes, and that piece of phenotype would already have a large number of design features, inherited from ancestral digit design. Once this sixth digit were in place, selection could then act on it to favor phenotypic characteristics that were different from the other digits, depending on their effects on fitness.

A scenario like this is probably how new photoreceptor pigments evolved in color vision, adding new pigments that could detect previously undetectable wavelengths of light, but that were modified from existing pigments (Bowmaker 1998). Marcus (2006) has proposed that such a duplication-plus-modification process might be common in the origin of new psychological adaptations. Human psychological modules are likely to be modified versions of previously existing modules that inherit much of their problem-solving machinery, and evolve against a background of pre-existing modules with which they must be able to interface.

Consistent with this scenario, humans and chimps exhibit extreme genetic overlap (though there are large differences in how genes are expressed – which genes are active, and when during development – in chimp and human brains; Enard *et al.* 2002). This does not mean that the number of new human capacities must be small, if by "new" one means "modified." It is also not inconsistent with the view that humans are cognitively quite different from their near relatives, though at the same time sharing many cognitive building blocks in common.

13.5.1   Mindreading as an example

One psychological capacity that has received substantial attention is the ability to make inferences about the intentions, goals, desires, and other psychological states of other individuals, a capacity broadly referred to as *mindreading*, or *theory of mind* (Baron-Cohen 1995; Nichols and Stich 2003). Mindreading has also been studied in a variety of other species, including nonhuman primates and carnivores (Hare *et al.* 2002). This has resulted in a vigorous debate about whether theory of mind is unique to humans (Heyes 1998).

It is increasingly coming to be recognized that much of this debate has been misguided because it mistakenly treats theory of mind as a single capacity rather than a conglomerate of specialized psychological adaptations, each with an evolutionary history (Nichols and Stich 2003). In the case of mind-reading, there is substantial evidence for the existence of multiple underlying components that carry out distinct functional subtasks which in normal every-day human cognition result in what appears to be, and phenomenologically feels like, a seamless capacity of intentional inference.

For example, mechanisms for computing the direction of others' gaze are likely to be phylogenetically widespread, and to play an important role in mindreading, even though they are not *sufficient* for mindreading (Baron-Cohen 1995). The evolutionary origins of an "eye direction detector" (EDD) are probably ancient, and the basic design may be highly conserved (Brothers 1995). However, how the EDD *interacts* with other systems might be highly variable across species: in some, it might merely trigger stereotyped behaviors like fleeing, whereas in humans, gaze is thought to be very important for sophisticated computation of others' mental states beginning in infancy (Tomasello 2000). The point is that while eye direction detection is clearly not the same as or sufficient for mindreading, the evolution of mindreading may depend on it as a precursor, and new mechanisms evolved to depend on such older mechanisms for tracking others' attention. This phenomenon of evolutionary synergy, of new mechanisms leveraging the outputs of existing mechanisms in the service of wholly new adaptive functions, is probably widespread. Thinking about how new adaptations leverage older ones will likely be critical for understanding human uniqueness in phylogenetic context: much of our unique intelligence may depend on novel combinations or modifications of older skills, as much or more than the evolution of entirely new ones.

13.6   The present and future state of evolutionary psychology

Evolutionary psychology research has described a wide range of psychological mechanisms. These include mechanisms involved in mate choice (Buss 1989), cooperation (Cosmides 1989), decision making (Gigerenzer *et al.* 1999), face recognition (Duchaine *et al.* 2006), mindreading (Baron-Cohen 1995), language acquisition and production (Pinker 1994), kin detection and kin-directed altruism (Lieberman *et al.* 2003), and emotions (Fessler 1999).

There are many other findings that are easily accommodated within an evolutionary framework because they either directly or indirectly imply the existence of an evolved mechanism, including findings on early developing cognition in infants (Baillargeon 2004; Spelke 2000). There are also many cases of psychological mechanisms that are often described as "domain general," but that clearly have a specialized function that probably has an evolved basis, such as mechanisms underlying working memory (Repovs and Baddeley 2006), specialized learning (Gallistel and Gibbon 2000), and executive functions such as inhibition (Leslie and Polizzi 1998). There is no reason why these kinds of mechanisms should not fall under the rubric of evolutionary psychology, as might much research in vision, emotion, social cognition, and neuroscience.

To date, research in evolutionary psychology and related fields has made substantial progress. However, the field is growing rapidly, and extending into new areas. Before concluding I suggest (by no means exhaustively) some directions which are likely to be important in future research.

The first and most obvious direction is to continue using adaptationist reasoning and knowledge of human evolutionary history to attempt to uncover new psychological capacities. While a substantial diversity of these have already begun to be described, there is no reason to suspect that there could not be many more capacities that we have not yet discovered. For example, many researchers both within and outside of evolutionary psychology agree that human social cognition is extremely sophisticated and complex, and likely makes use of capacities that have been modified substantially from those present in other animals. It is also widely agreed that a phenomenon that pervades human social life, and that probably involves uniquely elaborated psychological capacities, is the transmission and use of cultural information (Richerson and Boyd 2005; Tomasello 2000). This probably involves mechanisms that we do not yet understand, and research in this area is rapidly growing.

A topic that has received relatively little attention, and is likely to be important for a complete understanding of how the mind works, is how evolved mechanisms interact with each other. This will probably be key to understanding human mental flexibility. It could well be that a major part of this flexibility arises not just from the evolution of new psychological mechanisms in the sense that they are traditionally conceived, but also because of changes in how information is shared between systems within the mind, resulting in computational gains in trade. There have been a variety of proposals to this effect (Barrett, Cosmides, and Tooby 2007; Carruthers 2005; Cosmides and Tooby 2000; Jackendoff 2002), but so far, relatively little empirical work in this area using the conceptual tools of evolutionary psychology.

One set of possible adaptations that has received little attention is mechanisms for sharing information within the mind (Barrett 2005b). Jackendoff (2002) has proposed that the fact that we can talk about what we see implies the existence of specialized perceptual–linguistic interfaces. There must also be interfaces between perception, conceptual structure, and motor control (Carruthers 2005). Recent research in embodied cognition (Gibbs 2006) might provide a fruitful avenue for exploring the interface between motor systems, perceptual systems, and other cognitive mechanisms, especially if pursued from an evolutionary perspective.

An area of evolutionary research that is beginning to grow is the study of development (processes of growth and maturation) and the complex interactions between genes, genetic regulatory systems, the developing phenotype, and information that give rise to the mind. There is already much research on the developmental process in developmental psychology, developmental neurobiology, and related fields, and much of this work has an evolutionary component to it. However, there is need for a greater amount of research that explicitly asks how the evolved mechanisms that cause development have been shaped by the evolutionary process to produce adaptive phenotypic outcomes (Barrett 2007).

13.7 Conclusion

In this brief survey of evolutionary psychology I have tried to focus on evolutionary psychology as a way of thinking, a particular approach to incorporating both proximate and ultimate causal thinking in the generation and testing of hypotheses about the mind. From this perspective, it is not so much a field or subdiscipline of the cognitive sciences, but an approach that could be applied across fields, from neuroscience to language to development.

I have also tried to stress that the historical nature of the evolutionary process places unique demands on how we think about causation and proper causal explanations in evolutionary psychology. These demands do not necessarily apply to approaches that are entirely proximate in nature. For example, some accounts might try to explain human cognitive flexibility in purely proximate terms by appealing to neural plasticity alone. A complete evolutionary account, however, would need to explain how and why humans differ from other species whose brains are composed of neurons with essentially the same properties.

The existence of multiple levels of causation, proximate and ultimate, has implications for scientific explanations of the mind that are often not sufficiently appreciated. Causal explanations often imply a tacit framing which is satisfactory for some purposes but not others. A good example from perceptual psychology would be explanations in terms of "salience": e.g., an item was processed quickly because it was salient (more noticeable). But salience implies an interaction between the properties of the perceptual system and the properties of the stimulus, and these in turn need to be explained. Why is the perceptual system designed such that stimuli of the particular type in question are more noticeable? Similarly, we might state that an adult's competence in his or her language is due to social learning: the language was acquired from the surrounding social group. Surely this is true, but a full account of the adult competence would require our asking, why would a chimpanzee in the same circumstances not acquire the same competence? What are the underlying mechanisms involved, why do they have the properties they do, and how do these interact with the nature of the input (and how has that input itself been structured to facilitate learning)?

For some purposes, more proximate causal explanations will clearly suffice. For example, we might state that stock market crashes are caused by market panics, and that might be the correct explanation. However, to explain why humans are the way they are – why we have stock markets, why we are so sensitive to the panic of others – we need to go beyond proximate explanations alone and ask why we see these features of human psychology instead of other ones. Why are we not like chimps, or cows, or pigeons? A full answer to this requires thinking about causation at many, many time scales, and about the peculiar features of *evolutionary* causation, which is filtered through processes of genetic and environmental transmission. The ambition of incorporating these multiple levels of causation is a double-edged sword, because it renders the explanatory task of evolutionary psychologists more difficult but, when done right, more complete as well.

Further reading

Barkow, J. H., Cosmides, L., and Tooby, J. (eds.) (1992). *The Adapted Mind: Evolutionary Psychology and the Generation of Culture.* Oxford University Press. Perhaps the seminal founding text of modern evolutionary psychology. This edited volume includes chapters on many specific domains of human psychology, from mate choice to spatial navigation, as well as Tooby and Cosmides' "The psychological foundations of culture," which articulates the principles of evolutionary psychology.

Barrett, L., Dunbar, R., and Lycett, J. (2002). *Human Evolutionary Psychology.* Basingstoke: Palgrave. This edited volume offers a very broad view of evolutionary psychology, including many chapters on topics sometimes neglected in other evolutionary psychology texts, such as human behavioral ecology, culture–gene co-evolution, and niche construction.

Bjorklund, D. F. and Pellegrini, A. D. (2002). *The Origins of Human Nature: Evolutionary Developmental Psychology.* New York: American Psychological Association. A comprehensive introduction to the field of evolutionary developmental psychology, one of the most rapidly growing areas of evolutionary psychology.

Buss, D. M. (ed.) (2005). *The Handbook of Evolutionary Psychology.* New York: John Wiley. The most comprehensive recent edited volume that surveys the entire field of evolutionary psychology, with chapters covering virtually every major theoretical and empirical topic in the field.

Pinker, S. (1997). *How the Mind Works.* New York: W. W. Norton. This is a very accessible treatment of evolutionary psychology which blends computational approaches from cognitive psychology with evolutionary theory.

Richerson, P. and Boyd, R. (2005). *Not by Genes Alone: How Culture Transformed Human Evolution.* University of Chicago Press. A comprehensive survey of the field of culture–gene co-evolution, explaining what this field can contribute to an understanding of evolved psychological mechanisms for cultural transmission, as well as how culture shapes human psychology on historical time scales.

References

Baillargeon, R. (2004). Infants' physical world, *Current Directions in Psychological Science* 13: 89–94.

Baron-Cohen, S. (1995). *Mindblindness.* Cambridge, MA: MIT Press.

Barrett, H. C. (2005a). Adaptations to predators and prey, in D. M. Buss (ed.), *The Handbook of Evolutionary Psychology* (pp. 200–23). New York: John Wiley.

   (2005b). Enzymatic computation and cognitive modularity, *Mind and Language* 20: 259–87.

   (2007). Development as the target of evolution: A computational approach to developmental systems, in S. Gangestad and J. Simpson (eds.), *The Evolution of Mind: Fundamental Questions and Controversies* (pp. 186–92). New York: Guilford.

   (2009). Where there is an adaptation, there is a domain: The form-function fit in information processing, in S. M. Platek and T. K. Shackelford (eds.), *Foundations in Evolutionary Cognitive Neuroscience* (pp. 97–116). Cambridge University Press.

Barrett, H. C., Cosmides, L., and Tooby, J. (2007). The hominid entry into the cognitive niche, in S. Gangestad and J. Simpson (eds.), *The Evolution of Mind: Fundamental Questions and Controversies* (pp. 241–8). New York: Guilford.

Barrett, H. C. and Kurzban, R. (2006). Modularity in cognition: Framing the debate, *Psychological Review* 113: 628–47.

Bjorklund, D. F. and Pellegrini, A. D. (2002). *The Origins of Human Nature: Evolutionary Developmental Psychology.* New York: American Psychological Association.

Bowmaker, J. K. (1998). Evolution of colour vision in vertebrates, *Eye* 12: 541–7.

Boyd, R. and Richerson, P. (1985). *Culture and the Evolutionary Process.* University of Chicago Press.

Brothers, L. (1995). The neurophysiology of the perception of intentions by primates, in M. Gazzaniga (ed.), *The Cognitive Neurosciences* (pp. 1107–15). Cambridge, MA: MIT Press.

Buller, D. (2005). *Adapting Minds: Evolutionary Psychology and the Persistent Quest for Human Nature.* Cambridge, MA: MIT Press.

Buss, D. M. (1989). Sex differences in human mate preferences: Evolutionary hypotheses tested in 37 cultures, *Behavioral and Brain Sciences* 12: 1–49.

Carroll, S. B., Grenier, J. K., and Weatherbee, S. D. (2005). *From DNA to Diversity: Molecular Genetics and the Evolution of Animal Design* (2nd edn.). Oxford: Blackwell.

Carruthers, P. (2005). *The Architecture of the Mind*. New York: Oxford University Press.

Cosmides, L. (1989). The logic of social exchange: Has natural selection shaped how humans reason? Studies with the Wason selection task, *Cognition* 31: 187–278.

Cosmides, L. and Tooby, J. (2000). Consider the source: The evolution of adaptations for decoupling and metarepresentations, in D. Sperber (ed.), *Metarepresentations: A Multidisciplinary Perspective* (pp. 53–116). New York: Oxford University Press.

Daly, M. and Wilson, M. (1998). *The Truth about Cinderella*. London: Weidenfeld and Nicolson.

  (2005). The "Cinderella Effect" is no fairy tale, *Trends in Cognitive Sciences* 9: 507–8.

Duchaine, B., Yovel, G., Butterworth, E., and Nakayama, K. (2006). Prosopagnosia as an impairment to face-specific mechanisms: Elimination of the alternative hypotheses in a developmental case, *Cognitive Neuropsychology* 23: 714–47.

Enard, W., Khaitovich, P., Klose, J. *et al.* (2002). Intra- and interspecific variation in primate gene expression patterns, *Science* 296: 340–3.

Fessler, D. M. T. (1999). Toward an understanding of the universality of second order emotions, in A. Hinton (ed.), *Beyond Nature or Nurture: Biocultural Approaches to the Emotions* (pp. 75–116). New York: Cambridge University Press.

Fodor, J. (1983). *The Modularity of Mind*. Cambridge, MA: MIT Press.

Gallistel, C. R. and Gibbon, J. (2000). Time, rate and conditioning, *Psychological Review* 107: 289–344.

Gibbs, R. W. (2006). *Embodiment and Cognitive Science*. New York: Cambridge University Press.

Gigerenzer, G., Todd, P. M., and the ABC Research Group (1999). *Simple Heuristics that Make Us Smart*. New York: Oxford University Press.

Godfrey-Smith, P. (2003). *Theory and Reality: An Introduction to the Philosophy of Science*. University of Chicago Press.

Guski, R. (1992). Acoustic tau: An easy analogue to visual tau? *Ecological Psychology* 4: 189–97.

Hamilton, W. D. (1964). The genetical evolution of social behaviour I and II, *Journal of Theoretical Biology* 7: 1–52.

Hare, B., Brown, M., Williamson, C., and Tomasello, M. (2002). The domestication of social cognition in dogs, *Science* 298: 1636–9.

Heyes, C. M. (1998). Theory of mind in nonhuman primates, *Behavioral and Brain Sciences* 21: 101–34.

Jackendoff, R. (2002). *Foundations of Language: Brain, Meaning, Grammar, Evolution*. Oxford University Press.

Kaplan, H. S., Hill, K., Lancaster, J. L., and Hurtado, A. M. (2000). A theory of human life history evolution: Diet, intelligence, and longevity, *Evolutionary Anthropology* 9: 156–85.

Leslie, A. M. and Polizzi, P. (1998). Inhibitory processing in the false belief task: Two conjectures, *Developmental Science* 1: 247–54.

Lieberman, D., Tooby, J., and Cosmides, L. (2003). Does morality have a biological basis? An empirical test of the factors governing moral sentiments relating to incest, *Proceedings of the Royal Society, Biological Sciences* 270: 819–26.

Marcus, G. F. (2006). Cognitive architecture and descent with modification, *Cognition* 101: 443–65.

Neuhoff, J. G. (1998). Perceptual bias for rising tones, *Nature* 395: 123–4.

(2001). An adaptive bias in the perception of looming auditory motion, *Ecological Psychology* 13: 87–110.

Nichols, S. and Stich, S. P. (2003). *Mindreading.* New York: Oxford University Press.

Pinker, S. (1994). *The Language Instinct.* New York: William Morrow.

Repovs, G. and Baddeley, A. (2006). The multi-component model of working memory: Explorations in experimental cognitive psychology, *Neuroscience* 139: 5–21.

Richerson, P. and Boyd, R. (2005). *Not by Genes Alone: How Culture Transformed Human Evolution.* University of Chicago Press.

Schiff, W., Caviness, J. A., and Gibson, J. J. (1962). Persistent fear responses in rhesus monkeys to the optical stimulus of "looming," *Science* 136: 982–3.

Seifritz, E., Neuhoff, J., Bilecen, D. *et al.* (2002). Neural processing of auditory looming in the human brain, *Current Biology* 12: 2147–51.

Silk, J. B. (2002). Kin selection in primate groups, *International Journal of Primatology* 23: 849–75.

Spelke, E. S. (2000). Core knowledge, *American Psychologist* 55: 1233–43.

Sperber, D. (1994). The modularity of thought and the epidemiology of representations, in L. A. Hirschfeld and S. A. Gelman (eds.), *Mapping the Mind: Domain Specificity in Cognition and Culture* (pp. 39–67). New York: Cambridge University Press.

Stephens, D. W. and Krebs, J. R. (1986). *Foraging Theory.* Princeton University Press.

Tomasello, M. (2000). *The Cultural Origins of Human Cognition.* Cambridge, MA: Harvard University Press.

Tooby, J. and Cosmides, L. (1992). The psychological foundations of culture, in J. H. Barkow, L. Cosmides, and J. Tooby (eds.), *The Adapted Mind: Evolutionary Psychology and the Generation of Culture* (pp. 19–136). Oxford University Press.

14 Embodied, embedded, and extended cognition

Andy Clark

14.1 Introduction: world enough, and flesh

Flesh and world are surely flavors of the moment. Talk of mind as *intimately* embodied and *profoundly* environmentally embedded shimmers at the cusp of the cognitive scientific zeitgeist. But beneath the glamour and glitz lies a still-murky vision. For this is a view of mind that can seem by turns radical and trivial, interestingly true and outrageously false, scientifically important and a mere distraction, philosophically challenging and simply confused. This chapter is an attempt to locate some footholds in this new and at times treacherous landscape.

It is comforting to begin with a seeming truth. Human minds, it can hardly be doubted, are at the very least in deep and critically important contact with human bodies and with the wider world. Human sensing, learning, thought, and feeling are all structured and informed by our body-based interactions with the world around us. Thus when Esther Thelen, a leading proponent of the embodied perspective, writes that "to say that cognition is embodied means that it arises from bodily interactions with the world" (Thelen 2000, p. 4), no sensible person is likely to disagree. But surely that isn't *all* that it means?

Clearly, there is more to this than meets the eye. Here is how the quote continues:

From this point of view, cognition depends on the kinds of experiences that come from having a body with particular perceptual and motor capacities that are inseparably linked and that together form the matrix within which memory, emotion, language, and all other aspects of life are meshed. The contemporary notion of embodied cognition stands in contrast to the prevailing cognitivist stance which sees the mind as a device to manipulate symbols and is thus concerned with the formal rules and processes by which the symbols appropriately represent the world. (Thelen 2000, p. 4)

Some of the material in this chapter is drawn from *Supersizing the Mind: Embodiment, Action, and Cognitive Extension* (Oxford University Press, 2008). Thanks to the publishers for permission to use this material here. This chapter was prepared thanks to support from the AHRC, under the ESF Eurocores CNCC scheme, for the CONTACT (Consciousness in Interaction) project, AH/E511139/1.

In this much-quoted passage we begin to glimpse some of the key elements of a more radical view. But even here, there are plenty of claims with which no one is likely to take issue. As active sensors of our world, possessed of bodies with specific shapes and characters, it is relatively unsurprising if what we think, do, and perceive all turn out to be *in some sense* deeply intertwined. Nor is it all that surprising if much of higher cognition turns out to be in some sense *built on* a substrate of embodied perceptuo-motor capacities. But the notion of "meshing" that Thelen deploys should give us pause, suggesting as it does a kind of ongoing intermingling of cognitive activity with the perceptuo-motor matrix from which it putatively emerges.

Meshing and intermingling are likewise prominent in John Haugeland's benchmark assertion that

If we are to understand mind as the locus of intelligence, we cannot follow Descartes in regarding it as separable in principle from the body and the world... Broader approaches, freed of that prejudicial commitment, can look again at perception and action, at skillful involvement with public equipment and social organization, and see not principled separation but all sorts of close coupling and functional unity... Mind, therefore, is not incidentally but *intimately* embodied and *intimately* embedded in its world. (Haugeland 1998, pp. 236–7)

What this passage makes clear is that the core claim at issue is not primarily a claim about development and learning. Nor is it about the undoubted role of body and world in fixing the contents of thought, or in determining the sequence of thoughts, or even in determining what kinds of thing we find it worth thinking about. Rather, what is at issue is something to do with the separability of mind, body, and world, at least for the purposes of understanding mind as the "locus of intelligence." What Haugeland is selling is a radical package deal aimed at undermining a simple, but arguably distortive, model of mind. This is the model of mind as essentially inner and (in our case) neurally realized. It is, to put it bluntly, the model of mind as brain (or perhaps brain and central nervous system): a model increasingly prevalent in a culture where just about everything to do with thinking seems to be accompanied by some kind of image of the brain. Call this model BRAINBOUND.

According to BRAINBOUND the (non-neural) body is just the sensor and effector system of the brain, and the (rest of the) world is just the arena in which adaptive problems get posed and the brain–body system must sense and act. If BRAINBOUND is correct, then all thoughts and feelings, and all cognition properly so called, depend directly upon neural activity alone. The neural activity itself may, of course, in turn depend on worldly inputs and (extra-neural) bodily activity. But that would be merely what Hurley

(1998, pp. 10–11) usefully dubs "instrumental dependence," as when we move our eyes and get a new perceptual experience as a result. BRAINBOUND asserts, seemingly in opposition to the very possibility of non-instrumental forms of bodily and worldly dependence, that all that really matters as far as the actual mechanisms of cognition are concerned is what the brain does: body and world act merely as sources of input and arenas for output.

Maximally opposed to BRAINBOUND is a view according to which thinking, cognizing, and feeling may all (at times) depend directly and non-instrumentally upon the ongoing work of the body and/or the extra-organismic environment. Call this model POROUS. According to POROUS, the actual local operations that make cognizing possible and that give content and character to our mental life include inextricable tangles of feedback, feedforward, and feedaround loops that promiscuously criss-cross the boundaries of brain, body, and world. The local mechanisms of mind, if POROUS is correct, are not all in the head.

Why might anyone think that POROUS expresses a truth about the mind? As a quick and dirty example, consider the familiar practice of writing while problem solving. One way to conceive of this process is in terms of a BRAINBOUND cognitive engine, one that generates ideas that are then stored externally as a hedge against forgetting or as a ploy to enable the communal sharing of information. But while both these roles are real and important, many people feel as if the act of writing is playing some rather more active role, as if the act itself matters in some way that goes beyond the simple offloading of a previously formed thought. Here, for example, is a famous exchange between the physicist Richard Feynman and the historian Charles Weiner:

> Weiner once remarked casually that [a batch of notes and sketches] represented "a record of [Feynman's] day-to-day work," and Feynman reacted sharply.
> "I actually did the work on the paper," he said.
> "Well," Weiner said, "the work was done in your head, but the record of it is still here."
> "No, it's not a *record*, not really. It's *working*. You have to work on paper and this is the paper. Okay?" (Quoted in Gleick 1993, p. 409)

Feynman's suggestion is that the loop into the external medium is integral to the intellectual activity, to the *working*, itself. It is not just the contingent environmental outflow of the working, but actually forms part of it. If such loops are indeed integral to certain forms of intelligent activity, we need to understand when and why this can be so, and just what it might mean (if anything) for our general model of minds and agency. Do such examples lend support to a vision such as POROUS or are they better accommodated (as many critics believe) in some much more deflationary way?

14.2   Simple causal spread

In a range of interesting and important cases, there is clear evidence that the problem-solving load is spread out across brain, body, and (sometimes) world. To get the flavor of this, it is helpful to contrast various solutions to a single problem. Take the case of walking (powered locomotion).

Honda's walking robot Asimo is billed, perhaps rightly, as the world's most advanced humanoid robot. Boasting a daunting 26 degrees of freedom (2 on the neck, 6 on each arm, and 6 on each leg) Asimo is able to navigate the real world, reach, grip, walk reasonably smoothly, climb stairs, and recognize faces and voices. The name Asimo stands (a little clumsily perhaps) for "Advance Step in Innovative Mobility." And certainly, Asimo is an incredible feat of engineering: still relatively short on brainpower but high on mobility and maneuverability.

As a walking robot, however, Asimo is far from energy efficient. For a walking agent, one way to measure energy efficiency is by the so-called "specific cost of transport" (Tucker 1975) – viz., "the amount of energy required to carry a unit weight a unit distance" calculated as (energy used)/(weight)(distance traveled). The lower the resulting number, the less energy is required to shift a unit of weight a unit of distance. Asimo rumbles in (see Collins and Ruina 2005) with a specific cost of transport of about 3.2, whereas we humans display a specific metabolic cost of transport of about 0.2. What accounts for this massive difference in energetic expenditure?

Where robots like Asimo walk by means of very precise, and energy-intensive, joint-angle control systems, biological walking agents make maximal use of the mass properties and bio-mechanical couplings present in the overall musculoskeletal system and walking apparatus itself. Wild walkers thus make canny use of so-called "passive dynamics," the kinematics and organization inhering in the physical device alone (McGeer 1990). Pure passive dynamic walkers are simple devices that boast no power source apart from gravity, and no control system apart from some simple mechanical linkages such as a mechanical knee and the pairing of inner and outer legs to prevent the device from keeling over sideways. Yet despite (or perhaps because of) this simplicity, such devices are capable, if set on a slight slope, of walking smoothly and with a very realistic gait. The ancestors of these devices are, as Collins, Wisse, and Ruina (2001) nicely document, not sophisticated robots but children's toys, some dating back to the late nineteenth century: toys that stroll, walk, or waddle down ramps or when pulled by string. Such toys have minimal actuation and no control system. Their walking is a consequence not of complex joint movement planning and actuating, but of basic morphology (the shape of the body, the distribution of linkages and weights of components, etc.).

Behind the passive dynamic approach thus lies the compelling thought that

Locomotion is mostly a natural motion of legged mechanisms, just as swinging is a natural motion of pendulums. Stiff-legged walking toys naturally generate their comical walking motions. This suggests that human-like motions might come naturally to human-like mechanisms. (Collins *et al.* 2001, p. 608)

Collins *et al.* (2001) built the first such device to mimic human-like walking, by adding curved feet, a compliant heel, and mechanically linked arms to the basic design pioneered by McGeer (1990). In action, the device exhibits good, steady motion and is described by its creators as "pleasing to watch" (2001, p. 613). By contrast, robots that make extensive use of powered operations and joint angle control tend to suffer from "a kind of rigor mortis [because] joints encumbered by motors and high-reduction gear trains...make joint movement inefficient when the actuators are on and nearly impossible when they are off" (2000, p. 607).

What, then, of powered locomotion? Once the body itself is "equipped" with the right kind of passive dynamics, powered walking can be brought about in a remarkably elegant and energy-efficient way. In essence, the tasks of actuation and control have now been massively reconfigured so that powered, directed locomotion can come about by systematically pushing, damping, and tweaking a system in which passive dynamic effects still play a major role. The control design is delicately geared to utilize all the natural dynamics of the passive baseline, and the actuation is consequently efficient and fluid.

Some of the core flavor of such a solution is captured by the broader notion of *ecological control* (see Clark 2007) where an ecological control system is one in which goals are not achieved by micro-managing every detail of the desired action or response, but by making the most of robust, reliable sources of relevant order in the bodily or worldly environment of the controller. In such cases the "matching" (of sensors, morphology, motor system, materials, controller, and ecological niche) yields a spread of responsibility for efficient adaptive response: the details of embodiment take over some of the work that would otherwise need to be done by the brain or the neural network controller, an effect that Pfeifer and Bongard (2007, p. 100) aptly describe as "morphological computation." The exploitation of passive dynamic effects thus exemplifies one of several key characteristics of the embodied, embedded approach: a characteristic that Wheeler and Clark (1999) dubbed *non-trivial causal spread*. Non-trivial causal spread occurs whenever something we might have expected to be achieved by a certain well-demarcated system turns out to involve the exploitation of more far-flung factors and forces. When a Mississippi alligator allows the temperature of the rotting vegetation in which it lays its eggs to determine the sex of its offspring, we encounter some non-trivial causal spread. When the passive dynamics of the actual legs and body take care of many of the demands that we might otherwise have ceded to an energy-hungry joint angle control system, we encounter non-trivial causal spread. One of the big lessons of contemporary robotics is that the co-evolution of morphology (which can include sensor placement, body-plan, and even the choice of basic building materials, etc.) and control yields a truly golden opportunity to spread the problem-solving load between brain, body, and world. (For excellent discussion, see Pfeifer and Scheier 1999; Pfeifer 2000. For the possible importance of bedrock materials, see Brooks 2001.)

14.3   Action as information self-structuring

Ballard *et al.* (1997) describe a task in which you are given a model pattern of colored blocks that you are asked to copy by moving similar blocks from a reserve area to a new workspace. Using the spare blocks in the reserve area, your task is to recreate the pattern by moving one block at a time from the reserve to the new version you are busy creating. The task is to be performed using mouse clicks and drags on a computer screen. As you perform, eye-tracker technology is monitoring exactly where and when you are looking at different bits of the puzzle.

What problem-solving strategy do you think you would use? One neat strategy might be to look at the target, decide on the color and position of the next block to be added, then execute the plan by moving a block from the reserve area. This is, for example, pretty much the kind of strategy you'd expect of a classical Artificial Intelligence planning system. When asked how we would solve the problem, many of us pay lip service to this kind of neat and simple strategy. But the lips tell one story while the hands and eyes tell another. For this is emphatically not the strategy used by most human subjects. What Ballard *et al.* found was that repeated rapid saccades to the model were used in the performance of the task: many more than you might expect. For example, the model is consulted *both before and after* picking up a block, suggesting that when glancing at the model, the subject stores only one piece of information: either the color or the position of the next block to be copied.

To test this hypothesis, Ballard *et al.* used a computer program to alter the color of a block while the subject was looking elsewhere. For most of these interventions, subjects did not notice the changes even for blocks and locations that had been visited many times before, or that were the focus of the current action. The explanation was that when glancing at the model, the subject stores only one piece of information: either the color or the position of the next block to be copied (not both). In other words, even when repeated saccades are made to the same site, very minimal information is retained.

Instead, repeated fixations provide specific items of information "just in time" for use. The experimenters conclude that

In the block-copying paradigm . . . fixation appears to be tightly linked to the underlying processes by marking the location at which information (e.g., color, relative location) is to be acquired, or the location that specifies the target of the hand movement (picking up, putting down). Thus fixation can be seen as binding the value of the variable currently relevant for the task. (Ballard *et al.* 1997, p. 734)

Two morals matter for the story at hand. The first is that visual fixation is here playing an identifiable computational role. As the authors (p. 725) comment, "changing gaze is analogous to changing the memory reference in a silicon computer." The second is that repeated saccades to the physical model thus allow the subject to deploy what Ballard *et al.* dub "minimal memory strategies" to solve the problem. The idea is that the brain creates its programs so as to minimize the amount of working memory that is required, and that eye motions are here recruited to place a new piece of information into memory. Indeed, by altering the task demands, Ballard *et al.* were also able to systematically alter the particular mixes of biological memory and active, embodied retrieval recruited to solve different versions of the problem. They conclude that, in this kind of task at least, "eye movements, head movements, and memory load trade off against each other in a flexible way" (1997, p. 732). As a result, a Ballard-style approach is able

To combine the concept that looking is a form of doing with the claim that vision is computation [by] introducing the idea that eye movements . . . allow perceivers to exploit the world as a kind of external storage device. (Wilson 2004, pp. 176–7)

Bodily actions here appear as among the means by which certain (in this case quite familiar) computational and representational operations are implemented. The difference is just that the operations are realized not in the neural system alone, but in the whole embodied system located in the world.

Embodied agents are also able to act on their worlds in ways that conjure cognitively and computationally potent time-locked patterns of sensory stimulation. In this vein Fitzpatrick *et al.* (2003) show, using robot demonstrations, exactly how active object manipulation (the robots are able to push and touch objects in view) can help generate information about object boundaries and affordances. Similarly, in human infants, grasping, poking, pulling, sucking, and shoving create a flow of multi-modal sensory stimulation that has been shown (Lungarella and Sporns 2005) to aid category learning and concept formation. The key to such capabilities is the robot or infant's capacity to maintain coordinated sensorimotor engagement with its environment. Self-generated motor activity, such work suggests, acts as a "complement to neural information-processing" in that

The agent's control architecture (e.g. nervous system) attends to and processes streams of sensory stimulation, and ultimately generates sequences of motor actions which in turn guide the further production and selection of sensory information. [In this way] "information structuring" by motor activity and "information processing" by the neural system are continuously linked to each other through sensorimotor loops. (Lungarella and Sporns 2005, p. 25)

14.4 Cognitive extensions

So far, we have been seeing evidence of the important roles played by bodily form and bodily action in the solution of basic adaptive problems such as locomotion and learning. But what about mature thought and reason? Does embodiment and environmental embedding play a role here too?

Consider an accountant, Ada, who is extremely good at dealing with long tables of figures. Over the years, Ada has learned how to solve specific classes of accounting problems by rapidly scanning the columns, copying some numbers onto a paper scratchpad, then looking to and from those numbers (carefully arrayed on the page) back to the columns of figures. This is all now second nature to Ada, who scribbles at lightning speed deploying a variety of "minimal memory strategies" (Ballard *et al.* 1997). Instead of attempting to commit multiple complex numerical quantities and dependencies to biological short-term memory, Ada creates and follows trails through the scribbled numbers, relying on self-created external traces every time an intermediate result is obtained. These traces are visited and revisited on a "just-in-time, need to know" basis, briefly shunting specific items of information into and out of short term bio-memory in much the same way as a serial computer shifts information to and from the central registers in the course of carrying out some computation. This process may be analyzed in "extended functional" terms, as a set of problem-solving state-transitions whose implementation happens to involve a distributed combination of biological memory, motor actions, external symbolic storage, and just-in-time perceptual access.

Robert Wilson's notions of "exploitative representation" and "wide computation" (Wilson 1994, 2004) capture some of the key features of such an extended approach. Exploitative representation occurs when a subsystem gets by without explicitly encoding and deploying some piece of information, in virtue of its ability to track that information in some other way. Wilson gives the example of an odometer that keeps track of how many miles a car has traveled not by first counting wheel rotations then multiplying according to the assumption that each rotation $= x$ meters, but by being built so as to record x meters every time a rotation occurs:

> In the first case it encodes a representational assumption and uses this to compute its output. In the second it contains no such encoding but instead uses an existing relationship between its structure and the structure of the world. (Wilson 2004, p. 163)

Wilson's descriptions and central examples can make it seem as if exploitative representation is all about achieving success without representations at all, at least in any robust sense of representation. But this need not be so. Another, very pertinent, range of cases would be those in which a subsystem does not contain within itself a persisting encoding of certain things, but instead leaves that information in the world, or leaves encoding it to some other subsystem to which it has access. Thus Ada's biological brain does not create and maintain persistent internal encodings of every figure she generates and offloads onto the page, though it may very well create and maintain persistent encodings of several other key features (for example, some kind of running approximation that acts to check for gross errors). In much the same way as Ballard's block-puzzlers, Ada's biological brain may thus, via the crucial bridging capacities of available embodied action, key its own internal representational and internal computational strategies to the reliable presence of the external pen-and-paper buffer. Even robustly representational inner goings-on may thus count as exploitative insofar as they merely form one part of a larger, well-balanced process whose cumulative set of state-transitions solves the problem. In this way

> explicit symbolic structures in a cognizer's environment... together with explicit symbolic structures in its head [may] constitute the cognitive system relevant for performing some given task. (Wilson 2004, p. 184)

The use of various forms of exploitative representation immediately yields a vision of what Wilson dubs "wide computationalism," according to which "at least some of the computational systems that drive cognition reach beyond the limits of the organismic boundary" (2004, p. 165). Extended functional systems may include coupled motor behaviors as processing devices and more static environmental structures as longer-term storage and encoding devices. The larger systems thus constituted are, as Wilson insists, unified wholes such that "the resulting mind–world computational system itself, and not just the part of it inside the head, is genuinely cognitive" (2004, p. 167).

Extended functionalists thus reject the image of mind as a kind of input–output sandwich with cognition as the filling (for this picture, and many more arguments for its rejection, see Hurley 1998; see also Clark 1997a; Clark and Chalmers 1998). Instead, we confront an image of the local mechanisms of human cognition quite literally bleeding out into body and world. The traditional functionalist was interested in neural goings-on as the contingent means by which human beings manage to implement the specific functional organizations characteristic of the human mind. The extended functionalist takes this one step further. From an extended functionalist perspective, not just the brain, but also the (non-neural) body and world, are apt to provide the physical machinery that implements (some of) the abstract organizations that turn matter into mind.

14.5   Critical reactions

It is the claims concerning cognitive extension, rather than those concerning simple causal spread (which now seems widely accepted in both the philosophical and cognitive scientific communities), that have received the most critical attention. Insofar as the more basic claims (about embodiment and causal spread) have been subject to critical scrutiny, it has mainly consisted in worries about a non-essential accompaniment to those claims, viz., the tendency of some theorists to reject the appeal to internal representation and/or computation in the explanation of adaptive success. Thus Grush (2003) takes issue with what he describes as

a growing radical trend in current theoretical cognitive science that moves from the premises of embedded cognition, embodied cognition, dynamical systems theory and/or situated robotics to conclusions either to the effect that the mind is not in the head or that cognition does not require representation, or both. (Grush 2003, p. 53)

Grush's stalking horse is, in fact, a view that is in at least one crucial respect much more radical than POROUS itself. It is the view that

the mind is not essentially a thinking or representing thing: it is a controller, a regulator, an element in a swarm of mutually causally interacting elements that includes the body and environment whose net effect is adaptive behavior. (Grush 2003, p. 55)

POROUS, however, need not deny that the mind is essentially a thinking or representing thing. It is committed only to the weaker claim that the thinking, and even the representing, may in many cases supervene on activities and encodings that criss-cross brain, body, and world. The debate concerning internal representation is thus independent (or so I have argued: see Clark 1997) of many of the key claims concerning causal spread between brain, body, and world.

Concerning the putative extension of (some of) the machinery of mind and reason into the surrounding world, Rupert (2004) worries that not enough has been done to justify talk of genuine cognitive extension. For all that matters, in such cases, is fully captured (Rupert claims) by the more conservative claim that he terms the *hypothesis of embedded cognition* (HEMC). According to HEMC:

Cognitive processes depend very heavily, in hitherto unexpected ways, on organismically external props and devices and on the structure of the external environment in which cognition takes place. (Rupert 2004, p. 393)

In other words, Rupert wants to treat all the cases in the way we (above) treated cases of simple causal spread. One reason for this is that Rupert (see also Adams and Aizawa 2001) is impressed by the profound *differences* that appear to distinguish the inner and outer contributions to human cognitive success. Thus, for example, we read that "the external portions of extended 'memory' states (processes) differ so greatly from internal memories (the process of remembering) that they should be treated as distinct kinds" (Rupert 2004, p. 407).

Part of the problem here may stem from a persistent misreading of the so-called "parity claim" introduced in Clark and Chalmers (1998). This was the claim that if, as we confront some task, a part of the world functions as a process which, were it to go on in the head, we would have no hesitation in accepting as part of the cognitive process, then that part of the world is (for that time) part of the cognitive process. But far from *requiring* any deep similarity between inner and outer processes, the parity claim was specifically meant to *undermine* any tendency to think that the shape of the (present-day, human) inner processes sets some bar on what ought to count as part of a genuinely cognitive process. The parity probe was thus meant to act as a kind of veil of metabolic ignorance, inviting us to ask what our attitude would be if currently external means of storage and transformation were, contrary to the presumed facts, found in biology. Thus understood, parity is not about the outer performing just like the (human-specific) inner. Rather, it is about equality of opportunity: avoiding a rush to judgment based on spatial location alone. The parity principle was meant to engage our rough sense of what we might intuitively judge to belong to the domain of cognition – rather than, say, that of digestion – but to do so without the pervasive distractions of skin and skull.

This point is nicely recognized by Wheeler (2010) who notes that the *wrong* way to assess parity of contribution is

[to] fix the benchmarks for what it is to count as a proper part of a cognitive system by identifying all the details of the causal contribution made by (say) the brain [then by looking] to see if any external elements meet those benchmarks. (Wheeler 2010, p. 3)

To do things that way, Wheeler argues, is to open the door to the highly chauvinistic thought that only systems whose fine-grained causal profile fully matches that of the brain can be cognitive systems at all. Yet, just because some alien neural system failed to match our own in various ways we should surely not *thereby* be forced to count the action of such systems as "non-cognitive." The parity principle is thus best seen as a demand that we assess the bio-external contributions with the same kind of unbiased vision that we ought to bring to bear on an alien neural organization. It is misconstrued as a demand for fine-grained sameness of processing and storage. Rather, it is a call for sameness of opportunity, such that bio-external elements *might* turn out to be parts of the machinery of cognition *even if* their contributions are unlike (perhaps deeply complementary to) those of the biological brain.

It is also important to see that there is no need, in taking extended cognition seriously, to lose our grip on the more-or-less stable, more-or-less persisting, core biological bundle that lies at the heart of each episode of cognitive processing. Occasionally, under strict and rare conditions we may confront genuine extensions of even that more-or-less persisting core: cases where even the persisting, mobile resource bundle is augmented in a potentially permanent manner. But in most other cases, we confront only temporary medleys of information-processing resources comprising a dovetailed subset of neural activity and bodily and environmental augmentations. The mere fact that such circuits are temporary, however, does not provide sufficient reason to downgrade their cognitive importance. Many purely internal information-processing ensembles are likewise transient creations, generated on the spot in response to the particularities of task and context. As just one example, consider Van Essen, Anderson, and Olhausen's (1994) account according to which many neurons and neuronal populations serve not as direct encodings of knowledge or information, but as (dumb) middle managers routing and trafficking the internal flow of information between and within cortical areas. These "control neurons" serve to open and close channels of activity, and allow for the creation of a kind of instantaneous, context-sensitive modular cortical architecture. Control neurons thus weave functional modules "on the hoof," in a way sensitive to the effects of context, attention, and so on. As Jerry Fodor once put it, in such cases it is "*unstable instantaneous* connectivity that counts" (1983 , p. 118; see also Fodor 2001). The resulting soft-wired ensembles, in which information then flows and is processed in ways apt to the task at hand, do not cease to be important just because they are transient creations ushered into being by a preceding wave of "neural recruitment."

Rupert worries that, by taking seriously the notion of cognitive extension in the special subclass of transient cases where the newly recruited organizations span brain, body, and world, we lose our grip on the persisting systems that we ordinarily take to be our objects of study. For indeed, as Rupert (2008) points out, much work in cognitive and experimental psychology proceeds by assuming that subjects are "persisting, organismically bound cognitive systems." Fortunately, however, there is no incompatibility whatsoever between the claims about cognitive extension and the notion of a persisting common biological core. Nor does anything in such treatments threaten to deprive us of that common core as a proper object of scientific study. If our avowed goal is to discover the stand-alone properties of the neural apparatus, we might want to impede subjects from using their fingers as counting buffers during an experiment. Similarly, if our goal is to understand what the persisting biological organism alone can do, we might want to restrict the use of all non-biological props and aids. But if our goal is to unravel the mechanically modulated flow of energy and information that allows an identifiable agent (a Sally, Johnny, or Terry) to solve a certain kind of problem, we should not simply *assume* that every biologically motivated surface or barrier forms a cognitively relevant barrier, or that it constitutes an important interface from an information-processing perspective.

As philosophers and as cognitive scientists we should, I suggest, practice the black but important art of repeatedly flipping between these different possible perspectives (extended, organismic, neural), treating each as a lens apt to draw attention to certain features, regularities, and contributions while at the same time obscuring others.

14.6   Conclusions

In his famous (1982) treatment, *The Extended Phenotype*, Richard Dawkins (pp. 4–5) encourages readers to try a "mental flip." Where before we saw only whole organisms (albeit replete with smaller parts, and themselves forming and re-forming into larger groups and wholes) we now see transparent bodies and the near-seamless play of replicating DNA. The spider's web appears as a proper part of the spider's extended phenotype, and the organism emerges as no more (and no less) than an adaptively potent non-random concentration of DNA. This perspective, Dawkins (p. 1) concedes, is not compulsory, nor can it be simply proved (or disproved) by experiment. Its virtues lie rather in the new ways of seeing familiar phenomena that it may breed, in that flip of perspective that invites us to view the larger organism–environment system in new and illuminating ways.

Work on embodiment, embedding, and cognitive extension likewise invites us to view mind and cognition in a new and (I believe) illuminating manner. It invites us to cease to unreflectively privilege (as does BRAINBOUND) the inner, the biological, and the neural, while at the same time helping us better to understand the crucial contribution of the whole organism and (within that organism) of neural control systems in the production of intelligent, information-based response. As POROUS cognitive agents we are merciless exploiters of bodily and environmental structure, and inveterate conjurors of our own cognition-enhancing input streams. Somewhat paradoxically, then, sustained attention to embodiment and action renders the bounds of skin and skull increasingly transparent, revealing processes running through body and world as integral parts of the machinery of mind and cognition.

To unravel the workings of these embodied and extended minds requires an unusual mix of neuroscience, computational, dynamical, and information-theoretic understandings, "brute" physiology, ecological sensitivity, and attention to the stacked designer cocoons in which we learn, think, and act. This may seem a daunting prospect, but there is cause for optimism. In learning, development, and evolution, trade-offs between neural control, morphology, action, and the epistemic use of environmental resources and opportunities are regularly and reliably achieved. Since such solutions are reliably found, there is a good chance that they can be systematically understood. Better still, the sciences of the mind are already well on the way to developing frameworks and forms of analysis that make headway with this difficult task. A mature science of the embodied mind will, I have argued, need to combine so-called "dynamical" insights (such as the stress on various forms of coupled organism–environment unfolding) with a much better understanding of the broad space of adaptive trade-offs: an understanding probably best filtered through the more familiar lenses of computational, representational, and information-theoretic tools and constructs.

The appeal to embodiment, embedding, and cognitive extension, if this is correct, marks not so much a radical shift as a natural progression in the maturing of our understanding the mind. It does not call into question all forms of "machine metaphors," and need involve no rejection of (though it is by no means exclusively committed to) accounts couched in terms of representations and computations. Indeed, the most natural way to approach the tough task of understanding *just how* body and world contribute to our cognitive performances is (I have tried to suggest) by the use of what are still broadly speaking functional and information-theoretic perspectives. The hope is rather to add new layers to our functional and information-processing understandings, by revealing the role of complex coupled dynamics, non-neural resources, and embodied action in the very machinery of thought and reason.

Further reading

Adams, F. and Aizawa, K. (2008). *The Bounds of Cognition*. Oxford: Wiley-Blackwell. A concise and accessible critique of the various arguments meant to support the hypothesis of the extended mind.

Clark, A. (1997). *Being There: Putting Brain, Body and World Together Again*. Cambridge, MA: MIT Press. A broad integrative overview, ranging from robotics to language to economic institutions, delivered with a mildly philosophical slant.

(2008). *Supersizing the Mind: Embodiment, Action, and Cognitive Extension.* Oxford University Press. A detailed reworking of the central claims concerning the "extended mind" and a response to the main critiques.

Gallagher, S. (2005). *How the Body Shapes the Mind.* Oxford University Press. An excellent synthesis of empirical work and phenomenology.

Pfeifer, R. and Bongard, J. (2007). *How the Body Shapes the Way We Think.* Cambridge, MA: MIT Press. An inspiring and rich, robotics-based, overview.

Robbins, P. and Aydede, M. (eds.) (2008). *The Cambridge Handbook of Situated Cognition.* Cambridge University Press. A wonderful and diverse collection of entries concerning the embodied, situated, and extended mind.

Rowlands, M. (1999). *The Body In Mind.* Cambridge University Press. A careful yet broad overview, conducted with a keen philosophical eye.

Rupert, R. (2004). Challenges to the hypothesis of extended cognition, *Journal of Philosophy* 101: 389–428. An important critical treatment, that develops a novel "systems-based" objection to the idea that human minds extend beyond the bounds of the organism. For a fuller and even wider-ranging deployment of this important strategy, see Rupert, R. (2009). *Cognitive Systems and the Extended Mind.* New York: Oxford University Press.

Wheeler, M. (2005). *Reconstructing the Cognitive World.* Cambridge, MA: MIT Press. A wonderfully original take on the debates concerning embodiment and cognitive extension. Embodiment with a Heideggerian twist.

Wilson, R. A. (2004). *Boundaries of the Mind: The Individual in the Fragile Sciences – Cognition.* Cambridge University Press. A delightfully wide-ranging examination of the role of the individual in the sciences of mind, and a defense of the claim that the boundaries of the mind extend beyond the skin.

References

Adams, F. and Aizawa, K. (2001). The bounds of cognition, *Philosophical Psychology* 14: 43–64.

Ballard, D., Hayhoe, M., Pook, P., and Rao, R. (1997). Deictic codes for the embodiment of cognition, *Behavioral and Brain Sciences* 20: 723–67.

Brooks, R. (2001). The relationship between matter and life, *Nature* 409: 409–11.

Clark, A. (1997). *Being There: Putting Brain, Body and World Together Again.* Cambridge, MA: MIT Press.

(2007). Re-inventing ourselves: The plasticity of embodiment, sensing, and mind, *Journal of Medicine and Philosophy* 32: 263–82.

Clark, A. and Chalmers, D. (1998). The extended mind, *Analysis* 58: 7–19.

Collins, S. H. and Ruina, A. (2005). A bipedal walking robot with efficient and human-like gait, in *Proceedings of the IEEE International Conference on Robotics and Automation, Barcelona, Spain* (pp. 1983–8).

Collins, S. H., Wisse, M., and Ruina, A. (2001). A three-dimensional passive-dynamic walking robot with two legs and knees, *International Journal of Robotics Research* 20: 607–15.

Dawkins, R. (1982). *The Extended Phenotype*. Oxford University Press.

Fitzpatrick, P., Metta, G., Natale, L., Rao, S., and Sandini, G. (2003). Learning about objects through action: Initial steps towards artificial cognition, in *Proceedings of the IEEE International Conference on Robotics and Automation (ICRA), May 12–17, Taipei, Taiwan* (pp. 3140–5).

Fodor, J. A. (1983). *The Modularity of Mind*. Cambridge, MA: MIT Press.
  (2001). *The Mind Doesn't Work That Way*. Cambridge, MA: MIT Press.

Gleick, J. (1993). *Genius: The Life and Times of Richard Feynman*. New York: Vintage.

Grush, R. (2003). In defence of some "Cartesian" assumptions concerning the brain and its operation, *Biology and Philosophy* 18: 53–93.

Haugeland, J. (1998). Mind embodied and embedded, in J. Haugeland, *Having Thought: Essays in the Metaphysics of Mind* (pp. 207–40). Cambridge, MA: Harvard University Press.

Hurley, S. (1998). *Consciousness in Action*. Cambridge, MA: Harvard University Press.

Lungarella, M. and Sporns, O. (2005). Information self-structuring: Key principle for learning and development, in *Proceedings of the 4th IEEE International Conference on Development and Learning* (pp. 25–30).

McGeer, T. (1990). Passive dynamic walking, *International Journal of Robotics Research* 9: 68–82.

Pfeifer, R. (2000). On the role of morphology and materials in adaptive behavior, in J.-A. Meyer, A. Berthoz, D. Floreano, H. Roitblat, and S.W. Wilson (eds.), *From Animals to Animats 6: Proceedings of the 6th International Conference on Simulation of Adaptive Behavior* (pp. 23-32). Cambridge, MA: MIT Press.

Pfeifer, R. and Bongard, J. (2007). *How the Body Shapes the Way We Think*. Cambridge, MA: MIT Press.

Pfeifer, R. and Scheier, C. (1999). *Understanding Intelligence*. Cambridge, MA: MIT Press.

Rupert, R. (2004). Challenges to the hypothesis of extended cognition, *Journal of Philosophy* 101: 389–428.
  (2008). Innateness and the situated mind, in P. Robbins and M. Aydede (eds.), *The Cambridge Handbook of Situated Cognition* (pp. 96–116). Cambridge University Press.

Thelen, E. (2000). Grounded in the world: Developmental origins of the embodied mind, *Infancy* 1: 3–28.

Tucker, V. A. (1975). The energetic cost of moving about, *American Scientist* 63: 413–19.

Van Essen, D. C., Anderson, C. H., and Olshausen, B. A. (1994). Dynamic routing strategies in sensory, motor, and cognitive processing, in C. Koch and J. Davis (eds.), *Large Scale Neuronal Theories of the Brain* (pp. 271–99). Cambridge, MA: MIT Press.

Wheeler, M. (2010). Minds, things and materiality, in L. Malafouris and C. Renfrew (eds.), *The Cognitive Life of Things*. Cambridge: McDonald Institute for Archaeological Research.

Wheeler, M. and Clark, A. (1999). Genic representation: Reconciling content and causal complexity, *British Journal for the Philosophy of Science* 50: 103–35.

Wilson, R. A. (1994). Wide computationalism, *Mind* 103: 351–72.

  (2004). *Boundaries of the Mind: The Individual in the Fragile Sciences – Cognition*. Cambridge University Press.

15 Animal cognition

Sara J. Shettleworth

15.1 Introduction: history and present trends

Writings about animal minds date from at least the time of Aristotle, but like so much else in the biological sciences, the modern study of animal cognition began with Darwin. In *The Origin of Species* he said little about the implications of natural selection for the human species, but human evolution was the subject of his second great book, *The Descent of Man and Selection in Relation to Sex* (Darwin 1871), and the similarity of nonhuman to human "mental powers" was a central part of the argument. Chapter 2 of *The Descent of Man* in effect outlines a research program for comparative psychology. Nearly all the topics in it – from animal attention and memory to self-consciousness and the foundations of morality – are active areas of research today, and some of the themes and orienting attitudes that still provoke discussion in the early twenty-first century emerged very soon after 1871.

Obtaining convincing evidence for commonalities between nonhuman and human minds was an important task for early defenders of Darwinism, but initially much of that evidence – like that provided by Darwin himself – was anecdotal: descriptions of dogs that opened gates or found their way home from great distances, a monkey that cared for a kitten. The Darwinian agenda pursued by writers such as George Romanes encouraged anthropomorphic interpretations of such human-like behaviors. So, for example, a cat that opened a gate after observing people do so must have reasoned "by the logic of feelings," "If a hand can do it, why not a paw" (Romanes 1892). Critics of such unsupported anthropomorphism were not slow to appear, among them the American comparative psychologist Edward Thorndike. Thorndike's (1911/1970) experiments with puzzle boxes were based pretty directly on anecdotes about animals opening gates: his subjects escaped from cages by pushing levers, pulling strings, and the like. They scrambled around ineffectually until they performed the required response by chance, and then improved only gradually, learning by trial and error rather than reasoning or imitating.

Thorndike's findings doubtless helped to dampen interest in studying higher mental processes in animals throughout much of the twentieth century. The rise of behaviorism was another important factor (see Boakes 1984) in human as well nonhuman psychology. Among biologists too, sentimental anthropomorphism was replaced by a strictly behaviorist, mechanistic, approach to behavior. Arguably this attitude was essential to the development of ethology as a science in the 1930s and 40s (Burkhardt 2005). Of course, there were some attempts to investigate the cognitive processes underlying behavior, notably by E. C. Tolman (e.g., 1948) and by Wolfgang Kohler (1959) in his studies of chimpanzees' problem solving, but on the whole "animal psychology" focused on describing how the environment controlled behavior and how it came to do so through instrumental (or operant) and classical (or Pavlovian) conditioning, i.e., learning in which a response or a neutral stimulus, respectively, is associated with reward or punishment. That all began to change in the early 1970s. Following on from the success of the cognitive revolution in human psychology, animal behavior was now seen as a window onto processes of perception, memory, and representation. Initially, much of the research in the nascent field of animal cognition was done by people trained in the behaviorist tradition, using instrumental and classical conditioning procedures with pigeons and rats to look at basic processes such as memory, timing short intervals, or categorizing stimuli and to address theoretical questions such as whether animals form concepts or why forgetting occurs (e.g., Hulse, Fowler, and Honig 1978).

Research in the "animal learning" tradition is still going on (see Wasserman and Zentall 2006), but the contemporary study of animal cognition has many other ingredients in a rich mix from research traditions including ethology, behavioral ecology, anthropology, and behavioral neuroscience. Increasingly, research synthesizes elements from more than one of these traditions. In part this multidisciplinarity reflects independent developments in hitherto separate fields that have encouraged interest in one aspect or another of animal cognition. For example, at about the same time as cognitively inspired research was getting off the ground in animal learning laboratories, the distinguished biologist Donald Griffin (1976) began exhorting ethologists to start investigating animal consciousness. The research stimulated by Griffin's writings, referred to as *cognitive ethology* (Ristau 1991), thus dealt primarily with processes thought to be conscious rather than the broader type of cognition involved in natural behaviors. Meanwhile behavioral ecology was developing as an offshoot of ethology focused on testing precise models of the adaptive value of behavior. As it became apparent that understanding why animals forage or choose mates as they do requires understanding how their perception, learning, memory, and other cognitive processes work, behavioral ecologists began calling for a *cognitive ecology* (see Healy and Braithwaite 2000; Dukas and Ratcliffe 2009), a marriage between animal cognition and behavioral ecology research. At the same time, an explosion of field studies on primates and other species was providing a wealth of provocative observations on natural behavior begging to be followed up with closer analyses of underlying cognitive mechanisms. Both field experiments and more detailed observations with wild and captive groups are revealing much about animals' social knowledge (de Waal and Tyack 2003; Cheney and Seyfarth 2007), communication (Seyfarth and Cheney 2003), and tool using (e.g., chapters by Visalberghi and Fragaszy and by Kacelnik *et al.* in Wasserman and Zentall 2006). Finally, an important impetus for some high-profile contemporary research is the promise of the neurosciences that "animal models" will help in unraveling the neural and genetic bases of not only memory and learning but of distinctive states of consciousness in humans.

The next part of this chapter discusses some basic orienting attitudes that inform contemporary research and debate on animal cognition. Then research on four specific problems – memory in food-storing birds, conscious aspects of memory, numerical cognition, and animal theory of mind – is sketched to illustrate some important themes in current work. Finally we look briefly at where the field might go in the future.

15.2   Orienting attitudes

15.2.1   Anthropomorphism and Morgan's canon

Anthropomorphism – explaining behavior in terms of human-like mental processes – is almost a dirty word in the scientific study of animal cognition (Wynne 2007; Mitchell 2005). But although anthropomorphism as explanation may rarely be justified, evolutionary continuity justifies anthropomorphism as a source of hypotheses. After all, if other species share common ancestors with us, then we share an a priori unspecifiable number of biological processes with any species one cares to name. Just as with our genes and other physical characters, it is likely that some cognitive processes are shared with many other species, some with only a few, and some are uniquely human (Penn, Holyoak, and Povinelli 2008). One of the biggest challenges in studying animal cognition is to conceive of alternatives to proposed mentalistic, anthropomorphic explanations of the "clever" things animals do. For example, a chimpanzee or a crow poking a stick into a hole and pulling out a grub looks as if it understands how its tool works. What do we mean by "understanding," what could be going on instead, and how can possible alternative explanations be tested against each other?

Traditionally, a guiding principle here is *Morgan's canon*, after C. Lloyd Morgan, an early ethologist and Darwinian who is now best known for stating a principle commonly taken as forbidding unsupported anthropomorphism. Morgan's (1894) canon states "In no case may we interpret an action as the outcome of the exercise of a higher psychical faculty, if it can be interpreted as the outcome of the exercise of one which stands lower in the psychological scale." This prescription is clearly not without problems (Sober 2005). For example, what is the "psychological scale"? "Higher" and "lower" suggest classification in terms of more and less highly evolved, an erroneous idea insofar as it implies that evolution is linear rather than branching. In contemporary practice, "lower" usually means classical and instrumental conditioning or untrained species-specific responses. "Higher" is reasoning, planning, insight, or any representational process other than what is evident in associative learning. The field as it has developed in the past thirty to forty years has a very strong bias in favor of the "simple." The burden of proof is generally on anyone wishing to explain behavior otherwise. Although it could be said to be as simple to assume other species are just like us (Sober 2005), evolutionary theory does justify a bias toward explaining learned behaviors in terms of associative learning because basic conditioning mechanisms are very widespread in the animal kingdom, having been found in every animal in which they have been sought, from worms and fruitflies to primates. Thus they seem to be evolutionarily very old and present in species ancestral to all present-day animals, and they are probably adaptations to basic causal regularities in the world (Papini 2002, 2008).

15.2.2   Animal cognition and animal consciousness

As with humans, the first research with animals stimulated by the cognitive revolution consisted of inferring cognitive processes from input–output relations. Consciousness was not an issue. Just as this attitude changed with the legitimization of consciousness in the cognitive sciences more generally, so people studying animals became more willing to tackle processes that in humans are accompanied by distinctive states of awareness. Most researchers seem to assume that animals are conscious in the sense of having perceptual awareness, but aspects of reflective consciousness such as future planning, episodic memory, metacognition (section 15.3.2), and theory of mind (section 15.3.4) are more controversial. Because evidence for these processes in humans generally consists of what people say about their mental experiences, studying them in nonverbal species requires us to accept some behavior as equivalent to a verbal report. Clearly, we can never know whether this is correct or not, since we can never know the animal's private state. Therefore, the point of view of most researchers studying animal cognition is that how animals process information can, and should, be analyzed without making any assumptions about what their subjective experiences are like (Wynne 2007; Hampton 2005).

Considerations of evolution and function are not much help here. Evolutionary continuity suggests that some other species, most likely primates, must share some forms of consciousness with us. But because evolution has acted via the results of what creatures do, not directly on what they experience privately while doing it, there must be something promoting survival and reproduction that a conscious animal can do and one lacking consciousness cannot. However, it is difficult to find a situation for which the notion that an animal has a conscious belief or intention or is consciously manipulating information unambiguously predicts what it does (Dawkins 1993).

The gap between humans and other living species in language ability is also part of the discussion of human vs. animal consciousness. Most would now conclude that language is unique to humans (Fitch 2005), so if conscious thought requires language, neither animals nor preverbal children can possibly be conscious (Macphail 1998). Even when, as in the examples to be discussed later in the chapter, it is possible to agree on what patterns of nonverbal behavior would be functionally similar to behavior that serves as evidence for a given conscious process in humans, many researchers would go no further than saying that the animals that behave in such a manner behave only "as if" possessing metacognition, theory of mind, or whatever.

15.2.3   Comparative cognition?

The field of animal cognition is frequently referred to as *comparative cognition* (e.g., Wasserman and Zentall 2006), but in fact many of the comparisons made by researchers studying nonhuman animals do not go beyond testing whether individuals of some convenient species behave like humans when tested in a parallel way. Indeed, for over fifty years comparative psychologists have been complaining about how few species other than rats and pigeons find their way into psychology laboratories (Beach 1950; Shettleworth 2009). There are many signs that this is changing and that the developments sketched in section 15.1 are resulting in a more deeply comparative study of cognition.

For many years, the best-developed research program comparing any aspect of cognition among species was that of M. E. Bitterman on learning in a sample of species that included goldfish, turtles, pigeons, rats, and honeybees (Bitterman 2000). This research can be criticized for choosing species for no other reason than that they are phylogenetically diverse and relatively available for work in the laboratory without taking into account the natural context in which each one may need to learn (Shettleworth 2010; but see Bitterman 2000). Nevertheless, as in the recent discoveries of genetic commonalities across the animal kingdom, this approach has revealed important commonalities in learning mechanisms across species along with a few differences, notably in ways of adjusting to unpredictable rewards (Papini 2002, 2008). One important contribution it has made to theory development is to open our eyes to the sometimes radically different ways in which different species may solve the same information-processing problems (Mackintosh 1988). Equally important is its deep consideration of methodological issues that must be addressed in order to draw meaningful conclusions about underlying cognitive processes from comparisons of behavior in species that differ as drastically as fish, rats, and bees in perceptual, motor, and motivational mechanisms (see section 15.3.2).

Unlike traditional comparative research in psychology, several contemporary research programs focus directly on questions about the function and evolution of cognitive processes. As in evolutionary biology more generally, such questions can be addressed by looking both for divergence in close relatives with different ecologies and convergence in distantly related species with similar ecologies. An example of the former – the comparison of memory in birds that do and do not store food – is discussed in section 15.3.1. One very stimulating example of the latter is the comparison of tool using and aspects of social intelligence in primates vs. some of the larger-brained birds, especially members of the crow family, *corvids* (Emery and Clayton 2004; Balda and Kamil 2006). Some of this research is part of a larger enterprise comparing the cognitive abilities used to track social relationships in diverse species of mammals. Some time ago it was suggested that the supposedly great general intelligence of monkeys and apes evolved to meet the demands of social life (Jolly 1966; Humphrey 1976). But this "social theory of intellect" should apply to any species with a primate-like social life, i.e., with overlapping generations living in stable groups of individuals with differentiated social roles. Increasing information from long-term field studies about the social lives of hyenas, meerkats, whales, and a diversity of other species is fueling debate and discussion about whether these species solve similar social problems in similar ways (de Waal and Tyack 2003; Holekamp 2006).

15.2.4   Modularity or "general intelligence"?

Originally, the social theory of intellect was proposed to account for the apparently superior general problem-solving ability of monkeys and apes in learning tasks in the laboratory, most of which involved physical causal relations rather than social ones (Jolly 1966). The proposal that abilities evolved to solve social problems are available for solving physical ones assumes that animals have a general intelligence rather than distinct abilities that can evolve to some extent independently, i.e., modular intelligence. But the idea of animal, or even mammalian, "general intelligence" by which species can be ranked makes very little sense (Shettleworth 2010). Although "the modularity of mind" may be controversial in the cognitive sciences, organization into somewhat independent but interconnected parts is a basic property of complex systems and, accordingly, modularity is an accepted property of biological systems (Barrett and Kurzban 2006). Animal cognition can be seen as modular because different kinds of information demand different memory systems (Sherry and Schacter 1987) or learning modules (Gallistel 1998) with different rules of operation. For example, orienting by landmarks requires storing distance and direction, i.e., vector-like information, whereas tracking events through time to learn what predicts what, as in conditioning, requires computing temporal dependencies. Nowadays most discussions of cognitive modularity are supported by evidence of modularity in the brain, and as we see in section 15.3.1, brain parts with different functions evolve to some extent independently (Striedter 2005). In principle then, the study of animal cognition is of key relevance to evolutionary psychology in providing tractable models of how modular cognitive systems are organized (see Chapter 13).

15.3   Research programs

This section is a brief overview of four areas of research that together illustrate a broad sample of current issues and approaches. Sections 15.3.1 and 15.3.2 deal with contrasting aspects of memory: cross-species comparisons of spatial memory and its relation to ecology and brain evolution on the one hand, and attempts to investigate conscious aspects of memory in animals on the other. Sections 15.3.3 and 15.3.4 sketch research on two problems in which comparative and developmental psychology are intertwined – numerical cognition and theory of mind. The former is an example of deeply comparative research in which progress has been made by thinking in terms of component processes, some shared across human and nonhuman species and some unique to humans. The latter, while a hotbed of new findings from species as diverse as dogs, ravens, and chimpanzees, is also a hotbed of perhaps inevitable controversy arising from attempts to document human-like understanding in other species.

15.3.1   Adaptive specializations of memory in food-storing birds

Some birds store food and retrieve it days, weeks, or months later using memory. For example, Clark's nutcrackers make thousands of caches of pine seeds in late summer and retrieve them throughout the winter and into the next spring. Besides corvids like the nutcracker, the chickadees and tits (*Paridae*) have been extensively studied. The importance of successfully retrieving stored food for winter survival suggests that food storers have evolved spatial memory that is superior in some way to that of other birds. Beginning in the mid 1980s this hypothesis stimulated a substantial body of research comparing memory in corvids and parids that store different amounts of food in the wild. The most systematic and comprehensive such research compares the Clark's nutcracker and several species of food-storing jays that live in similar areas in the American Southwest (Balda and Kamil 2006).

Any attempt to test the apparently obvious conclusion that some animals have better memory than others has to confront some difficult problems long known in the traditional comparative psychology of learning. To begin with, species differences in sensory systems can influence the ability to discriminate among the stimuli being used. Then it has to be taken into account that even within a species speed or accuracy of performance on learning tasks can vary with motivation and type and amount of reward. Such *contextual variables* (Macphail 1987) can never be precisely equated across species. At best, their role can be addressed by systematically varying each factor suspected to influence the outcome within any given species (Bitterman 1975), for instance by looking at how the animals perform at a range of hunger levels and reward sizes. But this makes rejecting the null hypothesis that species don't differ cognitively an infinite process of systematically rejecting one candidate contextual variable after another as the cause of any observed difference in performance (Kamil 1988).

An alternative and arguably more productive approach is to vary the task, to see whether multiple tests of the same cognitive ability converge on a consistent pattern of species differences (Kamil 1988). This is the approach pursued by Balda and Kamil (2006) with the food-storing corvids. For example, nutcrackers outperform the other corvids studied in tests of memory for stored food in the laboratory, memory for locations of food hidden by the experimenters, and memory for locations of colored images on a video monitor. Importantly, nutcrackers do not perform differently from the other species on tests of memory for the colors of the images, showing that they are not just "smart" in general, better adjusted to life in the laboratory, or the like. Rather, these findings and comparable ones with chickadees and tits (Shettleworth and Hampton 1998) support the hypothesis that food-storing birds have evolved an adaptive specialization specifically of spatial memory.

This same idea – that natural selection shapes specific ecologically relevant aspects of cognition – has been tested with other groups of species thought to vary in their reliance on spatial memory in the wild, including cowbirds and several kinds of rodents (Sherry 2006). It also applies to differences within a species, as when males and females use different sized territories or different populations live in more or less spatially demanding circumstances (e.g., Pravosudov and Clayton 2002). However, comparing close relatives, or even members of the same species, does not necessarily escape the problem of contextual variables entirely. Persuasive evidence of a difference in cognition usually requires more than a single experiment, no matter how stimulating and plausible the results.

The idea that natural selection shapes specific aspects of cognition has also influenced studies of cognitive abilities thought to be used in social life. For example, transitive inference is thought to be useful for inferring dominance relations among members of a social group after observing their interactions. That is, after observing that animal *A* dominates *B* and *B* dominates *C*, an animal infers that *A* dominates *C*. Not only is one species of jay capable of this feat in the laboratory (Paz-y-Miño C. *et al.* 2004), but they outperform members of a less social species in an abstract operant version of the task (Bond, Kamil, and Balda 2003). Consistent with the notion that animal intelligence is modular, with distinct abilities evolving somewhat independently, the same corvids whose spatial memory has been compared have a different profile of species differences when it comes to social organization and, as far as they have been tested, of cognitive abilities related to sociality (Balda and Kamil 2006). Natural selection for behavior and cognition implies selection for underlying neural mechanisms. Because the hippocampus is known to be involved in spatial memory in mammals and birds there has been extensive examination of the possibility that hippocampal volume is correlated with the demand for spatial memory in the wild (Sherry 2006). The comparative method developed in evolutionary biology is applied here by taking into account species differences in overall brain or body size and correcting for different degrees of relatedness among the species being compared. This kind of analysis shows that food-storing species have much bigger hippocampi than expected for their overall brain and body size (Sherry 2006; Shettleworth 2010). The comparative method has been widely applied to look for relationships between brain areas and other specific behaviors and/or aspects of ecology (Sherry 2006; Healy and Rowe 2007). Within psychology, however, this approach, sometimes called *neuroecology*, has been surprisingly controversial, in part because spatial memory, hippocampus, and food storing are not always related precisely as predicted (Bolhuis and Macphail 2001). Certainly other kinds of research are needed to understand how any brain area works, but correlating brain development with ecological demands can provide valuable insights into what particular structures allow animals to do and, indirectly, into the course of cognitive evolution (Sherry 2006).

15.3.2   Memory and consciousness

The research on food-storing birds just reviewed, like most research on animal and human memory until recently, treats memory simply as a process that allows past experience to influence behavior. Whether or not animals are aware of their memories is not an issue. But with development of interest in aspects of memory that are accompanied by (or even defined by) distinct conscious experiences in humans, there has also come interest in looking for the same processes in other species. The two that have attracted the most research are metamemory (awareness of one's own memories) and episodic memory (recollection and "re-experiencing" of specific events in one's personal past). In both cases, as in other research discussed in section 15.3.4, because animals cannot talk to us about their subjective states, the challenge is to define behavior that is uniquely indicative of whatever kind of conscious process one is trying to identify in the animal. Even if, as in the case of metamemory, animals show behavior that is *functionally similar* (Hampton 2001) to human verbal report in that it varies similarly with independent variables, we still can never know whether the animal's subjective state resembles that of a human.

There is now a substantial body of work on metacognitive responses in animals, particularly rhesus macaques (see Smith *et al.* 2008; Hampton 2009). Metamemory entails reporting on the strength of one's memory, for example by saying "I know that phone number" and then dialing it correctly. Thus testing metamemory in animals requires looking for a relationship between two different responses within the same situation: a report on memory strength and a direct test of memory. When accuracy on the direct test of memory is manipulated, as by increasing the interval over which items must be remembered (the retention interval), the report on memory strength should change accordingly.

One way to encourage an animal to "report" its memory strength is to offer a choice between taking a memory test and avoiding it. A large reward is given for correct responses on the memory test and no reward for getting it wrong; avoiding the test always earns a mediocre reward. Thus, animals that can monitor their memory strength (i.e., that have metamemory) should choose the memory test when they "know that they know" the answer and otherwise accept the certain but mediocre reward. For instance, when the retention interval is lengthened, an animal with metamemory should avoid the memory test more often, but on trials when it does choose to take the test it should perform better than when forced to take the test. Rhesus monkeys show this pattern of relationships in several variations of such tasks. They also transfer their metacognitive "reports" from one task to another (e.g., Kornell, Son, and Terrace 2007). And in one experiment (Hampton 2001) monkeys immediately avoided memory tests on trials when nothing had been presented for them to remember, more consistent with behavior based on an internal state rather than external cues (Hampton 2009). In contrast, the repeated failure of pigeons to pass this and other tests passed by monkeys (Sutton and Shettleworth 2008) indicates that pigeons either have no metacognitive ability or do not readily use it. In that it is a kind of sensitivity to one's own internal state, metacognition is sometimes seen as a form of self-awareness. Since, as described next, some birds among the corvids show behavior consistent with other conscious aspects of memory and self-awareness it would be of interest to give them tests of metacognition. Mammals other than primates, too, remain to be given the range and depth of tests given to the monkeys.

Comparative research on metamemory provides an instructive contrast to that on episodic memory, or conscious recollection of episodes in one's personal past. More so than research on metamemory, research on animal episodic memory has been impelled by the promise of understanding its neural mechanisms in humans by studying "animal models." This is because loss of episodic memory is a hallmark of Alzheimer's disease and other forms of amnesia. A landmark here was the demonstration by Clayton and Dickinson (1998) that Western scrub jays, a food-storing corvid, remember what items they cached in which locations at a particular time in the past. Thus, the jays show memory for the what, where, and when of past events, called by Clayton and Dickinson "episodic-like" memory. This term acknowledges that although the jays meet certain behavioral criteria for episodic memory, we cannot know if they have the feeling of consciously "traveling back in time" to those events – something which has been claimed (e.g., by Tulving 2005) to be a defining feature of episodic memory in humans.

The report on the scrub jays stimulated an explosion of attempts to demonstrate what-where-when memory in rats and monkeys, but whereas these animals readily showed that they could remember what was where, the "when" (or relative time) aspect usually eluded them (but see Babb and Crystal 2006). However – and here is where the research is importantly different from that on metamemory – at the same time a number of other candidates for nonverbal analogues of episodic memory were proposed. These included the ability to answer an unexpected question (Zentall et al. 2001), memory for the spatial (as opposed to temporal) context in which something was experienced (Ergorul and Eichenbaum 2004), and ability to identify an event's position in a sequence of similar events (Eichenbaum et al. 2005). Another suggestion is that choices in a yes/no test of recognition memory should change with the relative effort required to make the two choices (i.e., bias factors) and that the shape of the function should change with hippocampal lesions. In a test of olfactory memory, rats behave as this hypothesis predicts, a nice example of memory varying with independent variables in a similar way across species (Eichenbaum et al. 2005).

One way to interpret this variety of results is to say that they converge on several shared aspects of human and animal memory for specific episodes (Eichenbaum et al. 2005; Crystal 2009). They can also be taken as highlighting ambiguities in the way human episodic memory is conceptualized and the difficulty (impossibility even) of drawing conclusions about the evolution or comparative distribution of a cognitive ability when a key part of its definition is human subjective experience. This problem is even more acute in discussions of whether species other than humans are capable of "mentally time traveling" into the future as well as into the past (e.g., Suddendorf and Corballis 2007). In effect, future time travel is planning ahead. However, an abundance of simple learning and timing mechanisms allow animals to prepare for future events on the basis of cues that reliably foretold the future in their ancestors' and/or their individual past. Genuine "planning" has been proposed to consist uniquely of a novel behavior or combination of behaviors that fulfills a need not present at the time of performance (Suddendorf and Corballis 2007). This rules out behaviors such as migrating in response to seasonal cues and learning with delayed reinforcement. So far, the most convincing candidate consists of a demonstration that scrub jays cache food in the evening in locations where it is most likely to be needed the next morning (Raby et al. 2007; but see Suddendorf and Corballis 2008). However, the folk-psychological notion of planning implies that it is general to a variety of events, and the scrub jays' ability may be confined to the food-storing system.

15.3.3 Numerical cognition

Perhaps because mathematics is a pinnacle of human intellectual achievement, attempts to answer the question "Can animals count?" are as old as the study of animal cognition. In the end, Clever Hans, the horse who seemed to count and do arithmetic, did not provide much evidence about animal numerical abilities because he proved to be responding to subtle aspects of the questioners' body language. But a century later, research on numerical cognition is a rich area of two-way interaction between comparative and developmental psychologists. The theoretical focus has moved away from the simplistic "Can animals count?" to a nuanced view of numerical cognition as consisting of several core systems shared among species, with an additional language-based system unique to humans. Much of this progress rests on the fact that babies and monkeys can be given virtually identical nonverbal tests of sensitivity to number (for review see Feigenson, Dehaene, and Spelke 2004; Shettleworth 2010).

One candidate core ability is precise tracking of small numbers of objects. For example, if two objects disappear behind a screen, an infant or a monkey expects to see two objects when the screen is removed, as shown by looking longer when one or three rather than two objects are revealed. Similarly, rhesus monkeys and toddlers who see small numbers of treats deposited successively into two containers prefer the container containing the larger number. But these subjects choose randomly when the containers have more than about three objects each, as if object-tracking has broken down. Clearly, verbal counting would allow a numerate human to continue choosing the larger number with larger quantities. A nice demonstration of this is a study of performance in several numerical tasks by members of an Amazonian tribe whose language lacks counting words for quantities above three or four (Pica *et al.* 2004). The tribespeople were as accurate as French controls in exact judgments of small quantities, but only up to about three, the limit of their naming ability. In contrast, the groups did not differ in judging which of two larger sets had more items, an ability taken as evidence for a second core system concerned with approximate discrimination among larger sets. In a variety of species, including rats, monkeys, pigeons, and people, such numerosity discrimination follows Weber's law, i.e., accuracy of discriminating between two quantities is a function of their ratios, not their absolute values. For example, 8 is judged to be more than 6 as often as 24 is judged to be more than 18.

The idea of analyzing broadly defined cognitive competences into core systems with specific "signatures" such as Weber's law-based discrimination for the approximate large number system and failure at three or four for the precise small number system provides a productive framework for comparative research. This same approach has been applied to spatial behavior (Wang and Spelke 2002; Shettleworth 2010). Here the intuitively appealing but vague notion that creatures navigate with reference to a cognitive map is replaced by understanding effective way-finding as depending on several well-specified and dissociable but interacting systems. These include path integration, landmark use, and orientation by the geometry of local space (Wang and Spelke 2002; Shettleworth 2010). Similarly, comparative research directed toward understanding the evolution of language has moved beyond asking "Can chimps use forms of human language?" to looking at the function and distribution across species of components of human linguistic ability (Fitch 2005; Seyfarth, Cheney, and Bergman 2005).

15.3.4   Theory of mind

In comparative cognition and child development, having a *theory of mind* means understanding that others have minds. Among other things, theory of mind entails understanding that seeing leads to knowing and that others' knowledge may be different from one's own, which confers the ability to practice intentional deception. The term was actually introduced by Premack and Woodruff (1978), who tested the language-trained chimpanzee Sarah to discover whether she understood the intentions of people filmed trying to overcome various obstacles. The study of theory of mind soon became a major topic in child development (e.g., Carruthers and Smith 1996). Children were found to develop various indices of theory of mind, such as appreciating that only someone who had seen where an object was hidden could know where it was, somewhere between the ages of three and four. Analogous tests were then developed for chimpanzees (see Shettleworth 2010). Perhaps the most extensive series of such tests probed whether chimpanzees understand something comparable to "If someone sees me, they know what I want" (Povinelli and Eddy 1996). The animals could beg for food from one of two people, only one of whom could see them. The other's eyes were averted or covered. Theory of mind should allow excellent performance as soon as the animal is tested in a novel situation sharing few if any specific stimulus features with past situations in which the animal succeeded, whereas reinforcement-based learning should require at least a few trials. Chimpanzees "passed" the tests only after extensive training, suggesting that they were not using theory of mind but rather learning to use cues such as "eyes visible" that predicted who would give them the food.

The conclusion that chimpanzees lack theory of mind flies in the face of naturalistic observations of chimpanzee society, in which they seem to routinely practice deception, form friendships and alliances, and generally behave as if understanding each other's states of mind (e.g., Byrne and Whiten 1988). One problem with laboratory studies such as Povinelli and Eddy's is that in effect the chimpanzees were expected to infer the state of mind of humans, not other chimpanzees. Another is that chimpanzees do not typically cooperate with one another over food but compete. To address both of these shortcomings, Hare, Call, and Tomasello (2001) let a dominant and a subordinate chimp compete over food. Sometimes the food was within sight of the dominant animal, sometimes it was out of the dominant's sight. When the two animals were allowed to go after the food, the subordinate typically behaved as if knowing what the dominant knew, for example preferring to approach the food that the dominant should have been ignorant about.

At first glance, the results of these experiments seem to show that chimpanzees use theory of mind when competing with each other. But on one view (Penn and Povinelli 2007) the question of animal theory of mind cannot be answered by any experiment like those described so far. Inferences about another individual's state of mind are necessarily inferences from their behavior. Any behavior, such as my attempting to deceive Sam, that might be based on my theory of mind ("Sam knows where the food is") is indistinguishable from behavior based on inferences directly from observable cues ("Sam is/was facing toward it with his eyes open"). Appropriate responses to such cues might be largely unlearned or abstractions from past experience; they do not require inferences about the other individual's state of mind. Therefore, one possible conclusion is that chimpanzees regulate their complex social interactions on the basis of inferences from external cues alone without human-like inferences about others' minds. Indeed, they may not interpret social or physical events in terms of unobservable causes (Povinelli 2004). The same goes for comparable behaviors in other species, such as food-storing birds that behave so as to prevent observers stealing their caches (Emery and Clayton 2004; Bugnyar and Heinrich 2005). Not surprisingly, such conclusions have not gone unchallenged (Call and Tomasello 2008), but so far no published experiment has escaped the compelling logic of the behavioral abstraction view (Penn and Povinelli 2007).

15.4   Concluding remarks

Besides being fascinating in its own right, the study of animal cognition is the area of the cognitive sciences most richly connected to all the others, and to behavioral and evolutionary biology besides. It has been growing recently and becoming more interdisciplinary and more deeply comparative. Of course, some of its appeal, and some important applications, lie in its implications for understanding the mechanisms and evolution of human cognition. For example, many discussions of the chimpanzee genome project allude to the importance of studying chimpanzee cognition for unraveling the meaning of chimpanzee–human genetic differences. In some areas (section 15.3.3), progress is being made by moving beyond traditional questions about human uniqueness with yes-or-no answers, such as "Do animals count?", to a more productive analysis in terms of the cross-species pattern of component abilities. In others (section 15.3.2), a major challenge for comparative research is defining patterns of animal behavior that can be taken as evidence for mental processes that people report on verbally. Indeed, throughout the field one of the biggest contemporary challenges may be remaining focused on objective analyses of behavior while at the same time finding a balance between the appeal of frank anthropomorphism and legitimate interest in the bases of human capabilities. But anthropocentrism does not provide the only rationale for studying cognition in other species. To quote the paraphrase of Darwin in an article on comparative development (Finlay 2007), "endless minds most beautiful" have arisen during evolution. A cognitive science that overlooks them is incomplete.

Further reading

Boakes, R. (1984). *From Darwin to Behaviourism*. Cambridge University Press. An informative, well-written, and well-illustrated history of the early days of research on learning and cognition in animals.

Comparative Cognition Society website: www.comparativecognition.org. This has links to online "cyberbooks" on spatial behavior and on avian visual cognition as well as to the society's online journal of reviews and websites of many researchers in the field, mainly in North American psychology departments.

Papini, M. (2002). Pattern and process in the evolution of learning, *Psychological Review* 109: 186–201. A thoughtful discussion of how comparative studies of learning can be better related to contemporary evolutionary biology. Greater depth in his 2008 book.

Penn, D. C., Holyoak, K. J., and Povinelli, D. J. (2008). Darwin's mistake: Explaining the discontinuity between human and nonhuman minds, *Behavioral and Brain Sciences* 31: 109–78. Analyzes a wide range of recent claims for human-like abilities in other species, arguing that no non-human species forms higher-order representations.

Shettleworth, S. J. (2010). *Cognition, Evolution, and Behavior* (2nd edn.). New York: Oxford University Press. A comprehensive review of comparative cognition, integrating material from biological and psychological research. Written for higher-level undergraduates, graduate students, and researchers.

Sober, E. (2005). Comparative psychology meets evolutionary biology: Morgan's canon and cladistic parsimony, in L. Daston and G. Mitman (eds.), *Thinking with Animals: New Perspectives on Anthropomorphism* (pp. 85–99). New York: Columbia University Press. This and similar articles by the same author thoughtfully analyze the relationships among Morgan's canon, anthropomorphism, and evolutionary biology.

Terrace, H. S. and Metcalfe, J. (2005). The *Missing Link in Cognition: Origins of Self-Reflective Consciousness*. New York: Oxford University Press. A stimulating collection of chapters by researchers working on both humans and animals dealing with metacognition and related topics.

Wasserman, E. A. and Zentall, T. R. (eds.) (2006). *Comparative Cognition: Experimental Exploration of Animal Intelligence*. New York: Oxford University Press. A substantial collection of reviews of contemporary research programs, with a few exceptions involving laboratory studies by psychologists.

Wynne, C. D. L. (2007). What are animals? Why anthropomorphism is still not a scientific approach to behavior, *Comparative Cognition and Behavior Reviews* 2: 125–35. This provocative article and the four commentaries that follow in the same issue of the journal debate the apparent revival of anthropomorphism in contemporary research on animal cognition. No further evidence is needed that controversy over the role of anthropomorphism is far from dead.

References

Babb, S. J. and Crystal, J. D. (2006). Discrimination of what, when, and where is not based on time of day, *Learning and Behavior* 34: 124–30.

Balda, R. P. and Kamil, A. C. (2006). Linking life zones, life history traits, ecology, and spatial cognition in four allopatric southwestern seed caching corvids, in R. G. Cook and M. F. Brown (eds.), *Animal Spatial Cognition*. Comparative Cognition Society. Cyberbook. www.comparativecognition.org.

Barrett, H. C. and Kurzban, R. (2006). Modularity in cognition: Framing the debate, *Psychological Review* 113: 628–47.

Beach, F. A. (1950). The snark was a boojum, *American Psychologist* 5: 115–24.

Bitterman, M. E. (1975). The comparative analysis of learning, *Science* 188: 699–709.

  (2000). Cognitive evolution: A psychological perspective, in C. Heyes and L. Huber (eds.), *The Evolution of Cognition* (pp. 61–79). Cambridge, MA: MIT Press.

Boakes, R. (1984). *From Darwin to Behaviourism*. Cambridge University Press.

Bolhuis, J. J. and Macphail, E. M. (2001). A critique of the neuroecology of learning and memory, *Trends in Cognitive Sciences* 5: 426–33.

Bond, A. B., Kamil, A. C., and Balda, R. P. (2003). Social complexity and transitive inference in corvids, *Animal Behaviour* 65: 479–87.

Bugnyar, T. and Heinrich, B. (2005). Ravens, *Corvis corax*, differentiate between knowledgeable and ignorant competitors, *Proceedings of the Royal Society B* 272: 1641–6.

Burkhardt, R. W. (2005). *Patterns of Behavior*. University of Chicago Press.

Byrne, R. W. and Whiten, A. (eds.) (1988). *Machiavellian Intelligence: Social Expertise and the Evolution of Intellect in Monkeys, Apes, and Humans.* Oxford: Clarendon Press.

Call, J. and Tomasello, M. (2008). Does the chimpanzee have a theory of mind? 30 years later, *Trends in Cognitive Science* 12: 187–92.

Carruthers, P. and Smith, P. K. (eds.) (1996). *Theories of Theories of Mind.* Cambridge University Press.

Cheney, D. L. and Seyfarth, R. M. (2007). *Baboon Metaphysics: The Evolution of a Social Mind.* University of Chicago Press.

Clayton, N. S. and Dickinson, A. (1998). Episodic-like memory during cache recovery by scrub jays, *Nature* 395: 272–4.

Crystal, J. D. (2009). Elements of episodic-like memory in animal models, *Behavioural Processes* 80: 269–77.

Darwin, C. (1871). *The Descent of Man and Selection in Relation to Sex.* London: John Murray.

Dawkins, M. S. (1993). *Through Our Eyes Only?* Oxford: W. H. Freeman.

de Waal, F. B. M. and Tyack, P. L. (eds.) (2003). *Animal Social Complexity.* Cambridge, MA: Harvard University Press.

Dukas, R. and Ratcliffe, J. M. (eds.) (2009). *Cognitive Ecology II.* University of Chicago Press.

Eichenbaum, H., Fortin, N. J., Ergorul, C., Wright, S. P., and Agster, K. L. (2005). Episodic recollection in animals: "If it walks like a duck and quacks like a duck . . . ," *Learning and Motivation* 36: 190–207.

Emery, N. J. and Clayton, N. S. (2004). The mentality of crows: Convergent evolution of intelligence in corvids and apes, *Science* 306: 1903–7.

Ergorul, C. and Eichenbaum, H. (2004). The hippocampus and memory for "what," "where," and "when," *Learning and Memory* 11: 397–405.

Feigenson, L., Dehaene, S., and Spelke, E. (2004). Core systems of number, *Trends in Cognitive Sciences* 8: 307–14.

Finlay, B. L. (2007). Endless minds most beautiful, *Developmental Science* 10: 30–4.

Fitch, W. T. (2005). The evolution of language: A comparative review, *Biology and Philosophy* 20: 193–230.

Gallistel, C. R. (1998). The modular structure of learning, in M. S. Gazzaniga and J. S. Altman (eds.), *Brain and Mind: Evolutionary Perspectives* (pp. 56–71). Strasbourg: Human Frontiers Science Program.

Griffin, D. R. (1976). *The Question of Animal Awareness.* New York: Rockefeller University Press.

Hampton, R. R. (2001). Rhesus monkeys know when they remember, *Proceedings of the National Academy of Sciences (USA)* 98: 5359–62.

  (2005). Can rhesus monkeys discriminate between remembering and forgetting?, in H. S. Terrace and J. Metcalfe (eds.), *The Missing Link in Cognition: Origins of Self-Reflective Consciousness* (pp. 272–95). New York: Oxford University Press.

(2009). Multiple demonstrations of metacognition in nonhumans: Converging evidence or multiple mechanisms? *Comparative Cognition and Behavior Reviews* 4: 17–28.

Hare, B., Call, J., and Tomasello, M. (2001). Do chimpanzees know what conspecifics know? *Animal Behaviour* 61: 139–51.

Healy, S. and Braithwaite, V. (2000). Cognitive ecology: A field of substance? *Trends in Ecology and Evolution* 15: 22–6.

Healy, S. D. and Rowe, C. (2007). A critique of comparative studies of brain size, *Proceedings of the Royal Society B* 274: 453–64.

Holekamp, K. E. (2006). Questioning the social intelligence hypothesis, *Trends in Cognitive Sciences* 11: 65–9.

Hulse, S. H., Fowler, H., and Honig, W. K. (eds.) (1978). *Cognitive Processes in Animal Behavior.* Hillsdale, NJ: Lawrence Erlbaum.

Humphrey, N. K. (1976). The social function of intellect, in P. P. G. Bateson and R. A. Hinde (eds.), *Growing Points in Ethology* (pp. 303–17). Cambridge University Press.

Jolly, A. (1966). Lemur social behavior and primate intelligence, *Science* 153: 501–6.

Kamil, A. C. (1988). A synthetic approach to the study of animal intelligence, in D. W. Leger (ed.), *Comparative Perspectives in Modern Psychology: Nebraska Symposium on Motivation* (vol. 35, pp. 230–57). Lincoln, NE: University of Nebraska Press.

Kohler, W. (1959). *The Mentality of Apes.* New York: Vintage Books.

Kornell, N., Son, L. M., and Terrace, H. S. (2007). Transfer of metacognitive skills and hint-seeking in monkeys, *Psychological Science* 18: 64–71.

Mackintosh, N. J. (1988). Approaches to the study of animal intelligence, *British Journal of Psychology* 79: 509–25.

Macphail, E. M. (1987). The comparative psychology of intelligence, *Behavioral and Brain Sciences* 10: 645–95.

(1998). *The Evolution of Consciousness.* Oxford University Press.

Mitchell, S. D. (2005). Anthropomorphism and cross-species modeling, in L. Daston and G. Mitman (eds.), *Thinking with Animals: New Perspectives on Anthropomorphism* (pp. 100–17). New York: Columbia University Press.

Morgan, C. L. (1894). *An Introduction to Comparative Psychology.* London: Walter Scott.

Papini, M. R. (2002). Pattern and process in the evolution of learning, *Psychological Review* 109: 186–201.

(2008). *Comparative Psychology.* New York: Psychology Press.

Paz-y-Miño C., G., Bond, A. B., Kamil, A. C., and Balda, R. P. (2004). Pinyon jays use transitive inference to predict social dominance, *Nature* 430: 778–81.

Penn, D. C., Holyoak, K. J., and Povinelli, D. J. (2008). Darwin's mistake: Explaining the discontinuity between human and nonhuman minds, *Behavioral and Brain Sciences* 31: 109–78.

Penn, D. C. and Povinelli, D. J. (2007). On the lack of evidence that non-human animals possess anything remotely resembling a "theory of mind," *Philosophical Transactions of the Royal Society B* 362: 731–44.

Pica, P., Lemer, C., Izard, V., and Dehaene, S. (2004). Exact and approximate arithmetic in an Amazonian indigene group, *Science* 306: 499–503.

Povinelli, D. J. (2004). Behind the ape's appearance: Escaping anthropocentrism in the study of other minds, *Daedalus* 133: 29–41.

Povinelli, D. J. and Eddy, T. J. (1996). What young chimpanzees know about seeing, *Monographs of the Society for Research in Child Development* 61: 1–152.

Pravosudov, V. V. and Clayton, N. S. (2002). A test of the adaptive specialization hypothesis: Population differences in caching, memory, and the hippocampus in black-capped chickadees (*Poecile atricapilla*), *Behavioral Neuroscience* 116: 515–22.

Premack, D. and Woodruff, G. (1978). Does the chimpanzee have a theory of mind? *Behavioral and Brain Sciences* 4: 515–26.

Raby, C. R., Alexis, D. M., Dickinson, A., and Clayton, N. S. (2007). Planning for the future by Western scrub-jays, *Nature* 445: 919–21.

Ristau, C. A. (ed.) (1991). *Cognitive Ethology: The Minds of Other Animals*. Hillsdale, NJ: Lawrence Erlbaum.

Romanes, G. J. (1892). *Animal Intelligence*. New York: D. Appleton and Company.

Seyfarth, R. M. and Cheney, D. L. (2003). Signalers and receivers in animal communication, *Annual Review of Psychology* 54: 145–73.

Seyfarth, R. M., Cheney, D. L., and Bergman, T. J. (2005). Primate social cognition and the origins of language, *Trends in Cognitive Sciences* 9: 264–6.

Sherry, D. F. (2006). Neuroecology, *Annual Review of Psychology* 57: 167–97.

Sherry, D. F. and Schacter, D. L. (1987). The evolution of multiple memory systems, *Psychological Review* 94: 439–54.

Shettleworth, S. J. (2009). The evolution of comparative cognition: Is the snark still a boojum? *Behavioural Processes* 80: 210–17.

　(2010). *Cognition, Evolution, and Behavior* (2nd edn.). New York: Oxford University Press.

Shettleworth, S. J. and Hampton, R. H. (1998). Adaptive specializations of spatial cognition in food storing birds? Approaches to testing a comparative hypothesis, in R. P. Balda, I. M. Pepperberg, and A. C. Kamil (eds.), *Animal Cognition in Nature* (pp. 65–98). San Diego: Academic Press.

Smith, J. D., Beran, M. J., Couchman, J. J., and Coutinho, M. V. C. (2008). The comparative study of metacognition: Sharper paradigms, safer inferences, *Psychonomic Bulletin and Review* 15: 679–91.

Sober, E. (2005). Comparative psychology meets evolutionary biology: Morgan's canon and cladistic parsimony, in L. Daston and G. Mitman (eds.), *Thinking with Animals: New Perspectives on Anthropomorphism* (pp. 85–99). New York: Columbia University Press.

Striedter, G. F. (2005). *Principles of Brain Evolution.* Sunderland, MA: Sinauer Associates.

Suddendorf, T. and Corballis, M. C. (2007). The evolution of foresight: What is mental time travel and is it unique to humans? *Behavioral and Brain Sciences* 30: 299–313.

(2008). New evidence for animal foresight? *Animal Behaviour* 25: e1–e3.

Sutton, J. E. and Shettleworth, S. J. (2008). Memory without awareness: Pigeons fail to show metamemory in matching to sample, *Journal of Experimental Psychology: Animal Behavior Processes* 34: 266–82.

Thorndike, E. L. (1911/1970). *Animal Intelligence.* Darien, CT: Hafner Publishing Company.

Tolman, E. C. (1948). Cognitive maps in rats and men, *Psychological Review* 55: 189–208.

Tulving, E. (2005). Episodic memory and autonoesis: Uniquely human?, in H. S. Terrace and J. Metcalfe (eds.), *The Missing Link in Cognition: Origins of Self-Reflective Consciousness* (pp. 3–56). New York: Oxford University Press.

Wang, R. F. and Spelke, E. S. (2002). Human spatial representation: Insights from animals, *Trends in Cognitive Sciences* 6: 376–82.

Wasserman, E. A. and Zentall, T. R. (eds.) (2006). *Comparative Cognition: Experimental Exploration of Animal Intelligence.* New York: Oxford University Press.

Wynne, C. D. L. (2007). What are animals? Why anthropomorphism is still not a scientific approach to behavior, *Comparative Cognition and Behavior Reviews* 2: 125–35.

Zentall, T. R., Clement, T. S., Bhatt, R. S., and Allen, J. (2001). Episodic-like memory in pigeons, *Psychonomic Bulletin and Review* 8: 685–90.

Glossary

actual domain A description of the set of current environmental circumstances that will cause an **adaptation** to be deployed. For psychological adaptations, the set of inputs or stimuli that the adaptation will process, if it is exposed to them. Compare **proper domain**.

adaptation Part of an organism that evolves to carry out a specific function that is useful in the survival and reproduction of the organism. Evolutionary psychology focuses on psychological adaptations, or modules (brain structures that carry out specific information-processing and behavior regulation functions that help the organism survive and reproduce).

adaptive problem A recurring situation or challenge in the physical or social environment that exerts selection on organisms when genetic variation appears that causes them to vary in how they respond to the situation. Over time, natural selection favors variants that lead to the highest fitness in response to the adaptive problem.

agency, sense of The experience that I am the author or cause of an action and that I control its course.

anthropomorphism The practice of treating animals as if they are human, as in explaining animal behavior as if it was generated by human cognitive processes.

appraisal A representation of an organism–environment relationship that bears on well-being.

behavioral ecology The subfield of ethology, the study of animal behavior, that focuses on formulating and testing precise models of the adaptive value and evolution of behavior.

blindsight Visual responsiveness, revealed by above chance performance, without reportable visual consciousness.

change blindness Failure to detect and report changes to a visual scene that one might otherwise expect to be salient.

classical computer A kind of computer, also known as a "conventional" computer, the paradigm of which is a "von Neumann" computer, a device with distinct components for memory, processing, and input–output that computes its input–output functions by executing its operations in accordance with a stored program or algorithm. A more abstract conception of a classical computer is a system with (1) representations with a combinatorial syntax and semantics, and (2) processes that operate on these representations in virtue of their syntactic structure.

classical view of concepts The traditional theory that concepts can be defined by necessary and sufficient conditions.

cognitive architecture A general proposal about the structures and processes that produce intelligent thought.

cognitive ecology The study of animal cognition in its ecological context, integrating behavioral ecology and comparative cognitive psychology.

cognitive ethology The study of animal behaviors thought to involve consciousness. (Term introduced by Donald Griffin.)

cognitive grammar A linguistic framework originated by, among others, Ronald Langacker, George Lakoff, and Leonard Talmy. Its fundamental premise is that the structure of language is driven by the structure of meaning, which in turn is built by domain-general cognitive processes.

cognitive neuroscience The subfield of neuroscience addressing the physiological mechanisms underlying cognition and behavior.

cognitive science (broadly construed) All of the fields (or subfields within them) of **cognitive science (narrowly construed)** are sometimes regarded as *cognitive sciences*, offering work that most often is not explicitly interdisciplinary but contributes to the overall goal of understanding intelligence.

cognitive science (narrowly construed) An interdisciplinary field focused on the understanding of intelligence, primarily human cognition but also animal cognition and artificial intelligence. Contributing disciplines include cognitive psychology, artificial intelligence, linguistics, philosophy, sociology, anthropology, developmental psychology, education, and neuroscience.

comparative cognition Strictly, the comparison of cognitive processes across species of animals, including humans. Also used to refer to research on animal cognition in general, whether or not involving explicit comparisons of two or more species.

computation A term used with a variety of meanings, ranging from arithmetic calculation to operations on discrete symbols. Thus, some cognitive scientists apply this term to a variety of models, including dynamic systems accounts of cognition, and others make a point of narrowing its meaning so as to explicitly exclude such accounts.

computational model A model of a biological or behavioral process expressed mathematically and/or run on a computer, providing a mechanistic explanation for an experimental observation and making predictions for further study. Like an experimental model, a computational model makes simplifying assumptions and controls a small number of dependent variables by manipulating a small number of independent variables.

computational neuroscience The application of mathematical or information-theoretic methods to the study of the brain, often in the form of connectionist modeling.

conceptual semantics An approach to meaning originated by Ray Jackendoff. Its premise is that linguistic meaning is grounded in human cognition, and that traditional notions of reference and truth must be grounded in human conceptualization of the world. Unlike **cognitive grammar**, conceptual semantics takes the position that syntactic structure is partly autonomous from meaning, and it takes seriously the possibility that some aspects of the language faculty are domain-specific, not just a consequence of general cognition.

connectionist computer A computer, consisting of a collection of simple computing units linked into a network that is capable of modifying the pattern of connectivity of those units. Sometimes referred to as a **neural network**.

construction grammar A linguistic framework originated by, among others, Charles Fillmore, Paul Kay, and Adele Goldberg. Its fundamental premise is that syntactic structures are not just the glue that ties words together; rather, syntactic structures themselves bear meaning. The framework is most commonly illustrated with idiosyncratic sentence types such as *Out the door with you!*

declarative memory Conscious memory for facts and past events.

deductive reasoning Reasoning in which the truth of the premises guarantees with certainty that the conclusion is true.

defeasible reasoning Reasoning in which the conclusion may be overturned by subsequent information.

design feature A property of an adaptation that is well suited to carrying out an evolved function, i.e., to solving an adaptive problem.

disjunctivism The class of views in the philosophy of perception according to which perceptual experiences and hallucinations do not belong to a common psychological kind or share a common core content.

dynamic neural field A **recurrent neural network** characterized by a smooth transition from net excitation between adjacent processing units to net inhibition between units farther apart. These networks are commonly used to model brain regions that encode continuous-valued features (e.g., spatial location).

ecological control A type of control in which goals are achieved, not by micro-managing every detail of the desired action or response, but by making the most of robust, reliable sources of relevant order in the bodily or worldly environment of the controller.

embodiment The idea that a mental capacity depends heavily upon a bodily response and interaction with the environment. Embodied cognition is cognitive processing that relies on the use of morphological structure and the active probing of the environment via the sense organs.

emotions Felt inner states that register matters of concern to an organism and help prepare for cognitive and behavioral response.

enactivism An approach to the nature of perception and perceptual content according to which action is constitutive of perception, and perceiving is a way of actively exploring an environment.

episodic memory Memory for specific episodes in one's personal past, as opposed to memory for facts and ideas (**semantic memory**). On one influential definition, episodic memory also involves conscious recollection or mentally "traveling back in time" to past experiences.

exemplar A remembered category member that is used for classification, inference, and other conceptual processes.

explanation, scientific A description of mechanisms or underlying structures and processes that produce the phenomena to be explained.

explanatory gap The view that, even if we were assured that a conscious experience is strictly identical with a neurophysiological event, we would still lack an explanation of why that event feels to its subject in the distinctive way it does.

exploitative representation The kind of representation employed in systems that get by without explicitly encoding certain pieces of action-relevant information by virtue of their ability to track or access that information in some other way. (Term coined by Robert Wilson.)

extended cognition Cognitive processing that includes elements outside of the brain/central nervous system.

function (1) A mathematical function is a mapping from one set of objects to another. (2) The "teleological" function of an entity, property, or event is, roughly, its purpose or aim. (3) In biology, the function of an entity, property, or process is frequently defined as the role it plays that has contributed to its genetic success and evolution.

functional role The causal or computational relations of a state or entity, such as a **mental representation**, within a larger system.

generative grammar On a broad reading, any theory of the grammar of natural language that attempts to be explicit in characterizing the range of utterances of a language, their structures, and their interpretations. On a narrower reading, any of the versions of generative grammar espoused by Noam Chomsky and his close associates, including transformational grammar of the 1950s through 1970s, the principles and parameters framework of the 1980s and the early 1990s, and the most recent minimalist program. All of these approaches are based on an algorithmic generation of syntactic structure, from which both sound and meaning are derived. They contrast with frameworks such as head-driven phrase structure grammar, lexical-functional grammar, and **construction grammar,** which view grammar as a system of constraints rather than an algorithm, and with **cognitive grammar,** which views the structure of language as driven by meaning rather than syntax.

ground (of mental content) The properties or relations that determine the content of a representation (see **mental representation**). The ground properties most often explored in the literature are resemblance, causal relations (both historical and nomological), and biological function.

Hebbian learning The hypothesis that learning is supported by **synaptic plasticity** driven by correlations between pre-synaptic and post-synaptic activity.

inattentional blindness Failure to detect and report objects and events in a visual scene to which one does not attend, even when one might otherwise expect those objects and events to be salient.

inductive reasoning Reasoning in which the truth of the premises confers only a higher plausibility on the conclusions.

information The term "information" is rooted in the rise of *information theory* in the 1920s to 1960s. Information theory offers a quantitative treatment of information transmission across channels subject to capacity limits, rate limits, and noise. For example, a *bit* is a unit of information sufficient to distinguish two messages. The term was adopted by psychologists, initially in applications of information theory to human performance, and later (from the 1960s on) in the context of *information-processing* accounts, which posit symbolic rules and representations (see **symbolic models**). Philosophers have also proposed *informational accounts of representational content*, in which content is claimed to be grounded in some form of co-variation or nomic dependency relation.

intention A mental state that represents some desired state of affairs and sets the subject on a course to bring that state of affairs about.

intentionality The property of having content or being "about" something.

internal model for action control An internal model is a neural process that simulates the response of the motor system in order to estimate the outcome of a motor command. An internal model combines an inverse model that takes as input a desired state and computes the motor commands necessary to reach that state and a forward model that takes as input a copy of the motor command output from the inverse model and yields as output a prediction of the state resulting from the execution of the motor commands. If the desired and predicted states differ, the difference can be fed back as an input into the internal model again so that an adjusted set of motor commands can be generated.

knowledge argument The argument made by Frank Jackson and others that, since someone could know all the scientific and other objective facts about a subject without being able to work out what it is like for the subject to be experiencing such-and-such a sensation, the latter fact cannot be accommodated within a purely scientific account of the mind.

logical form Broadly reading, the truth-evaluable aspects of sentence meaning. Within the principles and parameters framework of generative grammar, a covert level of syntactic structure in which quantifier scope is explicitly encoded, and which serves as the input to the rules that derive semantic interpretation.

long-term memory (LTM) Memory for items and events across extended periods of time, ranging from minutes through decades.

mechanism A system of related parts whose interactions produce regular changes.

mental logic The psychological theory of reasoning that assumes that various syntactic inference rules form part of the architecture of the mind.

mental models The psychological theory of reasoning that assumes that humans are logical in principle but that their reasoning can be systematically biased since they represent logical terms by the possible states of affairs they allow.

mental representation A state or structure within a cognitive system that stands for something else and thereby has content.

metamemory Awareness of the strength of one's own memories, as evident, for example, in a feeling of knowing whether or not one can answer a question correctly.

models, modeling An account intended to replicate salient parts and/or operations of a target system, allowing capacities and activities of that system to be simulated. Explanations and theories in cognitive science employ models of many types, including mathematical, computational, connectionist, semantic network, dynamical systems, and symbolic rules and representations.

Morgan's canon The doctrine that learned behaviors should be explained in terms of simple conditioning and species-specific predispositions rather than "higher" cognitive mechanisms. (Named after the late nineteenth-century comparative psychologist C. Lloyd Morgan, who held that behavior should be interpreted as due to the cognitively simplest mechanism possible.)

naturalistic Naturalistic properties are those commonly invoked in the physical and life sciences, such as those involved in physical and causal relations.

neural network An interconnected set of neuron-like processing units. Each unit sums its input signals and produces an output signal, but the interpretation of these signals depends on the level of biophysical detail in the network.

neuroecology The approach to comparative neuroanatomy and behavioral neuroscience that attempts to understand brain structure and evolution by analyzing relationships between brain areas and natural behaviors. Examples might include comparing relative sizes of relevant brain structures in species with different social systems or foraging ecologies.

parity claim The claim that if, as we confront some task, a part of the world functions in such a manner that, were it inside the head, we would unhesitatingly accept it as part of the cognitive process, then that part of the world is (for that time) part of the cognitive process. The claim is best seen as a request to try to decide what counts as a cognitive process in some way that is unbiased by knowledge of its location and material (e.g., biological or non-biological) constitution.

poverty of the stimulus An argument within the theory of language learning, concerning whether the input available to the child is sufficient for the child to extract the principles of grammar. The argument from the poverty of the stimulus suggests that the input alone is not enough – the stimulus is impoverished relative to the cognitive end result – and that therefore the child must come equipped with some principles of analysis and with innate expectations as to what the grammar of a language ought to be like.

probabilistic approach The psychological theory of reasoning that assumes that the human mind is adapted to dealing with an uncertain world and thus that human reasoning mechanisms are probabilistic.

procedural memory Memory for operations, skills, and procedures; "knowing *how*."

productivity The property of producing novel instances. A cognitive capacity is productive in the sense that once a person has the capacity in question, he or she is typically in a position to exercise it in a practically unlimited number of novel ways. For example, human minds are productive in that they can think a practically unlimited number of novel thoughts.

proper domain A description of the set of environmental circumstances that led to the evolution of an **adaptation**. For psychological adaptations, the set of inputs or stimuli that the adaptation evolved to process. Compare **actual domain**.

prototype A summary representation that describes category members in general, though not necessarily any particular member. The representation often involves properties of varying significance for category membership. More generally, "prototype theory" often refers to any theory of concepts that denies that concepts are well defined.

psychological essentialism The view that people assume that certain categories have an underlying microstructure or essence (e.g., atomic structure or genetics) that is responsible for category membership and that causally determines observable features.

recurrent neural network A neural network characterized by extensive feedback connectivity, comparable to the extensive collateral synaptic connectivity in brain structures such as the cerebral cortex and hippocampus.

representation bearer The aspect of a representation – usually a state or entity – that "bears" the representational properties of the representation. For example, the representation bearer of an inscription on paper is usually a pattern of ink marks.

representationalism In a broad sense, the view that minds employ **mental representations**. The term is also used to refer to the more specific claim that the phenomenal characteristics of an experience ("what it's like") supervene upon its representational properties.

semantic memory Organized knowledge about words, concepts, and rules.

semantics The term "semantics" is used in three senses: (1) to refer to the mapping rules that bestow content upon representations (i.e., the conditions that link a representation to what it represents); (2) to refer to the field (area of knowledge) that studies such rules, and (3) for **mental representation**, to refer to proposals concerning the **ground** or (usually naturalistic) basis of semantic mappings in sense (1).

sense-data Immediate or direct objects of acquaintance in sense perception. Traditionally believed to be private.

sensory qualities The qualitative features of which we are aware in sensory experience: colors, pitches, smells, textures, and the like.

short-term memory (STM) Memory storage over brief time periods, on the order of seconds.

state consciousness A mental state/event is a conscious state/event just in case its subject is directly aware of being in it.

symbol A discrete form (e.g., the word "stop" or a stop sign) that stands for (represents) something else.

symbolic models (symbolic architecture, symbolic computation) Models comprising (a) *representations* whose elements are discrete symbols and (b) *operations* on those representations that typically involve moving, copying, deleting, comparing, or replacing symbols. A *rule* specifies one or more operations, and the overall approach is often referred to as "rules and representations."

synaptic plasticity The change in strength of synapses due to pre-synaptic and/or post-synaptic activity.

theory of content determination A theory of the ground of the semantic properties of a representation or system of representation, namely, of the properties and relations that determine those semantic properties. Such a theory is often referred to as a "semantics" (as in "functional role semantics" or "indicator semantics").

transparency (diaphanousness) The putative feature of perceptual experience whereby the qualitative nature of the experience is introspectively indistinguishable from features of the object perceived. For example, the redness of a visual experience is simply the property of representing the apple itself as red.

universal grammar (UG) The set of principles and expectations that a normal child brings to the acquisition of language, such that he or she can acquire any human language given appropriate input. Often incorrectly confused with universals of human language, universal grammar provides a toolkit of possibilities for human languages, not all of which are used by every language.

working memory (WM) The cognitive structures responsible for our ability to use internal goal representations to direct the maintenance and manipulation of information even when that information is no longer present in the environment.

Index